GREGG TYPING 2

Advanced Course/
Series Eight

KEYBOARDING AND PROCESSING DOCUMENTS

ALAN C. LLOYD, Ph.D.
Director, Employment Testing,
The Olsten Corporation,
Westbury, New York

FRED E. WINGER, Ed.D.
Former Professor, Office Administration and
Business Education, Oregon State University,
Corvallis, Oregon

JACK E. JOHNSON, Ph.D.
Coordinator of Business Education,
Department of Vocational and Career Development,
Georgia State University,
Atlanta, Georgia

PHYLLIS C. MORRISON, Ph.D.
Professor of Administrative Management and
Business Education, Robert Morris College,
Coraopolis, Pennsylvania

REBECCA A. HALL, Ph.D.
Department Chairperson, Business and Office
Education, Centerville High School,
Centerville, Ohio

GREGG DIVISION/McGRAW-HILL BOOK COMPANY

New York Atlanta Dallas St. Louis San Francisco Auckland Bogotá Guatemala Hamburg
Lisbon London Madrid Mexico Montreal New Delhi Panama Paris
San Juan São Paulo Singapore Sydney Tokyo Toronto

Sponsoring Editors/Barbara N. Oakley, Gina M. Ferrara
Editing Supervisors/Julie A. Bokser, Matthew Fung, Elizabeth Huffman, Frances Koblin
Cover, Level Openings, and Interior Designer/Art and Design Supervisor/Patricia F. Lowy
Production Supervisors/Frank Bellantoni, Mirabel Flores

Technical Studio/Burmar Technical Corp.
Cover, Level Openings, and Text Photographer/Ken Karp

This edition of *Gregg Typing* is dedicated to Phyllis C. Morrison, who contributed much time, creativity, and hard work to the development of the manuscript and who passed away shortly before its publication.

Library of Congress Cataloging-in-Publication Data

Main entry under title:

Gregg typing 2: advanced course, series eight.

Includes index.
Summary: A textbook for a two-semester advanced course in typewriting for the secondary school. Includes processing of such forms as brochures, legal documents, and medical forms.
1. Typewriting. [1. Typewriting] I. Lloyd, Alan C.
Z49.G819 1987 652.3 85-23803
ISBN 0-07-038343-X

Gregg Typing 2, Advanced Course, Series Eight
Keyboarding and Processing Documents

4 5 6 7 8 9 0 DOCDOC 8 9 3 2 1 0 9

ISBN 0-07-038343-X

PREFACE

Series Eight is an all-new edition of the famous *Gregg Typing* programs. Developed with the needs of students and teachers in mind, *Series Eight* offers all the text and workbook materials needed for a comprehensive, modern typewriting program. It also offers many exciting features that make it an effective instructional system.

PARTS OF THE PROGRAM

Designed to meet the needs of one-semester, one-year, or two-year courses of instruction, *Series Eight* offers a variety of student's textbooks and workbooks, as well as a special Teacher's Edition for each student's text:

Gregg Typing 1. The first-year text offers 150 lessons of instruction. The first 75 lessons (one semester) are devoted to learning the keyboard and typing for personal use.

Gregg Typing 2. The second-year text includes a comprehensive Reference Section for students. It also includes, of course, Lessons 151 through 300 of the *Gregg Typing* program.

Gregg Typing, Complete Course. Specially designed for the two-year program of instruction, the *Complete Course* text offers all 300 lessons from *Typing 1* and *Typing 2* in one binding.

Teacher's Editions. The three separate Teacher's Editions—one for each of the student's texts—include all the pages in the corresponding student's texts plus annotations intended only for the teacher. Each Teacher's Edition also includes a separate section of teaching methodology, as well as lesson-by-lesson teaching notes for all the lessons in that text.

Learning Guides and Working Papers. Four workbooks—one for each 75 lessons of instruction—provide the stationery and forms needed for all text jobs and in-baskets and a variety of reinforcement and enrichment exercises correlated to the text copy and to the LABs (Language Arts for Business).

Instructional Recordings. The *Keyboard Presentation Tapes for Gregg Typing* are cassettes correlated to the textbook keyboard lessons in *Gregg Typing 1* and in *Gregg Typing, Complete Course.*

Transparency Masters. These teaching tools will enhance the classroom presentation. They contain the masters for the transparencies. In addition, there are teaching suggestions and annotated illustrations.

Test Book. A *Test Book* provides masters for production, LAB, and objective tests for all 12 levels of the program. They parallel the production tests in the textbook and may be reproduced for classroom use as formal tests.

Test Bank. A *Computer Test Bank* contains all the questions covered in the 12 objective tests. Teachers may use these questions to develop their own objective tests for the program.

Keys. Complete keys to all text jobs and projects (both in pica and elite) are in the *Resource Manual and Key for Typing 1* and the *Resource Manual and Key for Typing 2.*

Computer Teaching Suggestions Manual. If you are using microcomputers instead of typewriters in your classroom, this manual will provide instruction for adapting the lessons and the formatting directions.

FEATURES OF *GREGG TYPING, SERIES EIGHT*

The *Series Eight* program incorporates many time-tested features from past editions of *Gregg Typing;* at the same time, it introduces some new features. For example:

Diagnostic Exercises. Many timings utilize the Pretest/Practice/Posttest routine, which allows each student to diagnose areas in which additional skill development is needed. After taking a Pretest, students practice according to their specific needs (as diagnosed from the Pretest). After the Practice session, students take a Posttest, which enables them to see how the Practice session improved their skill.

Skill-Building Routines. In addition to the Pretest/Practice/Posttest routine, a variety of other skill-building routines are provided in the program. These routines help maintain student interest while developing the basic keyboarding skill.

Clinics. Clinics (every sixth lesson) are designed to strengthen skill development. Most Clinics use diagnostic routines.

Language Arts for Business (LABs). Concise, easy-to-understand LABs help students to review the basic uses of punctuation, capitalization, and abbreviations and to avoid the most common errors in using plurals, contractions, possessives, and so on. Students reinforce and apply the LAB rules as they type sentences and production assignments.

Cyclical Approach. In *Series Eight,* concepts are taught once and recycled several times, with each cycle building on the previous one and becoming progressively more complex. Each cycle is a "level," lasting five weeks. Thus the full two-year program includes 12 levels—6 per year.

Five-Week Tests. At the conclusion of each level of work, a test provides both the student and the teacher with an opportunity to check the student's level of performance. These tests may be used as informal or formal evaluations. Parallel tests are provided in the *Test Book.*

Information Processing. Word processing and data processing terminology and applications are integrated into the text. Students, for example, format (and later fill in) form letters, type from "dictated" copy, and prepare a word processing procedures manual. Technology notes throughout the text point out how electronic equipment simplifies formatting procedures.

Decision-Making Exercises. To simulate real-life business experience, the *Series Eight* program includes many exercises that require students to make realistic "on-the-job" decisions. The complexity of the decisions to be made increases as students progress through the program.

Various Input Modes. Students will format letters, memos, and so on, from various input modes—for example, from unarranged copy, from handwritten copy, from rough drafts, and from incomplete information.

The *Series Eight* program greatly reflects the comments, suggestions, and recommendations we received from many teachers who used *Series Seven* and participated in the extensive review process. We sincerely appreciate their contributions to the effectiveness of this publication.

The Authors

CONTENTS

INTRODUCTION

REFERENCE SECTION

LEVEL 7
GOAL: 41/5'/4e

LEVEL 8
GOAL: 43/5'/4e

LEVEL 9
GOAL: 45/5'/4e

LEVEL 10
GOAL: 47/5'/3e

LEVEL 11
GOAL: 49/5'/3e

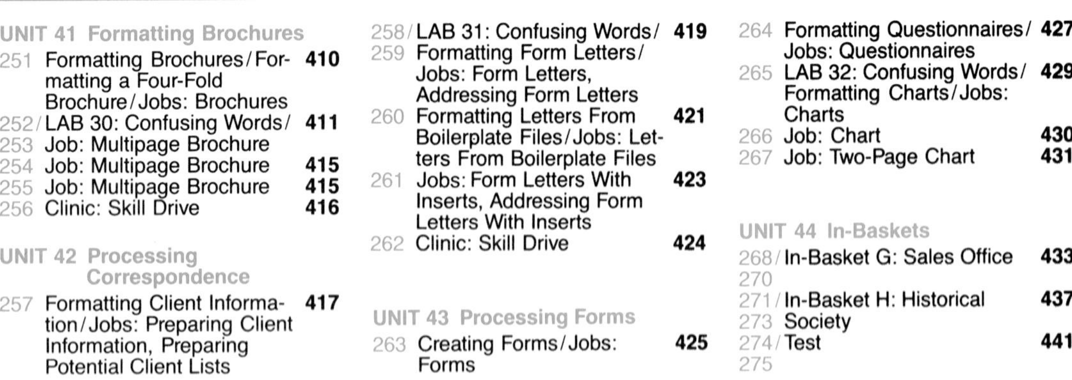

LEVEL 12
GOAL: 50/5'/3e

INDEX

Drills

Timings

Words	SI	Minutes	Page
120	1.40	3*	252
200	1.43	5*	254
200	1.45	5*	258
200	1.47	5*	263
200	1.45	5	270
123	1.50	3*	275
205	1.48	5	281
205	1.49	5*	285
205	1.51	5	291
210	1.55	5*	294
210	1.58	5	299
126	1.54	3*	304
215	1.56	5*	313
214	1.56	5	318
215	1.56	5	320
215	1.58	5*	324
215	1.54	5	328
220	1.59	5*	331
220	1.59	5	339
132	1.59	3*	343
135	1.57	3*	352
225	1.57	5*	358
225	1.58	5	362
225	1.59	5	366
230	1.57	5*	370
230	1.58	5*	382
138	1.63	3	387
235	1.64	5*	391
235	1.67	5	395
235	1.68	5*	398
235	1.72	5	402
235	1.72	5	406
240	1.66	5*	412
240	1.70	5	416
240	1.70	5	423
147	1.68	3*	426
245	1.68	5*	433
245	1.68	5	437
245	1.92	5	441
250	1.72	5*	448
250	1.73	5	453
250	1.74	5*	456
250	1.74	5	462
250	1.75	5	472
250	2.03	5	481

*Pretest/Practice/Posttest routine.

INTRODUCTION

The *Series Eight* program has been specially designed to help you develop your typewriting skills through a carefully planned, step-by-step process. To be sure that you understand the terms, the procedures, and the directions used throughout this book, as well as the operation of the machine you are using, be sure to read this introduction and refer to it whenever you have any question or problem.

GLOSSARY OF TERMS

The special terms and symbols used throughout this text are very easy to understand. Read the following glossary to be sure you know the meaning of the terms and symbols, and refer to the glossary whenever necessary.

GOAL STATEMENTS

Skill Goal. At the beginning of every unit, a skill goal is given—the goal you are aiming to achieve by the end of that unit. For example, the skill goal *To type 35/5′/5e* means "to type 35 words a minute for 5 minutes with 5 or fewer errors."

Production Goal. At the beginning of every lesson, one or more production goals are given for that lesson; for example, "To format a report from handwritten copy." Production goals alert you to the kinds of activities that you will type in each lesson.

FORMATTING INSTRUCTIONS

Formatting means arranging a document according to a specific set of rules.

A number of formatting terms and symbols are used to help you understand the directions for completing each activity in *Series Eight.* The most commonly used terms and symbols and their meanings are given below.

Single spacing (or *double* or *triple spacing*) tells you how to set your typewriter for that particular lesson.

40-, 50-, 60-, or 70-space line tells you the specific line length to use.

6-inch line or **60P/70E** indicates a 60-space line for typewriters with pica (P) type, a 70-space line for typewriters with elite (E) type.

5-space tab tells you precisely where to set your tab stops for a particular lesson—in this case, 5 spaces from the left margin.

Arrows in production work are used as follows:

→ This arrow is used in some tables to show you the vertical center of your work.

↓ 3 Arrows with numbers tell you how many lines down the next line should be typed—in this case, 3 lines.

Standard format will be stated in the directions for letters, tables, and so on, once you have learned the standard format for these kinds of jobs. To refresh your memory of the standard format, page numbers are often provided; for example, "Standard format (see page 209)."

Body 120 words tells you there are 120 words in the body of a letter. Knowing the approximate length of a letter will help you to adapt the standard format to position the letter on the page. Thus the number of words in the body of the letter is given to help guide you.

Workbook 86 indicates that a form or a letterhead for that specific job is provided in the *Learning Guides and Working Papers* workbook. If no workbook page is cited, then you are to use plain paper.

TECHNOLOGY NOTES

This symbol is used to point out a special feature on electronic equipment (electronic typewriters, word processors, computers) that makes formatting and keyboarding easier. For example, when you learn how to return the carriage or carrier, the technology note will describe *wordwrap,* which is an automatic return feature on electronic equipment.

SKILL-BUILDING ROUTINES

Typewriting is a skill, and a skill is best developed through directed practice. *Series Eight* provides a variety of effective skill-building routines to improve the speed and the accuracy of your typing, including the following:

A variety of **Pretest/Practice/Posttest** routines is offered—all designed to improve either speed or accuracy through a proven, step-by-step procedure. First the *Pretest* (a 2-, 3-, or 5-minute timing) helps you identify your speed or accuracy needs. Having identified your needs, you then do the *Practice* exercises—a variety of intensive improvement drills. After you have completed the *Practice* exercises, you take a *Posttest.* Because the Posttest is identical to the Pretest, the Posttest measures your improvement.

12-Second timings are routines in which you take a series of short timings to boost speed.

30-Second speed timings are slightly longer routines in which you take a series of short timings to boost speed.

30-Second "OK" timings help you build accuracy on alphabetic copy (that is, copy that includes all 26 letters of the alphabet). You take three 30-second timings on the copy to see how many error-free copies you can type.

SCALES AND INDEXES

Series Eight uses a variety of scales and indexes designed to help you (1) measure quickly—with little counting—how many words you have typed, (2) analyze whether you should practice speed drills or accuracy drills, and (3) identify the relative difficulty of the copy you are typing.

Word Count Scales. You get credit for typing a "word" whenever you advance 5 spaces. Thus when you have typed a 60-space line, you have typed 12 words. To save you time, word counts that appear at the right of a timing tell you the cumulative number of words you have typed at the end of each completed line.

The scale shown at the right, for ex- 12
ample, is used with timings that have 12 24
words a line. In production work the 36
scale at the right also gives you stroking 48
credit for using the tabulator, for center- 60
ing, and for other nonstroking move- 72
ments. 84

To quickly determine the words typed for *in*complete lines, use the scale that appears below each timing:

1 2 3 4 5 6 7 8 9 10 11 12

This scale quickly indicates the number of words typed. Just align the last word typed with the number on the scale.

When you take a 3- or 5-minute timing, use the speed markers (the small numbers above the copy) to quickly find your words-a-minute speed.

This special scale appears with 12-second timings:

5 10 15 20 25 30 35 40 45 50 55 60

It converts your typing speed during a 12-second timing into words a minute.

Practice Guide. In certain skill-building routines, you will use the following chart to find the drill lines you should type:

Pretest errors	0–1	2–3	4–5	6+
Drill lines	9–13	8–12	7–11	6–10

For example, if you made only 1 error in the Pretest, then the guide directs you to complete "Drill lines 9–13"; if you made 3 errors, you should complete "Drill lines 8–12"; and so on.

Syllabic Intensity (SI) Index. To indicate the relative difficulty of copy, syllabic intensity (SI) is often listed. The SI number is computed by dividing the number of actual words in the copy into the total number of syllables of all words. Thus 1.00 indicates copy that has one syllable per word; 1.50 indicates copy that has an average of one and a half syllables per word; and so on. The higher the number, the more difficult the copy.

LABs

Effective typewriting requires a knowledge of at least the basics of grammar, punctuation, and style. The *Series Eight* program provides Language Arts for Business (LABs) that offer concise, practical reviews and application exercises on punctuation, capitalization, and number use, for example. Thus you may review the most common language arts principles *as you type* sentences and production activities.

REFERENCE SECTION

MECHANICS OF CENTERING

HORIZONTAL CENTERING

Horizontal centering is used to position copy horizontally in the center of the paper—that is, so that there are equal margins on both sides of the copy. Remember that the width of standard-size paper is 85P/102E.

To center copy horizontally on standard-size paper:

1. Center the carriage or carrier.
2. As you say each pair of strokes to yourself (including spaces), depress the backspace key once for each *pair* of strokes. Do not backspace for an extra letter left over at the end.
3. Type the material. It should appear centered horizontally on the page.

VERTICAL CENTERING

Vertical centering is used to position copy between the top and the bottom margins—that is, so that there are equal margins above and below the copy. Remember that standard typewriting paper is 66 lines long from top to bottom.

To center copy vertically on a sheet of standard-size paper:

1. Count the number of lines (including blank ones) that will be used to type the copy.
2. Subtract that number from 66.
3. Divide the difference by 2 to find the line on which you should begin typing. (Drop any fraction you get when dividing by 2.)
4. Type the copy. It should appear centered vertically on the page.

MECHANICS OF CORRECTING ERRORS

CORRECTION DEVICES

Corrections can be made easily with an eraser, correction paper, or correction fluid. Typewriters equipped with correction ribbons make the task even simpler.

1. *Typewriter Eraser.* Before using a typewriter eraser, turn the platen so that the error is visible above the printing point indicator. Then move the carriage or carrier to the left if the error was made to the left of the center of the paper; move it to the right if the error was made to the right of the center of the paper. (Moving the carriage or carrier will keep eraser crumbs from falling into the mechanism.) Use a light up-and-down motion to erase the error. Return to the line; type the correction.
2. *Correction Paper.* Slips of paper containing a light coating of chalk can be used to make corrections. When an error is made, backspace to it and place the correction paper over the error between the typing paper and the typewriter ribbon. Strike the same key that was originally struck in error. The white chalk is transferred to the paper, concealing the error. Backspace and type the correct letter.
3. *Correction Fluid.* Correction fluid covers an error. Brush the correction fluid sparingly over the error until the ink is concealed. Give the fluid a few seconds to dry before typing the correction.
4. *Correction Tape.* Some typewriters are equipped with a correction device. When you strike the correcting key, the machine will backspace to the error. When you restrike the error, the correction device will engage a special tape that either lifts off or covers the error. The mechanism prevents the machine from spacing forward until the correct letter is struck.

SQUEEZING AND SPREADING WORDS

After erasing or covering an error, you may need to *squeeze,* for example, *six* characters into *five* spaces. In other cases you may need to *spread five* characters over *six* spaces. Use the following instructions for squeezing and spreading words:

1. *Squeezing Words.* To squeeze in a word with an extra letter, start the new word ½ space to the left of the position where the original word began, so that ½ space precedes and follows the new word. To do this, you must control the carriage or carrier movement by one of the following methods, depending on the make of your typewriter: (*a*) place your finger against the side of the carriage or carrier and move it back ½ space as you type each letter in the word, (*b*) partially depress the backspace key, or (*c*) depress the half-space key if your typewriter has one.
2. *Spreading Words.* To spread a word with one fewer letter, start the new word ½ space to the right of the position where the original word began, so that 1½ spaces precede and follow the new word. To do this, you must again control the carriage or carrier movement by one of the methods described for squeezing a letter.

PROOFREADERS' MARKS

Shown below are standard revision marks used in business to show changes that are to be made in draft copy. Revision marks with their definitions are shown in column 1. Column 2 shows an example of each mark in draft copy. Column 3 shows how the final copy should appear.

Proofreaders' Mark	Draft	Final Copy	Proofreaders' Mark	Draft	Final Copy
ss [Single-space	ss [first line / second line	first line / second line	Move as shown	it is (not)	it is
ds [Double-space	ds [first line / second line	first line / second line	Transpose	is/it so	it is not so
Move to left	let us	let us	Omit space	to gether	together
Move to right	it is so	it is so	Delete letter	errorr	error
5 Indent 5 spaces	5 Let it be	Let it be	Delete word	it may be	it may
][Center	]TITLE[	TITLE	new word / word Change word	and if it (so)	and so it
¶ Paragraph	¶ If he is	If he is	Delete and close up	judgement	judgment
○ Spell out	the only (1)	the only one	··· Don't delete	can we go	can we go
≡ Capitalize	mrs. Wade	Mrs. Wade	# Insert space	Itmay be	It may be
/ Lowercase letter (make letter small)	Business	business	∧ Insert word or letter	and ∧ it (so)	and so it
			V or ∧ Insert punctuation mark	Shes not	She's not,
			⊙ Insert a period	other way⊙	other way.

MECHANICS OF TYPING LETTERS AND ENVELOPES

LETTERS

LETTER PLACEMENT

Business letters are generally typed on a line 5 inches (50P/60E) long. The date line begins on line 15 and has 4 blank lines below it. However, depending on the length of the letter, the line length, the position of the date line, and other internal spacing may vary, as shown in the chart below.

Words in Body	Line Length	Date Typed on	From Date to Inside Address	Space for Signature
Under 100	5″ 50P/60E	Line 15	5–8 lines	3–6 blank lines
100–225	5″ 50P/60E	Line 15	5 lines	3 blank lines
Over 225	6″ 60P/70E	Lines 12–15	4–5 lines	2–3 blank lines

BUSINESS LETTER PARTS

A business letter contains a *heading,* an *opening,* a *body,* and a *closing.*

The *heading* consists of (1) the printed letterhead and (2) the date the letter is typed.

The *opening* includes (3) the inside address (the name and address of the party to whom the letter is being sent), (4) the attention line (if used, it directs the letter to a specific person or department), and (5) the salutation. If (6) a subject line is used, it is typed a double space below the salutation.

The *body* is (7) the message of the letter. Single-space lines, but use double spacing between paragraphs.

The *closing* includes the following parts: (8) the complimentary closing (such as *Yours truly, Sincerely yours,* or *Cordially yours,*), which is typed a double space below the last line of the body, (9) the handwritten signature of the person who composed the letter, (10) the signer's identification (name and title), and (11) the reference initials of the signer and/or typist. Note in the first illustration that a colon is typed after the salutation (5) and that a comma is typed after the complimentary closing (8). This use of the colon and comma after these opening and closing lines is known as "mixed punctuation style." If no punctuation marks are used after these lines, the style is known as "open punctuation style."

The closing may also include the following optional parts: (12) an enclosure notation (specifying that something is enclosed with the letter), (13) a carbon copy (*cc*) notation (specifying that copies of the letter have been sent to other parties), and (14) a postscript (an added message that, when used, is always typed as the final item in a letter). In addition, some companies include (15) the firm name, which, if used, is typed a double space below the complimentary closing in all-capital letters.

Two additional letter parts are the continuation-page heading and the blind carbon copy (*bcc*) notation. The continuation-page heading, used on continuation pages for long letters, indicates the addressee's name, the page number, and the date. The *bcc* notation is a copy notation that appears only on the copies—so that the addressee does not see who has received copies.

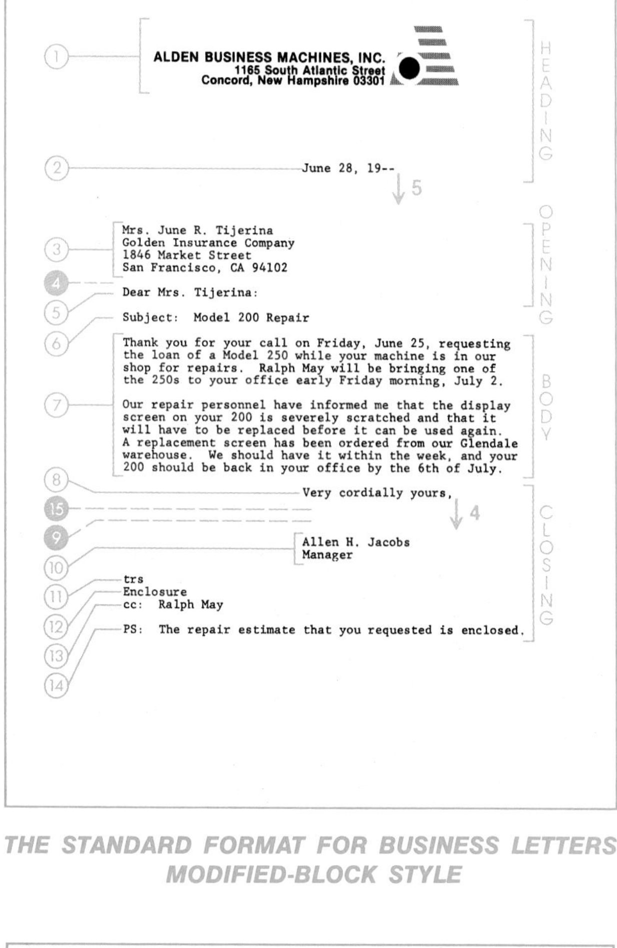

ALDEN BUSINESS MACHINES, INC.
1165 South Atlantic Street
Concord, New Hampshire 03301

June 28, 19--

Mrs. June R. Tijerina
Golden Insurance Company
1846 Market Street
San Francisco, CA 94102

Dear Mrs. Tijerina:

Subject: Model 200 Repair

Thank you for your call on Friday, June 25, requesting the loan of a Model 250 while your machine is in our shop for repairs. Ralph May will be bringing one of the 250s to your office early Friday morning, July 2.

Our repair personnel have informed me that the display screen on your 200 is severely scratched and that it will have to be replaced before it can be used again. A replacement screen has been ordered from our Glendale warehouse. We should have it within the week, and your 200 should be back in your office by the 6th of July.

Very cordially yours,

Allen H. Jacobs
Manager

trs
Enclosure
cc: Ralph May

PS: The repair estimate that you requested is enclosed.

THE STANDARD FORMAT FOR BUSINESS LETTERS: MODIFIED-BLOCK STYLE

PERSONAL-BUSINESS LETTER PARTS

A personal-business letter also has a heading, an opening, a body, and a closing, but the personal-business letter usually differs from the business letter in the following respects:

1. The heading is typewritten, not printed, and consists of the writer's full address (street, city, state, and ZIP Code) and the date the letter is typed.
2. The closing includes the complimentary closing and the writer's name. Reference initials are omitted.

Personal-business letters may also include carbon copy notations, enclosure notations, and so on.

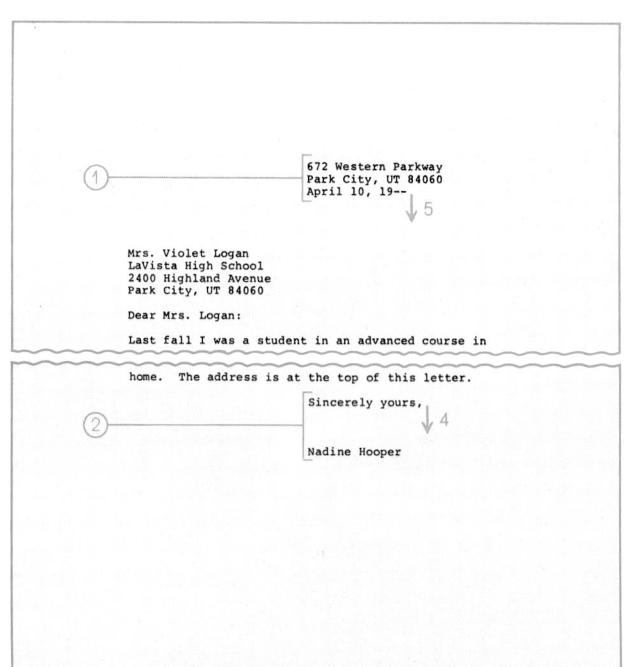

672 Western Parkway
Park City, UT 84060
April 10, 19--

Mrs. Violet Logan
LaVista High School
2400 Highland Avenue
Park City, UT 84060

Dear Mrs. Logan:

Last fall I was a student in an advanced course in

home. The address is at the top of this letter.

Sincerely yours,

Nadine Hooper

PERSONAL-BUSINESS LETTER

LETTER FORMATS

Standard Format. The most popular format for business letters is the modified-block style—the *standard format* used in business. As shown on the previous page, in the standard format the date line and the closing lines (complimentary closing and writer's name and/or title) begin at the center. All other lines begin at the left margin.

Other Letter Formats. Three other letter formats are illustrated below: (1) A *variation of the standard format* is to indent the start of paragraphs 5 spaces, rather than to type them at the left margin, as shown in the first illustration below. (2) The *block* format shows all lines beginning at the left margin. (3) The *simplified* format also has all lines beginning at the left margin. Simplified letters do not have salutations and complimentary closings; they always have all-capital subject lines (a triple space precedes and follows the subject line) and all-capital writer's identification lines (typed 5 lines below the body).

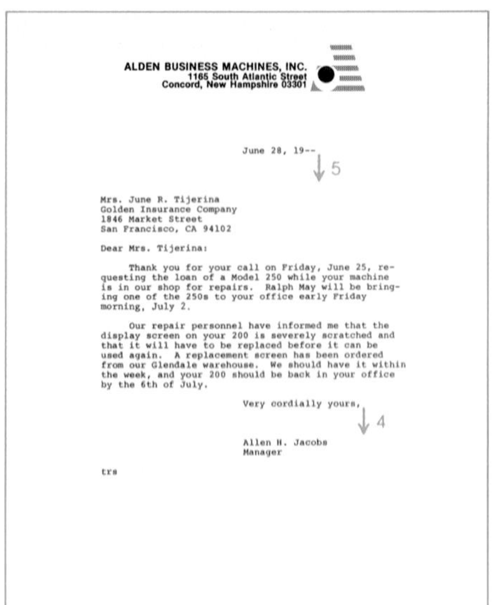

ALDEN BUSINESS MACHINES, INC.
1165 South Atlantic Street
Concord, New Hampshire 03301

June 28, 19--

Mrs. June R. Tijerina
Golden Insurance Company
1846 Market Street
San Francisco, CA 94102

Dear Mrs. Tijerina:

Thank you for your call on Friday, June 25, requesting the loan of a Model 250 while your machine is in our shop for repairs. Ralph May will be bringing one of the 250s to your office early Friday morning, July 2.

Our repair personnel have informed me that the display screen on your 200 is severely scratched and that it will have to be replaced before it can be used again. A replacement screen has been ordered from our Glendale warehouse. We should have it within the week, and your 200 should be back in your office by the 6th of July.

Very cordially yours,

Allen H. Jacobs
Manager

trs

STANDARD FORMAT WITH INDENTED PARAGRAPHS

ALDEN BUSINESS MACHINES, INC.
1165 South Atlantic Street
Concord, New Hampshire 03301

June 28, 19--

Mrs. June R. Tijerina
Golden Insurance Company
1846 Market Street
San Francisco, CA 94102

Dear Mrs. Tijerina:

Thank you for your call on Friday, June 25, requesting the loan of a Model 250 while your machine is in our shop for repairs. Ralph May will be bringing one of the 250s to your office early Friday morning, July 2.

Our repair personnel have informed me that the display screen on your 200 is severely scratched and that it will have to be replaced before it can be used again. A replacement screen has been ordered from our Glendale warehouse. We should have it within the week, and your 200 should be back in your office by the 6th of July.

Very cordially yours,

Allen H. Jacobs
Manager

trs

BLOCK FORMAT

ALDEN BUSINESS MACHINES, INC.
1165 South Atlantic Street
Concord, New Hampshire 03301

June 28, 19--

Mrs. June R. Tijerina
Golden Insurance Company
1846 Market Street
San Francisco, CA 94102

MODEL 200 REPAIR

Thank you for your call on Friday, June 25, requesting the loan of a Model 250 while your machine is in our shop for repairs. Ralph May will be bringing one of the 250s to your office early Friday morning, July 2.

Our repair personnel have informed me that the display screen on your 200 is severely scratched and that it will have to be replaced before it can be used again. A replacement screen has been ordered from our Glendale warehouse. We should have it within the week, and your 200 should be back in your office by the 6th of July.

ALLEN H. JACOBS, MANAGER

TRS

SIMPLIFIED FORMAT

Stationery Sizes

Most business letters are typed on standard-size paper. However, other sizes, such as monarch and baronial, may also be used. All three sizes (with placement guidelines) are illustrated below.

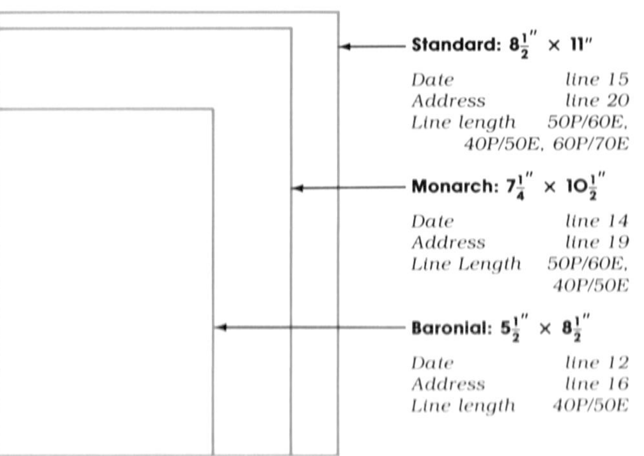

Two-Page Letters

A second-page heading for a letter should be typed on plain paper and should include the addressee's name, the page number, and the date. Start typing the heading on line 7; use one of the styles illustrated below. Triple-space after the heading before continuing the letter.

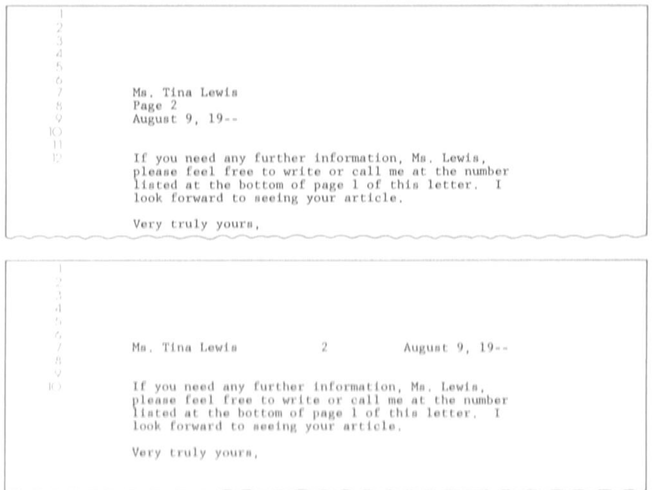

Ms. Tina Lewis
Page 2
August 9, 19--

If you need any further information, Ms. Lewis, please feel free to write or call me at the number listed at the bottom of page 1 of this letter. I look forward to seeing your article.

Very truly yours,

Ms. Tina Lewis 2 August 9, 19--

If you need any further information, Ms. Lewis, please feel free to write or call me at the number listed at the bottom of page 1 of this letter. I look forward to seeing your article.

Very truly yours,

ENVELOPES

ADDRESSING ENVELOPES

Every envelope should include the writer's name and *return address* and the addressee's full *mailing address.*

Return Address. A printed return address gives the company name, street address, and city, state, and ZIP Code. The writer's name should be typed above the printed return address, aligned at the left with the top line of printing.

If the return address is not printed, then it should be typed blocked and single-spaced, beginning on line 3, 5 spaces from the left edge.

Mailing Address. An envelope addressed to a person at his or her place of business generally includes the addressee's name and business title, the company name, and the complete company address (street address plus city, state, and ZIP Code). An envelope addressed to a person at home usually includes his or her name, street address, and city, state, and ZIP Code. In either case, a courtesy title (such as *Ms.* or *Mr.*) should precede the addressee's name.

On a small envelope, begin typing the addressee's name on line 12, 2 inches (20P/24E) from the left edge. On a large envelope, begin typing the addressee's name on line 14, 4 inches (40P/48E) from the left edge. Single-space the mailing address, and block all lines on the left. Leave only 1 space between the state and the ZIP Code.

Special Directions. Type on-arrival directions (such as *Attention: District Manager*) on line 9 in capital and lower-case letters. Underscore the direction, and align it with the return address. Type mailing directions (such as *Special Delivery* and *Express Mail*) on line 9 below the stamp, on the right side of the envelope. Try to end the mailing direction about 5 spaces from the right edge.

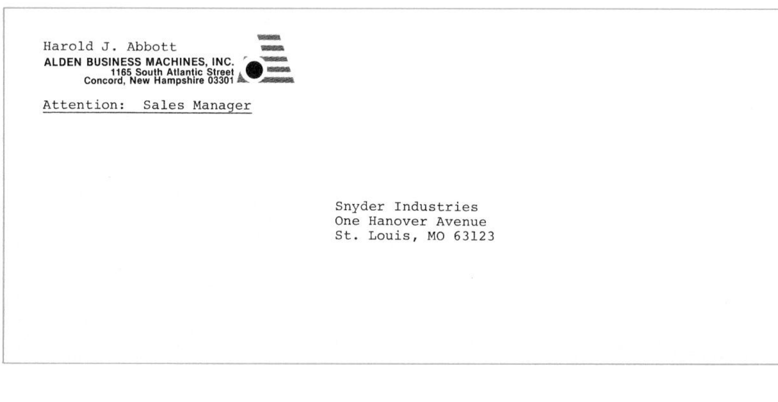

Harold J. Abbott
ALDEN BUSINESS MACHINES, INC.
1165 South Atlantic Street
Concord, New Hampshire 03301

Attention: Sales Manager

Snyder Industries
One Hanover Avenue
St. Louis, MO 63123

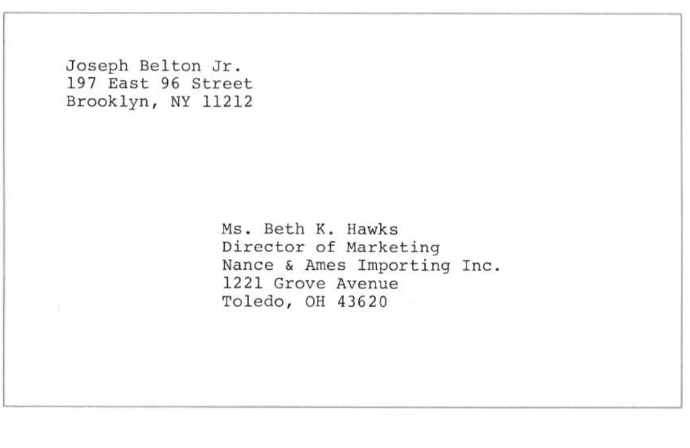

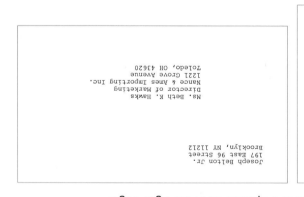

Joseph Belton Jr.
197 East 96 Street
Brooklyn, NY 11212

Ms. Beth K. Hawks
Director of Marketing
Nance & Ames Importing Inc.
1221 Grove Avenue
Toledo, OH 43620

FOLDING LETTERS

For Small Envelopes, No. 6¾ (6½ by 3⅝ inches)

1. Fold up the bottom edge to ⅜ inch from the top edge.
2. Fold the right-hand third over to the left.
3. Fold the left-hand third over to ⅜ inch from the right edge.
4. Insert the last crease into the envelope first, with the flap facing up.

For Large Envelopes, No. 10 (9½ by 4⅛ inches)

1. Fold up the bottom third of the letter.
2. Fold the top third down to ⅜ inch from the bottom edge.
3. Insert the last crease into the envelope first, with the flap facing up.

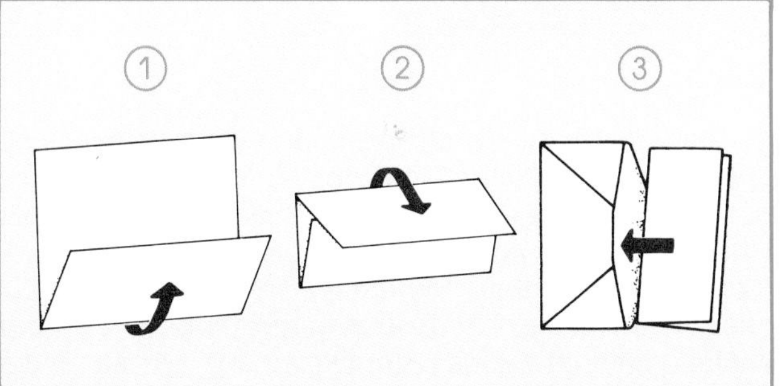

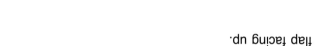

MECHANICS OF TYPING FORMS

ALIGNMENT

Forms have printed guide words to show where to type names, dates, and so on. Align typed insertions with the bottom of the printed guide words, 2 spaces after the printed word (or the colon that follows the word). When one guide word is below another, begin the insertions at the same point.

To align properly, you must know how close your typewriter prints to its aligning scale. Type the alphabet and study the space between the typing and the scale. You will then know how much to adjust the paper (using the variable line spacer) whenever you are aligning the typed words with the guide words of a form.

When you type on ruled lines, the ruled line should be in the position of the underscore.

MEMOS

1. Set your left margin at the point where you begin the fill-ins in the heading.
2. Set your right margin so that it is the same width as your left margin.
3. Begin the body a triple space below the last line of the heading.
4. Type the writer's initials at the same tab used for the second column in the heading.

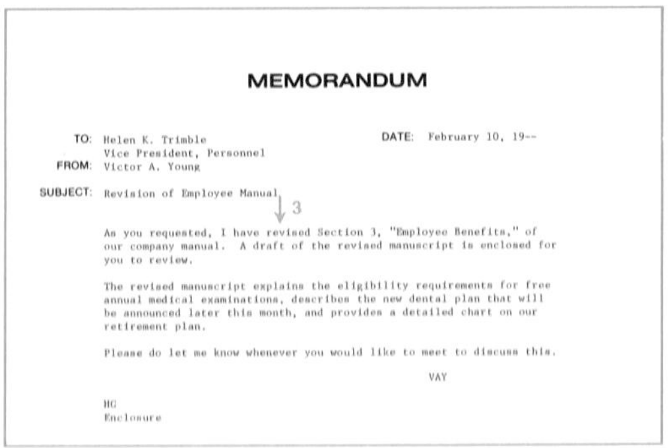

MEMORANDUM

TO: Helen K. Trimble
Vice President, Personnel
DATE: February 10, 19--
FROM: Victor A. Young

SUBJECT: Revision of Employee Manual

↓ 3

As you requested, I have revised Section 3, "Employee Benefits," of our company manual. A draft of the revised manuscript is enclosed for you to review.

The revised manuscript explains the eligibility requirements for free annual medical examinations, describes the new dental plan that will be announced later this month, and provides a detailed chart on our retirement plan.

Please do let me know whenever you would like to meet to discuss this.

VAY

HG
Enclosure

BILLING FORMS

1. Align number columns on the right; center visually within the column.
2. Align word columns on the left; begin 2 spaces after the vertical rule.
3. Double-space; single-space turnover lines and indent them 3 spaces.
4. Align total lines with the *D* in *Description.*
5. Do not type the symbol *$* in money columns.

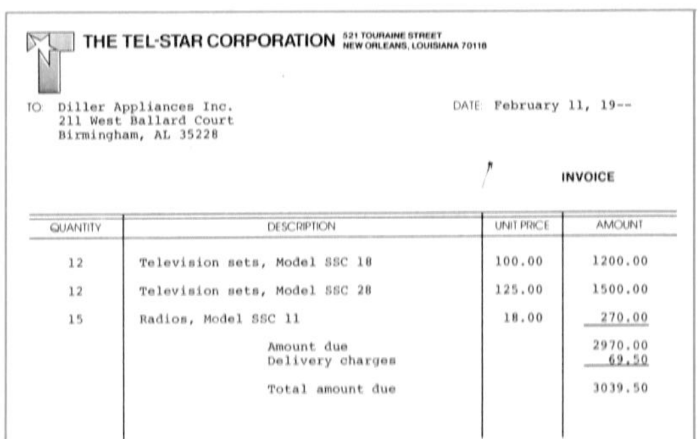

THE TEL-STAR CORPORATION 521 TOURAINE STREET NEW ORLEANS, LOUISIANA 70118

TO: Diller Appliances Inc.
211 West Ballard Court
Birmingham, AL 35228

DATE: February 11, 19--

INVOICE

QUANTITY	DESCRIPTION	UNIT PRICE	AMOUNT
12	Television sets, Model SSC 18	100.00	1200.00
12	Television sets, Model SSC 28	125.00	1500.00
15	Radios, Model SSC 11	18.00	270.00
	Amount due		2970.00
	Delivery charges		69.50
	Total amount due		3039.50

MECHANICS OF TYPING TABLES

OPEN TABLES

Of all the different table styles, the *open* style is the easiest to set up and type. Open tables are commonly used in business offices.

Table Parts

1. Title—Centered in all capitals.
2. Subtitle—Centered with first and main words in capital and lowercase letters.
3. Column Headings—Centered over the column (may be blocked at the start of the column in drafts).
4. Body—The contents of the table.

*Key Line—The longest item in each column (the longest item will sometimes be the column heading), plus the number of spaces between columns.

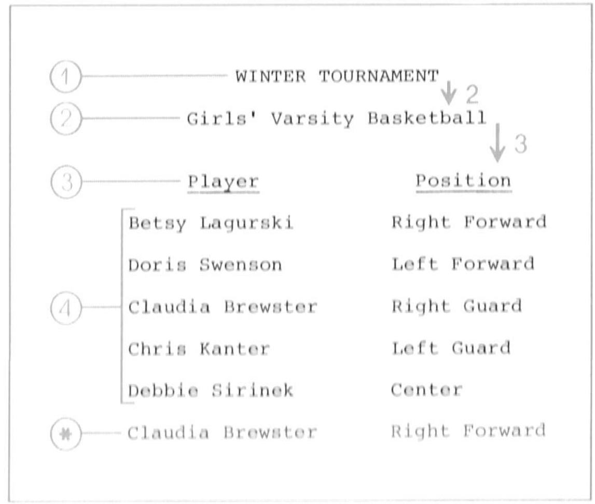

(1) WINTER TOURNAMENT

↓ 2

(2) Girls' Varsity Basketball

↓ 3

(3) Player	Position
Betsy Lagurski	Right Forward
Doris Swenson	Left Forward
(4) Claudia Brewster	Right Guard
Chris Kanter	Left Guard
Debbie Sirinek	Center

(*) Claudia Brewster Right Forward

Format

1. Use 6 spaces between columns (unless there is a special reason for using more or fewer spaces).
2. Underscore all words in the column headings.
3. Sequence the items, when appropriate, by putting them in alphabetic order, putting them in numeric order, arranging them by dollar amount, and so on.
4. Use a 1-inch (10P/12E) line to separate a footnote from the body of the table.

INTERNATIONAL TREATIES AND AGREEMENTS*

↓3

Name	Year Adopted	Number of Countries
Common Market	1957	9
Commonwealth of Nations	1931	43
NATO	1949	15
OAS	1948	28

*Warsaw Pact and Yalta not included.

RULED TABLES

Ruled tables are often used for formal reports and research papers. The ruled lines (solid lines of underscores) are typed before and after the column headings and also at the end of the table.

Format

1. Type the ruled lines the exact width of the table.
2. Single-space before each ruled line, and double-space after each ruled line.
3. If the table ends with a Total line, type a ruled line before and after the Total line.

SALES ANALYSIS

Borden Manufacturing Company ↓1

ss / ds ↓2

Salesperson	Units	Sales
Robert Brazinski	10	$ 427.70
Carol Dawkins	18	769.86
Janice Greene	20	855.40
Jose Herrera	17	727.09
TOTAL	65	$2780.05

BOXED TABLES WITH BRACED HEADINGS

Boxed tables contain both horizontal and vertical rules. The vertical rules are used to highlight the columns of the table. A braced column heading is centered over two or more columns.

Format

1. When typing a table with braced headings, type the column headings first; then turn back the paper and type the braced heading above the horizontal ruled line.
2. Center the braced heading over the column headings it braces.
3. Vertical rules should stop at the bracing line. Horizontal rules for the braced columns should extend only over the columns that are braced.

SALES ANALYSIS

Borden Manufacturing Company

June 30, 19-- ↓1

	1st Quarter		2d Quarter	
Salesperson	Units	Gross Sales	Units	Gross Sales
Robert Brazinski	10	$ 427.70	29	$1240.33
Carol Dawkins	18	769.86	17	727.09
Janice Greene	20	855.40	28	1197.56
Jose Herrera	17	727.09	24	1026.48
Diane Keester	15	641.55	25	1069.25
Joe Yeung	19	812.63	32	1368.64
TOTAL	99	$4234.23	155	$6629.35

LEADERED TABLES

Leadered tables have typed rows of periods between the columns. The periods "lead" the reader's eyes from column to column within the table.

Format

1. Type rows of solid periods (no space between periods).
2. Leave 1 blank space before the first and after the last period in each row.
3. Use at least three periods in a row of leaders.

SUMMER SEMINAR SCHEDULE

"Time Management" .... June 7-8

"Financial Planning" .... June 11-13

"Budgeting Techniques" .... July 6-9

"Advertising Principles" ...... July 16-18

4. **Note:** You must look at your work as you type leadered tables to be certain you type the exact number of periods for each row.

MECHANICS OF TYPING REPORTS

Reports are very commonly used communications—both in schools and in business. The parts listed below typically appear in most reports. Special pages that appear in longer reports—title pages, contents pages, and so on—are discussed later.

Parts of a Report

1. *Title*—Centered in all capitals on line 13.
2. *Subtitle*—Centered in capital and lowercase letters on line 15.
3. *Byline*—Centered in capital and lowercase letters on line 17.
4. *Side Heading*—At left margin in all capitals, preceded by 2 blank lines and followed by 1 blank line.
5. *Short Quotation* (not longer than three typed lines)—Typed in quotation marks as part of the text of the report.
6. *Paragraph Heading*—Indented, in capital and lowercase letters, underscored, and followed by a period.
7. *Page Numbers*—Backspaced from the right margin on line 7. Triple-space to the text of the report. (**Note:** Do not type the number on the first page.)
8. *Long Quotation* (longer than three typed lines)—Single-spaced, preceded and followed by a blank line, and indented 5 spaces from each margin.
9. *Separation Line*—To separate footnotes from the text of the report, type a rule 20P/24E spaces long, beginning at the left margin. Use a minimum of a single space before the separation line, and always use a double space after it.
10. *Footnote*—Type footnotes at the bottom of the page from margin to margin; single-space, with a double space between footnotes. Indent the first line of the footnote 5 spaces. **Note:** Footnotes may also be placed in their entirety on a separate page at the end of the report. See "Endnotes" on page 493.

Format. Observe the following rules when typing reports:

1. *Spacing*. Double is used. Single may be used to save space.
2. *Line Length.*
   - **a.** For unbound reports—6-inch line (60P/70E).
   - **b.** For bound reports—shift both margin stops (and center tab) 3 spaces to the right.
3. *Paragraph Indention.* 5 spaces.
4. *Top Margin.* Leave 12 blank lines on first page; 6 blank lines on other pages.
5. *Bottom Margin.* Leave between 6 and 9 blank lines.

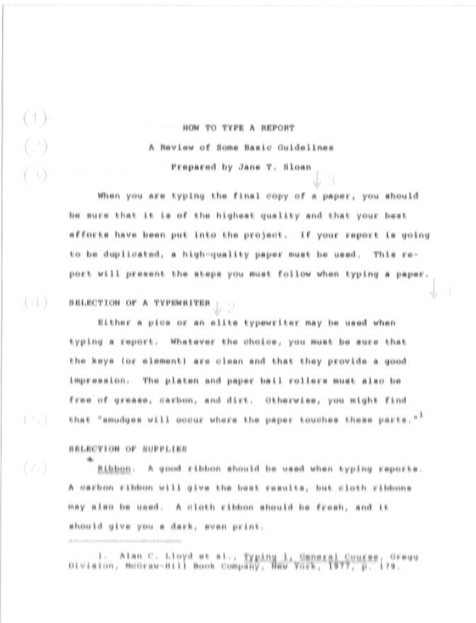

(1) HOW TO TYPE A REPORT

(2) A Review of Some Basic Guidelines

(3) Prepared by Jane T. Sloan

When you are typing the final copy of a paper, you should be sure that it is of the highest quality and that your best efforts have been put into the project. If your report is going to be duplicated, a high-quality paper must be used. This report will present the steps you must follow when typing a paper.

(4) SELECTION OF A TYPEWRITER

Either a pica or an elite typewriter may be used when typing a report. Whatever the choice, you must be sure that the keys (or element) are clean and that they provide a good impression. The platen and paper bail rollers must also be free of grease, carbon, and dirt. Otherwise, you might find (5) that "smudges will occur where the paper touches these parts."[1]

SELECTION OF SUPPLIES

(6) Ribbon. A good ribbon should be used when typing reports. A carbon ribbon will give the best results, but cloth ribbons may also be used. A cloth ribbon should be fresh, and it should give you a dark, even print.

1. Alan C. Lloyd et al., Typing 1, General Course, Gregg Division, McGraw-Hill Book Company, New York, 1977, p. 179.

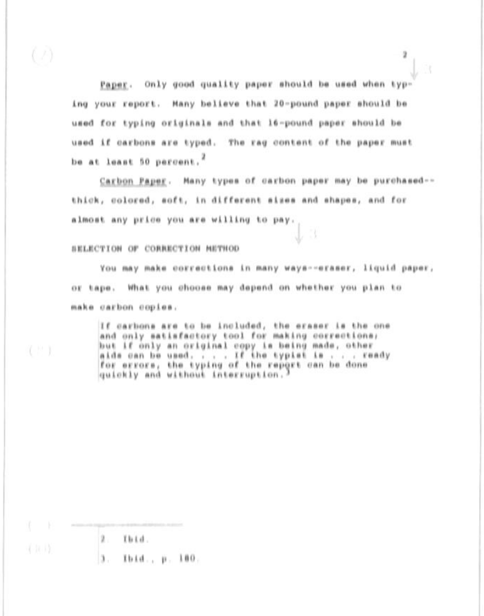

(7) 2

Paper. Only good quality paper should be used when typing your report. Many believe that 20-pound paper should be used for typing originals and that 16-pound paper should be used if carbons are typed. The rag content of the paper must be at least 50 percent.[2]

Carbon Paper. Many types of carbon paper may be purchased--thick, colored, soft, in different sizes and shapes, and for almost any price you are willing to pay.

SELECTION OF CORRECTION METHOD

You may make corrections in many ways--eraser, liquid paper, or tape. What you choose may depend on whether you plan to make carbon copies.

(8) If carbons are to be included, the eraser is the one and only satisfactory tool for making corrections; but if only an original copy is being made, other aids can be used. . . . If the typist is . . . ready for errors, the typing of the report can be done quickly and without interruption.[3]

(9)

(10) 2. Ibid.

3. Ibid., p. 180.

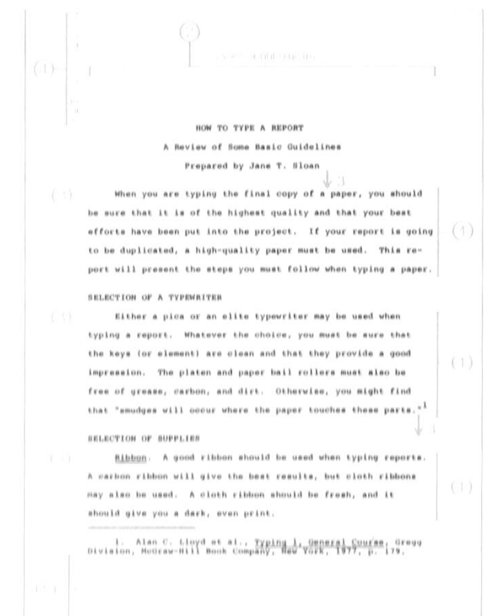

HOW TO TYPE A REPORT

A Review of Some Basic Guidelines

Prepared by Jane T. Sloan

When you are typing the final copy of a paper, you should be sure that it is of the highest quality and that your best efforts have been put into the project. If your report is going to be duplicated, a high-quality paper must be used. This report will present the steps you must follow when typing a paper.

SELECTION OF A TYPEWRITER

Either a pica or an elite typewriter may be used when typing a report. Whatever the choice, you must be sure that the keys (or element) are clean and that they provide a good impression. The platen and paper bail rollers must also be free of grease, carbon, and dirt. Otherwise, you might find that "smudges will occur where the paper touches these parts."[1]

SELECTION OF SUPPLIES

Ribbon. A good ribbon should be used when typing reports. A carbon ribbon will give the best results, but cloth ribbons may also be used. A cloth ribbon should be fresh, and it should give you a dark, even print.

1. Alan C. Lloyd et al., Typing 1, General Course, Gregg Division, McGraw-Hill Book Company, New York, 1977, p. 179.

SPECIAL REPORT PAGES

A long report contains the following special pages: (1) title page, (2) contents, and (3) bibliography.

Title Page. Title page information may vary greatly, depending on the purpose of the report. Formal reports, for example, often require additional information. Note the following guidelines:

For School Reports and Most Business Reports

1. In the top half of the page, center the title of the report and the name of the person who prepared the report.
2. In the lower half of the page, center the name of the course (for a school report) or the name of the company (for a business report), the name of the person to whom the report is being submitted, and the date.

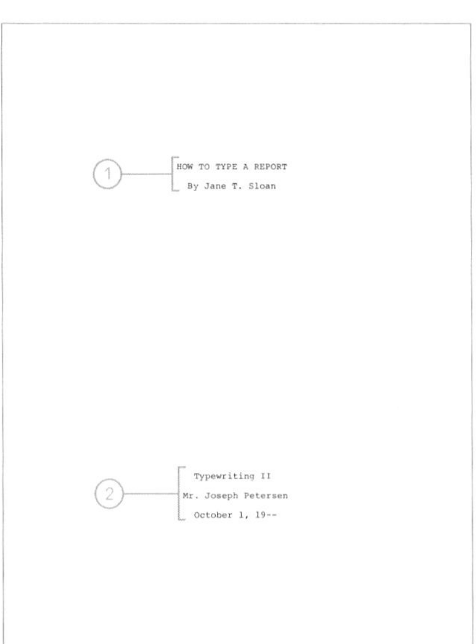

For More Formal Reports

1. Center the report title in all caps on line 13.
2. Center the subtitle or the first line of a multiline subtitle on line 15 in capital and lowercase letters. Single-space additional lines in the subtitle.
3. Center in capital and lowercase letters the author's name and title, department name, and company name, centered vertically on the page.
4. Center the date on line 54 (13 lines from the bottom of the page).

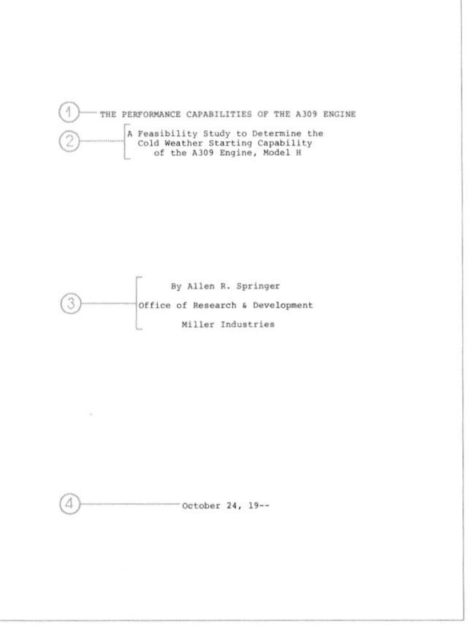

Contents. The contents page follows the title page of the report.

1. Center *CONTENTS* or *TABLE OF CONTENTS* on line 13 in all capitals; triple-space after the heading.
2. Type each entry in the contents (a chapter, a major section, and so on) in capital and lowercase letters.
3. Precede each entry with a roman numeral (*I, II,* and so on). Use leaders between each entry and its page number.
4. Number the contents page or pages with lowercase roman numerals (*ii, iii,* and so on), and center each number 6 lines from the bottom of the page.
5. Use the same margins as you used for the report.

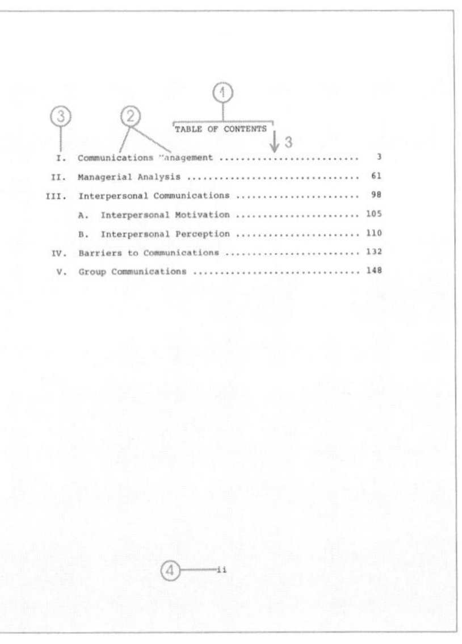

SPECIAL REPORT PAGES (CONTINUED)

Bibliography. A bibliography identifies all the sources that were used in preparing the report and all the sources cited in the footnotes. It is the last major section of a report. To format a bibliography page:

1. Center *BIBLIOGRAPHY* on line 13 in all capitals; triple-space after this heading.
2. Use margins identical with those used in the body of the report.
3. Alphabetize all entries by authors' last names.
4. Single-space all entries, but use a double space between individual entries.
5. Begin the first line of each entry at the left margin; indent additional lines for each entry 5 or 10 spaces from the left margin.
6. List the name of the first author in each entry in inverted order (last name first).
7. Follow the report style for page numbers.

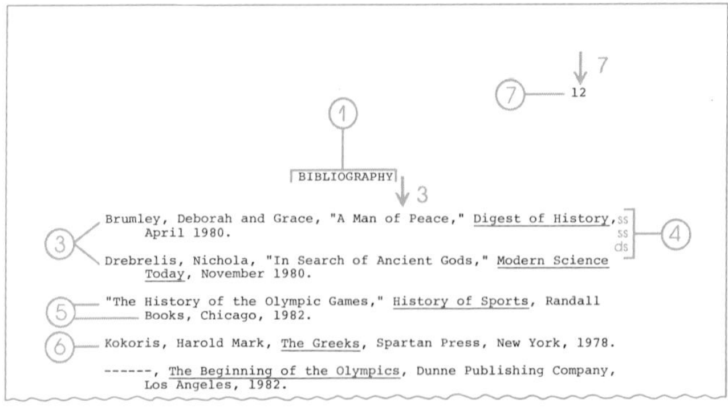

12

BIBLIOGRAPHY

Brumley, Deborah and Grace, "A Man of Peace," Digest of History, April 1980.

Drebrelis, Nichola, "In Search of Ancient Gods," Modern Science Today, November 1980.

"The History of the Olympic Games," History of Sports, Randall Books, Chicago, 1982.

Kokoris, Harold Mark, The Greeks, Spartan Press, New York, 1978.

------, The Beginning of the Olympics, Dunne Publishing Company, Los Angeles, 1982.

Endnotes. Footnotes placed in a special section at the end of a report are called *endnotes.* To format endnotes:

1. Center *NOTES* on line 13 in all capitals; triple-space after this heading.
2. Use the same margins that were used to type the body of the report.
3. Single-space each note, and leave 1 blank line between individual notes.
4. Indent the first line of each note 5 spaces. Additional lines within the same note should begin at the left margin.
5. Number the endnote page(s) in the same way you numbered the report.

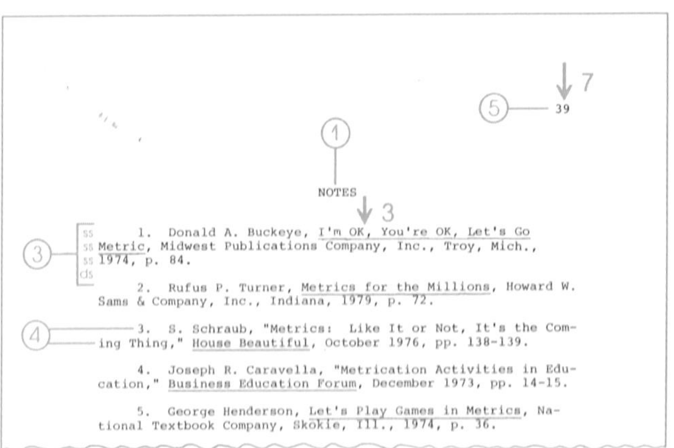

39

NOTES

1. Donald A. Buckeye, I'm OK, You're OK, Let's Go Metric, Midwest Publications Company, Inc., Troy, Mich., 1974, p. 84.

2. Rufus P. Turner, Metrics for the Millions, Howard W. Sams & Company, Inc., Indiana, 1979, p. 72.

3. S. Schraub, "Metrics: Like It or Not, It's the Coming Thing," House Beautiful, October 1976, pp. 138-139.

4. Joseph R. Caravella, "Metrication Activities in Education," Business Education Forum, December 1973, pp. 14-15.

5. George Henderson, Let's Play Games in Metrics, National Textbook Company, Skokie, Ill., 1974, p. 36.

SPECIAL REPORT FORMATS

Variations of the report format are used for minutes of a meeting, magazine articles, and legal documents.

Minutes of a Meeting. The minutes of a meeting usually consist of three parts—*ATTENDANCE, UNFINISHED BUSINESS,* and *NEW BUSINESS*—which are typed as side headings in all caps at the left margin. Minutes are usually saved in a three-ring binder, so the margins for a bound report should be used. Three space-saving rules for typing minutes of a meeting are:

1. Type the title on line 7.
2. Use single spacing in the body.
3. Leave 1 blank line before and after each side heading.

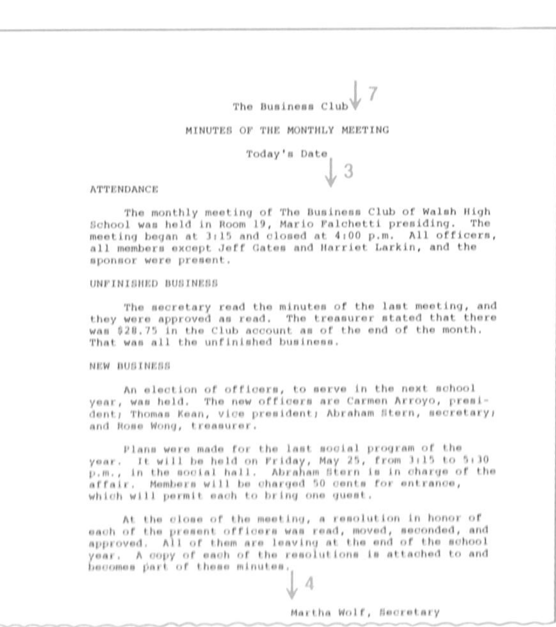

The Business Club

MINUTES OF THE MONTHLY MEETING

Today's Date

ATTENDANCE

The monthly meeting of The Business Club of Walsh High School was held in Room 19, Mario Falchetti presiding. The meeting began at 3:15 and closed at 4:00 p.m. All officers, all members except Jeff Gates and Harriet Larkin, and the sponsor were present.

UNFINISHED BUSINESS

The secretary read the minutes of the last meeting, and they were approved as read. The treasurer stated that there was $28.75 in the Club account as of the end of the month. That was all the unfinished business.

NEW BUSINESS

An election of officers, to serve in the next school year, was held. The new officers are Carmen Arroyo, president; Thomas Kean, vice president; Abraham Stern, secretary; and Rose Wong, treasurer.

Plans were made for the last social program of the year. It will be held on Friday, May 25, from 3:15 to 5:30 p.m., in the social hall. Abraham Stern is in charge of the affair. Members will be charged 50 cents for entrance, which will permit each to bring one guest.

At the close of the meeting, a resolution in honor of each of the present officers was read, moved, seconded, and approved. All of them are leaving at the end of the school year. A copy of each of the resolutions is attached to and becomes part of these minutes.

Martha Wolf, Secretary

SPECIAL REPORT FORMATS (CONTINUED)

Magazine Article. To determine the line length for typing a magazine article, get a printed copy of the magazine to which the article will be submitted, and count the total number of characters and spaces in ten random full lines in a printed article. Compute the average number of spaces per line, and use this figure for the line length. (**Reason:** Typing the article to this line length will help the magazine editor to determine how many columns or pages the article requires.) Or use a 50-space line.

Follow the standard report format for the article title and the byline. In parentheses below the byline, type the total number of lines in the article and the line length used, as shown in the illustration. On all pages except the first, type the author's last name and the page number at the right margin. As shown in the illustration, use a diagonal to separate the author's name from the page number.

TYPING AN ARTICLE
By Allen R. Davis
(30 Lines of 50 Spaces)

If you ever have to type a magazine article as part of your job, there are a few rules that you should always follow. As you can see by the rules in this article, the layout of the page is very similar to the typing of a report. There are some differences, however, between typing reports and typing magazine articles. These minor differences are explained in this magazine article.

1. Find a copy of the magazine to which the article is going to be submitted for publication. Count the number of lines in the article to see how long the article should be.

2. To determine what line length to use, count the number of strokes appearing in ten full lines of the article. The average of these ten lines will be the line length you should use for the article. Set your left and right margins for that precise line. When you type the article, do not exceed by more than two strokes the exact line length you have chosen. For example, assume that you have found

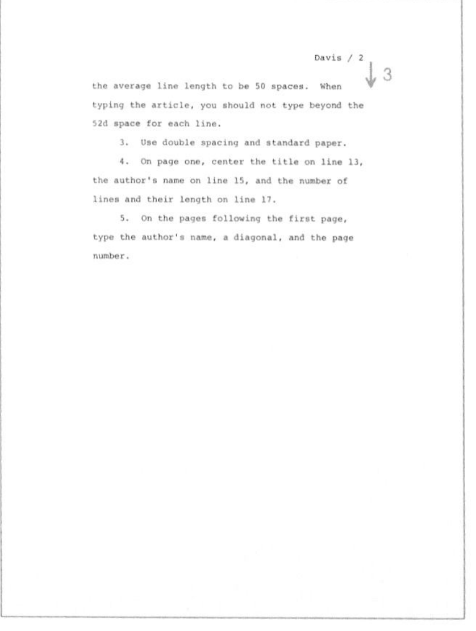

Davis / 2

the average line length to be 50 spaces. When typing the article, you should not type beyond the 52d space for each line.

3. Use double spacing and standard paper.

4. On page one, center the title on line 13, the author's name on line 15, and the number of lines and their length on line 17.

5. On the pages following the first page, type the author's name, a diagonal, and the page number.

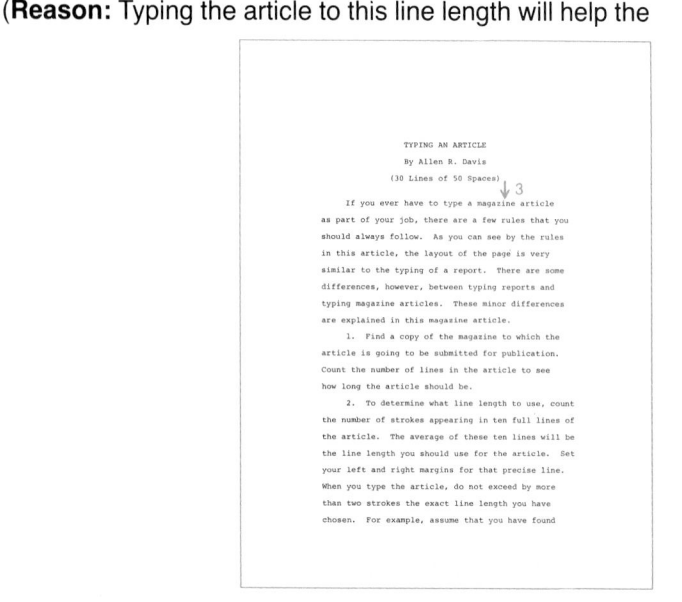

Legal Document. Legal typing differs from other report typing in several ways.

1. Use legal paper, which has a double vertical line 14P/17E spaces from the left edge and a single vertical line 4P/5E spaces from the right edge.
2. Double-space the body.
3. Indent paragraphs 10 spaces.
4. Set margins 2 spaces inside the vertical ruled lines.
5. Leave a top margin of 12 blank lines on page 1; 9 blank lines on other pages.
6. Center page numbers about 6 lines from the bottom of the page. Paginate as follows: "Page 1 of 3," "Page 2 of 3," and so on.

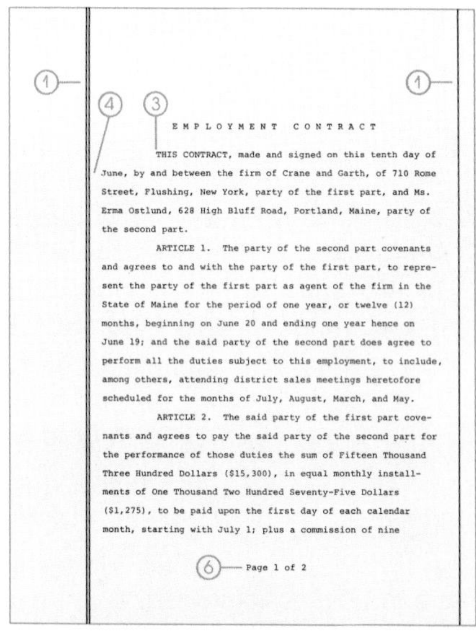

E M P L O Y M E N T   C O N T R A C T

THIS CONTRACT, made and signed on this tenth day of June, by and between the firm of Crane and Garth, of 710 Rome Street, Flushing, New York, party of the first part, and Ms. Erma Ostlund, 628 High Bluff Road, Portland, Maine, party of the second part.

ARTICLE 1. The party of the second part covenants and agrees to and with the party of the first part, to represent the party of the first part as agent of the firm in the State of Maine for the period of one year, or twelve (12) months, beginning on June 20 and ending one year hence on June 19; and the said party of the second part does agree to perform all the duties subject to this employment, to include, among others, attending district sales meetings heretofore scheduled for the months of July, August, March, and May.

ARTICLE 2. The said party of the first part covenants and agrees to pay the said party of the second part for the performance of those duties the sum of Fifteen Thousand Three Hundred Dollars ($15,300), in equal monthly installments of One Thousand Two Hundred Seventy-Five Dollars ($1,275), to be paid upon the first day of each calendar month, starting with July 1; plus a commission of nine

Page 1 of 2

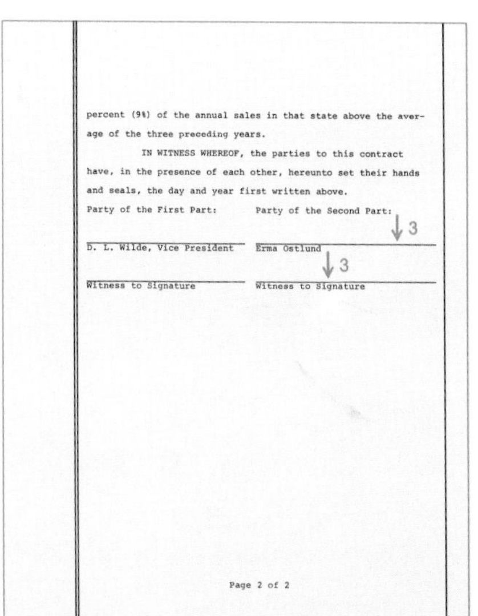

percent (9%) of the annual sales in that state above the average of the three preceding years.

IN WITNESS WHEREOF, the parties to this contract have, in the presence of each other, hereunto set their hands and seals, the day and year first written above.

Party of the First Part: Party of the Second Part:

D. L. Wilde, Vice President   Erma Ostlund

Witness to Signature   Witness to Signature

Page 2 of 2

GOALS

1. Demonstrate keyboarding speed and accuracy on straight copy with a goal of 41 words a minute for 5 minutes with 4 or fewer errors.
2. Correctly proofread copy for errors and edit copy for revision.
3. Apply production skills in keyboarding and formatting copy for reports, correspondence, tables, and forms from a variety of input modes—arranged, unarranged, rough draft, handwritten, incomplete, and/or unedited.
4. Apply rules for subject/verb agreement in written communications.

MAGAZINE ARTICLE

SELL YOUR MANUSCRIPTS

By Jean B. Hall

The way in which a magazine story is typed can help or hurt its chance for acceptance. Why is this so? Well, all editors get many more stories than they can publish, so they are prejudiced in favor of the infrequent article that looks as though it were the polished handiwork of some expert on the staff who got it ready for printing. When editors are pushed for time, they will use what is easiest to use, other things being equal.

So, if you want to sell a magazine article, story, or feature, look at it the way the editor will. Simply imagine, if you can, what editors have to know about your contribution and what they may have to modify before it can be published.

For example, they have to know how many lines of space your article will fill, what headings it may require, and what style touches must be injected. When you type the manuscript, try to solve as many of these problems as you can.

Here is what the professional would do:

1. Acquire an issue of the journal in which you hope to see your writing. Find a similar story and count how many lines it has; that figure will be your target for the length of your article.
2. Count the number of strokes printed in ten full lines in the columns of the magazine. Average the figure so that you know how long a line to use. Set the stops exactly for that line (do not add the usual extra 5 spaces). Do not let any line go more than 2 spaces beyond that line length.
3. Use double spacing and standard paper.
4. On page 1, center the title in all caps on line 13, the author's name on line 15, and the number of lines and the line length on line 17.
5. On each page after the first, type the name of the author, a diagonal, and the page number.
6. If you need side headings or other displays, show them in the style used in the magazine.

A lot of trouble to go to? Perhaps, but not nearly as much trouble as writing and typing an article that earns a rejection slip instead of an acceptance.

MINUTES OF A MEETING

Personnel Committee

MINUTES OF THE SPECIAL MEETING

[Today's date]

ATTENDANCE

A special meeting of the Personnel Committee was held in the office of Ms. Quinn, who presided at the meeting. The session began at two o'clock and was adjourned at four. All members were there except Alan Schmidt, who was represented by Helen Sampson.

UNFINISHED BUSINESS

The secretary read the minutes of the last monthly conference, and they were approved.

Mr. Stern reported on the survey of ages of company employees; a copy of the survey is attached to these minutes.

NEW BUSINESS

Ms. Quinn introduced the need for planning a campaign to let job applicants know about the new openings in our office. It will be studied further at our next meeting.

Bob Dawson, Secretary

UNIT 25 Keyboarding Skills Review

UNIT GOAL 40/5′/4e

■ **GOALS**
To build speed on the alphabetic keyboard using two practice routines.
To type 40/3′/3e.

■ **FORMAT**
Drills: Single spacing 60-space line
3-Minute Timings: Double spacing 5-space tab

KEYBOARDING SKILLS

Type lines 1–4 once. Then practice using your shift lock when typing line 5. Repeat lines 1–4, or take a series of 1-minute timings.

Speed	1	When did he go to the city and pay them for the world maps?	12
Accuracy	2	Max and Kay reviewed the subject before giving Phil a quiz.	12
Numbers	3	Read Chapters 10, 29, and 38; summarize Chapters 47 and 56.	12
Symbols	4	We bought 10 balls @ 56¢; he bought 29 @ 38¢ and 100 @ 47¢.	12
Technique	5	I WANT to PRACTICE my SHIFT-LOCK TECHNIQUE using THIS LINE.	

| 1 | 2 | 3 | 4 | 5 | 6 | 7 | 8 | 9 | 10 | 11 | 12

12-SECOND TIMINGS

Type each line three times, or take three 12-second timings on each line. For each timing, type with no more than 1 error.

6 A sign of their blame is the half audit they did for Nancy.
7 If that form is for the men, then the eight may sign today.
8 A small dog and a girl ran down the long lane to the shore.

5 10 15 20 25 30 35 40 45 50 55 60

PRETEST

Take two 3-minute timings on lines 9–19. Circle and count your errors on each.

9 Word processing happens in three office situations, so 12
10 when you try to define what word processing is, you must be 24
11 careful to explain all three of these versions and not just 36
12 one kind you know about. 41
13 In a big office several of the machines may be concen- 53
14 trated in one location, called a center. The typists spend 65
15 most of their time on letter projects. Some organizations, 77
16 to bring the equipment closer to the work, put the machines 89
17 in clusters where the typists turn out letters and reports. 101
18 The third version is the office that has one machine; it is 113
19 used to produce all kinds of work. 120

| 1 | 2 | 3 | 4 | 5 | 6 | 7 | 8 | 9 | 10 | 11 | 12 SI 1.40

acquire the skill of listening to others? The experts tell us that there are ten steps we need to follow to really become good listeners. Let's look at a few of these.

SLIDE 2

First, when someone speaks to you, stop talking. It's really okay to be quiet for a few minutes, and when you stop to think about it, it's hard to hear someone speak over the sound of your own voice — so, stop talking!

SLIDE 3

Next, put the person at ease. Now, how can you do this? You can look the person in the eye. You can turn yourself toward the person. You can let this person know, by using your eyes, that you like him or her. Let the person know that he or she is important to you.

SLIDE 4

Another important point is to be patient. Often when people are trying to tell you something that is important to them, it takes them time to get their thoughts together. So be patient and LISTEN!

SLIDE 5

Next, ask questions! This is the easiest way to really get into another's thoughts. And your questions will alert the person to your interest in what he or she has said. You will become a better listener by learning to ask the right questions.

If you apply just these few ideas to your everyday life, you will find that your friends will want to talk to you. Your popularity will increase. Why? Because everyone wants to be liked; and if your friends feel that you really like them, they will like you.

PRACTICE

Type lines 20–28 three times each.

20 they lend duck coal wish pane form risk sign lens fish turn
21 dish lamb tidy jams when cork them name duty envy kept such
22 then tick maid keys firm gown both flay bush fuel goal work

23 their hairy angle endow right bugle gland chair laugh ivory
24 panel girls turns rotor fight world field shape eight forms
25 audit signs blame slept tithe shame visit gowns title burns

26 usual amend firms widow usury giant prism vigor whale vials
27 spend handy forks blend roams eight right field forms forks
28 profit enrich eighty handle theory island ambush enrich and

Type lines 29–32 four times as a group; then type lines 33–36 four times as a group.

29 robber beggar common arrive jobber bigger commas errors all
30 middle letter snooze supper fiddle little smooth puppet see
31 bubble gummed bottle happen effect agreed bullet middle zoo
32 dinner issues sizzle accord annoys puzzle keeper muffle off

33 breed flood class drill putty cliff offer witty hilly asset
34 goods green skill added seeks proof small radii guess dizzy
35 fluff abbey rummy ditto apple gummy petty upper sleep shall
36 issue floor speed essay gloss broom occur staff funny happy

POSTTEST

Take another 3-minute timing on lines 9–19 on page 252 to see how much your skill has improved.

CARE OF THE EQUIPMENT

If using a **typewriter:** (1) remove the paper using the paper release, (2) center the carriage on a typebar machine, (3) turn off the typewriter.

If using a **computer:** (1) save the document on a disk, (2) exit the program, (3) remove the disks from the computer and store them in sleeves, (4) turn off the computer system. **Note:** Steps 2 and 3 may be reversed on some computers.

Always cover the equipment at the end of the last period; dust with a soft cloth at the end of the week.

LESSON 152

■ GOALS

To type 40/5′/4e.

To identify and practice the alphabetic keys on which more drill is needed.

■ FORMAT

Drills: Single spacing 60-space line

5-Minute Timings: Double spacing 5-space tab

KEYBOARDING SKILLS

Type lines 1–4 once. Then practice your space bar technique by typing line 5 twice. Repeat lines 1–4, or take a series of 1-minute timings.

Speed 1 The goal of the rich girls is to fix a bicycle for the man. 12
Accuracy 2 Jack would pay for fixing my novels if Elizabeth requested. 12
Numbers 3 Mark the chalkboards at 10, 29, 38, 47, and 56 centimeters. 12
Symbols 4 She bought 56 books @ $47; he bought only 38 records @ $29. 12
Technique 5 z y x w v u t s r q p o n m l k j i h g f e d c b a ; / , .

| 1 | 2 | 3 | 4 | 5 | 6 | 7 | 8 | 9 | 10 | 11 | 12

SPEECH 1

WHAT DO YOUR CLOTHES SAY ABOUT YOU?

By Anne Clardy

While you're walking down the halls of school, do you ever wonder why the other students dress as they do? You've probably noticed the well-dressed and most fashionable students. They're really eye-catching, aren't they? Their clothes are usually the latest fad or fashion. Their hair is groomed just right, and they always look neat. You just know

TRANSPARENCY 1

they never do anything to make a mess of themselves. It's interesting how these people are always "in tune" with what is going on in the fashion world.

Those students who do not always wear the latest in fashion, though, can also be admired by other students. They are often admired by others because of the courage it takes to be different.

Regardless of the manner in which you dress, your clothes do say something about you as an individual. If you wear what's in fashion, if you like a lot of contrast in your colors, if you prefer the earth tones or pastels—all of these choices will convey to others who you are.

TRANSPARENCY 2

Experts in communications have studied the effects of nonverbal communications on personal relationships. We give others a nonverbal message by the clothes we wear; many have called this communications an "object language." It refers to our use of "objects" such as clothing to communicate with those around us.

TRANSPARENCY 3

Yes, our clothes do say something about us as individuals. If you want to convey a message to your friends, put some thought into the clothes you wear. The impression you make on other people will be a lasting one, so make a wise choice in the clothes you wear.

SPEECH 2

ARE YOU LISTENING

By Gilbert Sanchez

Have you ever had anyone tell you to do something and ten seconds later you couldn't recall what that person said? Or have you had an incident described, and you couldn't remember the details? Situations such as these can be attributed to a failing that many of us have — and it has to do with not listening to others. We are often so preoccupied with the thoughts that are going on in our own heads that we cannot hear what others are saying.

SLIDE 1

Another aspect of this syndrome is when someone is telling you something and you interrupt that person to give your own thoughts. Again, you're not listening! How can you

(Continued on next page)

PRETEST

Take two 5-minute timings on lines 6–22. Circle and count your errors on each.

In many firms, the text-editing[1] equipment has[2] replaced 12
the typewriter[3] and is used for all the normal[4] typing tasks. 24
Since[5] the machine is not part[6] of a center or cluster, it[7] is 36
called a standalone.[8] It is an expensive typewriter,[9] but it 48
is so efficient[10] that in many offices[11] it more than pays off.[12] 60
The main value of word[13] processing equipment is[14] that it 72
makes correcting[15] and retyping very easy.[16] Surveys show that 84
more[17] than half of the papers typed[18] by a good typist will[19] be 96
retyped for some reason.[20] Any machine that can[21] speed up the 108
process is,[22] of course, extremely helpful[23] in the office--and[24] 120
just as much so for a standalone[25] as for the other machines.[26] 132
A modern WP[27] unit can increase enormously[28] the output of 144
any office[29] worker, but one must[30] realize that there can't[31] be 156
an increase if there[32] is not plenty of work to[33] do. You need 168
the equipment[34] to get more work done,[35] not to make it pretty.[36] 180
A standalone unit is cost-effective[37] only when used by those[38] 192
who cannot otherwise[39] get their work done.[40] 200

| 1 | 2 | 3 | 4 | 5 | 6 | 7 | 8 | 9 | 10 | 11 | 12 SI 1.43

PRACTICE

Type each line twice. Then study the errors you made on the 5-minute timings above. Identify the letters you are keyboarding incorrectly. Practice these letters by typing the appropriate drill lines twice.

A art amp acts aide amen asked alive about again amend assert
B bad bat bite brag brim brand bland black banks blank begins
C cat car caps crop crew check could claim corps chair change
D dad dye duet drag down drums digit doing dance dread disown

E elm eve ears etch east erase eight empty exact enter effect
F fir fan feud fame from flown favor fruit fancy fable female
G gap gag gale game glow glory gauge grain green gates govern
H hat has hope have hold helps hoist hitch hobby heavy hustle

I its imp ills into ibex ideal inept issue input ivory island
J jar joy joke jump join juice judge jokes jeers juror jackal
K key kit kids kiln kill kings keeps knows kayak kicks kindly
L lob lie line late lake laugh labor light lucid lumps lagoon

M mat mad maze more mist music month money minus metal mighty
N nor not nags norm noon nasty night noise nutty nymph nickel
O oak old odor over oath olive opens ought ounce opera occupy
P pat pay paid pour past proud piano plain plane plump photos

(Continued on next page)

REPORT 2 (CONTINUED)

SUMMARY

Based on the findings of this study, the main reason for missing classes as most answered by students is that the class is not interesting. Illness is the other main reason for missing, followed by weather conditions and oversleeping. The findings of this study reveal further that over 1/2 of the students do not miss classes and fewer than 1/3 miss more than one class during the length of the course.

RECOMMENDATIONS

Based on the findings of this study, it is reccommended that:

1. Instructors strive to add interest and enthusiasm in class lectures.

2. The absentee policy at Central State College be strictly enforced.

3. Absentee records be ~~included~~ placed on the grade sheets.

FOOTNOTES

Place footnotes at the bottom of appropriate pages.

1. Thomas Haynes Bayly, Five Thousand Quotations for All Occasions, Garden City Books, Garden City, N.Y., 1952, p. 1.

2. General Catalog, College Press, State College, Pa., 1981, p. 34.

3. Ibid., p. 35.

4. Ibid., p. 36.

CONTENTS

Provide the missing page numbers after you have finished typing the report.

TABLE OF CONTENTS

TITLE PAGE

Prepare a title page for the report. Include on it the following:

1. Report title
2. Author's name
3. Date of report
4. Your name as typist

Q 39 quo que quad quip quid quick quits quire quite quote quaint
R 40 row rip ride reap rake right ready reach roads razor record
S 41 sit sky sips sing stay sting sweet scale stone state savory
T 42 top try team tame task throw tests teams tense tales tactic

U 43 urn use ugly upon used unite under usual untie upset unique
V 44 vet vex vats vote vase vague verve voice vital veins vertex
W 45 was wow wage when what white water wedge weave waves wealth

X 46 tax six axes oxen axis exact exist taxis exits vexes exerts
Y 47 you yet yell yard year young yield yours youth yacht yellow
Z 48 zap zig zinc zeal zest zooms zebra zones zonal zeros zodiac

POSTTEST

Take another 5-minute timing on lines 6–22 on page 254 to see how much your skill has improved.

LESSON 153

■ **GOALS**
To recognize subject-verb agreement while typing sentences.
To build skill in keyboarding numbers.

■ **FORMAT**
Drills: Single spacing 60-space line
2-Minute Timings: Double spacing

LAB 17

Subject-Verb Agreement

Type lines 1–4 once. Then repeat lines 1–4 or take a series of 1-minute timings. Note subject-verb agreement as you type each line (verbs are underscored).

1 Only Lisa DePasquale knows the combinations to these safes. 12
2 Most employees want us to close this store earlier than 10. 12
3 Joe Nizer begins his six-week vacation on December 1 or 12. 12
4 All our sales representatives talk with customers each day. 12

| 1 | 2 | 3 | 4 | 5 | 6 | 7 | 8 | 9 | 10 | 11 | 12

A verb must agree with its subject in number and person. The letter *s* is usually added to a verb to indicate the third person singular.

	Singular		Plural	
First person	I	run	We	run
Second person	You	run	You	run
Third person	He, She, It	runs	They	run
	A child	runs	Children	run

A plural verb is always required after *you*, even when *you* is singular.

Correct: You [meaning "one"] run fast. *Wrong:* You runs fast.

12-SECOND TIMINGS

Type each line three times, or take three 12-second timings on each line. For each timing, type with no more than 1 error.

5 I know those four girls can swim across the lake with ease.
6 Please take one of these big boxes down to the post office.
7 May we go to the game with you, or do you have other plans?

5 10 15 20 25 30 35 40 45 50 55 60

REPORT 2 (CONTINUED)

FINDINGS

As a by-product of this research, it was revealed that nearly 1/2 the students did not miss classes during the school year, and about 1/3 of the students missed only one class per course. For those who ~~that~~ missed classes, 57 percent believed that their absence did not affect their grades. ¶Reasons students gave for missing classes were quite varied, and this data is revealed in Table 1. Most of the students, 34 percent, felt that the class's being not interesting was their main reason for missing a class. The 2nd most common reason for missing classes was illness. As was quoted from the college catalog ~~on page 1~~ of this report, this is the only reason given by the students that the college accepts as an excused absence.

TABLE 1

REASONS FOR MISSING CLASSES

Reason	Percentage*
1. Class is not interesting	34
2. Illness	29
3. Weather	14
4. Oversleeping	13
5. Attendance not taken	12
6. Grade in class is not as important as grade in other classes	12
7. Take off early for weekends	9
8. Other	3

* The percentages total more than the number of participants because students were allowed to give more than one reason.

(Continued on next page)

PRETEST

Your goal on number-filled copy is 30/2′/2e.

Take two 2-minute timings on lines 8–12. Circle and count your errors on each.

8 The class of 1980 will hold its spring reunion on August 16 12
9 with a dinner at the Quinton Hotel, 4422 West 66 Street, in 24
10 High Tor. The cost is only $33 per couple; reserve a table 36
11 by calling one of these persons: Zoe Strum (555-8416), Rex 48
12 Strength (555-7934), or Dr. Mary Jane Scholneck (555-8190). 60

| 1 | 2 | 3 | 4 | 5 | 6 | 7 | 8 | 9 | 10 | 11 | 12

PRACTICE

Can you keyboard the number keys while keeping your eyes on the copy?

Type lines 13–20 twice each.

13 tie 583 toe 593 toy 596 top 590 tip 580 wet 235 woe 293 293
14 pie 083 pet 035 pot 095 pow 092 row 492 rye 463 rue 473 473
15 rut 475 rot 495 roe 493 ire 843 ore 943 owe 923 ewe 323 323
16 eye 363 out 975 our 974 owe 923 per 034 pit 085 toe 593 593

17 your 6974 pour 0974 pout 0975 rout 4975 rope 4903 ripe 4803
18 wipe 2803 pipe 0803 were 2343 wore 2943 wire 2843 wiry 2846
19 pure 0743 pore 0943 port 0945 pert 0345 tore 5943 tire 5843
20 tier 5834 pier 0834 purr 0744 prow 0492 toot 5995 prop 0490

Clear your tabulator. Set seven tab stops, each one 8 spaces apart, beginning at the left margin. Type lines 21–28 twice—or more. Circle your errors, if any, as your teacher reads the copy.

21	235	236	237	238	239	240	241	242
22	599	598	597	596	595	594	593	592
23	632	633	634	635	636	637	638	639
24	480	479	478	477	476	475	474	473
25	788	789	790	791	792	793	794	795
26	334	333	332	331	330	329	328	327
27	993	992	991	990	989	988	987	986
28	878	879	880	881	882	883	884	885

POSTTEST

Take another 2-minute timing on lines 8–12 to see how much your skill has improved.

GOALS

To identify subject-verb agreement while typing sentences.
To build skill in keyboarding symbols.

FORMAT

Drills: Single spacing 60-space line
2-Minute Timings: Double spacing

LAB 17

Subject-Verb Agreement

Type lines 1–4 once. Then repeat lines 1–4 or take a series of 1-minute timings.

1 Six buyers plan to distribute dozens of catalogs very soon. 12
2 One buyer plans to distribute dozens of catalogs very soon. 12
3 Bob orders jade rings from Algonquin Jewelers in Tennessee. 12
4 They order jade rings from Algonquin Jewelers in Tennessee. 12

| 1 | 2 | 3 | 4 | 5 | 6 | 7 | 8 | 9 | 10 | 11 | 12

If a student has an excessive number of absences, heor she may be dropped from a class. Excessive absences are those that ocurr three times in a class that meets three times a week, three times in a class that meets two times a week, and three times in a class that meets once a week.[4]

(Type PROBLEM here - see below for comment!)

PROCEDURES

An equal number of Freshman, Sophomore, Junior, and Senior students provided the population for this survey. A total of 25 students from each class was asked too complete a questionnairre on student absenteeism. The students were randomly chosen in several locations at Central State College. Of the 120 questionnaires that were completed, 88 could be used. The findings of the study are based on 88 percent of the totalnumber of students sampled.

(The PROBLEM should appear before the PROCEDURES in your report.)

PROBLEM

The problem of this study is to determine reasons for student absenteeism at Central State College. It is hoped that the findings of this study will reveal the most prevalent reasons for student absences and may be used by both students and faculty in eliminating the problem of excessive absences from certain classes at Central State College.

(Continued on next page)

12-SECOND TIMINGS

Type each line three times, or take three 12-second timings on each line. For each timing, type with no more than 1 error.

5 The one problem is that he might not wish to take the work.

6 We know that they can do this work as well as we can do it.

7 Why did Joe and the dog not see you at the end of the path?

5 10 15 20 25 30 35 40 45 50 55 60

PRETEST

Take two 2-minute timings on lines 8–12. Circle and count your errors on each.

8 I am writing to ask you to check on an order of 16 machines 12

9 worth $48,000. I placed my order (#738) with Wes & Benson, 24

10 a company that as of this date (9/26) sells office supplies 36

11 in a wide range of prices (the majority @ $5 to $10). Make 48

12 sure that I get the starred (*) 2% pay-as-you-can discount. 60

| 1 | 2 | 3 | 4 | 5 | 6 | 7 | 8 | 9 | 10 | 11 | 12

PRACTICE

Type lines 13–32 twice each. Then repeat any of the lines that stress the symbol errors you circled in the Pretest.

@ 13 sws sw2s s2s s2@s s@s s@s @s@ @s@ s@s @22 2@2 22@ @2@2 2@2@

14 She bought 10 @ 56, 29 @ 47, 38 @ 38, 47 @ 29, and 56 @ 10.

¢ 15 juj ju6j j6¢j j¢j¢ ¢j¢j j¢j j¢j ¢j¢ ¢j¢ j¢j 66¢ 77¢ 88¢ 99¢

16 Pretzels are 56¢, sweet rolls are 47¢, and cookies are 38¢.

* 17 kik ki8 k8k k8*k k*k* *k*k k*k k*k k*k k*k k*k 88* *88* 7*7

18 Nancy,* Henry,* Sarah,* and Gregory* were chosen to attend.

19 ded de3 d3d d3#d d#d# d#d# d#d 3#3 #4# #5# #6# #7# #8# d#d#

20 Check my lists for #56, #47, #38, #29, #10, #7, #8, and #9.

$ 21 frf fr4 f4f f4$f f$f f$f f f f$f $44 4$4 $444 $555 $666

22 Our game tickets should cost us $10, $29, $38, $47, or $56.

% 23 ftf ft5 f5f f5%f f%f% %f%f f%f f%f 55% 55% 44% 33% 22% %f%f

24 Let's hope to get a discount of 10%, 29%, 38%, 47%, or 56%.

& 25 juj ju7 j7j j7&j j&j& &j&j j&j j&j &8& &9& &1& &2& &3& &7&7

26 Bennett & Shea, DeLuca & Nucci, and Brim & Todd sent gifts.

( ) 27 lol lo9 19(l(l l(l (l(;p; ;p) ;p) ;); ;););) (9) (0) (;)

28 Donna (Adams), Gene (Ponti), and Helen (Yeo) came to visit.

Hyphen – 29 ;p; ;p- ;p- ;-; ;-; 8-9 -;- 3-4 ;-;- 1-10 -;-; -76- ;-; p-p

30 Her phone is 412-555-4808; her other phone is 412-555-8975.

Diagonal / 31 ;/; ;/; /;/ /;/ ;/; 7/8 8/9 9/0 1/2 2/3 3/4 4/5 5/6 ;/; ;/;

32 Check these dates: 7/8/88, 8/19/89, 10/23/90, and 12/5/91.

POSTTEST

Take another 2-minute timing on lines 8–12 to see how much your skill has improved.

REPORT 2
Side-bound report.

ABSENTEEISM AT C. S. C.

Written by Charles T. Tulland

March 19, 19--

INTRODUCTION

Thomas Haynes Bayly said that "absence makes the heart grow fonder."[1] The quote most certainly applies to the absence of a loved one, but it does not definitely pertain to a classroom environment. Thelevel of absenteeism at central state college has created problems for administrators, faculty, and students; and it warrants an in-depth look at the reasons why students are absent from classes.

BACKGROUND

According to the academic procedures at Central State College, students are expected to be present for all class meet ings in courses for which they are enrolled."[2] According to current policy, faculty are to allow students who miss classes because of excused absence every opportunity to make up the work that was missed during the absence. Absences excusable are as follows:

1. Student participation in an authorized university activity.
2. Confinement of the student due to illness. This confinement must be verified by a physician.
3. Death in the student's immediate family.
4. Legal obligation where a student must participate in legal proceedings.[3]

(Continued on next page)

LESSON 155

■ **GOALS**
To correct errors in subject-verb agreement while typing sentences.
To type 40/5′/4e.
To build keyboarding skills.

■ **FORMAT**
Drills: Single spacing 60-space line
5-Minute Timings: Double spacing 5-space tab

LAB 17

Subject-Verb Agreement

Type lines 1–4 once, correcting verbs if necessary to ensure subject-verb agreement. Edit your copy as your teacher reads the answers. Then retype lines 1–4 from your edited copy.

```
1 Kay want several dozen more boxes to store all your files.
2 They needs Joseph's approval before they order this machine.
3 Helene signs all purchase requisitions as soon as possible.
4 The managers buys all their supplies from Craig & Craig Inc.
```

12-SECOND TIMINGS

Type each line three times, or take three 12-second timings on each line. For each timing, type with no more than 1 error.

```
5 Mark can type fast on these words:  the, for, but, can, go.
6 Sue says that she can fix the vase that fell from the desk.
7 The four of them had to get to the bus by the time it left.
```

5 10 15 20 25 30 35 40 45 50 55 60

PRETEST

Take two 5-minute timings on lines 8–22. Circle and count your errors on each.

8 If you work in a word processing center, you will work with several 15
9 typists and a supervisor, which means that you will always have someone 29
10 willing and able to extend aid and assistance if needed. 40
11 Most of the machines are assigned to the routine work, even though they 56
12 have the extra features needed for special projects. It is a relief to know that 72
13 someone can help you to use the features. 80
14 Much of the work in a center consists of transcription from recordings. 96
15 The writer of a letter, for example, will phone the center and dictate a 110
16 message. One of the typists then transcribes it. 120
17 Because of the ease with which WP equipment can change or correct 134
18 information, it is widely used for mailing lists and price lists and similar 150
19 information that needs updating on a regular basis. 160
20 There is a wide variety of work typed in a center, but every person who 175
21 works there will probably become an expert in just one type of production 190
22 and become recognized as one of the specialists. 200

| 1 | 2 | 3 | 4 | 5 | 6 | 7 | 8 | 9 | 10 | 11 | 12 | 13 | 14 | 15 SI 1.45

REPORT 1 (CONTINUED)

TITLE PAGE

Prepare a title page for the report. Include on it the following:

1. Report title
2. Author's name
3. Date of report
4. Your name as typist

8. It is definitely more difficult to find a parking space on a Monday, Wednesday, or Friday than on a Tuesday or Thursday.

RECOMMENDATIONS

Based on the findings of this survey, the follwoing recomendations are made.

1. Parking space allotments should be reviewed each year to determine shifts in driver status in each of the five driver classifications. categories.

2. Parking places should be clearly marked and should be painted regularly.

3. A study ofan open parking system should be considered and undertaken.

4. Additional parking space should be provided for students who purchase green permits for $6.00 per year.

5. An alternate parking system should be enforced so that more green parking spaces are alowed on Monday, Wednesday, and Friday -- the peak traffic days.

SS with ds between items.

PRACTICE

Type lines 23–25 three times as a group and lines 26–28 three times as a group.

Accuracy

23 My fine ax just zipped through the black wood quite evenly.
24 Roxie picked off the amazing yellow jonquils by the cavern.
25 Jane gave my excited boy quite a prize for his clever work.

26 Kay bought five or six cans to award as equal major prizes.
27 Six big Kansas jewelers have imported quartz for my clocks.
28 Alex A. Bishop may want foreign jade and zinc very quickly.

Type lines 29–34 three times each.

Speed

29 Did she pay the neighbor to fix the oaken box for the coal?
30 I am to go to work for the audit firm by the eighth of May.
31 When she got to the lake, the girl paid for the oak panels.

32 I envy the six firms, for they fight for the right element.
33 Jane and the girl kept their title to the island cornfield.
34 The man got a snap of an authentic whale by the big island.

POSTTEST

Take another 5-minute timing on lines 8–22 on page 258 to see how much your skill has improved.

LESSON 156

CLINIC

GOALS
To improve competency on selected reaches.
To type 40/5′/4e.

FORMAT
Drills: Single spacing 60-space line
Timings: Double spacing 5-space tab

KEYBOARDING SKILLS

Type lines 1–4 once. Then type each word in line 5 two times, returning your carriage or carrier before starting to type the next word. Repeat lines 1–4, or take a series of 1-minute timings.

Speed 1 Look and see how well his fingers are flying over the keys. 12
Accuracy 2 Poor Jack was vexed about my long and quite hazy falsehood. 12
Numbers 3 Alice put markers at 10 km, 29 km, 38 km, 47 km, and 56 km. 12
Symbols 4 Some stores are offering 20% off; some are giving only 10%. 12
Technique 5 next pear lead yelp made near lame keep jade hard part open

| 1 | 2 | 3 | 4 | 5 | 6 | 7 | 8 | 9 | 10 | 11 | 12

PRETEST 1

Take two 2-minute timings on lines 6–9. Circle and count your errors on each.

6 Stewart deserves to get a big reward after saving the girl. 12
7 Seven bears rested at the water's edge after the hard swim. 24
8 Barbara wore a dark red sweater to the fair in Texas today. 36
9 Edward said the test was extra hard and feared the results. 48

| 1 | 2 | 3 | 4 | 5 | 6 | 7 | 8 | 9 | 10 | 11 | 12

REPORT 1 (CONTINUED)

PROCEDURES

A pilot questioairre was sent and prepared toa sample of 25 students and 10 faculty members who had campus parking permits. The question naire was designed after a meeting with Central State Security and after studying the campus motorvehicle regulations.

After minor changes were made too the questioairre, it was distributed to the following people: 73 persons with green permits, 3 persons with brown permits, 2 persons with white permits, 2 persons with red permits, and 20 persons with blue permits. The nubmer chosen for each color in the sample corresponded to that colors percentage of the whole (the total number of issued stickers by the college).

FINDINGS

Based on the responses received from the questionnaires, the following findings were obtained:

1. About 75% of the student and faculty live off-campus.
2. About 80% of the students and faculty drive to school.
3. Faculty have fewerproblems in finding a parking space.
4. Students have more problems in finding a parking space.
5. About 66% of the students feel that faculty recieve to much parking space.
6. Over 50% of those surveyed have received at least one parking ticket in the last year.
7. Over 50% of those surveyed feltthat open parking should be allowed.

(Continued on next page)

PRACTICE 1

Type lines 10–15 four times.

```
10 acts west cards drafts started greatest beverages afterward
11 read gates serve acreage created erasers rewarded decreased
12 tract state seats grave aware fever brave eager areas after

13 texts waste verbs tests saved great fewer stage weave wears
14 eats dear base acre rare text star ward grew verb fact safe
15 sad age bed ads dad wax tea war bet bar are ear cat tax wet
```

POSTTEST 1

Take another 2-minute timing on lines 6–9 on page 259 to see how much your skill has improved.

PRETEST 2

Take two 2-minute timings on lines 16–19. Circle and count your errors on each.

```
16 The surprised judge thanked her for getting the desk files.   12
17 Watch just to see who else puts anything on the two floors.   24
18 Thinking people have studied a multitude of needless words.   36
19 I hope the enclosed idea can keep the guests in the course.   48
   | 1 | 2 | 3 | 4 | 5 | 6 | 7 | 8 | 9 | 10 | 11 | 12
```

PRACTICE 2

Type lines 20–25 four times.

```
20 old used word think watch hidden studied thinking multitude
21 how need seem noted shown arises thanked needless surprised
22 dry just puts floor meant counts implied invested forwarded

23 use else grow files judge formed closest anything effective
24 kit loan step shown table plenty private journals scheduled
25 yes park very token total school program patients physician
```

POSTTEST 2

Take another 2-minute timing on lines 16–19 to see how much your skill has improved.

5-MINUTE TIMING

Take one 5-minute timing on lines 8–22 on page 258.

UNIT 26 Formatting Review of Reports

UNIT GOAL 40/5'/4e

■ **GOALS**
To correct errors in subject-verb agreement while typing sentences.
To review formatting outlines and enumerations.

■ **FORMAT**
Single spacing   60-space line

LAB 17

Subject-Verb Agreement

Type lines 1–4 once, correcting verbs to ensure subject-verb agreement. Edit your copy as your teacher reads the answers. Then retype lines 1–4 from your edited copy.

```
1 Federal law prohibit discrimination because of age or sex.
2 Many employees complains about these six billing procedures.
3 Only Joanne like the new offices better than the old ones.
4 Liza and Al Aqualina gives superb talks on money management.
```

REPORTS

REPORT 1
Unbound report.

PARKING PROBLEMS AT CENTRAL STATE COLLEGE

Type heading in two lines.

By Juanita S. Sanchez

INTRODUCTION

The Central State College campus has a total student body of 9600, a faculty of 400, and a staff of 600. Campus parking consists of six major areas. A parking sticker issued by the Cnetral State Security Department is required to park in any of these areas. These stickers are issued for one year, and in most cases they cost $6.

The parking stickers are issued in five collors: blue, brown, red, white,and green. Blue permits are always issued to full -time faculty and staff members; brown permits are issued to assistant instructors and to part-time employees. Red permits are issued to sorority house residents and to dis abled persons. Administrative personnel and visitors to the campus receive white permits. All students not issued a blue, brown, red, or green sticker may purchase a white permit for approximately $6 each year. During the last five years, 7400 students purchased green permits. Green permits were by far the most popular permit issued at Central State College.

THE PROBLEM

The problem of this study is to reveal the statsu of parking at Central State College and to determine if any parking problems exist atthe college.

PURPOSE OF THE STUDY

The purposes of this study are is to determine (1) the status of parking, (2) if problems exist in the parking present situation, (3) if any people are not satisfied with parking, and (4) where and for whom improvements are needed.

(Continued on next page)

FORMATTING REVIEW

Outlines

1. Margins: Center the longest line horizontally.
2. Title: Centered; triple-space after.
3. Roman-numeral lines in all caps—2 blank lines before, 1 blank line after.
4. Single-space other lines.
5. Align the periods after the roman numerals.
6. Indent each subdivision 4 more spaces, thus:

I.
    A.
        1.
            a.

JOB 157 A. OUTLINE

Standard format (see review in margin). Full sheet of paper.

YEAR-END SALES REPORT ON CLOCK RADIOS
I. RECORD SALES
A. New Models This Year
1. AM/FM Digital Clock Radio
a. Snooze Control
b. Earphone Jack
2. AM/FM Electronic Clock Radio
a. LED Readout Display
b. Alarm With Automatic Shutoff
c. Cassette Tape Recorder
B. New Outlets This Year
II. FORECAST FOR NEXT YEAR
A. Foreign Imports
B. Inflation
III. LONG-RANGE PLANNING

Enumerations

1. 5-inch line.
2. Center vertically or begin on line 13.
3. Title: Centered; triple-space after.
4. Single-space enumerated items; double-space between items.

Hanging-Indented Format

5. Type numbers at left margin; indent turnover lines.

Paragraph Format

6. Indent first line of each numbered item 5 spaces; type turnover lines at the left margin.

JOB 157 B. ENUMERATION

Hanging-indented format (see review in margin). Full sheet of paper.

FORM LETTERS 7

In these days of mass mailings, form letters are especially 21
effective. Form letters have many excellent features, such 33
as the following: 37
1. A form letter can be stored on a machine, such as a word 51
processor, and reproduced automatically at rapid rates. 64
2. Since the form letter is already written, it can be sent 78
out immediately whenever it is needed. 87
3. One letter can be sent to hundreds of people by changing 101
the inside address (and sometimes other variables). 112

JOB 157 C. ENUMERATION

Paragraph format (see review in margin). Full sheet of paper.

Title: WORD PROCESSING 9

There are many ways a word processor can assist writers in the writing 26
process. Here are a few of them: 33
1. Making changes is easy. The writer can add to, delete from, 48
and move around the text quickly and simply by pressing the appropriate 63
keys. The changes are displayed at once on the video screen, and there 77

(Continued on next page)

MEMO 4

DATE: August 13, 19--
TO: EMANUEL T. PETERSON, Business Department
FROM: ALICE R. HAYEN, Dean
SUBJECT: Phi Chi Luncheon

It was a thrill for me to inform the other members of our executive board that you will address the group on October 15. Thank you, Dr. Peterson, for agreeing to speak at our meeting.
Our theme this year is "The 80s - A Decade of Change." We hope to have the privilege of listening to your excellent thoughts for about 30 to 60 minutes. And, yes, we will have a projector and screen available for you during your speech.
Thank you again, Dr. Peterson, for accepting our invitation. ARH

MEMO 5

(Date) December 4, 19--, (To) J.D. Hill, Personell Director, (From) Matthew S. Sanchez, Training directer, (Subject) Part-Time Workers

Cooper School has just recently informed me that they will being sending (2) young people to us for the next (6) to (8) weeks. as you recall, we agreed to provide some practicle workexperience for the education office students at Cooper.

The students will be with us from 9-12 daily. Could you have some one from your office meet with them to inform her of our personnel policies? MSS, (Your initials)

is no longer the need to edit copy by crossing out 87
words or writing changes in the margin of the 97
manuscript. 99

2. Retyping whole pages is unnecessary. If 110
an error is discovered or a sentence must be re- 120
written after the manuscript has been printed, all 130
the writer needs to do is bring up the original 139
copy on the video screen, make the needed 148
change, and print a new page. Simple changes 157
take only a few minutes, and most of that time is 167
spent waiting for the printer. 173

3. Returning the carriage is not needed. Most 185
word processing programs automatically move 194
the words to the next line when the right-hand 203
margin is reached. This feature is called wrap- 213
around. In this way the words can flow—the 222
writer uses the carriage return key only when he 231
or she wants to start a new paragraph. 239

■ **GOALS**
To type 40/5′/4e.
To review formatting reports, references, and footnotes.

■ **FORMAT**
Drills: Single spacing 60-space line
5-Minute Timings: Double spacing 5-space tab

KEYBOARDING SKILLS

Type lines 1–4 once. Then practice using your shift lock by typing line 5 twice. Repeat lines 1–4, or take a series of 1-minute timings.

Speed 1 The six forms she got from the firm may do for the problem. 12
Accuracy 2 Jacqueline was vexed by the folks who got the money prizes. 12
Numbers 3 Adele moved from Rooms 10, 29, and 38 into Rooms 47 and 56. 12
Symbols 4 Recheck the invoices for Boxes #10, #29, #38, #47, and #56. 12
Technique 5 The SHIFT LOCK helps YOU to make ALL CAPS for DISPLAY work.

| 1 | 2 | 3 | 4 | 5 | 6 | 7 | 8 | 9 | 10 | 11 | 12

PRETEST

Take a 5-minute timing on lines 16–33 on page 263. Circle and count your errors. Use the chart below to find the number of errors you made on the Pretest. Then type each of the designated drill lines four times. Take a 5-minute Posttest on lines 16–33 on page 263.

PRACTICE

Pretest errors	0–1	2–3	4–5	6+
Drill lines	9–15	8–14	7–13	6–12

Accuracy
6 it's July quite depends comedies programs shutdown stations
7 operas there's outside outdoor revealed Thursdays homeowner
8 escape camping because hundred business companies broadcast
9 quiz enough license favorite majority Icelanders television
10 enjoy relies survey pleases employed picnicking commercials

Speed
11 Iceland living which their makes down this work bit for all
12 persons during devote color when them that have big buy the
13 people enough time tell have used city pays soap zany of us
14 viewing watch money favor shuts shows never been less to go
15 comedies course month extra dark want less most sun who set

MEMO 1

[*Date*] May 7, 19—, [*To*] Alphonso R. Rossetti, Sales Representative, [*From*] Pamela T. Wayne, District Manager, [*Subject*] Quarterly Budgets

Enclosed are next year's budget figures for your service area. Please review these figures and send me your response no later than May 15.

Al, you might want to review the final page of the budget and compare it closely with last year's report. Notice that we have a 5 percent cut in travel funds for the final quarter. Since we transferred Waco to another district, the travel funds were cut in proportion to the accounts we lost in the Waco region. PTW

MEMO 2

[*Date*] May 12, 19—, [*To*] Pamela T. Wayne, District Manager, [*From*] Alphonso R. Rossetti, Sales Representative, [*Subject*] Your May 7 Memo

Pam, all the figures you mentioned in your memo agree with my sales budget for next year with the exception of the travel funds for the last quarter.

As you know, we are holding our regional conference in Dallas during the last quarter, and we'll have to make a number of trips to Dallas to finalize this meeting. Thus my travel funds for the last quarter reflect a $1400 expense that your budget did not include. ARR

MEMO 3

DATE: August 10, 19--

TO: Alice R. Haynel, Dean

FROM: Emanuel Peterson, business department

SUBJECT: Phi Chi Luncheon

It will be a distinct pleasure for me to speak to your group no October 15 at the Student Ballroom. As a former member of this fine group myself, I like always to attend the anual busniess meeting

Please let me know what theme you wishme to address during my presentation adn how long you want me to "entertain" your gruop. Would it be possible foryou to have available a projector and screen for my presentation?

I lookforward to meeting you on October 15.

Every July, Iceland shuts down its television stations 12
because all the people employed in this work want to escape 24
on their vacations. July is one month in Iceland when it's 36
never dark, which makes it the ideal time for Icelanders to 48
go outside and enjoy the extra sun. 55

The Icelanders devote July to outdoor living, camping, 67
and picnicking. The vast majority of them tell us that the 79
shutdown pleases them. A survey of several hundred persons 91
who live in one city revealed that most of them favor a bit 103
less television. Of course, these people have been used to 115
less viewing time because during the year the stations have 127
no programs on Thursdays. Although each homeowner pays for 139
a license for each color set, there's not enough money from 151
all sources to broadcast all week. 158

Television is quite a big business that relies on lots 170
of companies to buy time for their commercials. It relies, 182
too, on you to view your favorite shows: soap operas, zany 194
comedies, quiz and game shows. 200

| 1 | 2 | 3 | 4 | 5 | 6 | 7 | 8 | 9 | 10 | 11 | 12 SI 1.47

POSTTEST

Take another 5-minute timing on lines 16–33 to see how much your skill has improved.

FORMATTING REVIEW

Workbook 275–278.

Reports

1. Use a 6-inch line (60P/70E).
2. Margins:
   a. Top margin on page 1—2 inches (↓ 13).
   b. Top margin on other pages—1 inch (↓ 7).
   c. Bottom margin on all pages—1 to 1½ inches (6 to 9 blank lines).
3. Double spacing.
4. Title: Centered, all caps, line 13.
5. Subtitle: Double-space before; triple-space after.
6. Side headings (if used): All caps; triple-space before; double-space after.
7. Paragraph headings (if used): Initial caps, underscored, followed by a period and 2 spaces.

References and Footnotes

1. Text references: Type the appropriate superscript figure (raised, like this[1]) following the word, phrase, or sentence for which there is a footnote.
2. Separation line: At the left margin, a single space below the last line of a full page of text, 2 inches (20P/24E) long.
3. Footnotes: A double space below the line, indented 5 spaces. Type the number on the line of writing, followed by a period and 2 spaces, then the reference.
4. Single-space footnotes; double-space between them.

LETTER 14

Business letter. Standard format, with indented paragraphs, second-page heading, display, and enclosure and *cc* notations. Body 318 words.

Mr. Richard Cohen, President, Jacksonville Tile and Shingle Co., 8091 21st Street, NW, Jacksonville, FL 33024

Dear Mr. Cohen: I have gone over the books for the month of september and can report to you and the owners that you have had a most successful month: a net in come of 10,130.00 on sales of $96,595.00 which is 10.5 per cent. I tip my hat to you and your staff.

A comparison of the August and september figures shows that, with the about the same sales, you doubled the net income in September. Here are the summary figures for the 2 months:

	August	September
Net Sales	$89,600.00	$96,595.00
Cost of Goods Sold	58,320.00	60,099.00
Gross Profit	$31,280.00	$36,496.00
Operating Expenses	26,235.00	26,366.00
Net Income	$ 5,045.00	$10,130.00

This comparison shows with only $7000 more sales that in August, you were able to hold the line on expenses and therefore transfer 5000 of the $7000 to the bottom line as more net income. An income statement for the month is ynclosed.

I looked into your expenses items but could find no weakspot. Your delivery wspenses went up about $150 more than expenses, but supply cost was down about $150, which made a stand off. It seems to me that you are working really close to the line.

As you know from our many conferences you must get you sales to the $10,000 mark each month to stay in the blank and up to the $102,000 mark if you are to give the owners the return that they need to sustain there confidence in your management. The benifit that came from the $7000 increase proves the point.

So it seems to me that you will have to take some big steps to boost your sales. I know of no way you can cut expenses more that you have; to set up a sales promotion account as a knew expense in attracting them. They won't happen. Congradulations on a good month! Sincerely yours, Paula Pirece, Management Consultant, Florida Accounting Services Inc, Enclosure, cc: Ms. Helen Green, Mr. Arthur Henley, ms. Clara Downs

JOB 158 A. UNBOUND REPORT WITH FOOTNOTES

Standard format (see review on page 263).

WORD PROCESSING 9

A concept known as word processing has led the way toward making the 26
office worker more productive. Word processing can be defined in many 40
ways, but the main concept is to use people, procedures, and machines to 55
speed business communications.[1] 63

HISTORY 67

The first true word processing machine was placed on the market in 81
1965. It was an automatic editing typewriter that could store typed copy 96
and replay it, error-free, at 150 words per minute.[2] Later, a newer model 113
that recorded on plastic cards was devised. Office workers began to see 128
that word processing had many benefits: easier revision of copy, mass 142
production of form letters that did not look like form letters, and faster 157
handling of mailing lists. 163

VOCABULARY 167

Like any specialized industry, word processing has its own terms that 182
can be confusing to the untrained. For example, "floppy disks" are thin 196
platters of magnetic tape used for information storage. Printing is often 211
done with a "daisy wheel"—a typing element shaped like a wheel with a 226
solid black center and type on the outside edge—which can print at the rate 241
of 55 characters per second. 247

SHOPPING FOR EQUIPMENT 254

Office managers offer these pointers to those who are thinking of buying 269
word processing machines: 275

1. Consider the change fully. Word processing is not just fast typewrit- 292
ers; it is a change in the way the office operates. 305
2. Get expert help from the beginning, and test the equipment in your 322
own office. 325
3. Be sure the type of machine you buy is simple to operate and easy to 342
repair. 344

Footnotes:

1. Ralph Reiss, "Word Processing in Today's Office," National Busi- 126
ness Weekly, January 15, 1986, p. 45. 138

2. Delores Chaffee, "Electronic Equipment in the Office," Business 158
Review, November 1985, pp. 73–74. 168

LETTER 13 (CONTINUED)

1. In the first five years of operation, assuming normal office renovations, the open office concept will save A. B. Grant $14,000. In the first ten years, that savings will grow to $75,000. The lower savings in the first five years is due to investments needed for new office equipment and furniture.

2. The open office plan will provide a smoother work flow and communications flow.

3. The open office plan will decrease your operating expenses for heating and cooling. See attachment 2 for these figures.

4. The open office plan will increase A. B. Grant's tax savings. See attachment 3 for this data.

5. The movement of personnel and office due to the addition of 75 employees in the next five years will be less expensive with an open office plan. See attachment 4 for this data.

Please study the office layout plan we have enclosed. We urge you and your staff to analyze and compare the savings you will realize with our plan. If you have any questions on this data, please feel free to call me so that we can discuss in more detail our rationale for doing what we did on this layout design.

Overall, I think we have a very workable plan here, and one that you will be quite satisfied with in actual use. We would like to meet with you after you have had a chance to study this plan in detail. Would it be possible to meet on the 18th, next Wednesday, to review the plan? I'll call you early next week to set a time.

Thank you again, Mr. Christie, for giving us the opportunity to design your office layout for you.

Sincerely yours, Nancy R. Mabry, Office Consultant, 4 Enclosures: 1. Office layout, 2. Operating expenses, 3. Tax analysis, 4. Relocation analysis, cc: Mr. Hopper, Mr. James

LESSON 159

■ **GOALS**
To recognize subject-verb agreement while typing sentences.
To review formatting speeches and minutes of a meeting.

■ **FORMAT**
Single spacing 60-space line

LAB 18

Subject-Verb Agreement

Type lines 1–4 once. Then repeat lines 1–4 or take a series of 1-minute timings. Note subject-verb agreement as you type each line (verbs are underscored).

```
1  Alex does his work very well, according to Frank Zimbulski.   12
2  Alex and James do their work very well, according to Frank.   12
3  She is quite interested in learning to operate the machine.   12
4  They are quite interested in learning to operate a machine.   12
   | 1 | 2 | 3 | 4 | 5 | 6 | 7 | 8 | 9 | 10 | 11 | 12
```

The verbs *to be, to do,* and *to have* need special attention because these irregular verbs are very commonly used. Note how these verbs agree with pronouns and with singular or plural nouns:

	Singular	Be	Do	Have	Plural	Be	Do	Have
First person	I	am	do	have	we, you, they, the clerks	are	do	have
Second person	you	are	do	have				
Third person	he, she, it, the clerk	is	does	has				

30-SECOND "OK" TIMINGS

This version of a 30-second timing is used to build your accuracy on alphabetic copy. Type as many "OK" (errorless) timings as possible out of three attempts on lines 5–7.

```
5  Jean gave our boy quite a prize for his clever work, and he   12
6  is very excited about it.  I hope that he will continue the   24
7  fine work because he is trying to be the best in his major.   36
   | 1 | 2 | 3 | 4 | 5 | 6 | 7 | 8 | 9 | 10 | 11 | 12
```

FORMATTING REVIEW

Speeches

1. 50-space line.
2. Standard top and bottom margins.
3. Triple-space for easier reading.
4. If audiovisual materials, such as slides, are to be used, indicate in the copy where they occur by centering *Slide 1, Slide 2,* and so on.

JOB 159 A. SPEECH

Standard format (see review in margin).

Mailroom Addressing for Automation 21

January 10, 19-- 34

5 I am delighted to be with you today. It isn't often that mail- 48
room personnel are given the opportunity to have a get-together 61
and discuss the mail. So I ~~trust~~ hope that my brief review of 72
how to address the mail will make your jobs easier *and keep you* 85
up to date. 87

(Continued on next page)

LETTER 12

Business letter with subject line and *cc* notation. Body 115 words.

Athletic Department, Springs High School, 1800 Keystone Road, Sand Springs, OK 74063, Ladies and Gentlemen: Subject: Gymnastics Competition

¶ We have recently learned that Springs High School is planning to start a gymnastics squad for next fall's competition. We are members of the gymnastics Conference, and we are pleased to welcome you to our league. ¶ As a first-year member, you are probably in the middle of planning your competition schedule. We would like to plan a meet with you on November 15 or 18. Would you be interested in a meet on either of these two dates? ¶ We can arrange to meet either in the afternoon or during the evening. Because of the distance between our schools, an evening meet might be more convenient for us. ¶ Please let me hear from you soon. Very truly yours, Conrad Simpson, Athletic Manager, cc: League Office

LETTER 13

Business letter. Special parts: Second-page heading, subject line, indented enumerations, enclosure notation, and *cc* notation. Body 396 words.

Mr. Ross Christie, Facilities Planner, A.B. Grant, Inc., 356 Highland Avenue, Montclair, NJ 07043, Dear Mr. Christie: Subject: Office Layout

The suggestions we have for the blueprints you submitted to us for review appear below. Before we start, though, we want to take this opportunity to thank you for selecting Office Design, Inc., to plan the office layout for your new store in Wayne, New Jersey.

The office layout that is enclosed reflects the open office concept you suggested in your letter to us last June. The plan has been designed to accommodate all 150 employees specified in the personnel report you submitted, and it will also accommodate the additional 75 employees to be added in the next five years.

We have suggested the open office concept over the traditional office for several reasons:

(Continued on next page)

Slide 1 187

5 Remember: You are doing essentialwork. You are the focal point 102
of a large part of your company's communicattions effort. how 114
well the mailroom functions has a major affect on how your com- 126
pany loooks in the eyes of its customersand how well it prospres. 140
By making sure that your mail is prepared for sorting by the Postal 153
Service's computerised sorting equipment, you'll promote better busi- 167
ness, improve communications, and enhance your own job perfromance. 181

Here is a correctly addressed envelope. Note that the ad- 200
dress arae should be in blocked form--all lines begin at the left 212
margin. 214

Sliee 2 221

5 Mail addressed to occupantsof multi unit buildings should include 235
dthe number of the apartment, room,suit or other unit. The unit 248
number should appear immediately after the stree address on the 261
same line--never above below, or in front of the street address. 275

Slide 3 281

The city, state, and ZIP Code should appaer inthat sequance 294
on the bottom line of the address block. This is where automatic 307
sorting equipment for this information. Mail presorted by ZEP 324
Codes by passes many processing steps in the postoffice and get 336
get to it's destination quicker. 343

is instructed to look

Slide 4 350

Window envelopes must be matched If the insert slides around 369
in the envelope the envelope can not be delivered. Always check 382
the window enevlope to be sure the address on the insert is fully 396
visible. 398

with the address on the insert.

Slide 5 404

When a postal station name is shown it should be entered on the sameline 420
as the box number. Correct spelling of street names is essentail, 433
since some postal machines compare the address name with address names 448
programmed in the computer's memory. 455

One last reminder: You can increase the machin handling of 468
your mail by usings two-letter abbreviation for state names. 481

Thank you for your attention and for coming to this workshop. 494

LETTER 9 (CONTINUED)

should clarify the ~~last~~ electricity bill

you received on your ~~August~~ through December statements.

From (Aug.) 1 to (Aug.) 31 you used 2348 kilowts at. This is based on an August 1 reading of 57,574 and a n August 31 reading of 59,922. Based on a rate of $ .068 per KWH, your total bill of $ 160.29 is correct. Your August through December readings are also summarized below:

August	2348	kWh	$160.29
September	2215	kWh	150.62
October	1755	kWh	119.34
November	1094	kWh	74.39
December	566	kWh	38.49

If you have any further questions on your statements, please feel free to again (call me) at 555-8956.

Very sincerely yours, John T. Crane, Acounts Recievable, cc: Customer Service

LETTER 10

Business letter. Special part: Table. Body 133 words.

Mr. Joseph T. Fortenberry, Miller's Nursery, 298 Meyers Road, Reno, NV 89506, Dear Mr. Fortenberry:

It appears that the trees you planted in front of our new office building on Commercial Row possibly may not survive. Of the 52 that were planted, 10 haven't shown any life now for at least three weeks, and they'll have to be replaced. The affected trees are described in the table below.

TREES TO BE REPLACED

Tree	Date Planted	Number
Box Elder	11/1	3
Wild Cherry	11/5	2
American Elm	11/15	2
Mountain Ash	11/20	2
Red Mulberry	11/30	1

Would you please bring replacements for these trees and have them replanted by the end of next week. We are having an open house for our new executive building on the 10th, and we would like to have all the replacements made by that date.

Yours truly, Denise T. Gordon, General Manager

LETTER 11

Business letter with subject line and postscript. Body 73 words.

Mr. Roberta Matsno, American Testing Agency, 160 (E.) Kellog (Blvd.), St. Paul, Mn 55101, Dear Ms. Matson: Subject: Typing Tests

Last week you mentioned that your agencie has been developing ~~a~~ an employment test for office typists. I would like to learm more about the test. We have for many years used 5- and 10-minute tests for all our applicants. How ever, we have found that there is little corelation between anapplicant's performance on the test and performance on the job. I hope that you will write to tell us about your test. Sincerely, Roberta Hendricks, Personnel Department, PS I'm enclosing a stamped envelope for writing me about your testing program.

FORMATTING REVIEW

Minutes of a Meeting

1. 6-inch line (see note below).
2. Title and subtitle lines include the name of the group and the date. Begin the title on line 7.
3. Single-space. All-cap side headings; double-space before and after.
4. Closing lines begin at center; 3 blank lines for signature.

Note: Minutes are usually kept in a binder. Shift margins and centering point 3 spaces to the right as for bound reports.

JOB 159 B. MINUTES OF A MEETING

Standard format (see review in margin).

Downtowners Club 10
Minutes of the December Meeting 32
December 6, 19— 44
Attendance 49
The annual dinner meeting of the 57
Downtowners Club was held at the 64
Press Club on Friday, December 3, 71
at 6 p.m. After dinner President 78
Solonchek called the meeting to 84
order. All members were present, 91
except Esther Falk and Ben Collard. 98
Unfinished Business 103
President Solonchek asked for ideas 112
on ways to raise money to pay for the 120
College scholarship fund that the Club 128
voted in November to support. The fund is 136
to be for a worthy student-writer who wants 145
to major in communications. Several 153
plans were put forth. President Solonchek 161
asked for members to serve on an ad 168
hoc committee to follow up on the 175
suggestions, and four members 181
volunteered: Susan Strauss, Nick 188
Pappas, Rupert Nosel, and Ann Zogg. 195
New Business 199
Since this is the final meeting of the 209
year, there was no new business. President 218
Solonchek thanked all her officers who 225
served with her during the past year: 233
Mike Epson, First Vice President; Rachael 242
Brewer, Second Vice President; Scott 249
Carter, Secretary; and Jay Suggard, 256
Treasurer. 259
The meeting adjourned at 8:30 p.m. 268
Scott Carter, Secretary 276

LETTER 7 (CONTINUED)

time, we have ~~always~~ received satisfactory shipments from your Omaha warehouse.

However, since you implemented your new shipping procedures last month, ~~no fewer than~~ at least 4 of our rush orders have been delayed ~~enroute~~. If we recieve delays in our future RUSH orders, we will have no other ~~alternative~~ choice but to seek another supplier.

Yours very truly, Grace R. Drake, General Manager, cc: Bill Burton, Faye Hunt

We ~~certainly~~ hope that this will not be necessary, because during the past six years we have developed some very excellent business relationships between our companies.

LETTER 8

Business letter. Special part: *bcc* notation. Body 99 words.

AKC Kennels, 2856 Washington Avenue, Baton Rouge, LA 70802, Ladies and Gentlemen:

We are opening a new warehouse and yard at 306 Sands Avenue next month. We'd like to purchase from your kennel three guard dogs that could protect our property after business hours and during weekends. Several owners have recommended that we contact you for our request.

We would like to have AKC German shepherds at this location and would prefer that they complete your protection training course (Level 2) prior to active duty.

I would like to observe these dogs during one of their training sessions. Would it be possible to visit the kennel on June 16 at 10 a.m. during one of your training periods?

Yours truly, Carmen T. Davis, Warehouse Manager, bcc: Samuel Adams

LETTER 9

Business letter. Special parts: Display, *cc* notation. Body 113 words.

(Date: January 16, 19--) Mrs. Jayne Barnes, 520 Dewey Avenue, St. Louis, MO 63161, Dear Ms. Barnes:

As you requested over the telephone on January 10, the following information

(Continued on next page)

LESSON 160

■ GOALS
To identify subject-verb agreement while typing sentences.
To review formatting magazine and newsletter articles.

■ FORMAT
Single spacing   60-space line

LAB 18

Subject-Verb Agreement

Type lines 1–4 once. Then repeat lines 1–4 or take a series of 1-minute timings. Note subject-verb agreement as you type each line (subjects and verbs are underscored).

```
1  Victor Mazurki has six copies of the required instructions.  12
2  Both managers have assistants to help them to analyze data.  12
3  I am sure that Gary Jeffers will be there for the luncheon.  12
4  Bryant and Darlene are now at a data processing convention.  12
   | 1 | 2 | 3 | 4 | 5 | 6 | 7 | 8 | 9 | 10 | 11 | 12
```

12-SECOND TIMINGS

Type each line three times, or take three 12-second timings on each line. For each timing, type with no more than 1 error.

```
5  Nancy works well with their plants:  iris, ivy, and laurel.
6  Ellen hopes to come back and assist her class with the job.
7  Les saw the ship as he was walking over the hill near here.
       5    10   15   20   25   30   35   40   45   50   55   60
```

FORMATTING REVIEW

Articles

1. Double spacing.
2. 50-space line (or match magazine).
3. Heading includes title, the author's name, and the number of lines and their length.
4. Top margins: 2 inches on page 1; 1 inch (6 lines) on all other pages. Bottom margins: 1–1½ inches.
5. Beginning with page 2, backspace from the right margin the page number and the author's name, separated by a diagonal.

Note: When you finish typing the article, count the lines and insert the number in the heading.

JOB 160 A. MAGAZINE ARTICLE

Standard format (see review in margin). 5-space and center tabs. Read the job before typing it.

YOUR PHONE CAN MAKE LIFE EASIER 19

By Adrienne Reifmueller 35

(00 Lines of 50 Spaces) 57

Teams of engineers, accountants, and marketing persons are working on 68
new services and equipment planned for telephone customers. When the 82
company will offer these new services and how much they will cost are not 97
known; but the company is planning to sell new phone and computer-based 111
equipment that will give its customers a variety of new ways to use its 125
phones. Here are some of the special uses. 134

Voice Storage. A computer will replace phone answering machines. 154
Besides taking messages, the new device will dial preselected phone num- 168
bers and return a call with a recorded message. For example, suppose you 183
put an ad in your newspaper to sell your used car, and you get ten calls 198
while you are outside showing your car to a potential buyer. The computer 213
will select the calls related to your ad and return these calls with a recorded 229
message, giving the caller all the needed information about your auto, such 244
as mileage and condition. 249

(Continued on next page)

LETTER 4

Business letter. Special part: Subject line. Body 94 words.

Ms. Barbara James, 206 Talmadge Avenue, Springfield, IL 62701, Dear Ms. James: Subject: Overdue Account #629-458901-RC

Ten days ago we sent you an overdue notice on the account referenced above. The notice was sent by registered mail, and your signature on the return receipt indicates that you did receive the notice.

Have you overlooked your payment on this account? The $45.89 you owe us is for purchases you made on 5/4, 5/9, and 6/2. If you have any questions on this account, please call me at (217) 555-3479. If you have no questions, please remit your payment by August 15.

We hope to be hearing from you in the near future. Cordially yours, Rodney P. Arnez, Collection Department

LETTER 5

Business letter. Special part: Enclosure notation. Body 137 words.

Mr. Ron Ferguson, 2368 Raintree Drive, Colorado Springs, CO 80911, Dear Mr. Ferguson:

Welcome to the gorgeous land of the Rocky Mountains. We wish you success in your new job and hope that you enjoy it and Colorado Springs so much that you will decide to live in our state for many years to come.

We would like to serve your banking needs here in Colorado Springs. In addition to our checking and savings services, we offer additional services to our customers. For instance, we have a 13-lane motor bank, 24-hour automated banking services, bank-by-mail privileges, and much more.

The enclosed brochure describes in greater detail all that Rocky Mountain National Bank can provide for you. If you have any questions about any of our services, please feel free to call me at 555-3490. We hope to have the privilege of serving you at our bank.

Sincerely yours, Brenda L. Vick, Vice President, Enclosure

LETTER 6

Business letter. Special part: Attention line. Body 57 words.

Metro Equipment, Inc., 1752 Big Hill Road, Dayton, OH 45439, Attention: Mr. Raymond P. Cruze, Ladies and Gentlemen:

Thank you for demonstrating your American Front Loader at our Irving Avenue construction site last Wednesday. This skid-steer loader is certainly one of the finest on the market, and we would like to purchase two for our Dayton yards.

Would you please have two Model H-290s delivered to 3578 Patterson Boulevard South on Tuesday, September 10. Yours truly, Layne S. Ramon, Manager

LETTER 7

Business letter. Special part: *cc* notation. Body 68 words.

```
Mr. Gordon P. Howell, Sales manager,
Bolts Best, Inc., 4538 Dodge St.
Omaha, NE 68132, Dear Mr. Howel:
     You've been supplying us with
hex head bolts, lag screws, and wash-
ers for the past 6 years.  During that
```

(Continued on next page)

Meter Reading and Protection Service. Using sensors and more wiring 278
tied to your phone, the company can call your home or business and read 293
your meters: water, gas, and electricity. Also, sensors in doorways and 308
windows of a home or place of business can self-activate the phone to 322
signal the police during a robbery. 329

Selective-Call Forwarding. Instead of all your phone calls being trans- 354
ferred to a place you plan to be, a computer system will select only the calls 370
you want to get through. Suppose you are a sales representative who is out 385
of the office a great deal, but you are expecting an extremely urgent call 400
from an important customer. You don't have to wait by your telephone. 415
You can leave instructions with the telephone company for calls to be 429
forwarded to wherever you plan to be. Only the call you were waiting for 443
will get through; the others will be answered by an automatic answering 458
system. 460

Electronic Yellow Pages. Linking the phone to the TV set opens up a 484
wealth of shopping-at-the-office or shopping-at-home services. Using a 498
separate keyboard attached to the phone, the customer can turn on the TV 513
set, ask to see a certain catalog listing, and order by phone. 525

JOB 160 B. UNEDITED NEWSLETTER ARTICLE

Standard format for a magazine article without subtitles. Edit the copy as you type. (That is, correct spelling, capitalization, and punctuation errors.)

FOCUS ON OUR PEOPLE—MEET CYNTHIA BERANEK

Cynthia Beranek is blind, but that hasn't prevented her from becoming a whiz at the keyboard of her automatic typewriter. For the passed 6 years, Cynthia has been typing up a storm in the word processing group of the office services section at great falls steel corporation's headquarters offices in pittsburgh.

She types letters, memos, and other documents that are phoned in by enginers, buyers, lawyers, and other company employees. Because they dictate onto a tape cassette most of her "audio" bosses have never had the opportunity to meet or talk directly to her. If they could, they would discover a delightful young woman who is very profishent in her job.

Cynthia produces accurate, neat work with an automatic typewriter and a transcribng unit the same as those used by other typists in the group. She types by touch and has master her machine through training, determenation, and a fine sense of recall.

When she begins a job, Cynthia slips the tape casette into the transcribing unit, puts on her earpiece, and listens to find out what format is desired. Then she types the job with speed and accuracy. Dictation requireing tabular work is handled by other typist.

Cynthias' timesaving machine permits her to mechanicaly correct conscieous typing errors on a line-by-line basis instead of having to retype the entire page. For fast character count-offs, she relyes on an abacus. The end result is a piece of final copy that is free of eraseres or any other types of correction marks. Although her work is checked by the group leader, it rarely needs addtional revision—a tribute to her fine typing skills.

CORRESPONDENCE

LETTER 1

Personal-business letter. No special parts. Body 63 words.

1079 61st Avenue, SW, Fort Lauderdale, FL 33317, Ms. Andrea Taylor, Customer Services, Friedman Supply Company, 11005 Stirling Road, Fort Lauderdale, FL 33328, Dear Ms. Taylor:

Thank you for crediting my account (No. 501 612 28) for $37.17 to reflect the payment I made on May 4. There had been some confusion in my May statement as to whether or not I had actually paid it, and it was a relief to see that the problem had been resolved.

It is certainly a pleasure to do business with you. Sincerely yours, Ricardo Santos

LETTER 2

Personal-business letter. Special part: Enclosure notation. Body 67 words.

701 Columbia Avenue East, Battle Creek, MI 49015, MR. Pete Johnson, Manager, Hunter Jewelry Store, 1870 Washington Avenue, Ann Arbor, MI 48104, Dear Mr. Johnson:

Enclosed is a Time Write watch that I purchased at your store on June 27. It stopped running after only three weeks' use, and the battery may have malfunctioned. Is it possible that the watch had been running on that battery in the showcase before I purchased it? Please replace the battery, if that is the problem, and return the watch to my home address, which appears above. Very truly yours, Kathryn E. Davis, Enclosure

LETTER 3

Personal-business letter. Special part: Postscript. Body 56 words.

P.O. Box 3606, Kingman, KS 67086, Pretoria Ticket Agency, 278 Main Street South, Witchita, KS 67202, Ladies and Gentlemen:

Please send me four $15 tickets to the Kenny Rogers concert on September 8, 19--. I would like the tickets charged to my autochecque card, No. 340-562-397.

If possible, I would like the seats to be selected from Section H in the auditorium. If this section is no longer available, Section G or Section I would be my ~~next~~ alternate choices.

Very Cordially yours, Paula B. Brown

PS: Please select 4 seats that are together, as we all would like to be seated by each other for the concert.

■ **GOALS**
To correct errors in subject-verb agreement while typing sentences.
To type 40/5′/4e.
To review formatting itineraries.

■ **FORMAT**
Drills: Single spacing   60-space line
5-Minute Timings: Double spacing   5-space tab

LAB 18

Subject-Verb Agreement

Type lines 1–4 once, correcting verbs if necessary to ensure subject-verb agreement. Edit your copy as your teacher reads the answers. Then retype lines 1–4 from your edited copy.

```
1 Mr. Zimbalist are excited about your ideas for our magazine.
2 Those real estate agencies is eager to purchase this land.
3 Madeline has not yet returned from her vacation in Jamaica.
4 Yes, she do have quite large land holdings in California.
```

PREVIEW PRACTICE

Type each line twice as a preview to the 5-minute timings below.

```
Accuracy  5 surveys example require repetitive responsible standardized
Speed     6 their forms with work hand turn such but may and the own to
```

5-MINUTE TIMINGS

Take two 5-minute timings on lines 7–21.

7 In some companies, some departments need to have their own centers, 15
8 with just a few word processing machines—this center is called a cluster, 30
9 and the production done is only for that department. 40
10 If the office belongs to the manager of the department that has the sur- 55
11 veys on viewers' likes and dislikes for the local TV station, for example, 70
12 the work of the cluster will be tables or reports. 80
13 On the other hand, a department responsible for making collections on 95
14 overdue bills will have a great deal of mail and just a few tables and reports 111
15 to be produced by typists within this cluster. 120
16 For one more example: A cluster that serves the legal department will 135
17 turn out a great many long documents, along with the forms that require 150
18 fill-ins, such as court papers, contracts, and wills. 160
19 Thus the work of one cluster will differ from the work of any other, but 176
20 the work within a cluster is standardized and repetitive. Although the work 191
21 may seem dull, it really is quite interesting. 200

| 1 | 2 | 3 | 4 | 5 | 6 | 7 | 8 | 9 | 10 | 11 | 12 | 13 | 14 | 15 | SI 1.45

TABLE 10
Multicolumn, with braced heading and footnote.

SUMMER SALE ITEMS
Harrison's Department Store
July 1, 19–, to July 31, 19–

ITEM	Description		
	Catalog Number	Regular Price	Sale Price
Fabric Hammocks	D80817	$ 59.99	$ 49.99
Lawn Dining Set*	D05069	69.99	59.99
Lawn Umbrella	D82345	97.99	87.99
Porch Swing*	D31002	72.99	64.99
3-Seat Lawn Sofa	D46701	139.99	124.99

*Quantities limited.

TABLE 11
Multicolumn, with braced heading and total line.

Type the regions in numerical order, with Region 1 first.

QUARTERLY MILEAGE REPORT
Driscoll Enterprises, Inc.
July 1, 19--, to June 30, 19--

Provide missing mileage figures.

Region	Quarterly Reimbursed Mileage			
	First	Second	Third	Fourth
3d Region	278,640	213,591	256,307	241,895
1st Region	?	484,267	453,109	492,361
4th Region	209,873	?	243,087	215,690
2d Region	346,519	391,564	?	338,165
TOTAL	1,294,135	1,380,887	11,260,782	?

FORMATTING REVIEW

Itineraries

1. 6-inch line (60P/70E).
2. Title, name, date, and cities displayed in 3 lines, double-spaced.
3. Day and date underscored at left margin.
4. Times of events indented 5 spaces from left margin.
5. Tab 25 spaces from left margin for details of trip; indent turnover lines 2 spaces.
6. Single-space turnover lines; double-space between entries.
7. Use names of airports only when there is more than one servicing a city.

JOB 161 A. ITINERARY

Type the itinerary below, making the changes shown in handwriting. Standard format (see review in margin).

ITINERARY

Insert (A)

Monday, March 6

Insert (B) 8:00 p.m.	Registration, Oceanview Room
9:00 p.m.	Reception, Ballroom A
	Accommodations: San Juan International, Headquarters for Governors' Conference
Reminder	Sign up for group meeting at the time of registration.

Tuesday, March 7

7:30 a.m.	Governors' Breakfast, Ballroom A
9:30 a.m.	First General Session, Ballroom B
12:00 noon	Luncheon, Garden Restaurant, lower level
2:00 p.m.	Keynote Address, Ballroom B
4:00 p.m.	Individual Group Meetings
8:00 p.m.	Dinner at the El Greco Club; shuttle buses from hotel.

Wednesday, March 8

7:30 a.m.	Breakfast with members of individual group meetings
9:30 a.m.	Second General Session, Ballroom B
12:00 noon	Lunch at the Golf Club
1:30 p.m.	Golf tournament or afternoon of sight-seeing. Participants in golf tournament should sign up early for a starting time; buses for sight-seers will leave from the Golf Club.
7:00 p.m.	Governors' Banquet at Villa Cavallino; the restaurant is across the street from the hotel.

Thursday, March 9

9:30 a.m.	Individual Group Meetings
12:00 noon	Luncheon and Closing Session, Ballroom A

Insert (C)

Inserts (A) Gov. Sam Rosen. March 6, 19--
(Boston—Puerto Rico)

(B) 8:31 a.m.	Depart Boston, Global Airlines Flight 351
1:41 p.m.	Arrive San Juan, Puerto Rico
(C) 3:00 p.m.	Depart hotel for the airport
4:43 p.m.	Depart San Juan, Global Airlines Flight 64
9:50 p.m.	Arrive Boston

TABLE 8
Multicolumn, with braced headings.

Southwestern States

Selected Statistics

State	Elevations		miles Across	
	Highest Points	Lowest Points	East/West	North/South
Arizona	12,670 ft	100 ft	340	390
New mexico	13,160 ft	2,871 ft	350	390
Oklahoma	4,980 ft	300 ft	460	203
Texas	8,750ft	Sea level	770	800

TABLE 9
Multicolumn, with braced headings and total line.

Type person with highest average total sales for both quarters first, followed by second highest average, etc.

SALES ANALYSIS

Borden Manufacturing Company

June 30, 19--

Salesperson	1st Quarter		2d Quarter	
	Units	Gross Sales	Units	Gross Sales
Robert Brazinski	10	$ 427.70	29	$1240.33
Carol Dawkins	18	769.86	17	727.09
Janice Greene	20	855.40	28	1197.56
Jose Herrera	17	727.09	24	1026.48
Diane Keester	15	641.55	25	1069.25
Joe Yeung	19	812.63	32	1368.64
TOTAL	99	$4234.23	155	$6629.35

LESSON 162

CLINIC

■ **GOAL**
To improve keyboarding skills by practicing right-hand words and down reaches.

■ **FORMAT**
Single spacing   60-space line

KEYBOARDING SKILLS

Type lines 1–4 once. Then use your margin release to finish typing line 5. Repeat lines 1–4, or take a series of 1-minute timings.

Speed 1 Clair may wish to blame me for both of their big work jams. 12

Accuracy 2 Jeff quietly moved his dozen boxes with Angy's power truck. 12

Numbers 3 Bob lost checks Nos. 10, 29, and 38; I lost Nos. 47 and 56. 12

Symbols 4 Bring me #10, #29, #38, and #47, but leave #56 for Jeffrey. 12

Technique 5 The director of the panel may wish to amend the audit form slightly.

| 1 | 2 | 3 | 4 | 5 | 6 | 7 | 8 | 9 | 10 | 11 | 12

PRETEST 1

Take two 2-minute timings on lines 6–9. Circle and count your errors on each.

6 It is their opinion that Jimmy will join the union at noon. 12

7 Phyllis knows her pumpkins will soon look similar to yours. 24

8 Phillip enjoys looking at and collecting only common coins. 36

9 Jon gave all patrons pure stones from that pioneer village. 48

| 1 | 2 | 3 | 4 | 5 | 6 | 7 | 8 | 9 | 10 | 11 | 12

PRACTICE 1

Type lines 10–13 four times.

10 kink lily oily nook only pill upon yolk honk join limp kiln

11 hill pink hook pool moon join noon milk mill lion look junk

12 poppy hilly onion pupil pulpy nylon milky phony plump lumpy

13 jolly imply phylon minimum million homonym opinion nonunion

POSTTEST 1

Take another 2-minute timing on lines 6–9 to see how much your skill has improved.

PRETEST 2

Take two 2-minute timings on lines 14–17. Circle and count your errors on each.

14 Barbara called the clinic to get vitamins for Liza and Max. 12

15 Grace wants to buy nine boxes of memos and carbons at cost. 24

16 Cathy agreed to leave early to meet our staff at our place. 36

17 Daniel cannot remove those trunks for another month or two. 48

| 1 | 2 | 3 | 4 | 5 | 6 | 7 | 8 | 9 | 10 | 11 | 12

PRACTICE 2

Type lines 18–21 four times.

18 fvf five viva very avid favor jmj jams many main mean major

19 dcd cede dice code dock occur sxs exit next taxi text taxes

20 aza maze haze hazy lazy azure jnj Jane June Joan Jean Janet

21 fbf beef fibs buff fobs fiber l.l Mr. Dr. Ms. Mrs. Sgt. Lt.

POSTTEST 2

Take another 2-minute timing on lines 14–17 to see how much your skill has improved.

TABLE 6
Multicolumn, with rules, decimals, and total line.

ANALYSIS OF LAST YEAR'S SALES

JULY 1 THROUGH JUNE 30

BRANCH	BUDGET	ACTUAL	PERCENT
CLEVELAND	$ 150,000	$ 150,000	100.0
DALLAS	255,000	244,000	95.7
MADISON	175,400	180,400	102.9
MINNEAPOLIS	215,400	177,500	82.4
PORTLAND	195,700	183,100	93.6
SAN FRANCISCO	300,500	278,300	92.6
TOTAL	$1,292,000	$1,213,300	94.5 %

TABLE 7
Multicolumn, with rules, total line, and footnote.

EMPLOYEE VACATION AND SPENDING HABITS

(Summer, 19--)

Vacation ~~Site~~	Number ~~O~~of Employees	Percent of Employees	Average Daily Expenses
Metro~~plo~~politan City	(24)	27	$55.00
Sea side resort	(25)	23	70.00
Mountain resort	(35)	~~2~~16	42.00
Motor Trip	22	14	88.~~5~~00
Lake Resort	10	6	48.50
(Misc.)	21	14*	41.~~00~~25
Total	155	100	$57.(64)

*A total of 1~~8~~4 percent of the employees collectively had other kinds of vacations.

UNIT 27 Formatting Review of Correspondence

UNIT GOAL 41/5'/4e

■ GOALS
To correct errors in subject-verb agreement while typing sentences.
To review formatting letters and envelopes, subject and attention lines.

■ FORMAT
Single spacing 60-space line

LAB 18

Subject-Verb Agreement

Workbook 279–280.

Type lines 1–4 once, correcting verbs to ensure subject-verb agreement. Edit your copy as your teacher reads the answers. Then retype lines 1–4 from your edited copy.

```
1  Their programs has great appeal, but they are hard to see.
2  The table is walnut, but the chairs is a variety of maple.
3  The books is selling quickly, and the buyers are jubilant.
4  She do good work for her boss, Mr. Zambrix, in personnel.
```

30-SECOND "OK" TIMINGS

Type as many 30-second "OK" (errorless) timings as possible out of three attempts on lines 5–7.

```
5  If there is a blaze in a home near us, we can be so excited   12
6  that we want to dash to see it.  So many observers may come   24
7  that they quite often jeopardize the work of fire fighters.   36
   | 1 | 2 | 3 | 4 | 5 | 6 | 7 | 8 | 9 | 10 | 11 | 12
```

FORMATTING REVIEW

Workbook 281–283.

Letters (Standard Format)

1. 5-inch line. (50P/60E)
2. Date: Line 15.
3. Inside address: 5 lines below date.
4. Salutation: Double-space before and after.
5. Complimentary closing: Begin at the center, a double space below the body.
6. Writer's identification (name and title): 4 lines below closing.
7. Typist's initials: At left margin, double space below writer's identification.

JOB 163 A. LETTER

Standard format (see review in margin and on page 274). Address a No. 10 envelope. Workbook 285–286. Body 137 words.

[*Today's date*] / Mr. Gregory Cocagi / 7224 London Drive / Raleigh, NC 18
27608 / Dear Mr. Cocagi: 24
Now you can hear stereo music on AM radio. That's right—AM stereo. 39
Last week in Washington, stereo broadcasting by AM radio stations was 53
approved. This action will permit broadcasters to give listeners like you the 68
full range of stereo, which up to this time you have been able to hear only 84
on FM radio. 86
While your present car radio, for example, will be able to pick up the 102
music played on AM stereo, you will not be able to enjoy stereo sound 116
because a new radio receiver will be required. 125
As you know, VISTA has been a leading maker of AM/FM radios for 139
many years. We are proud to inform you that all our new radios have AM 153
stereo capability. 157
Visit your VISTA dealer today and select your new car radio so that you 173
will hear relaxing stereo on both AM and FM broadcasts. / Sincerely 188
yours, / Ms. Elizabeth McDowell / Advertising Director / [*Your initials*] 205

TABLE 4
Multicolumn, with leaders.

New Mexico Gift Shop Inc.

SALES REPORT FOR NORTHERN REGION

City	This Year	Last Year	Increase
Albuquerque	$11,368	$10,476	$892
Gallup	5,029	4,775	254
Las Vegas	5,728	5,550	178
Raton	2,301	2,017	284
Santa Fe	7,204	6,852	352
Tucumcari	4,279	3,740	539

TABLE 5
Multicolumn, with footnote.

NATIONAL MONUMENTS

State of Colorado

6 spaces between columns

Name	Acres	Location	Outstanding Feature
Black Canyon of the Gunnison	13,690	Montrose	Steep canyon
Colorado	17,660	GrandJunction	Sand stone Formations
Dinousaur*	206,233	Dinosaur	Fossils
Florisant Fossil Beds	5,992	Florissant	Fossils
Great Sand Dunes	36,740	Hopper	Sand dunes
Hoven weep*	505	Cortez	Cliff Dwellings
Yucca House	110	Towoac	Pueblo indian

*Shared with Utah.

FORMATTING REVIEW (CONTINUED)

No. 10 envelope

Begin addressee's name and address on line 14, 4 inches (40P/48E) from left edge.

Subject line

1. Follows the salutation; double-space before and after.
2. Adds 20 words to body count.

Attention line

1. Between inside address and salutation; double-space before and after.
2. Adds 20 words to body count.

Women's titles

Respect a woman's preference in using *Miss, Mrs.,* or *Ms.* If not known, use the title Ms.

JOB 163 B. LETTER WITH SUBJECT LINE

Standard format (see review in margin). Workbook 287–288. Body 65 words.

[Today's date] / Mr. Chester Hartzell / R.R. 1 / St. 14
Augustine, FL 32084 / Dear Mr. Hartzell: / 23
Subject: Town Meeting / I will be holding a 34
town meeting in Interlachen on Thursday, 40
January 15, from 6:30 to 7:30 p.m. in 49
the council chambers of the Interlachen 57
Municipal Building. I hope that you and 66
members of your family can attend. ¶ 75
Thomas Jefferson said that the basis of our 83
government is the opinion of our people, 91
and that is why I will be in Interlachen-- 99
to get your opinions and to answer your 107
questions. / Sincerely yours, / Sylvia Nyhart / 120
United States Senator / [Your initials] 129

JOB 163 C. LETTER WITH SUBJECT AND ATTENTION LINES

Standard format (see review in margin). Workbook 289–290. Body 84 words.

(Today's date) / Hektor Plastics / 200 Saint Paul Street / 16
Denver, CO 80026 / Attention: Director of Advertising / 27
Ladies & Gentlemen: / Subject: The People Delivers System / 41
Have you seen our new median program entitled "The People 54
Delivery System, which is being shown this Week at the Clear 65
Reach Inn? Our station, WPIT-am/FM, together wit the CBC 77
Radio Network, build this display to call attention to the 89
the fact that we attract more than thirteen million listeners 99
a week! ¶ Before you plan your advertising budget for next 113
year, see this presentation. It will convince you that radio 125
advertising pays off--for the prince of one prime-time 30- 136
second spot you can buy 14 network radio spots. / Yours very 150
truly, / Harvey S. Grimes / Station Manager / (Your initials) 165

TABLES

TABLE 1
Multicolumn, with rules and long column headings.

Number of
TOTAL NEWSPAPERS

Morning and evening editions

Name of State	Morning	Evening
California	21	100
Illinois	22	71
Indiana	7	72
Ohio	8	89
Pennsylvania	13	80
Texas	25	89

TABLE 2
Multicolumn, with rules and two-line column headings.

CHIEF JUSTICES OF THE SUPREME COURT ds
Appointed During 1920 to 1970

Name	Year Appointed	State of Residence	President
Warren E. Burger	1969	Virginia	Nixon
Charles E. Hughes	1930	New York	Hoover
Harlan F. Stone	1941	New York	F. D. Roosevelt
William H. Taft	1921	Connecticut	Harding
Frederick M. Vinson	1946	Kentucky	Truman
Earl Warren	1953	California	Eisenhower

TABLE 3
Multicolumn, with rules and two-line column headings.

LARGEST U.S. NATIONAL PARKS

(Over 700,000 Acres)

Name of National Park	Acres	Location	Outstanding Feature
Yellowstone	2,221,800	Wyoming	Geysers
Mount McKinley	1,939,500	Alaska	Highest Mountain
Everglades	1,400,500	Florida	Wilderness
Glacier	1,013,100	Montana	Glaciers
Olympic	896,600	Washington	Wilderness
Yosemite	761,300	California	Waterfalls
Big Bend	708,200	Texas	Chisos Mountains

LESSON 164

■ **GOALS**
To type 41/3'/3e.
To review formatting letter styles and postscripts.

■ **FORMAT**
Drills: Single spacing 60-space line
3-Minute Timings: Double spacing 5-space tab

KEYBOARDING SKILLS

Type lines 1–4 once. Then do what line 5 tells you to do. Repeat lines 1–4, or take a series of 1-minute timings.

Speed	1	It is his fault if he does not help us find the six orders.	12
Accuracy	2	Jumping quickly from the taxi, Hazel brushed a woven chair.	12
Numbers	3	Please get some price tags for 10¢, 29¢, 38¢, 47¢, and 56¢.	12
Symbols	4	"Why must I leave?" she asked. "Well," we said, "why not?"	12
Technique	5	Type line 3 in all-capital letters using the shift lock.	

| 1 | 2 | 3 | 4 | 5 | 6 | 7 | 8 | 9 | 10 | 11 | 12

PRETEST

Take a 3-minute timing on lines 6–17. Circle and count your errors.

6 In the more than one hundred years since its invention 12
7 by Alexander Graham Bell, the telephone has changed the way 24
8 people all over the world communicate. It has also spawned 36
9 an ever-growing business. 41

10 Today the major goal of this business is to serve with 12
11 efficiency our increasing demand for more service—although 24
12 we in this country already own about half of the telephones 36
13 used in the entire world. 41

14 Tomorrow telephones will be required to do more things 12
15 for you. Technology is zeroing in on many new uses of your 24
16 telephone in the home and at work. Phones are vital to all 36
17 parts of our daily lives. 41

| 1 | 2 | 3 | 4 | 5 | 6 | 7 | 8 | 9 | 10 | 11 | 12 SI 1.50

PRACTICE

Take a 1-minute timing on each paragraph of the Pretest.

POSTTEST

Take another 3-minute timing on lines 6–17 to see how much your skill has improved.

TRANSPOSITION ERRORS (*we* for *ew*)

1 few hew new anew blew crew drew grew renews reviews viewing
2 owe wed weak weed week weld went west weary wedding western
3 Few in the weary crew knew that the weed grew in wet grass.
4 A crew grew weak and weary viewing wet weather in the west.

TRANSPOSITION ERRORS (*er* for *re*)

1 real rent reason regard regress relate relish remain remedy
2 ever leer alter fever lever lover sheer steer desert sorter
3 A store merchant had reasons for renting the camera to her.
4 He regretfully returned the sheer dress to the store clerk.

TRANSPOSITION ERRORS (*rt* for *tr*)

1 try trot true trade tribe trust truth travel truant trouble
2 art cart dart mart part tart alert heart shirt start cohert
3 The tattered tramps toiled to tow the trailer to the truck.
4 The new report revealed that the river had started to rise.

TRANSPOSITION ERRORS (*po* for *op*)

1 drop flop hoop hope loop opal open rope opera optic operate
2 poem poet pork port pose post porous porter portion posture
3 Those poems the poor poet composed were popular with Polly.
4 A job of the sponsor is to appoint the proper, polite poet.

TRANSPOSITION ERRORS (*u* for *i*; *i* for *u*)

1 fire hire inch milk mine pile size light limit waist finish
2 blue glue hulk much plug rust true lunch plump plush unhook
3 Jim Hunter had a delicious dinner with Muriel Mire at noon.
4 Hugh and Ivy Lute will visit their cousin in Biloxi in May.

TRANSPOSITION ERRORS (*o* for *i*; *i* for *o*)

1 light might quick nights simple identify quantity imaginary
2 hold home move once only crows occurs oppose people follows
3 A diary is a precise daily record of your personal actions.
4 A highlight at the spring fashion fair is an Oriental suit.

TRANSPOSITION ERRORS (*a* for *s*; *s* for *a*)

1 his lose loss lost miss mist pose rose snip snow stop knows
2 all ate way bake cake fake lake make rank take wait trained
3 Adam ate all the cake Barbara baked, but James had no cake.
4 Ms. Sarah Sands must stop at the Custer Museum some Sunday.

TRANSPOSITION ERRORS (*e* for *d*; *d* for *e*)

1 did lid duds duly duty card lard doubt drool ballad discard
2 elk east easy eves ebony empty emblem empire enchant energy
3 A dedicated editor decided to edit an address on education.
4 Ed Dodds read the report that Ted Edward prepared on weeds.

TRANSPOSITION ERRORS (*m* for *n*; *n* for *m*)

1 not now news note plan known night noble noise notch nickel
2 mad maid mail main male malt meal more maize magnet magnify
3 Ned nominated his nephew to navigate a nice, new steamship.
4 My magnificent machine managed to mangle the massive metal.

TRANSPOSITION ERRORS (*l* for *o*; *o* for *l*)

1 oak out coke cope home only open took cooked copper objects
2 lap let lip nil dell lace land lard lash large rifle ladder
3 I opened the cupboard doors and saw oranges and other food.
4 A large lumberjack loaded the last of the long, light logs.

FORMATTING REVIEW

Block Format

All lines begin at left margin.

Standard Format With Indented Paragraphs

Date and closing lines begin at center; paragraphs indented (usually 5 spaces). All other lines begin at left margin.

Postscripts

1. Double-space below last notation; begin with *PS:*.
2. Use paragraph style used in letter (block or indent).

JOB 164 A. LETTER WITH ATTENTION LINE

Block format (see review in margin). Workbook 291–292. Body 134 words.

[*Today's date*] / Voluntccr Fire Fighters of Summerville / P.O. Box 10 / 18
Summerville, PA 15864 / Attention: Fire Chief Rudy Pedder / Dear 33
Friends: 35
I am writing to thank all the volunteer fire fighters in your company who 51
assisted Troopers Woolworth, Hachmeister, Heimer, and Eaton last eve- 64
ning in our search for little Suzie Bathurst. Because of your immediate 79
response to our call for help, we were able to find the child before dark. 94
I especially want to commend Fire Fighter Cunningham, who volun- 108
teered to be lowered into the old Pitville mine shaft to look for Suzie. 122
Although he risked his life, he accepted the assignment with courage; and 137
when his efforts failed to find Suzie, he continued with us to search the 152
area. 153
The citizens of Summerville are fortunate to have a group of volunteers 169
who work closely with the State Police in any emergency in order to pro- 183
tect the lives of the people in this county. / Sincerely, / Captain Carl 201
McKune / Station Commander / [*Your initials*] 208

JOB 164 B. LETTER WITH ATTENTION LINE AND POSTSCRIPT

Retype Job 164 A. Standard format with indented paragraphs. Add the postscript below as the last item in the letter (see review in margin). Workbook 293–294.

PS: I am nominating Fire Fighter Cunningham for our community's Outstanding Citizen Award.

LESSON 165

■ GOALS
To recognize subject-verb agreement while typing sentences.
To review formatting two-page letters.
To review formatting letters on monarch and baronial stationery.
To review formatting enclosure notations.

■ FORMAT
Single spacing 60-space line

LAB 19

Subject-Verb Agreement

Type lines 1–4 once. Then repeat lines 1–4 or take a series of 1-minute timings. Note subject-verb agreement as you type each line (subjects and verbs are underscored).

```
1 One of the real reasons for quick rejection is poor health.   12
2 The prices of the new model are set by the board this year.   12
3 One of you is to be nominated for this new office tomorrow.   12
4 Her experience as adviser to adults gives her all the zest.   12
  | 1 | 2 | 3 | 4 | 5 | 6 | 7 | 8 | 9 | 10 | 11 | 12
```

Phrases and clauses between a subject and verb do not affect the number of the verb. If the subject is singular, use a singular verb; if the subject is plural, use a plural verb.

The lost *box* of new letterheads *has been found.*

Use a singular verb after a phrase beginning with *one of* or *one of the:*

One of the books *has been lost.* (Singular verb agrees with the subject *one*.)

5-LETTER WORDS

1 abide affix alarm bakes blade blend cakes charm civic dealt
2 desks dough eight ended equal fancy fifth flags gleam grant
3 guess happy heirs helps issue items ivory labor lapse lathe
4 magic maple mayor occur ought owned parks photo plane range
5 rocks royal sense shade shape taken thank title visit vital
6 voted waist wants whale yacht yield youth acute blank chest

SPACE BAR DRILLS

1 a b c d e f g h i j k l m n o p q r s t u v w x y z a b c d
2 aa bb cc dd ee ff gg hh ii jj kk ll mm nn oo pp qq rr ss tt
3 aaa bbb ccc ddd eee fff ggg hhh iii jjj kkk lll mmm nnn ooo
4 1 2 3 4 5 6 7 8 9 0 1 2 3 4 5 6 7 8 9 0 1 2 3 4 5 6 7 8 9 0
5 11 22 33 44 55 66 77 88 99 00 11 22 33 44 55 66 77 88 99 00
6 111 222 333 444 555 666 777 888 999 000 111 222 333 444 555

TABULATOR KEY DRILLS

Set tab every 8 spaces.

1 aid air and ant apt bid big bit
2 bow bud bus but cod cow cut did
3 dig dog due dug dye end eye fir
4 fit fix foe for fur jam key lay
5 man map may oak own pay rid rob
6 rod row rub she sit six sod the

CAPITALIZATION DRILLS

1 A Alex B Barb C Carl D Dawn E Earl F Faye G Glen H Hope Hal
2 I Inez J Jeff K Kate L Lory M Mike N Nell O Opel P Phil Pam
3 R Rona S Suzy T Troy A Alan B Beth C Chad D Drew E Eric Eva
4 A Alvin B Betty C Carol D David E Edwin F Frank G Garth Gus
5 H Helen J Joann K Kevin L Lloyd M Mavis N Nancy O Olive Ora
6 P Patsy R Randy S Sarah T Twila V Viola R Ronny S Steve Sam

ACCELERATION SENTENCES

1 She is busy with the work but is to go to town for the pen.
2 Jan got the forms for the firm and may also work with them.
3 He may wish to pay them if and when they go to work for us.
4 Both the men may go to town if he pays them for their work.
5 The name of the firm they own is to the right of the forms.
6 The coal firm also pays them when they load down rock jams.

NUMBER DRILLS

1 101 191 181 171 161 151 141 131 121 202 292 282 272 262 252
2 242 232 212 303 393 383 373 363 353 343 323 313 404 494 484
3 474 464 454 434 424 414 505 595 585 575 565 545 535 525 515
4 606 696 686 676 656 646 636 626 616 707 797 787 767 757 747
5 737 727 717 808 898 878 868 858 848 838 828 818 909 989 979
6 969 959 949 939 929 919 090 080 070 060 050 040 030 020 010

SYMBOL DRILLS

1 a!a s@s d#d f$f f%f j&j k*k l(l ;); ;'; ;"; ;-; ;_; ;=; ;+;
2 aq!a sw@s de#d fr$f ft%f ju&j ki*k lo(l ;p); ;p-; ;p_; ;=+;
3 a!!a s@@s d##d f$$f f%%f j&&j k**k l((l ;)); ;--; ;__; ;++;
4 $56 $47 $38 $29 $10 56# 47# 38# 29# 10# 1/2 1/3 1/4 1/5 1/6
5 56% 47% 38% 29% 100% 1 & 2 & 3 & 4 & 5 & 6 & 7 & 8 & 9 & 10
6 (1)* (2)* (3)* (4)* (5)* 1-2 3-4 5-6 7-8 9-10 1 + 2 + 3 = 6

FORMATTING REVIEW

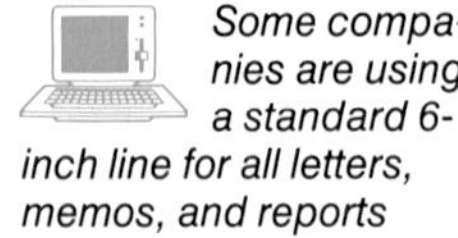

Some companies are using a standard 6-inch line for all letters, memos, and reports typed on 8½- by 11-inch paper.

Variable Letter Placement

Words in body	−225	225+
Date on line	15	12–15
Lines to inside address	5–8	4–5
Lines to signature	4–7	3–4
Line length	5″	6″

Second-Page Heading

1. Include name of addressee, page number, and date.
2. Block style: Begin addressee's name on line 7, page number (with word *Page*) on line 8, date on line 9, all typed at left margin.
3. Centered style: All parts typed on line 7—name at left margin, page number centered, date ending at right margin.
4. Leave 2 blank lines between the heading and the body of the letter.

Special Stationery Sizes

Monarch	
Size	7¼″ by 10½″
Line length	4″ or 5″
Date on line	14
Lines to inside address	5
Baronial	
Size	5½″ by 8½″
Line length	4″
Date on line	12
Lines to inside address	4

JOB 165 A. TWO-PAGE LETTER

Standard format (see review above). Workbook 295–296. Body 409 words.

[*Today's date*] / Station WXTC-TV / Skyline Drive / Nashville, TN 37215 / Attention: Mr. Ali Alrashead / Ladies and Gentlemen:

Are your personal computers really meeting your needs at Station WXTC-TV? As you know, personal computers have appeared on millions of desks and have taken a vital role in thousands of businesses. But now, as their businesses grow, some companies have stopped buying additional personal computers. Instead, they are buying what is known as a multiuser system.

A multiuser system consists of a powerful microcomputer connected to several terminals and a hard disk, which stores a company's data. This way, several workers can use the same computer, sharing information on the disks without having to copy it separately for each computer. Small businesses in particular are concluding that a multiuser system is more cost-effective than a mainframe computer and is cheaper and more useful than a whole lot of unconnected personal computers.

In an effort to serve this trend, UNITEX Corporation has developed a low-priced multiuser system that can cost you less than $10,000 and includes a microcomputer with a hard disk, two terminals, and a printer. Although buying one personal computer is far cheaper than buying a multiuser system, prices will look better when you consider that several users are involved. UNITEX lets several users share expensive peripherals such as printers and hard disks.

There is no doubt that for small businesses, the current stage of advancement of multiuser systems provides room for growth. In every application of the equipment, the size of the user group can grow. One of your neighboring stations, WDTN, bought a UNITEX system six months ago. It has been so useful that now they are planning to buy a second because they have found our system to be perfect for handling their business.

Our company also sells software that lets groups of users do word processing, data-base management, and spreadsheets—the kinds of tasks they have been doing on personal computers. Software for the UNITEX is in good supply. Increasing use of multiuser systems has brought about an increase in programming for multiuser systems. More software is coming on the market each day, and our unique control system makes it easier for software programmers to write programs.

Why not call and let a member of our sales staff visit your offices and demonstrate the advantages of

(Continued on next page)

RIGHT-HAND WORDS

1 mum pun lip yolk lion look loom lump oily holly jolly nippy
2 hip hop him join kink moll poll pink hook hilly lymph puppy
3 mom mop nip loll milk mill noon noun hull milky mummy poppy
4 kin joy oil honk holy hymn hook hunk loop lumpy union onion
5 pin you nun hoop link jump limp lily loin hooky nylon pupil
6 ink ill inn only pool pull pump upon pill knoll jumpy imply

LEFT-HAND WORDS

1 act bad car acre babe beat cage data ears gates safes taste
2 ads bag cat acts beet beds card date ease great seats taxed
3 are bar ear adds bags beef care draw east grade serve tests
4 ate bat eat ages bare bees cars dear edge grace staff texts
5 art bed far area bats best case debt eggs greet state tract
6 ade bet fed arts bear beer cast deed ever grate sweet trade

ALTERNATE-HAND SENTENCES

1 The lane to the lake may make the auto turn and go to town.
2 The man and the dog did go to the lake to dig for the dock.
3 The duck, the fox, and the fish make problems for the girl.
4 They may wish to blame me for the fight to end the problem.
5 She is busy with the work but is to go to town for the pen.
6 I am to go to work for the audit firm by the eighth of May.

DOUBLE-LETTER WORDS

1 burr ebbs eggs been less need fill look keep soon well tool
2 book will seem toss sees feel pool good pass mill miss ball
3 goods green skill added seeks proof small radii guess dizzy
4 fluff abbey sunny ditto apple gummy petty upper sleep shall
5 succeeds quitters withhold slowness grammar vacuums shopper
6 possible followed carriage occasion shipper accused cabbage

2-LETTER WORDS

1 ad am an as at ax be by do el go ha he hi ho id if in is it
2 la ma me my no of oh or ow ox oz pa re so to up us we ye yo

3-LETTER WORDS

1 aid air and ant apt bid big bit bow bud bus but cod cow cut
2 did die dig dog due dug dye end eye fir fit fix foe fur got
3 jam key lay man map may men oak own pay pep rid rob rod row
4 rub she sir sit six sod sue the tie tow via wit woe ago jet
5 bay can cad ink lab max van age boy fly had one par put sky
6 act add ads are art egg eve fee few sad sat saw see set sew

4-LETTER WORDS

1 able acid also bake bale band cake came chat days dial diet
2 else eyes fair fame felt firm game gift girl hair half halt
3 idle jury kept keys lake lame land mail make maps nail name
4 owns paid pair push rich ride rise self send sick tame than
5 vote wait want ants arms auto bird bite boat cite clay coal
6 does down dust fish flat fuel glad goal grow hand help horn

JOB 165 A. (CONTINUED)

the UNITEX multiuser system. We do not allow anyone to just buy a multiuser system. We insist on showing buyers what UNITEX can do for their businesses on their premises. Call today—555-5000. There is no obligation. / Cordially yours, / Felix Alapic / Sales Manager / [*Your initials*]

JOB 165 B. LETTER ON MONARCH STATIONERY

Standard format (see review on page 277). Workbook 297–298. Body 114 words.

Retype the first and last paragraphs of Job 165 A as a letter on monarch stationery.

FORMATTING REVIEW

Enclosure Notations

A single space below the reference initials, at the left margin.

JOB 165 C. LETTER ON BARONIAL STATIONERY

Standard format (see review on page 277). Workbook 299 top. Body 71 words.

(Today's date) / Mr. James Moreno / 186 West Girard Road / 16
Dunkirk, ny 14048 / Dear Mr. Moreno: / Thank you for your kidn 30
comments bout the BL Camptent. It is satisfying to ~~us~~ that an 44
experenced camper has found our product to be as good as we claim 57
it too be. 59

Enclosed is a copy of our ~~latest~~ catalog, which lists all the 73
products we made. The BL agent in your ~~town~~ is ~~that~~ Weekender 85
Sports Company, at 1125 Addison Avenue, they carry ~~the~~ full line 98
of ~~our~~ products. / Sincerely yours, / Patricia J. O'Keefe / 110
Customer Service Manager / (Your initials) / Enclosure 120

■ GOALS
To identify subject-verb agreement while typing sentences.
To review formatting memos on plain paper and printed forms.

■ FORMAT
Single spacing 60-space line

LAB 19

Subject-Verb Agreement

Type lines 1–4 once. Then repeat lines 1–4 or take a series of 1-minute timings. Note subject-verb agreement as you type each line (subjects and verbs are underscored).

1 The <u>books</u> on the shelf <u>have</u> a quick resale value next week. 12
2 <u>One</u> of us <u>has</u> to go to town to investigate the BART system. 12
3 The <u>students</u> at the school <u>are trying</u> to settle the matter. 12
4 <u>One</u> of the students <u>works</u> in the office of zoning problems. 12
| 1 | 2 | 3 | 4 | 5 | 6 | 7 | 8 | 9 | 10 | 11 | 12

ALPHABETIC WORDS (CONTINUED)

Q
33 quid quit quack quake queen quest quill quote quiet quavers
34 quip quiz quail quart quell quick quilt quirt quash quintet

R
35 rage raid read rest rink ripe roam roar rule rung rate ream
36 ranch raise reign reach rough round rainy recap rigid royal

S
37 sail said scar scan seal serf shin show skim soft span star
38 saint sauce scare scold serve share since slang smart solve

T
39 tale tart test teak them thus tilt time tone toil trap turn
40 taste taunt tempt tease there theme torch touch trade twist

U
41 urge used ugly undo uses unless unload unkind unfair unfold
42 undue upset union urban unite usher uncle until using under

V
43 vane vase veal veer vice view volt vote vast verb vine vise
44 vague verse value valve voice vault vocal verge vouch vowel

W
45 wade walk west were when whip word work wrap wise weld wing
46 waist waved weigh wedge wheat while worst would wreck wrist

X
47 flex hoax jinx apex text exam axle taxi axis exit waxy foxy
48 fixed mixed sixth exact extra relax sixty exile latex toxic

Y
49 yarn yawn yard year yell yelp yoke yolk your yule yowl yoga
50 yeast yield young yours yacht yearn youth yummy yucca yards

Z
51 zig zest zeal zinc zing zone zoom zero zany zips zoos zebra
52 zigzag zinnia zipper zodiac zircon zoology zealous zucchini

ALPHABETIC SENTENCES

1 Quietly, six zebras jumped back over the eight brown rafts.
2 Park my gray, bronze jet and quickly wax it for five hours.
3 Five more wax jugs have been glazed quickly for two people.
4 Jo quoted two dozen passages from Val's chemistry textbook.
5 The disc jockey won six bronze plaques for helping Mr. Van.
6 Ben auctioned off the pink gems and my quartz jewelry next.

SPEED SENTENCES

1 The book is new and will not be sold at the fair next year.
2 It is not the right time for us to talk about all the work.
3 The juice in that glass was cold, clear, and good to drink.
4 The light is dim, but it will give us all the light I need.
5 The bird flew way up in the sky to get away from the smoke.
6 We would like to know if you are going to the play at five.

12-SECOND TIMINGS

Type each line three times, or take three 12-second timings on each line. For each timing, type with no more than 1 error.

```
5  A red fox in the barnyard ran away and into the high grass.
6  We have a lot of work to do before we will be able to vote.
7  If it does not rain, I hope to go to his house to get them.
       5    10   15   20   25   30   35   40   45   50   55   60
```

30-SECOND SPEED TIMINGS

Take two 30-second speed timings on lines 8 and 9. Then take two 30-second speed timings on lines 10 and 11. Or type each sentence twice.

```
8  We will go to the fair in the city for the rest of the play   12
9  and stay to hear the band, view the parade, and have lunch.   24

10 The desk was moved over to the left and was not moved back,   12
11 but all of us who worked at the desk liked it on the right.   24
   | 1 | 2 | 3 | 4 | 5 | 6 | 7 | 8 | 9 | 10 | 11 | 12
```

FORMATTING REVIEW

You can create a form on a word processor or a computer. You can then enter data on the electronic form just as you would on a typewriter. When the copy prints out, it will print out the filled-in form.

Memos: Plain Paper

1. Use a 6-inch line, tab 10 spaces from left margin, center tab.
2. Type the title (MEMORANDUM) in all caps, centered, on line 7. Triple-space after the title.
3. Guide words: typed at left margin in all caps, double-spaced. Words that follow guides are typed at the 10-space tab.
4. Triple-space after the heading. Single-space the body; double-space between paragraphs.
5. Writer's initials typed in caps at the center, double space below the body.

Memos: Form

1. Set left margin 2 spaces after colon following longest guide word at the left side of the form.
2. Make right margin the same width as the left.
3. Set a tab 2 spaces after the colon following longest guide word at the right side of the form.
4. Writer's initials typed in caps at tab for guide words on the right side of the form.

JOB 166 A. MEMO

Standard format (see review above). Plain paper.

MEMORANDUM / DATE: [*Today's*] / TO: Camera Crew / FROM: Herbert Schelling, Producer / SUBJECT: Videotaping at South Park High School

Tomorrow we will videotape the students at South Park High School throughout the day in various classes, beginning at 8 a.m. We have volunteered to do this taping as part of our public service program, "Our Schools in Action."

Since many parents and community leaders will judge the school by what they see on television, I hope that you will be sure to involve as many teachers and students as possible in the planning of what will be taped in the classroom. We want to do an outstanding job so that the school will invite WXYR-TV again whenever they anticipate participating in a program of public interest.

The tape will be shown on Sunday, [*insert a Sunday date about two weeks from the date of the memo*], at 2 p.m. Students, teachers, and administrators will be invited to visit the studio at that time. / HS / [*Your initials*]

DRILLS

ALPHABETIC WORDS

A
1 ache aged aide arch aunt able acid acre afar ajar alas apex
2 aisle abide about above abuse acorn actor acute adapt agent

B
3 baby bias body busy bare bark bike bell belt bend beak brag
4 batch beach birch black board boast braid burst brave bride

C
5 calm cent chap clam coat crew curb czar cane cede cord cuff
6 caulk cease chant clang coast crane curve catch chief cling

D
7 damp deal dine done drag dust deck dent disk down drip dime
8 dance depth ditch dodge draft drove doubt dread drawl drone

E
9 each earn ease east edge else etch easy echo ever evil emit
10 earth eaves eight elect erase evoke event excel every entry

F
11 fact feat file flaw folk from fuse fang fend film flip form
12 false fence first flare force frame frost fault field flour

G
13 gain germ gift glib goat grim gulf gait gear girl glad gown
14 gauge ghost gland glare gouge grand grind guest grain grape

H
15 hail hear hike hold hulk hark helm hide honk huge hire howl
16 harsh heist hoist hutch haste hence horse hunch hotel husky

I
17 inch itch idle into iron item idea imps ills irks ibex iris
18 icing ideal igloo image imply index inept inert infer inlet

J
19 jest jilt jinx join joke jump jugs just jury jade jail jabs
20 jaunt jeans joist judge juice jelly jewel joker jolly juror

K
21 keel knot keep kelp kemp kick kiss kite knew knee knit knob
22 knack knead knife knock kayak kitty knows kinks khaki karat

L
23 lace left lick loft lump lynx lack lash lend lens life loud
24 lapse large ledge leave lodge lymph lapel legal logic lower

M
25 made mast mesh melt mild mint mole mold mule must mask mere
26 month midst march match merge mound mouth movie music motor

N
27 name nail near news none nose numb next nice noun note neck
28 nerve niece night ninth noise north notch nurse nudge noble

O
29 once oath ouch oboe odor oily obey open only omit oval odds
30 ought ounce ocean offer often orbit olive order onion other

P
31 page pale pail perk peat pert pile pike pine plea plop plot
32 paint pants paste pearl peach peace place plate pound pride

JOB 166 B. MEMO

Standard format. Workbook 299 bottom.

[Date:] (Today's date) / [To:] JoAnne Jones, Group
Leader / [From:] Ruth Lee, Chairperson / [Subject:] Fund
Drive for Handicapped Children / Thank you for your
excellent report, JoAnne. You, Sybil, and Dick
did a marvelous job! It is gratifying to know
that all employees supported the drive and that
we exceeded our goal of $800. ¶ Don't forget
to take the money to the computer center
before Friday. Last year we missed the
deadline, and so our group did not receive any
recognition for their hard work. ¶ If I can be of
assistance to you in any way, please let
me know. Remember to request a receipt
when you release our contributions. / R.L.

JOB 166 C. MEMO ON PRINTED FORM

Standard format. Retype Job 166 A, page 279, on a printed form. Workbook 301.

■ GOALS
To correct errors in subject-verb agreement while typing sentences.
To type 41/5′/4e.
To compose and type memos.

■ FORMAT
Drills: Single spacing 60-space line
5-Minute Timings: Double spacing 5-space tab

LAB 19

Subject-Verb Agreement

Type lines 1–4 once, correcting verbs to ensure subject-verb agreement. Edit your copy as your teacher reads the answers. Then retype lines 1–4 from your edited copy.

```
1 The managers in this factory has high expectations for me.
2 One of the programmers have created software to do this job.
3 Swimmers in the race was quick to zip off the pool's edge.
4 One of the items ordered have been delivered to you on time.
```

TIMING 11

Productivity measurement techniques are frequently employed in today's word processing installations to evaluate the amount of output that is produced. This technique will allow management to compare active work loads with inactive work loads that will improve scheduling and work dispersal.

Productivity measurement can also aid a company by recording, calculating, and tracking employee production over a period of time. Supervisors are then able to set performance standards made just for their own particular company. This method of measurement can then be used to help management in making decisions pertaining to salary increases and promotion of word processing personnel.

A measure of production might also help more able people in a great number of ways. For instance, when they are compared to their peers, their true abilities and successes will be accented. Using this particular technique, all employees are evaluated on a parallel basis. Therefore, just the very talented workers are rewarded. Finally, this measurement technique can assist in removing subjectivity that is often predominant in company measurement systems used in evaluating employees.

SI 1.85

TIMING 12

Electronic communications is a recent development that allows individuals to transmit messages electronically from one location to another. This method of communications can sometimes be referred to as electronic mail. Messages that are sent by electronic mail are transmitted from station to station via electronic signals.

Other distribution systems that are very popular today are the telex system in which information is transmitted by teletypewriter from terminal to terminal, and the Teletypewriter Exchange Service, commonly referred to as TWX. Both of these information systems communicate with one another.

Another popular method of electronic communications is Mailgram. To utilize the service, just telephone the Western Union office and dictate your complete message over the telephone. Your message is then transmitted electronically to a post office near the address on the message.

A final communications technology is the communicating word processor. If two word processors are linked together electronically, you can transmit your message between these two terminals. The unique advantage of using the word processor as a communication tool is that you can rapidly send large amounts of information.

SI 1.94

PREVIEW PRACTICE

Type each line twice as a preview to the 5-minute timings below.

Accuracy 5 exact magazine techniques alphabetic assignment distributed
Speed 6 signature format maybe with what make memo down name and to

5-MINUTE TIMINGS

Take two 5-minute timings on lines 7–24.

7 Editors of newspapers and magazines must read all copy 12
8 for publication to be sure of the content; they select what 24
9 will be final copy. The typist is the person who must make 36
10 sure that the final copy is completely free of errors. 47
11 The proofreading techniques you use will be determined 59
12 by the kind of typing assignment you have completed. Is it 71
13 a legal description of an estate or a brief memo to someone 83
14 down the hall? Have you just typed a copy of a letter that 95
15 will be distributed at a conference to hundreds of persons? 107
16 Maybe you have just typed the corporate budget with columns 119
17 of million-dollar figures. You must proofread the numbers, 131
18 as well as the alphabetic copy, for accuracy. 140
19 Another concern of the typist must be how to make time 152
20 available for proofreading. If your typing jobs are mostly 164
21 letters, pay attention to dates. Check that the months are 176
22 spelled correctly and the years are exact. Be sure to read 188
23 the name, address, subject, and signature lines. Check the 200
24 format of the letter too. 205

| 1 | 2 | 3 | 4 | 5 | 6 | 7 | 8 | 9 | 10 | 11 | 12 SI 1.48

JOB 167 A. MEMO

Standard format. Workbook 303 top.

[*To:*] Phillip Hamilton, General Manager / 7
[*Date:*] July 12, 19— / [*From:*] Kelly McGuire, 15
Maintenance / [*Subject:*] No. 2 Ski Lift / We 24
have finished regular inspection of our No. 2 33
lift, and it appears to be in good working order. 43
However, one of the cables is beginning to show 53
signs of wear and should be replaced. Although 62
it would pass inspection by the state safety engi- 72
neers, it could cause a problem when it is sub- 81
jected to heavier use in the next few months. 91
I recommend that we order a new cable from 100
StaCo Products Company, Denver. Delivery 109
takes six to eight weeks, and repairs to the lift 119
can be completed in one day. / KM / [*Your ini-* 127
tials] 129

JOB 167 B. MEMO

Standard format. Workbook 303 bottom.

[*To:*] Kelly McGuire, Maintenance / [*Date:*] 5
July 13, 19— / [*From:*] Phillip Hamilton / [*Sub-* 14
ject:] Replacement Cable for No. 2 Ski Lift / As 25
you recommended, we will replace the cable on 34

(Continued on next page)

TIMING 9

	1'	3'
Dinosaurs were giant reptiles that roamed the earth at	12	4
least 65 million years ago. Actually, they literally domi-	24	8
nated every other creature for over 160 million years. The	36	12
dinosaurs were so very powerful that they terrified most of	48	16
the other animals. Scientists have learned about dinosaurs	60	20
from all the fossils discovered in the earth.	69	23
The most ferocious meat-eating dinosaur was the Tyran-	81	27
nosaurus. This particular giant dinosaur was classified as	93	31
a meat eater because of its predatory habits.	102	34
Dinosaurs lived quite often on land that was mostly of	114	38
a subtropical nature. Most of the land mass was covered by	126	42
swamps which provided all kinds of vegetation for the great	138	46
appetites of these creatures. The swamps were also used by	150	50
numerous plant-eating dinosaurs as a refuge from all of the	162	54
meat-eating dinosaurs. Some dinosaurs were very small, not	174	58
much bigger than small reptiles. Others, however, were gi-	186	62
gantic creatures that grew much larger than an elephant. A	198	66
few dinosaurs grew enormous horns like a rhinoceros, others	210	70
carried bodies of armor, and others had large clubbed tails	222	74
for protection.	225	75

1' | 1 | 2 | 3 | 4 | 5 | 6 | 7 | 8 | 9 | 10 | 11 | 12 SI 1.70
3' | 1 | 2 | 3 | 4

TIMING 10

	1'	3'
Whenever you have an opportunity to look for your very	12	4
first job, you would undoubtedly have to complete an inter-	24	8
view before securing the position. Although all interviews	36	12
may vary significantly, most employers try to identify cer-	48	16
tain aspects of your background and personality.	58	19
Communications skills are considered to be critical in	70	23
most interviews. Many job applicants will not perform well	82	27
while communicating because they do not know how to express	94	31
themselves when asking and answering questions, because the	106	35
vocabulary they use during the interviewing session doesn't	118	39
reveal a command of the English language, and because their	130	43
listening skills are not developed well enough.	139	46
Employers also express quite an interest in an employ-	151	50
ee's maturity level. This is especially critical if you're	163	54
applying for a position in which you will work closely with	175	58
other people. It is also important if you are applying for	187	62
a position in which you will be involved in making critical	199	66
decisions that require good judgment. Employers will often	211	70
devote considerable time and effort to find this particular	223	74
person to work for their company.	230	77

1' | 1 | 2 | 3 | 4 | 5 | 6 | 7 | 8 | 9 | 10 | 11 | 12 SI 1.80
3' | 1 | 2 | 3 | 4

JOB 167 B (CONTINUED)

our No. 2 ski lift. Please prepare a purchase req- 44
uisition for the cable and any other parts you 53
think you will need. 58

You suggested that we order the cable from 67
StaCo Products, Denver. The last time we tried 77
to order parts for our Skyway equipment, they 86
wrote us that they no longer had the Skyway 95
dealership. Will you please check into this mat- 104
ter and locate a suitable supplier of the cable. / 114
PH / [*Your initials*] 119

JOB 167 C. MEMO

Compose a response to the electronic message shown below. Standard format. Plain paper.

```
DATE:  [TODAY'S DATE]
TO:    ALL STUDENTS
FROM:  SCHOOL DIETITIAN
SUBJ:  LUNCHEON MENUS

THIS YEAR THE WEDNESDAY MENU WILL BE
KNOWN AS "STUDENTS' CHOICE."  PLEASE
SEND ME YOUR SUGGESTIONS FOR THE STU-
DENTS' CHOICE MENU AS WELL AS FOR OUR
REGULAR MENUS.
```

CLINIC

GOALS
To build competency on selected keyboard reaches.
To type 41/5′/4e.

FORMAT
Drills: Single spacing 60-space line
Timings: Double spacing 5-space tab

KEYBOARDING SKILLS

Type lines 1–4 once. Then use the shift lock to capitalize the words in line 5. Repeat lines 1–4, or take a series of 1-minute timings.

Speed	1	I came to work for that firm and have been here since then.	12
Accuracy	2	When Zeth requested a bill, did Jack pay for fixing my van?	12
Numbers	3	Please clean Rooms 10, 29, and 38, but not Rooms 47 and 56.	12
Symbols	4	We will paint Rooms #10 and #29 (but not Rooms #38 or #56).	12
Technique	5	Do NOT type any CAPITAL in lowercase; always use UPPERCASE.	

| 1 | 2 | 3 | 4 | 5 | 6 | 7 | 8 | 9 | 10 | 11 | 12

PRETEST

Take two 2-minute timings on lines 6–15. Circle and count your errors on each.

6 You could spot certain kinds of treasure hunters among 12
7 any group of people. One unique kind of treasure hunter is 24
8 found among people liking the open spaces. Such people use 36
9 unique tools to come upon metal treasures which are covered 48
10 with soil. Schoolgrounds, public parks, even barren fields 60
11 are common areas surveyed by these fervid treasure hunters. 72
12 There are certain kinds of old mine detectors for sale 84
13 which permit the use of loop coils built to detect objects. 96
14 Jewels and old coins are common finds, but metal things and 108
15 all kinds of mineral products are welcomed by most hunters. 120

| 1 | 2 | 3 | 4 | 5 | 6 | 7 | 8 | 9 | 10 | 11 | 12 SI 1.44

TIMING 7

	1′	3′
There are specific language arts skills which everyone	12	4
must know. Such skills assist us in improving our speaking	24	8
and writing skills and will ultimately permit us to express	36	12
ourselves much better. The language arts skills emphasized	48	16
throughout this course have made us cognizant of the unique	60	20
role grammar plays in improving our methods of expression.	72	24
In previous lessons you learned when to capitalize and	84	28
when not to capitalize. You learned, for example, that all	96	32
proper nouns are capitalized and that a specific place such	108	36
as a city, town, county, or state is also capitalized. You	120	40
learned that numbers from 1 through 10 are spelled out, but	132	44
figures are used for numbers above 10. Several rules exist	144	48
on how and when to use the comma. For instance, commas are	156	52
used when three or more items appear in succession. Commas	168	56
are also used at the end of an introductory clause which is	180	60
followed by a main clause. Words such as if, as, when, and	192	64
although frequently introduce these particular clauses, and	204	68
therefore, commas are added.	210	70

1′ | 1 | 2 | 3 | 4 | 5 | 6 | 7 | 8 | 9 | 10 | 11 | 12 SI 1.49

3′ | 1 | 2 | 3 | 4

TIMING 8

	1′	3′
Proofreading skills are certainly the most critical as	12	4
well as the most ignored skills a person can possess. Many	24	8
of us have opportunities to write letters. In addition, we	36	12
sometimes must prepare term papers and do projects for some	48	16
classes. If our assignment is to prepare a report or write	60	20
a memo, we must identify and correct every error if we want	72	24
the product to create the necessary impact.	81	27
Everyone should try quite hard to improve proofreading	93	31
skill. Before removing a page from the typewriter, we must	105	35
proofread it. We should read every word, every phrase, and	117	39
every line. After completing this activity, we should look	129	43
closely for any spelling, capitalization, and typographical	141	47
errors. Next, the page has to be read sentence by sentence	153	51
in order to find punctuation and grammar mistakes. Lastly,	165	55
a page is read paragraph by paragraph to be sure all errors	177	59
have been erased completely and retyped.	185	62
By employing these methods of proofreading, we will be	197	66
certain to produce copy that is free of any errors. Error-	209	70
less copy or copy with corrected errors is your goal.	220	74

1′ | 1 | 2 | 3 | 4 | 5 | 6 | 7 | 8 | 9 | 10 | 11 | 12 SI 1.59

3′ | 1 | 2 | 3 | 4

PRACTICE

If you made three or fewer errors on the Pretest on page 282, type each line four times. If you made more than three errors on the Pretest, type lines 16–20 four times as a group; then type lines 21–25 four times as a group.

Right-hand sequences

```
16 oil coils boiler boiling doilies toiletry oilcloth oilskins
17 min mines naming eminent reminds claiming criminal mingling
18 oin coins doings joining appoint pointing pointers ointment
19 ion onion vision auction billion millions national opinions
20 ill still chilly skilled stilled thrilled fulfills instills
```

Adjacent-key sequences

```
21 po ports report airport spotted portrays powerful reporting
22 re where figure foreign prepaid reporter required therefore
23 sa sands usable sandals salable passable messages satisfied
24 we newer jewels jewelry viewers weighing weighted welcoming
25 lk yolks folksy milking walkers stalkers caulking milkshake
```

POSTTEST

Take another 2-minute timing on lines 6–15 on page 282 to see how much your skill has improved.

5-MINUTE TIMINGS

Take two 5-minute timings on lines 6–20 on page 285.

UNIT 28 Formatting Review of Tables and Forms

UNIT GOAL 41/5'/4e

■ **GOALS**
To correct errors in subject-verb agreement while typing sentences.
To review formatting invoices, purchase requisitions, and purchase orders.

■ **FORMAT**
Single spacing 60-space line

LAB 19

Subject-Verb Agreement

Type lines 1–4 once, correcting verbs if necessary to ensure subject-verb agreement. Edit your copy as your teacher reads the answers. Then retype lines 1–4 from your edited copy.

```
1 One of the computers are programmed to zero in on any error.
2 Jack's figures on this diagram is extra and quite useless.
3 One of them has a copy of the reforms that I would promote.
4 Advertisers who are listed in the yearbook is our friends.
```

FORMATTING REVIEW

Business Forms

A. Purchase Requisitions
B. Purchase Orders
C. Invoices

1. Align fill-ins in headings 2 spaces after guide words.
2. Visually center information in number columns.
3. Begin information in description (or word) columns 2 spaces after the vertical rule.
4. Set a tab stop for the most frequently used digit in the Unit Price and Amount columns.
5. Single-space entries; double-space between entries.
6. Align the word *Total* with *D* in *Description*, a double space below the last entry.

	1′	3′

TIMING 5

It's considered true for many that a troublesome punc- 12 4
tuation placement rule is where we should put the quotation 24 8
marks when they're used with periods or commas. If we just 36 12
follow some very basic rules, we'll soon recognize that the 48 16
exact placement of quotation marks is quite easy to do. 59 20
The first general rule we should recall is that commas 71 24
and periods always go inside the closing quotation mark. A 83 28
good example would be to place in quotation marks the final 95 32
word in this sentence, such as "this." Notice that even if 107 36
the last word in the sentence is placed in quotation marks, 119 40
the period is typed before that final quotation mark. When 131 44
quotation marks appear in the middle of the typed line, the 143 48
comma at the end of that quotation would appear as follows: 155 52
The package was labeled "Pizza," so the delivery person was 167 56
very careful not to jar the package when it was moved. Our 179 60
job of using quotation marks should become quite easy. 190 64

1′ | 1 | 2 | 3 | 4 | 5 | 6 | 7 | 8 | 9 | 10 | 11 | 12 SI 1.47
3′ | 1 | 2 | 3 | 4

	1′	3′

TIMING 6

Many people have often wondered what might possibly be 12 4
the greatest structure on earth. The tallest buildings and 24 8
the longest bridges and the mightiest dams might be closely 36 12
examined in an attempt to identify an answer to this diffi- 48 16
cult question. In the minds of many people, though, one of 60 20
the greatest structures ever built may be the Great Wall of 72 24
China. It's well established that its features are so very 84 28
overwhelming that astronauts could view the Wall from their 96 32
spaceship portholes. 100 33
The structure was built primarily by mixing just earth 112 37
and bricks. It is wide enough at the top to permit several 124 41
people to walk abreast on it. It winds for miles through a 136 45
large section of the country, over mountains and across the 148 49
valleys. It was constructed to keep out unwelcomed tribes. 160 53
It is believed that building the Wall required the labor of 172 57
many, many thousands of persons for many dozens of decades. 184 61
Actually, the Wall was built during the reign of many vari- 196 65
ous tribal dynasties. 200 67

1′ | 1 | 2 | 3 | 4 | 5 | 6 | 7 | 8 | 9 | 10 | 11 | 12 SI 1.50
3′ | 1 | 2 | 3 | 4

JOB 169 A. BUSINESS INVOICE

Standard format (see review on page 283). Workbook 305 top.

[*Date: Today's*] / [*To*] Station WXYR-TV / 3800 West Carmen Avenue / Milwaukee, WI 53209

Quantity	Description	Unit Price	Amount
4	Plastic stackable file-cabinet boxes #1975—beige	24.95	99.80
3 boxes	File folders #6176, 50 count	16.24	48.72
	Total		148.52
	Delivery		11.10
	Total amount due		159.62

JOB 169 B. PURCHASE REQUISITION

Standard format (see review on page 283). Workbook 305 bottom.

Purchase Requisition 4862. [*Date:*] July 15, 19—. To repair Skyway Ski Lift No. 2, Kelly McGuire, maintenance superintendent, needs the following items by September 15:

1 Transfer case gear, S&B #809297
3 Flexible tubing, 25-ft rolls
1 Overhaul gasket set, S&B #37-4037W

Recommended supplier: Thor Manufacturing Co., 2041 Hawthorne Boulevard, Torrance, CA 90503.

JOB 169 C. PURCHASE ORDER

Standard format (see review on page 283). Compute the total. Workbook 307 top.

Purchase Order 3576. [*Date:*] July 16, 19—. Thor Manufacturing Co. [*Ship via:*] United Parcel Service

1 Transfer case gear, S&B #809297, for Model 776W, @ $295.00 = $295.00
3 Plastic flexible tubing, 25-ft rolls, #33-674-11, @ $79.95 = $239.85
1 Overhaul gasket set, S&B #37-4037W, for Model 776W, @ $22.50 = $22.50
Total

JOB 169 D. INVOICE

Standard format (see review on page 283). Compute the total amount due. Workbook 307 bottom.

[*Date:*] September 24, 19— / [*To:*] Skyway Ski Resort / P.O. Box 7 / Vail, CO 81657

1 Transfer case gear, S&B #809297, for Model 776W
[*Unit price*] $295.00 [*Amount*] $295.00
3 Plastic flexible tubing, 25-ft rolls, #33-674-11
[*Unit price*] $79.95 [*Amount*] $239.85
1 Overhaul gasket set, S&B #37-4037W, for Model 776W
[*Unit price*] $22.50 [*Amount*] $22.50
Total amount due

JOB 169 E. INVOICE

Standard format (see review on page 283). Workbook 309 top.

[*Date: Today's*] / [*To:*] South Park High School / Pleasant Street / Milwaukee, WI 53213

The school has purchased 4 student terminals for a Mitronics Computer, LCS-90, Model II, @ $3967.50 each. There is no tax or delivery charge. Complete the Amount column by calculating the cost of the 4 terminals.

	1′	3′

TIMING 3

Autumn in the "northlands"[1] is very exciting.[2] You jump 12 4
up in the early[3] morning; walk out under[4] a clear, azure blue 24 8
sky;[5] and feel the strong chill[6] in the air. The leaves[7] have 36 12
lost their brilliant[8] green. It appears that[9] they have been 48 16
tinted by[10] someone passing by. The[11] truth is that during the[12] 60 20
night hours a frost has[13] painted the green to hues[14] of brown, 72 24
yellow, red,[15] and orange. It is really[16] a breathtaking pano- 84 28
rama[17] in technicolor. The[18] leaves barely move in the[19] quietly 96 32
persistent breeze.[20] Then, suddenly, a brisk[21] puff lifts them 108 36
from the[22] limbs and carries them[23] gently like feathers to the[24] 120 40
ground below. You watch[25] as legions of leaves jump[26] free and 132 44
float to the[27] earth, covering it like a[28] quilted blanket that 144 48
looks[29] much like moss. When[30] you walk on top of the[31] blanket, 156 52
it cushions each[32] step you take as though you[33] are walking on 168 56
top of[34] air. 170 57

1′ | 1 | 2 | 3 | 4 | 5 | 6 | 7 | 8 | 9 | 10 | 11 | 12 SI 1.30
3′ | 1 | 2 | 3 | 4

	1′	3′

TIMING 4

Every so often you[1] may inadvertently find a[2] typewriter 12 4
with something[3] very unique about it; the[4] thing might simply 24 8
be[5] some trays for a pencil or[6] eraser, or just an extra[7] key. 36 12
Or perhaps you[8] might find a machine with[9] small numbers 48 16
in the[10] place of the symbols on the[11] upper row; these are for[12] 60 20
things like footnote[13] annotations and citations in[14] the text. 72 24
You might[15] even find a machine that[16] has a light instead 84 28
of a[17] bell to signal the approach[18] to the margin; the[19] machine 96 32
is intended for[20] someone who's deaf or very[21] hard of hearing. 108 36
In a[22] hospital you might find[23] a typewriter mounted on a[24] 120 40
special contraption that[25] holds the keyboard where[26] a patient 132 44
flat on his or[27] her back is able to[28] manipulate all the keys. 144 48
But[29] the most dazzling and[30] unique of the surprise[31] items 156 52
is the discovery[32] that you have keys with[33] accent marks--just 168 56
what's[34] needed for typing the project[35] in a foreign language.[36] 180 60

1′ | 1 | 2 | 3 | 4 | 5 | 6 | 7 | 8 | 9 | 10 | 11 | 12 SI 1.42
3′ | 1 | 2 | 3 | 4

LESSON 170

■ **GOALS**
To type 41/5′/4e.
To type purchase requisitions, purchase orders, and invoices.

■ **FORMAT**
Drills: Single spacing 60-space line
5-Minute Timings: Double spacing 5-space tab

KEYBOARDING SKILLS

Type lines 1–4 once. Then concentrate on your space bar technique in line 5. Repeat lines 1–4, or take a series of 1-minute timings.

Speed 1 Show her what a nice day it is so that she may take a walk. 12
Accuracy 2 The many jovial men expressed a quick welcome to big Fritz. 12
Numbers 3 Those five passengers are 10, 29, 38, 47, and 56 years old. 12
Symbols 4 Write to A/B/C Ltd., Rube & Dodd, and Hill's Inc. for bids. 12
Technique 5 q z p / w x o . e c i , r v u m t b y n a ; s l d k f j g h

| 1 | 2 | 3 | 4 | 5 | 6 | 7 | 8 | 9 | 10 | 11 | 12

PRETEST

Take a 5-minute timing on lines 6–20. Circle and count your errors.

6 Would you like to write for a magazine? The first and most important 15
7 requirement for staff writers is knowing how to type; most successful jour- 30
8 nalists and other writers compose right at the machine. 41
9 Composing on the typewriter saves time. When a writer types his or her 15
10 first draft of an article, the writing can be corrected easier than copy in 31
11 script. Final copies of a manuscript must be typed. 41
12 Learning to use the typewriter as a tool requires some practice and real 16
13 desire. Begin first by expressing simply an idea or thought you have about 31
14 some topic. Try to write a short paragraph or two. 41
15 Once you have mastered typing your thoughts, you might decide that 14
16 you ought to pursue a career in writing. Today writers with talent can be 29
17 utilized and appreciated in many kinds of business offices. 41
18 If you want magazine editors to read your writings, be sure to format 15
19 your copy in manuscript form. Also, send an introductory letter. Naturally, 31
20 you will edit your work so that there are no errors. 41

| 1 | 2 | 3 | 4 | 5 | 6 | 7 | 8 | 9 | 10 | 11 | 12 | 13 | 14 | 15 SI 1.49

PRACTICE

Take a 1-minute timing on each paragraph of the Pretest.

POSTTEST

Take another 5-minute timing on lines 6–20 to see how much your skill has improved.

SUPPLEMENTARY MATERIAL

TIMINGS

TIMING 1

	1′	3′
Raising dogs can be a combination of both fun and hard	12	4
work. Before you even start, you have to decide just which	24	8
breed can best adapt to your life-style. If you need a dog	36	12
to protect your house, a dachshund will not give you enough	48	16
protection. If you are in your own apartment, a collie may	60	20
be too large. When you have chosen the dog for you, expect	72	24
to have to train it. This can be done quickly with a zesty	84	28
puppy that is willing to learn.	90	30
	SI 1.25	

TIMING 2

	1′	3′
When the snow begins to fall and the temperatures drop	12	4
far below freezing, avid sports fans in the cold country of	24	8
the far north alter what they do for sport. Gone are golf,	36	12
tennis, and hiking. In place of these sports are those for	48	16
which that cold weather is just right. The best suited for	60	20
this weather is ice fishing. It is a sport in which almost	72	24
all people can take part. A fact known to very few is that	84	28
the sport is not very expensive, not even for the beginner.	96	32
	SI 1.25	

JOB 170 A. PURCHASE REQUISITION

Standard format. Workbook 309 bottom.

Purchase Requisition 4869. [*Date:*] November 7, 19—. To expand the Gift Shop at Skyway Ski Resort, Madeline Strom, manager, needs the following by December 15:

1 Showcase, 8′ × 2′ × 3′—all glass
3 Glass shelves, 8′ × 2′
2 Round display tables, 22″ diameter
4 Revolving display racks, 5′ tall

Recommended supplier: Alpine Products, 4720 South Tacoma Way, Tacoma, WA 98409.

JOB 170 B. PURCHASE ORDER

Standard format. Compute the Amount column and total. Workbook 311 top.

Purchase Order 3577. [*Date:*] November 8, 19—. Alpine Products. [*Ship via:*] Greyhound Express

1 Decorative showcase, Style #6784, 8′ × 2′ × 3′, all glass with metal trim, @ $867.50
3 Glass shelves with beveled edges, 8′ × 2′, @ $88.00
2 Round tables, Style #8407, 22″ diameter, plastic top with metal base, @ $72.60
4 Revolving display racks, aluminum, brown, Style #441R, @ $102.50

JOB 170 C. INVOICE

Standard format. Compute the Amount column and total amount due. Workbook 311 bottom.

[*Date:*] December 8, 19— / [*To:*] Skyway Ski Resort / P.O. Box 7 / Vail, CO 81657

400 T-shirts, assorted colors and sizes, with Vail logo [*Unit price*] $8.95
250 Ski caps, assorted colors, with Vail logo [*Unit price*] $10.75
50 Pairs ski goggles, assorted colors and sizes [*Unit price*] $12.60
Total amount due

LESSON 171

■ GOALS
To recognize subject-verb agreement while typing sentences.
To review formatting tables.

■ FORMAT
Single spacing   60-space line

LAB 20

Subject-Verb Agreement—Compound Subjects

Type lines 1–4 once. Then repeat lines 1–4 or take a series of 1-minute timings. (Subjects and verbs are underscored.)

```
1  Sally and Joe are expected to become accountants this year.   12
2  Both Jean and Katherine have a reputation for quick typing.   12
3  Every man and woman in Zambrian County has a right to vote.   12
4  Apple pie and ice cream is an American dessert that I like.   12
   | 1 | 2 | 3 | 4 | 5 | 6 | 7 | 8 | 9 | 10 | 11 | 12
```

If the subject consists of two singular words connected by *and* or by *both . . . and*, the subject is plural and requires a plural verb.

Mr. Johnson and Mr. Bruce have received promotions.
Both the collection and the delivery of mail *are* to be curtailed.

If a subject consisting of two singular nouns connected by *and* refers to the same person or thing or is preceded by *each, every, many a,* or *many an,* a singular verb is used.

Corned beef and cabbage is our Monday special.
Each boy and girl has a ticket to the game.

JOB 299/300 B. FORM LETTER

Standard format. Needs editing.

we hope that you are enjoying the new automobile that you purchased from us this year it is always our intention to give our customers the best possible service *paragraph* with this in mind we would like to respectfully remind you that it is time for your 12,000-mile or your annual checkup on the items listed below *paragraph arrange in two columns without headings Column 1* transmission check *Column 2* brake check *Column 1* cooling system check *Column 2* general tuneup *Column 1* oil/lubrication *Column 2* wheel balancing and alignment *Column 1* emission control test *Column 2* catalytic converter test *new paragraph* please give us a call in the next two weeks so that we may help you keep your automobile running in top shape

JOB 299/300 C. COMPOSED LETTER

Select appropriate format. Workbook 717–718.

You have just received a new shipment of the newest compact economy cars—all American-made. You want to promote them to past customers. Compose a form letter promoting the car. Use your own creativity to describe the car, and give reasons why past customers might want to purchase another car at this time. Use the following subject/salutation instead of an inside address: Notice to our special customers.

JOB 299/300 D. OUTPATIENT RECORD

An employee of Monarch Motors slipped at work, fell, and broke his ankle. Prepare an outpatient form, using the information below. Workbook 719–720 top.

Jim Schwartz; Phone 555-9317; Age 27; Birthdate 3/27/69. Lives at 155 North Avenue, Chicago 60637, and is an automobile mechanic. Personal History: Patient is a healthy male, no serious illnesses. Present Illness: fracture of the left tarsus on May 15, 19—, while at work. Physical Examination: Patient's left ankle was badly swollen and bruised; patient was unable to put any weight on the left foot; mobility was severely restricted. X rays showed a simple fracture of the left tarsus. Bone was set and a cast applied. Physician: Dr. Ciano.

JOB 299/300 E. INVOICE

Standard format. Compute the unit prices. Workbook 719–720 bottom.

[To:] Mr. Jeffrey Snyder
485 Walnut Avenue
Cincinnati, OH 45218

For replacing thermostat, $9.00; replacing 2 gal. coolant, $12.00; replacing two hoses, $27.50; and labor, $25.00. (Add 5% sales tax on parts only, and total the invoice.)

JOB 299/300 F. TABLE

Select appropriate format.

This is the work schedule of the service department for the week of May 18, 19—. There are two shifts: 6 a.m. to 2 p.m. and 12 noon to 8 p.m. There are four work stations, which can be labeled "Station 1," "Station 2," and so forth. The schedule begins with Monday and runs through Saturday. The first shift will be Michael Bippus, Wan Chong, Bridget Vagades, and Leslie Trezise assisted by Eric Thomson, Julie Toma, Anthony Viola, and James Tomallo. The second shift will be Jeffrey Myers, Joseph Lavigne, Cynthia Detter, and Jessanne Attalla assisted by Michael Dean, Alison Akers, Cynthia Spoor, and Stacey Vreeland. *Assign stations and assistants alphabetically.*

30-SECOND SPEED TIMINGS

Take two 30-second speed timings on lines 5 and 6. Then take two 30-second speed timings on lines 7 and 8. Or type each sentence twice.

5 Kaye and Max have reviewed the subject and will give Paul a 12
6 quiz; and if the test is easy, Paul will not fail it today. 24

7 Ken promptly requested five dozen jugs of wax for the group 12
8 and found that it was not enough for all the artists there. 24

| 1 | 2 | 3 | 4 | 5 | 6 | 7 | 8 | 9 | 10 | 11 | 12

FORMATTING REVIEW

Workbook 313–314.

Open Tables

1. Center vertically and horizontally.
2. Double spacing.
3. Title: Centered, all caps. Subtitle(s): Centered; double-space before, triple-space after the entire subtitle.
4. Identify the key line—longest entry in each column, plus the spaces between the columns (usually 6).
5. Backspace to center the key line; set the left margin.
6. Space across to the start of the next column; set a tab stop. Continue for as many columns as needed.
7. Column heads are typed in initial caps, underscored, centered over their column; double-space after.

Reminder

Paper turned lengthwise has the following dimensions:
Width—110 pica spaces, 132 elite spaces
Depth—51 lines

JOB 171 A. TWO-COLUMN TABLE

Standard format (see review in margin). Half sheet of paper.

RADIO WXZR-FM

Your Fine Music Station

Schedule for Saturday, January 14, 19--

Time	Program
7-9 a.m.	A Morning of Music
9-Noon	Around the Town
Noon-4 p.m.	Absolutely Jazz
4-6 p.m.	For the Love of Music
6-9 p.m.	Symphony Hall
9-Midnight	Piano Personalities

JOB 171 B. FOUR-COLUMN TABLE

Standard format. (Notice that time is given on a 24-hour basis, including seconds.) Half sheet of paper.

TELEVISION SPORTS THIS WEEK

September 9-15, 19--

Sport	Day	Time	Channel(s)
Baseball	Monday	20:00:00	2, 6
Boxing	Friday	21:00:00	4
Football	Saturday	13:00:00	11
Tennis	Saturday	14:30:00	7
Golf	Saturday	16:00:00	6

JOB 171 C. FIVE-COLUMN TABLE

Retype Job 171 B, adding the information below as the third column (between *Day* and *Time*). Standard format. Full sheet of paper turned lengthwise.

Event, Detroit at New York, Davis vs. Watts, Ohio State vs. Purdue, French Open, Kemper Open

JOB 299/300 A. LEASE AGREEMENT

Standard legal format. Workbook 713–716.

NONMAINTENANCE LEASE AGREEMENT

Monarch Motors, Lessor, who*se* address is *419 Southdale Drive, Chicago, IL 60637*, agrees to lease to *Shihir Tadros*, Lessee, whose address is *1549 Calhoun St., Gary, IN 46401*, and Lessee agrees to lease from lessor, subject to the terms set ~~from~~ *forth* below, the following described motor vehicle, attachments, and accessories, delivery and acceptance of which is hereby acknowledged in good order by Lessee, for a term of *12* months, commencing on the date of ~~executive~~ *execution* of this lease as shown below.

19— Pontiac red Sunbird with automatic transmission, tinted glass, and luxury interior package.

The Lessee represents that this lease is entered into primarily for business or commercial use.

The Lessee agrees to pay *$160* per month for lease of the above-mentioned vehicle. Total monthly payment will be due on the *15th* of each month beginning with *June 15, 19—*.

The lease grants the Lessee the right to drive this vehicle for as many as *12,000* miles during the full term of this lease without incurring a charge for ~~execussive~~ *excessive* mileage. In the event of premature lease termination the number of mi(el)ls that the Lessee will be ~~tntitles~~ *entitled* to drive without incurring a charge for excessive mileage is *to* be determined by prorating the mileage allowed for the full lease term according to the proportion of the full lease term presented by the number of months the lease was in effect prior to premature termination. The lessee will be billed for excessive mileage at a rate of *18* cents per mile for each mile driven in excess of the mileage herein allowed. *Executed this 15th day of June 19—.*

Lessor ____________________ Lessee ____________________

LESSON
172

■ GOALS
To identify subject-verb agreement while typing sentences.
To review formatting ruled and leadered tables.
To review formatting footnotes in tables.

■ FORMAT
Single spacing   60-space line

LAB 20

Subject-Verb Agreement—Compound Subjects

Type lines 1–4 once. Then repeat lines 1–4 or take a series of 1-minute timings. (Subjects and verbs are underscored.)

```
1  Each horse and rider has a chance to win the race tomorrow.  12
2  Mr. Qucinich and Mr. Flexer of New Haven are in the office.  12
3  Both Mary and Ellen have the ability to zoom ahead on this.  12
4  Peanut butter and jelly makes a good sandwich for children.  12
   | 1 | 2 | 3 | 4 | 5 | 6 | 7 | 8 | 9 | 10 | 11 | 12
```

30-SECOND "OK" TIMINGS

Type as many 30-second "OK" (errorless) timings as possible out of three attempts on lines 5–7.

```
5  Both girls and boys are quite sure we will not expect their  12
6  speeds to zoom ahead for three minutes before they can jump  24
7  ahead to higher speeds for half a minute or a whole minute.  36
   | 1 | 2 | 3 | 4 | 5 | 6 | 7 | 8 | 9 | 10 | 11 | 12
```

FORMATTING REVIEW

Ruled Tables

1. Center horizontally and vertically.
2. Type the ruled lines (underscores) the exact width of the table.
3. Single-space before and double-space after each ruled line.
4. End the table with a single line, typed from the left margin to the right margin.

Leaders in Tables

1. Used to spread a narrow table to a wider width or when entries in the first column differ greatly in length.
2. Precede and follow the rows of periods with 1 blank space.
3. Backspace 2 spaces from the start of the second column to find the point on the scale where the final period will be typed.

Two-Line Column Headings

1. Center each line—subtract the number of characters in the shorter line from the number of characters in the longer line.
2. Divide the difference by 2 (drop any fraction); indent the shorter line that number of spaces.
3. Underscore each word in open tables; do not underscore in ruled tables.

(Continued on next page)

JOB 172 A. RULED TABLE

Standard format. Full sheet of paper.

MEDIA LIBRARY
Videotapes on Industrial-Safety Measures

Tape No.	Subject	Minutes
7624	Industrial Safety Is a Must	15
7629	Industrial Safety Means Better Wages	15
7630	Safety and Electric Lights	12
7631	Safety and Floors	12
7632	Safety and Housekeeping	12
7641	Working With Machines	9
7643	Working With Others	9
7657	Knowing About the Law	13

TEST

■ **GOALS**
To type 50/5'/3e.
To demonstrate competency in producing appropriately formatted communications from unarranged, handwritten, rough-draft, unedited, and incomplete copy.

■ **FORMAT**
Drills: Single spacing 60-space line
5-Minute Timings: Double spacing 5-space tab

PREVIEW PRACTICE

Type each line twice as a preview to the 5-minute timings below.

1 quality processing description opportunities administrative
2 senior analyst variations photocomposition phototypesetting
3 grammar formatting keyboarding punctuation responsibilities

5-MINUTE TIMINGS

Take two 5-minute timings on lines 4–24.

4 Job titles and [1]descriptions for personnel [2]working with 12
5 word [3]processing continue to grow. [4]Several different titles 24
6 show [5]job opportunities [6]depending upon the size of a [7]center. 36
7 One group of [8]titles and descriptions [9]focuses on people 48
8 whose [10]major responsibilities are [11]tied to the keyboarding of [12] 60
9 documents. There are [13]eight categories of [14]personnel listed: 72
10 a word [15]processing trainee who must have [16]entry-level skills; 84
11 a [17]competent word processing [18]operator; a specialist who [19]does 96
12 some formatting [20]variations and understands [21]total operations 108
13 of the [22]center; a phototypesetting [23]specialist who enters the [24] 120
14 special codes for [25]photocomposition systems; a [26]word process- 132
15 ing trainer [27]who controls quality and [28]teaches; a proofreader 144
16 who [29]checks text for spelling, [30]punctuation, grammar, [31]format, 156
17 and content; a word [32]processing supervisor [33]who directs oper- 168
18 ation of [34]a section; and a word [35]processing manager who takes [36] 180
19 responsibility for the [37]operations of the entire [38]center. 191
20 The other group [39]of titles and descriptions [40]encompasses 203
21 mainly [41]administrative positions. [42]Six categories are listed [43] 215
22 for this division: [44]administrative secretary, [45]senior admin- 227
23 istrative [46]secretary, administrative [47]supervisor, administra- 239
24 tive [48]manager, staff analyst, [49]and information manager. [50] 250
| 1 | 2 | 3 | 4 | 5 | 6 | 7 | 8 | 9 | 10 | 11 | 12 SI 2.03

FORMATTING REVIEW (CONTINUED)

Footnotes in Open Tables

1. Separate footnote from table with a 10P/12E line.
2. Single-space before line; double-space after.
3. Block short footnotes; single-space between them.
4. Indent long footnotes 5 spaces; type turnover lines at left margin.

Single-space footnotes; double-space between them.

Footnotes in Ruled Tables

1. Begin a double space below bottom line.
2. Follow Steps 3 and 4.

JOB 172 B. RULED TABLE WITH LEADERS

Standard format. Full sheet of paper.

Seminar for Safety Engineers
March 2, 19—

Topics	Speakers
Accident Investigations	W. Schuerle
Eye Protection	S. Cavallo
Fire Prevention	M. Dulac
Injuries	J. Volauski
Inspections	S. Tucci
Safe Job Procedures	K. Allerman
Safety Belts	S. Graham

JOB 172 C. RULED TABLE WITH LEADERS AND FOOTNOTE

Standard format. 30-space line. Half sheet of paper.

Expectation of Life in the U.S.*

Age	Number of Years
0–1	73.3
15	59.7
35	41.0
55	23.5
65	16.4

*1980 estimates.

JOB 172 D. TABLE WITH FOOTNOTE

5 by 3 index card.

MEDICAL DIRECTORS AT BRANCH PLANTS

Dr. Lee Kjelson, Colorado*	303-555-8200
Dr. Margaret Wenner, Utah	801-555-9393
Dr. Carl Zahn, California	213-555-3800

*On leave of absence. Dr. Margaret Tyhonas is Acting Medical Director.

LESSON 173

GOALS
To correct errors in subject-verb agreement while typing sentences.
To type 41/5′/4e.
To review formatting alphabetic file cards and tables.

FORMAT
Drills: Single spacing 60-space line
5-Minute Timings: Double spacing 5-space tab

LAB 20

Subject-Verb Agreement— Compound Subjects

Type lines 1–4 once, correcting verbs if necessary to ensure subject-verb agreement. Edit your copy as your teacher reads the answers. Then retype lines 1–4 from your edited copy.

1 For no reason at all, one of ten cats and dogs have run away.

2 Both the teacher and the principal has agreed to help Zoe.

3 We think that Quinton and Justin are planning a trip South.

4 Betty and Bob has an apartment near the college next year.

TURNAROUND TIME

The Word Procesing Center is operating with five word processing operators and a word processing center supervisor. The center is serving over ~~four hundred~~ 400 authors who have 24-hour access to the dictating facilities.

PRIORITY AND CONFIDENTIAL COMMUNICATIONS

Communications ~~which~~ that are marked priority and/or confidential ordinarily come from the Management Division. The turnaround time for these documents will not exceed 3 hours.

ROUTINE COMMUNICATIONS

Rputine correspondence is normally received from the supervisory personnel and makes up the majority of the word processing work load. The turnaround time for these documents will not exceed 5 hours.

LONG DOCUMENTS

Long documents such as procedures manuals and company reports come from all levels of the company. ~~The~~ Such documents usually ~~will~~ require numerous revisions before a final draft is ~~accomplished.~~ completed.

Turnaround time cannot be predicted since it depends upon the nature of the document and the number of revisions needed for completion.

This page is placed last because it was not determined where it should go in the manual. *You decide* where it should go.

[*you decide*] section, corrections and revisions

Responsibility for the accuracy of all documents rests with both the author and the word processing operator.

1. The author will clearly dictate and/or handwrite copy with all relevant information to complete the document.
2. The word processing operator will proofread all material before it is returned to the author. The author, however, should also proofread material when it is returned.
3. When a correction is necessary, note lightly on the copy in pencil any corrections in spelling, typing, punctuation, or content. Minor corrections may not require rerunning the document.
4. Return the original document and the copy on which the corrections are indicated to the word processing center. This is accomplished via the special word processing mail runs or by hand-carrying the document to the word processing center.
5. Do not accept work of inferior quality. Feedback to the supervisor of the word processing center is important and appreciated.
6. Revision of documents will be channeled according to the same priority as the original documents unless otherwise indicated. Thus a routine letter that has been revised will be processed as a routine letter again, a priority letter will be processed again as a priority letter, and so on.

PREVIEW PRACTICE

Type lines 5 and 6 twice on page 281 as a preview to the 5-minute timings.

5-MINUTE TIMINGS

Take two 5-minute timings on lines 7–24 on page 281.

FORMATTING REVIEW

Alphabetic File Cards

1. Name on line 2, 4 spaces from left edge of the card.
2. Type the person's last name first, followed by the first name and middle initial or middle name (if any).
3. Type all titles (*Ms., Mr., Dr., Mrs.*) in parentheses after the name.
4. Tab-indent the other lines 3 spaces, a double space below name.

JOB 173 A. ALPHABETIC FILE CARDS

Format a card for each name listed below. All live in Chattanooga, TN, so only the ZIP Code is given. But you must be sure to include the city and state on each card. Standard format (see review in margin). Workbook 315–317.

Mr. Lowell Cramer, 130 Glenview Street, 37408
Dr Albert E. Etzell, 230 Jefferson Avenue, 37408
Mrs. Ellie Frontino, P.O. Box 2671, 37407
Dr. Janice S. Oshie, 225 Wood Lane, 37415
Mr. McGrundy Barnes, 3000 Westside Drive, 37404
Ms. Pearl Ordway, 144 Crescent Circle, 37407
Mr. Hans Humperdinck, 14 Oweeda Terrace, 37415
Professor Lenora Trenton, 220 Harding Road, 37415

JOB 173 B. TABLE

Alphabetize the file cards prepared in Job 173 A. Format a three-column table. Head column 1 *Name* (first names first); column 2, *Address;* column 3, *ZIP Code.* Standard format. Double spacing. Title the table *CUSTOMERS IN CHATTANOOGA.* Full sheet of paper.

TEST

■ GOALS
To type 41/5′/4e.
To demonstrate competency while typing correspondence, forms, tables, and reports.

■ FORMAT
Double spacing   60-space line   5-space tab

PREVIEW PRACTICE

Type each line twice as a preview to the 5-minute timings on page 291.

```
Accuracy 1  size require gazette graphics extremely rewarding community
   Speed 2  elements printing subject profits paper focus their with is
```

5-MINUTE TIMINGS

Take two 5-minute timings on lines 3–22 on page 291.

1. gathering reference material this includes the letter or memo you are answering all necessary names and addresses and any information you may need from files reports and so on
2. establish your purpose decide your objective first load your brain before firing your mouth have clear in your own mind why this dictation is necessary
3. prepare an outline after some experience in some cases a mental run-through of points you wish to cover is the only outline you need you may wish to underline important points in the letter or memo you are answering to or write notes in the margin you may want a detailed outline for the first few tries
4. be concise clear and complete make sure your outline is adequate before you begin dictating break up paragraphs that are too long

REMEMBER GOOD LETTERS JUST DON'T HAPPEN—THEY ARE PLANNED THAT WAY

Workflow section, mailing procedures

1. Pickup and delivery. Pickup and delivery between the center and the various departments occurs every hour on the half hour, beginning at 9:30 a.m. and ending at 3:30 p.m. with the exception of 11:30 a.m. (lunch period). These times are subject to change as more departments begin to use the word processing center. Each department using the center has special input and output bins for routing work to and from the center:

Input: Completed documents are delivered.
Output: Revised or handwritten documents are picked up.

If a document is confidential, place it in an interoffice envelope and seal it with a secure-a-tie. Address the envelope to "Confidential" and place it in the output bin. It will be delivered directly to the "Confidential" word processing specialist. You may also hand-carry your document to the word processing supervisor.

2. Dating of correspondence. Material transcribed after 2:30 p.m. is automatically dated for the next working day, unless the author designates it as a rush or requests a specific date for the document.

3. Priorities. Work is processed in the following order:

a. Rush requests. A rush may be requested through the dictation system or by hand-carrying the document to the word processing center.
b. Corrections and retypes.
c. Routine work. This is processed on a first come, first served basis.
d. Forms.

Remember: Plan ahead to eliminate rushes. Rushes are subject to the approval of the word processing supervisor.

Formatting section, manuscripts and reports

Manuscripts are typed on a 6-inch line. The first page begins 2 inches from the top of the page, and all succeeding pages begin 1 inch from the top of the page. Titles are typed in all capitals, and side headings are typed in all capitals. Both are preceded by a triple space. All pages should have a 1-inch bottom margin. All manuscripts will be double-spaced unless otherwise designated.

479

Most successful [1]newspapers are large [2]businesses with a 12
big staff and [3]a lot of readers; there [4]are now an increasing 24
[5]number of smaller papers, [6]however, whose aim is to [7]focus on 36
one community or [8]subject. 41

All the [9]aspects of large-scale [10]publishing are involved 53
in smaller [11]papers and have the same [12]ingredients: graphics,[13] 65
words, and photos--[14]elements that are reflected by [15]the style 77
of the writing [16]and layout. 82

Advertising [17]is crucial to a newspaper [18]of any size. It 94
is [19]the money from advertisements, [20]as well as from the [21]sales 106
at the newsstands, [22]that brings in the profits. [23]All the ads 118
must be [24]neatly formatted. 123

A [25]small, well-produced paper [26]that will serve its local[27] 135
public is extremely [28]challenging and rewarding for [29]those who 147
are in the [30]business. Newspapers, after [31]all, give all of us 159
a [32]vehicle for free speech. 164

[33]With newer methods of [34]typesetting and offset [35]printing, 176
it is quite [36]feasible for people to start up [37]their own small 188
gazette. [38]Even a small-scale venture [39]would require a rather[40] 200
large investment, [41]though. 205

| 1 | 2 | 3 | 4 | 5 | 6 | 7 | 8 | 9 | 10 | 11 | 12 SI 1.51

JOB 174/175 A. LETTER

Block format. Workbook 319–320. Body 169 words.

[*Today's date*] / Ms. Rita DiClemente / Village 14
Tribune / 1624 Aquasco Drive / Middlebury, VT 22
05753 / Dear Ms. DiClemente: 29

The present system of filing checks cashed 38
every day, retrieving them and placing them in 48
an envelope at the end of the month, and then 57
mailing them to our customers has become so 66
expensive that in November we plan to initiate 75
Free Check Storage Accounts for our commer- 83
cial customers. 87

With this system we anticipate saving about 2 97
cents a check because canceled checks will not 106
be processed numerically and returned to cus- 115
tomers. Instead, these checks will be stored here 125
at the bank and may be retrieved by the customer 135
if it is necessary to produce evidence of pay- 144
ment. 146

If you would like additional information about 156
this new system, we invite you to attend a semi- 165
nar to learn how this program will operate. Just 175
come to the branch office nearest you on Satur- 185
day, October 28, at 9 a.m. 190

The meeting will last about an hour, and you 200
will have the opportunity to inspect our storage 210
areas. Do plan to attend. / Sincerely yours, / Zvi 224
Greenman / President / [*Your initials*] 229

Formatting section, forms

All forms processed by the center must have been designed with common horizontal and vertical measurements. (The vertical placement must be 1, 1½, 2, 2½, or 3 line spaces.) The horizontal placement must accommodate as many common tab stops as possible. The memo invoice form that follows illustrates all these principles.

OFFICE SYSTEMS INC.

DATE [*Current date*]

TO Research Division

FROM Word Processing Center

SUBJECT Procedures Manual

500	Printed procedures manuals @ $10	5 000 00
500	Special-design covers @ $2	1 000 00
	Total amount due	6 000 00

Workflow section, data input

Work is received in the word processing center in the following ways:
1. Via the telephone. Dictating into one of the dictating systems (available to the authors 24 hours a day, 7 days a week).
2. Via Form 6700. Request for form (repeat or model) letter. Mailed to the center through the special word processing mail runs.
3. Via Form 6800. Request for word processing service. Mailed to the center through the special word processing mail runs. This form must accompany all work sent to the center except for form letters, corrections, and retypes.
4. Corrections and retypes. Mailed to the center through the special word processing mail runs.

Dictation section, the system

the following are features of the word processing center's dictating system
1. the dictating equipment is voice-activated the tape moves only when you talk no pauses during replay
2. the recorder levels volume automatically alternate shouts and whispers sound essentially the same on replay the equipment also filters out high- and low-frequency background noises outside the normal voice range
3. dictated material is processed on a first-in first-out basis this sequence may be altered to accommodate priorities
4. your current dictation may be played back however to ensure privacy you as well as anyone else are locked out of prior dictation it is impossible for one author to play back anothers dictation
5. when you have access to a recorder you will hear a beep tone when you are in a dictate mode but not talking you will hear a continuous tone
6. if the recorders are busy you will get a regular busy signal hang up don't wait long to try again
7. your communications with the exception of some tabulated materials will come back faster from the word processing center if they are processed through the dictation system specialists can transcribe dictation much faster and more nearly free of errors than they can transcribe handwritten copy

Dictation section, techniques

dictating is a learned skill as in the case of all skills it requires planning practice and careful execution the following four techniques will help you dictate better communications

JOB 174/175 B. LETTER ON MONARCH STATIONERY

Standard format. Workbook 321–322. Body 81 words.

(Today's date) / Mr. Edward T. MacLean / 13
330 Oxford Street / London, UK W1R 1TD / 20
England / Dear Ed: 24
~~I want to~~ congratulate ~~you for~~ the 30
splendid series of articles you wrote 38
for your newspaper The London Times. 52
Luckily, our mutual friend, Neil Kline, 60
brought the clippings--otherwise, I 67
would have missed the series. Your 76
report, Ed, isthe best coverage I have 84
~~ever~~ read on the subject of education 92
improvment through the use of compu- 100
ters in the class room. 104
Certainly you must send copies of the 115
London Times to Dr. Hightower. She 129
will be extremely pleased (I know) to 134
learn your achievements. / Sincerely, / 144
Harold Zumerelli / (Your initials) 153

JOB 174/175 C. INVOICE

Standard format. Compute the Amount column, the total, and the total amount due. Workbook 323 top.

[*Date: Today's*] / [*To:*] Weekender Sports Company / 1125 Addison Avenue / Dunkirk, NY 14048 /
12 BL Campstoves, Model BT30, @ $29.95
24 BL Camptents, Model ND72, @ $85.00
10 BL Campside Tool Kits, Model TL05, @ $15.95
10 BL Campside Tool Kits, Model TL08, @ $19.95
Total / Less 20% discount / Total amount due

JOB 174/175 D. MEMO

Standard format. Workbook 323 bottom.

[*Date: Today's*] / [*To:*] Managers, Office Tech- 4
nology / [*From:*] Lionel Schmidt-Matzen / [*Sub-* 16
ject:] Software Buying 20
Don't buy software without trying it first. Good 32
vendors will arrange a trial demonstration for 42
you. It is reasonable to ask for one. It is also 52
reasonable to ask for the names of other organi- 61
zations already using the kind of software you 71
are considering. It is worth the effort to solicit a 81
few opinions. You will find that the computer 91
users world is very friendly, rather like the old 101
CB radio world. / LSM / [*Your initials*] 109

JOB 174/175 E. RULED TABLE

Standard format for a ruled table. Half sheet of paper.

Sales by Region, January–June 19__

Region	Actual Sales*	Budgeted Sales*
Eastern	$121.5	$119.6
Southern	113.6	109.2
Western	97.5	97.0
Mid-Continent	101.9	100.0
Average	108.6	106.5

*In thousands.

JOB 174/175 F. MAGAZINE ARTICLE

Standard format. Type the body of Job 174/175 D (memo) as the last paragraph of the article. Use the author of the memo in the byline.

SOFTWARE BUYING BASICS

You can get the most satisfaction from your computer if you address your attention to identifying software that is well suited to your needs. The key to satisfaction lies in the precision with which you are able to match your needs to the features of any given software package. Documentation refers to the instructions that come with a software package. Software documentation should be reviewed closely because even the best features in the world are no good if you can't figure out how to use them. Two or three things to look for include (1) a step-by-step instruction manual, (2) training diskettes that prompt the learner, and (3) training workshops for employees.

The more familiar you are with your needs, the more likely you will be to ask the right questions. Ask the manufacturer about service and support, the "bugs" in the program, and what hardware the program will operate on.

Formatting section, envelopes for routine correspondence

Window envelopes are used for the majority of all direct correspondence leaving the center. This procedures is used for several reasons:

1. Elimination of typing time.
2. Elimination of possible typing errors on envelopes.
3. Elimination of a matching problem of envelopes and correspondence.

The typing of the inside address is set up to allow the complete address to show through the window of the envelope.

A window envelope will accompany all direct correspondence unless the word processing supervisor is directed otherwise by the author.

Whenever a window envelope is too small to accommodate the correspondence, the word processing supervisor will instruct the operator to type the address on a gum label. The gum label can then be placed on a larger envelope.

Formatting section, tables and charts

Only routine tabulated data should be dictated. It is strongly recommended that long and detailed tabulated information be sent to the center in handwritten drafts.

All tabulated data will be typed as designated by the author. Please be specific with your directions concerning the formatting. Examples of a ruled table and a leadered table follow:

Word Processing Center Input

Type of Document	Turnaround Time
Priority/Confidential	3 hours
Routine Correspondence	5 hours
Long Documents	Varies*

*Depends upon number of revisions required.

Word Processing Center Personnel

Supervisor . . . . Shannon Murphy
CRT Operator . . . . Lori Otten
CRT Operator . . . . Janet Copenhefer
CRT Operator . . . . Lloyd James
CRT Operator . . . . Lisa Shepherd
CRT Operator . . . . Albert Daniels

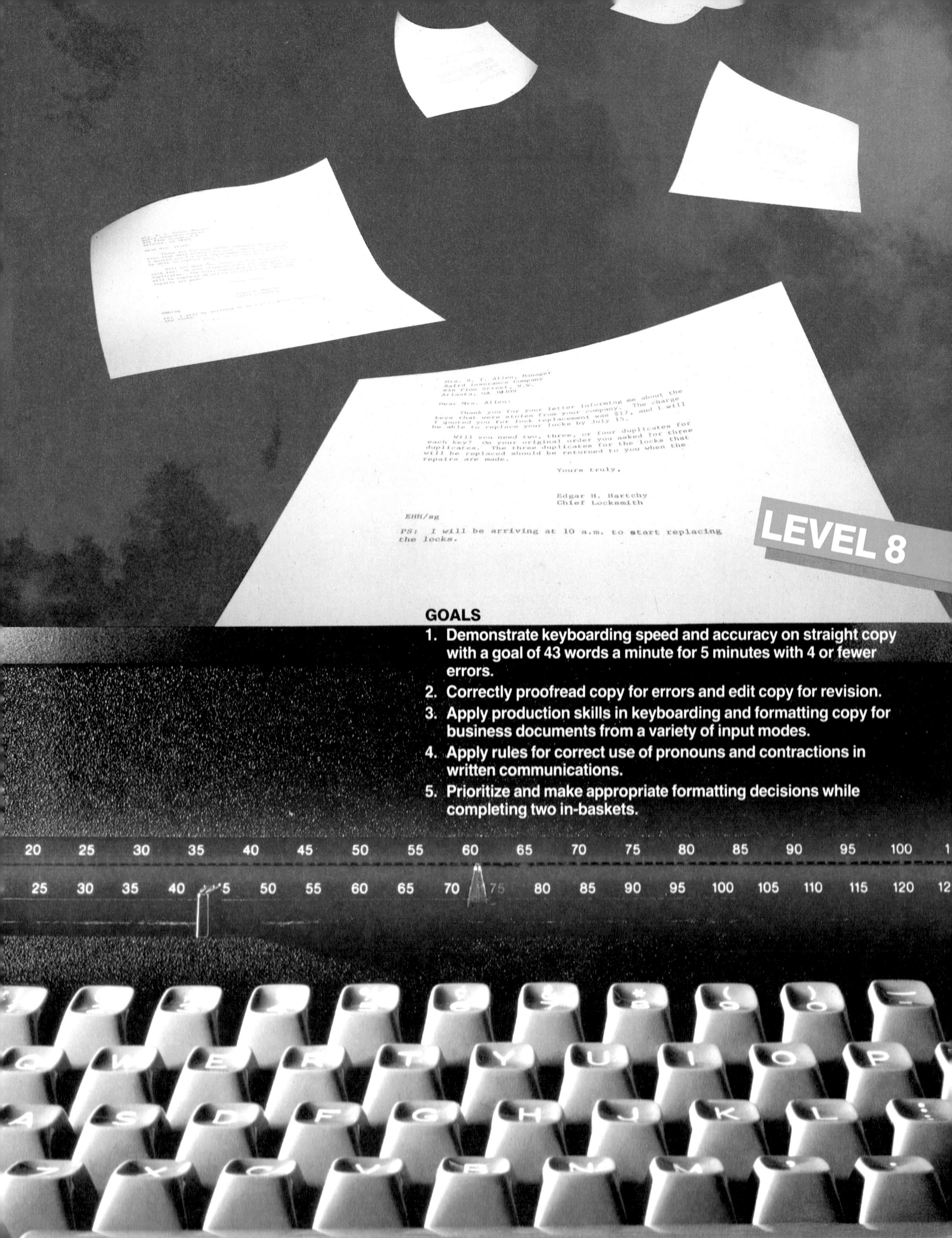

Mrs. R. T. Allen, Manager
Baird Insurance Company
956 Pine Street, N.W.
Atlanta, GA 30309
Dear Mrs. Allen:
Thank you for your letter informing me about the keys that were stolen from your company. The charge I quoted you for lock replacement was $17, and I will be able to replace your locks by July 15.
Will you need two, three, or four duplicates for each key? On your original order you asked for three duplicates. The three duplicates for the locks that will be replaced should be returned to you when the repairs are made.
Yours truly,
Edgar H. Hartchy
Chief Locksmith
EHH/sg
PS: I will be arriving at 10 a.m. to start replacing the locks.
20 25 30 35 40 45 50 55 60 65 70 75 80 85 90 95 100
25 30 35 40 45 50 55 60 65 70 75 80 85 90 95 100 105 110 115 120

LEVEL 8

GOALS

1. Demonstrate keyboarding speed and accuracy on straight copy with a goal of 43 words a minute for 5 minutes with 4 or fewer errors.
2. Correctly proofread copy for errors and edit copy for revision.
3. Apply production skills in keyboarding and formatting copy for business documents from a variety of input modes.
4. Apply rules for correct use of pronouns and contractions in written communications.
5. Prioritize and make appropriate formatting decisions while completing two in-baskets.

Workflow section, organizational chart

Arrange a full-page display of the information flow for the center from this handwritten draft.

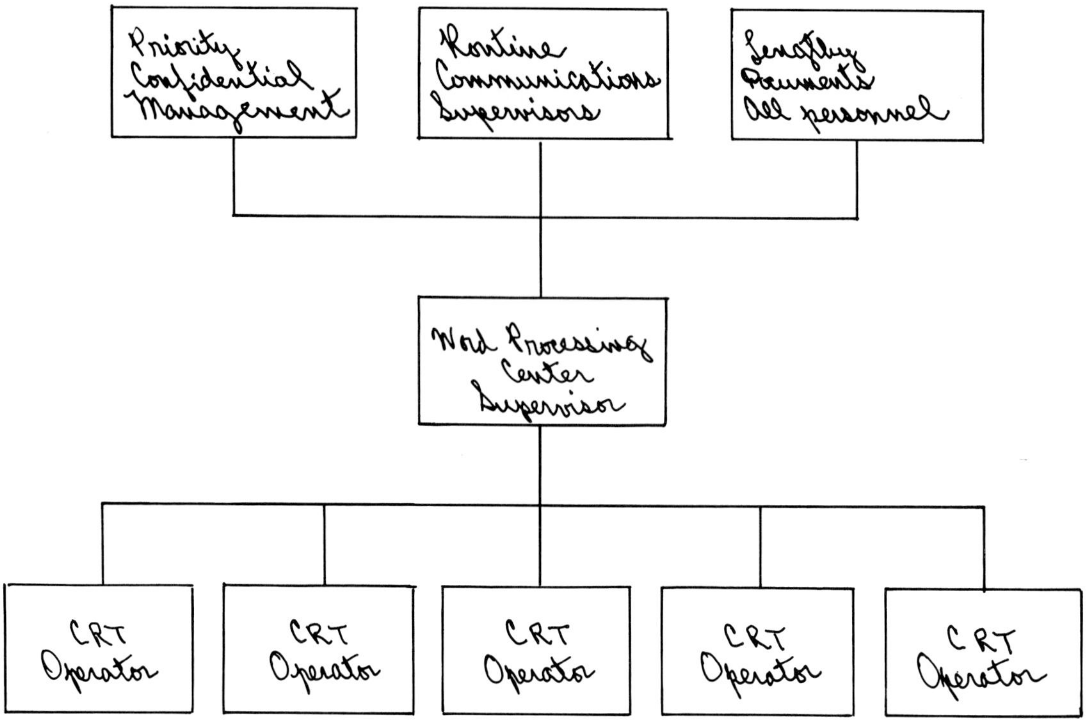

Formatting section, letters

```
Formatting section, letters

All routine letters will be typed on a 6-inch line with the date
displayed at the center of the writing line, 15 lines down from the
top of the page. The inside address will be placed 5 lines below the
dateline and against the left margin. All paragraphs of letters will
be blocked and single-spaced with double spacing between paragraphs.
All closing lines begin at the center, and all other notations (reference initials, enclosures, postscripts, etc.) will
be typed below the typed name, against the left margin. Note the
following example:
```

Ms. Marilyn Spangenberg, 1536 Princewood Court, Cincinnati, OH 45223, Dear Ms. Spangenberg: Your request for additional information concerning the new data processing laboratory has been referred to our district manager. There are four different systems that our company can offer, and an analysis of your school's needs will have to be conducted before any recommendations can be made.

You can expect to hear from Mr. Thomason within the next two to three weeks. In the meantime, I have enclosed a description of each system. Sincerely, Mark A. Johnson, Marketing Representative, Enclosure

UNIT 29 Formatting Reports

UNIT GOAL 42/5′/4e

■ **GOALS**
To correct errors in subject-verb agreement while typing sentences.
To type 42/5′/4e.
To type an itinerary.

■ **FORMAT**
Drills: Single spacing 60-space line
5-Minute Timings: Double spacing 5-space tab

LAB 20

Subject-Verb Agreement—Compound Subjects

Workbook 325–326.

Type lines 1–4 once, correcting verbs to ensure subject-verb agreement. Edit your copy as your teacher reads the answers. Then retype lines 1–4 from your edited copy.

1 Both Mr. Axmans and Dr. Garrett has been to visit us here.
2 Zeke and Annabelle is working on the design of a computer.
3 Every doctor and nurse need to check each chart carefully.
4 Jan and I does all we can to help the students with the quiz.

PRETEST

Take a 5-minute timing on lines 5–23. Circle and count your errors. Use the chart on page 295 to determine which lines to type for practice.

5 Today, with more and more people traveling by airplane 12
6 around the world, the airlines have become large companies, 24
7 employing thousands of workers. These corporations attempt 36
8 at all times to ensure safety throughout the system. A big 48
9 part of this safety effort comes from the pilots. 58
10 Strict medical standards have been established to make 70
11 sure that pilots will have ample physical as well as mental 82
12 abilities. A pilot must pass regular health exams to avoid 94
13 being grounded. Since the cost of training jet pilots runs 106
14 around a half million dollars, grounding of a pilot implies 118
15 a loss of revenue for the airlines. 125
16 Pilots work under a great deal of stress--and get very 137
17 little exercise. Extreme fatigue can set in and then add a 149
18 lot to health problems. Some airlines have started classes 161
19 to teach their employees the values of physical fitness. A 173
20 few offer exercises to strengthen the mind and body against 185
21 the problems that result from jet lag, which does interfere 197
22 with quality performance. 202
23 Physical health is vital--prize it. 210

| 1 | 2 | 3 | 4 | 5 | 6 | 7 | 8 | 9 | 10 | 11 | 12 SI 1.55

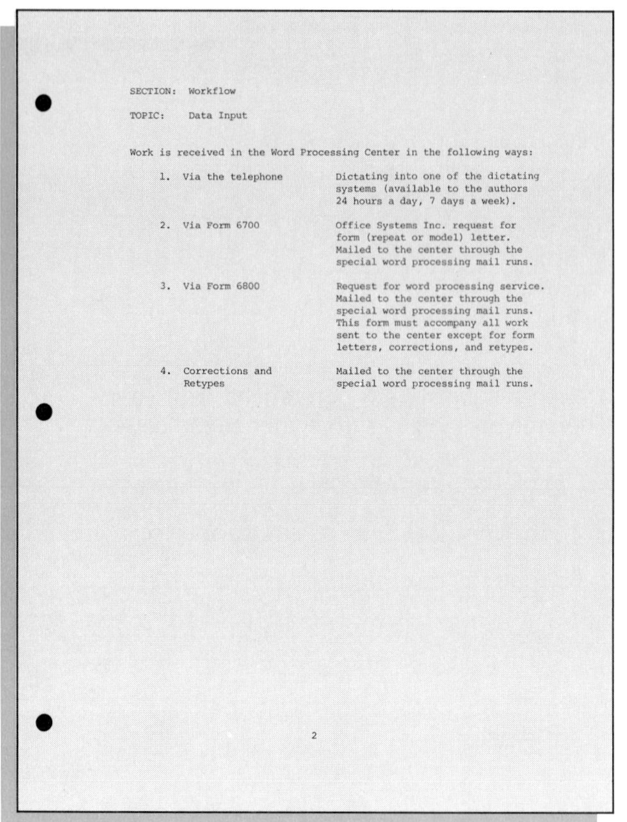

SECTION: Workflow

TOPIC: Data Input

Work is received in the Word Processing Center in the following ways:

1. Via the telephone — Dictating into one of the dictating systems (available to the authors 24 hours a day, 7 days a week).
2. Via Form 6700 — Office Systems Inc. request for form (repeat or model) letter. Mailed to the center through the special word processing mail runs.
3. Via Form 6800 — Request for word processing service. Mailed to the center through the special word processing mail runs. This form must accompany all work sent to the center except for form letters, corrections, and retypes.
4. Corrections and Retypes — Mailed to the center through the special word processing mail runs.

2

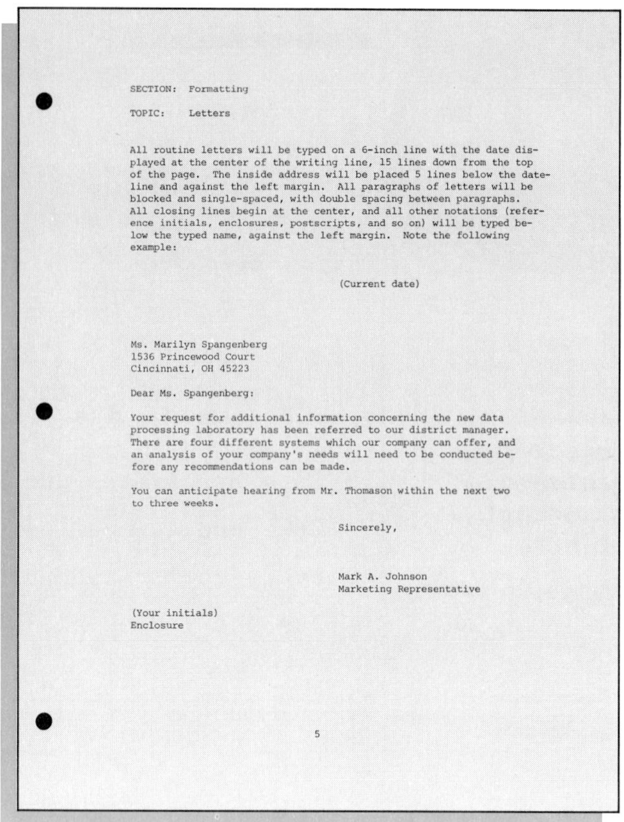

SECTION: Formatting

TOPIC: Letters

All routine letters will be typed on a 6-inch line with the date displayed at the center of the writing line, 15 lines down from the top of the page. The inside address will be placed 5 lines below the dateline and against the left margin. All paragraphs of letters will be blocked and single-spaced, with double spacing between paragraphs. All closing lines begin at the center, and all other notations (reference initials, enclosures, postscripts, and so on) will be typed below the typed name, against the left margin. Note the following example:

(Current date)

Ms. Marilyn Spangenberg
1536 Princewood Court
Cincinnati, OH 45223

Dear Ms. Spangenberg:

Your request for additional information concerning the new data processing laboratory has been referred to our district manager. There are four different systems which our company can offer, and an analysis of your company's needs will need to be conducted before any recommendations can be made.

You can anticipate hearing from Mr. Thomason within the next two to three weeks.

Sincerely,

Mark A. Johnson
Marketing Representative

(Your initials)
Enclosure

5

Dictation section, guidelines for dictation

1. identify yourself by name division and group
2. state what you are dictating letter memo report rough draft form
3. spell out names and addresses use phonetic alphabet for initials spell out numbers that might be confusing (for example fifty and fifteen)
4. use the proper method of dictating an address
5. indicate the end of the subject line
6. use the proper method for capitalization
7. indicate end of sentence punctuation only
8. say "operator" before giving special instructions
9. spell out all mechanical instructions—paragraphs to be indented beyond the regular margins quotes to be given special margin treatment columns of figures and charts (give headings that go across paper then all data in each column [under each heading] across like it will be typed) entries to be numbered and typed under one another and titles to be underlined
10. spell out any words that might give trouble
    a. homonyms—accept, except; council, counsel; elicit, illicit
    b. other words that might be misunderstood—fiscal, physical
    c. medical and technical terms—myocardial, infarction
    d. uncommon words—rectify, aforementioned, indebtedness, reiterate
11. maintain voice control
    a. use a relaxed, normal conversational tone
    b. do not go too fast (especially on material that's familiar to you)
    c. avoid mumbling, smoking, chewing gum, fumbling with instruments—moving phone around causes chopping of words
    d. use appropriate inflections and pauses
12. dictate the copies of the letter in the order in which you want them to appear on your document (by rank, alphabetical, by sex, and so on)
13. indicate the end of the document

PRACTICE

In the chart below find the number of errors you made on the Pretest. Then type each of the designated drill lines four times.

Pretest errors	0–1	2–3	4–5	6+
Drill lines	27–33	26–32	25–31	24–30

Accuracy

24 have exams safety result implies against exercise traveling
25 large prize system quality medical workers fatigue problems
26 pilots stress started million training interfere strengthen
27 offer values revenue extreme physical employees performance
28 great strict classes regular grounded standards established

Speed

29 mental people world today their with loss that well all the
30 around health since comes under more work does will jet lag
31 airplane dollars fitness become these cost been part big is
32 abilities little being which ample pass make body for by it
33 companies ensure avoid vital times runs some half and to of

POSTTEST

Take another 5-minute timing on lines 5–23 on page 294 to see how much your skill has improved.

JOB 176 A. ITINERARY

Standard format (see page 271). Make two carbon copies.

Mayor Richard Ginallo ITINERARY *Oct. 24, 19--*

(Des Moines -- Switzerland)

Monday, October 24

12:10 p.m., CDT Depart Des Moines, United Flight 260, lunch served

5:30 p.m., EDT Arrive New York, Kennedy International Airport

7:10 p.m. Depart New York, Kennedy International Airport, TNA Flight 455

Tuesday, October 25

10:15 a.m. Arrive Geneva, Switzerland
3:00 p.m. Tour watch factory
Accommodations: Hotel Geneva

Wednesday, October 26

9:00 a.m. Depart Geneva, train to Bern
1:00 p.m. Visit Castle of Chillon
5:15 p.m. Depart Bern, bus to Baden
Accommodations: Schweiz Hotel

Thursday, October 27

9:30 a.m. Tour Forrer Electronics
11:30 a.m. Depart Baden, bus to Basel
2:00 p.m. Tour Rebound Chemicals
Accommodations: Vanil-Noir Hotel

Friday, October 28

9:40 a.m. Depart Basel, train to Zurich
2:00 p.m. Tour Swiss Credit Bank
6:20 p.m. Depart Zurich, overnight train to St. Moritz

(Continued on next page)

PRETEST Take a 5-minute timing on lines 8–29 on page 472. Circle and count your errors.

PRACTICE In the chart below find the number of errors you made on the Pretest on page 472. Then type each of the designated drill lines six times.

Pretest errors	0–1	2–3	4+
Drill lines	32–35	31–34	30–33

Accuracy

```
30 ticket airline computer originally technology international
31 growth options property associated management comprehensive
32 assist examine pleasure collection businesses experimenting
```

Speed

```
33 estate which agent banks lists small lack that with and the
34 obtain quick store every would local very main data for use
35 access files costs their where items want lost them can are
```

POSTTEST Take another 5-minute timing on lines 8–29 on page 472 to see how much your skill has improved.

IN-BASKET I: Word Processing Center

Office Systems Inc. has operated a word processing center for about 6 months. During this time various procedures have been set up and tested for effectiveness and efficiency. As an employee of the center, you will now prepare the final draft of a procedures manual that the center has decided to use. Since you are an experienced operator, you have been given some responsibility for the general formatting of the manual. Arrange the material so that it will be a good reference manual.

TIME LOG

Read the entire document before beginning work. The pages are not necessarily in the correct order. You must decide the correct order. Be sure to keep an accurate time log as you complete each job. Workbook 707–711.

General Layout There are 12 pages to the manual as well as a cover page and a table of contents. There are three sections: Workflow, Formatting, and Dictation. The Workflow section has three pages: a one-page organizational chart, a page explaining how to input data, and a page explaining mailing procedures. The Formatting section has one page each for envelopes, letters, forms, tables, and reports. The Dictation section has a page explaining the system, a page for techniques, and a page for guidelines. You decide the sequence of the various sections. You also decide which section should include the page on corrections and revisions. On page 475 are sample pages from a procedures manual. Use this format or create one of your own. Once you decide on a format, be consistent in using it for all 12 pages.

Cover Page The key elements of a word processing operation are people, procedures, and equipment. Design a cover using these terms as well as the name of the center.

Table of Contents Prepare a table of contents that will make it easy to find information in the procedures manual.

Saturday, October 29

9:00 a.m.	Tour St. Moritz
2:44 p.m.	Depart St. Moritz, train to Appenzell
	Accommodations: Helvetia Inn

Sunday, October 30

7:51 a.m.	Depart Appenzell, train to Zurich
2:05 p.m.	Depart Zurich, TNA Flight 611
5:05 p.m., EST	Arrive New York, Kennedy International Airport
7:00 p.m.	Depart New York, United Flight 927, dinner served
10:59 p.m., CST	Arrive Des Moines

■ GOAL
To format and type a report in space-saving style.

■ FORMAT
Single spacing 60-space line

KEYBOARDING SKILLS

Type lines 1–4 once. Practice using the shift lock in line 5. Then repeat lines 1–4 or take a series of 1-minute timings.

Speed	1	The home row keys are easy to find as you type, type, type.	12
Accuracy	2	Joan saw six azure kites quickly drift by very huge maples.	12
Numbers	3	The party governed during 1910, 1929, 1938, 1947, and 1956.	12
Symbols	4	Los Angeles (California) and Chicago (Illinois) are cities.	12
Technique	5	He TYPES for BIG companies and EARNS a GREAT DEAL of MONEY.	

| 1 | 2 | 3 | 4 | 5 | 6 | 7 | 8 | 9 | 10 | 11 | 12

30-SECOND "OK" TIMINGS

Type as many 30-second "OK" (errorless) timings as possible out of three attempts on lines 6–8. Then repeat the effort and try to improve on the first score.

6 Max had a zest for quiet living and placed work before joy, 12
7 which caused his family to gripe. His son Zeke is very sad 24
8 because he and his sister do not often play with their Dad. 36

| 1 | 2 | 3 | 4 | 5 | 6 | 7 | 8 | 9 | 10 | 11 | 12

FORMATTING REVIEW

Reports in Space-Saving Style

1. 6½-inch line (65P/75E).
2. Title on line 10; double-space after.
3. Single-space; double-space between paragraphs.
4. Leave 1 blank line above and below side headings, or use paragraph headings instead.
5. If your machine has vertical half spacing, use 1/2 blank line wherever you usually use 1 blank line.

JOB 177 A. TRIP REPORT

Type the report on page 297. Space-saving style with paragraph headings.

Time frame proposed for writing courseware ______

______

Time frame proposed for testing courseware ______

______

List any additional resources necessary for completion of the writing of the courseware. (6 ruled lines)

C. Prepare the committee checklist form for the writing guide. Use a 6-inch line. Precede the first line of each item with a ruled line. Begin the items 1½ inches from the left margin. Leave 2 spaces between the rule and the start of the item. Single-space items; double-space between them.

]COMMITTEE CHECK LIST[

The General guidelines are clearly stated.

The General guidelines include all items that we agreed to have stated.

The guidelines for testing, revising, and adopting are clearly stated.

The guideslines for testing, revising, and adopting include all items that we agreed to have stated.

the guidelines for the Elementary level are clearly stated.

The guidelines for the middle schoIl level are clearly stated.

The middle school level draft includes all items that we agreed to have stated.

The elementary level draft includes all items that we agreed to have stated.

The ~~middle~~ guidelines for the high school level are clearly stated.

The high school level draft includes all items that we agreed to have stated.

The application form is clearly designed.

The total draft includes all necessary items and is stated clearly.

The draft needs revision. (If you check this item, please list specific revision(s).)

d.s.

______

______

______

______

The application form includes all the information that we agreed to have included.

LESSONS 293–298

UNIT 48 In-Basket

UNIT GOAL 50/5′/3e

GOALS

To type 50/5′/3e.

To prioritize and determine format for a word processing procedures manual.

FORMAT

Drills: Single spacing 60-space line

5-Minute Timings: Double spacing 5-space tab

KEYBOARDING SKILLS Type lines 1–5 on page 471.

REPORT OF TOUR OF SWITZERLAND
Mayor Richard Ginallo, Des Moines, IA
October 24-30, 19--

Purpose. I was one of 23 mayors of third-class cities in the United States who were seleced by the State department to spend one week in Switzer land studying that country government, factories, and business. Switzerland was choosen because it's not large, has no unemployment, and si govern by a body of representetives from each of it's 25 cantons.

Switzerland depends no imports to feed it's pupulation, which is about 6,000,000 million people. These people are a mixture of langage and culture, which breaks down some what like this:

Language	Percent of Population
German	69.0
French	19.0
Italian	10.0
Rumanish	0.9

Constitutional safe guards prevent any one person, group or canton from becoming too powerful. The Swiss president serves a one-year term and maynot immediately succeed him self or herself. By living small but thinking big Switzerland has forged a people of many tongues and diverse cultures into one nation; and from Switzer-lnad's lesson, there is much we can learn.

Geneva. Our first stop was Geneva, head quarters fo 51 internation bodies, including the International Cross. We visited the archives of the Central Training Agency where more than 15 million names are cross-fill ed on 45 million cards. During world war II, the IORC kept track of captives, making contact with next of kin. These cards were color-coded--pink for Germans, white for Americans, and blue for British.

Crafts workers began building clocks and watches in Geneva more than 400 year ago. Many of Switzerland't 515 watch-assembling plants are small and scattered To maintain consistenly high standards, they still do a lot of the most exacting work by hand. Even on on small assembly lines there is no compromisy with precision.

Today they produce almost half the world's watches — 67 million a year.

Baden. In Baden, a few miles northest of Zurich, large industries flourish and are dramatic proof that Swiss industryalso thinkg big. At Lyck, Inc., we watched spirals of steel spin off a huge lathe-like machine, operated by a master machinest with 27 years experience. He earns 20,0000 francs a year, the equivelent of $4,600, which is excellent pay by Swiss standards.

Basel. The Next to machinery, the most important export is chemicals. The hub of this industry Basel. Since the early 1900s the industry has branched in all types of chemical products--dyes, drugs, pesticides, plastics, inks, and rare metals. During the 1930s Switzerland began making vitmins and today is the world's largest producer.

Zurich. In Zurich, Switzerland's biggest city, we visited the headquarter of one of the country oldest and largest banks, the Swiss credit bank. In the foreign exchange section teletypewriters clattered, while a dozen buyers with direct lines to London, rome, and New York bargained for blocks of sterling, lira, and dollar currencies. Bank employees are allowed by law to reveal information about depsoitors. The name of a numbered-acount depositor is known only to 2 or 3 of the bank's top officials.

St. Moritz. This citys industry is recreation--plush hotels bobsled andtoboggan runs, ski jumps, and facilitiesfor the whole gamut of snow-and-ice sprots--a winner among the world's winter resorts.

Appenzell. One of the last areas in Switzerland where mostpeople still work the land, this this valley is green and fruit ful. In the winter, families work at small embroidery factory is town.

Conclusion. This trip was a great privi-ledge, and I learned many things that we can incorporate in our developmental plan for Des Moines.

With the growth of information and the technology that 12
permits management of it, data banks are cropping up every- 24
where. Data banks are comprehensive collections of data in 36
library form. Data is stored so that it can be accessed by 48
quick, efficient use of computer terminals. 57

Numerous businesses have acquired access to data banks 69
and use them as the main service components of their opera- 81
tions. Airline ticket agents make reservations by consult- 93
ing a computer data bank for obtaining flight times, ticket 105
costs, passenger lists, and seating options. A terminal is 117
accessed to get the information the agent needs, and reser- 129
vations are confirmed or adjusted. 136

Real estate listing used to be very laborious, and the 148
sale of property could be lost because of lack of knowledge 160
of certain opportunities. Multiple listings allow an agent 172
to examine national and international offerings through the 184
data banks, which store most real estate that is available. 196

Data banks were originally associated with large files 208
of information containing millions of citations. Now small 220
communities are experimenting with smaller banks of data to 232
aid local businesses and citizens who want special informa- 244
tion for work or for pleasure. 250

| 1 | 2 | 3 | 4 | 5 | 6 | 7 | 8 | 9 | 10 | 11 | 12 | SI 1.75

JOB 291/292 A. WRITING GUIDE

Complete the writing guide you started in Lessons 289/290 on pages 468–471.

JOBS 291/292 B AND C. APPLICATION AND CHECKLIST FORMS

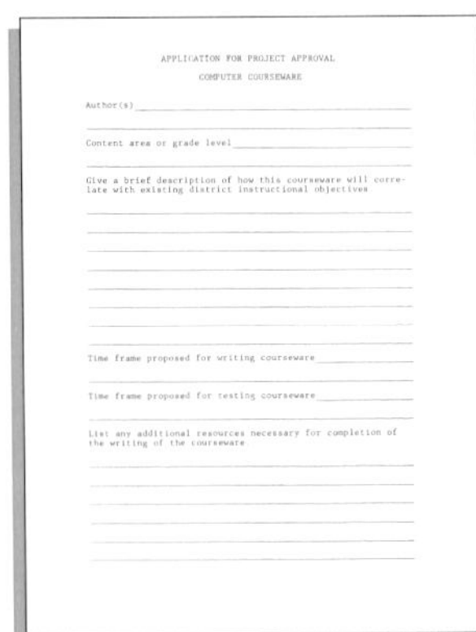

APPLICATION FOR PROJECT APPROVAL

COMPUTER COURSEWARE

Author(s) ____________________

____

Content area or grade level ____________________

____

Give a brief description of how this courseware will correlate with existing district instructional objectives

____________________ (8 lines)

Time frame proposed for writing courseware ____________________

____

Time frame proposed for testing courseware ____________________

____

List any additional resources necessary for completion of the writing of the courseware

____________________ (6 lines)

Application

COMMITTEE CHECKLIST

_______ The general guidelines are clearly stated

_______ The general guidelines include all items that we agreed to have stated

_______ The guidelines for testing, revising, and adopting are clearly stated.

_______ The guidelines for testing, revising, and adopting include all items that we agreed to have stated

_______ The guidelines for the elementary level are clearly stated

_______ The elementary level draft includes all items that we agreed to have stated

_______ The guidelines for the middle school level are clearly stated

_______ The middle school level draft includes all items that we agreed to have stated

_______ The guidelines for the high school level are clearly stated

_______ The high school level draft includes all items that we agreed to have stated

_______ The application form is clearly designed

_______ The application form includes all the information that we agreed to have included

_______ The total draft includes all items necessary and is clearly stated.

_______ The draft needs revision. (If you check this item, please list specific revision(s).)

Checklist

B. Prepare the application form for the writing guide. Use a 6-inch line. Single-space items; double-space between items. Ruled lines should all be double-spaced.

APPLICATION FOR PROJECT APPROVAL
COMPUTER COURSEWARE

Author(s) ____________________

____

Content area or grade level ____________________

____

Give a brief description of how this courseware will correlate with existing district instructional objectives.

(8 ruled lines) (Continued on next page)

LESSON 178

■ GOALS
To recognize pronouns and their antecedents while typing sentences.
To format and type a side-bound report.

■ FORMAT
Single spacing   60-space line

LAB 21

Pronouns

Type lines 1–4 once. Then repeat lines 1–4 or take a series of 1-minute timings. (The pronouns are underscored.)

1 Sheila reports that her books are on the shelves at school. 12

2 Jennifer and I are taking our unique exam at the city hall. 12

3 Next month all the employees hope that they can get a pass. 12

4 The Johnsons and Zonks are going to their school's reunion. 12

| 1 | 2 | 3 | 4 | 5 | 6 | 7 | 8 | 9 | 10 | 11 | 12

A pronoun must agree with its antecedent (the word for which the pronoun stands) in person (I, you, he), number (he, they), and gender (he, she).

Frank said that he could do the job alone.
The managers believe that they will settle this matter today.

12-SECOND TIMINGS

Type each line three times, or take three 12-second timings on each line. For each timing, type with no more than 1 error.

5 The men may fix their antique auto and go downtown with it.
6 The girls held a social to pay for their visit to the lake.
7 It is the duty of the eight men to cut down the large oaks.

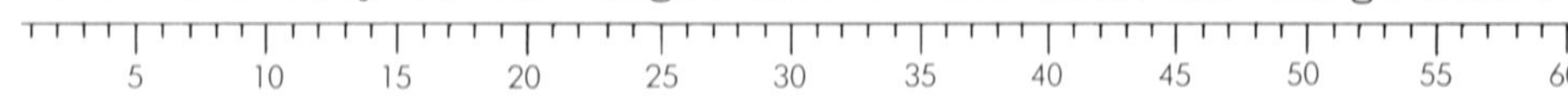

30-SECOND SPEED TIMINGS

Take two 30-second speed timings on lines 8 and 9. Then take two 30-second speed timings on lines 10 and 11. Or type each sentence twice.

8 It is not the size of your fingers or your hands that gives 12
9 you speed in stroking; you build quick stroking day by day. 24

10 Try to practice keyboarding at a steady pace; practice your 12
11 drills evenly and smoothly without pausing or wasting time. 24

| 1 | 2 | 3 | 4 | 5 | 6 | 7 | 8 | 9 | 10 | 11 | 12

FORMATTING REVIEW

Side-Bound Reports

Move margins and the centering point 3 spaces to the right to allow room for binding at the left.

JOB 178 A. SIDE-BOUND REPORT

Retype the trip report on page 297. Change paragraph headings to side headings. Make one carbon copy. Bound format (see review in margin).

4. *Items B and C remain the same.*
5. *In Item D after* will lead to, *change wording to read* interdisciplinary coordination, teachers who will be affected by the necessary coordination should be involved in the initial planning of the courseware.
6. *Item E remains the same.*
7. *In Item F after* enhancement of, *change wording to read* writing skills, calculating skills, and decision-making skills.
8. *The rest of the page needs no changes.*

Page 5

Use the copy of page 4. Mark the following changes on the page, and then type page 5.

1. *Change the title to* CONTENT GUIDELINES FOR HIGH SCHOOL.
2. *Change the introductory paragraph to read* high school, *instead of* middle school, *and focus on* computer programming and computer applications. *Change* as a tool for calculating and writing *to* to manipulate data in a more efficient manner than would be possible without it.
3. *In Item A change* in a different way *to* in a more efficient manner.
4. *Add the following sentence to Item B:* Changes may be requested as a result of the materials which are developed.
5. *Items C, D, and E remain the same.*
6. *In Item F after* should be, *change the rest of the item to read* writing programs that will allow students to complete tasks more efficiently and using commercially prepared software to complete tasks more efficiently. Students should understand that the computer are a tool to help solve a problem. It may be solved by writing a customized program or by using previously prepared software.
7. *The rest of the page remains the same except that it will extend to a second page in order to accommodate all the changes.*

■ GOALS
To type 50/5'/3e.
To complete the writing guide.
To prepare application and checklist forms.

■ FORMAT
Drills: Single spacing 60-space line
5-Minute Timings: Double spacing 5-space tab

KEYBOARDING SKILLS

Type lines 1–4 once. Then punctuate line 5 as you type it. Repeat lines 1–4, or take a series of 1-minute timings.

Speed	1	As soon as we had tried on the blue suits, we had to leave.	12
Accuracy	2	Brown jars prevented the mixture from freezing too quickly.	12
Numbers	3	No. 101 is 29 mm wide, 38 cm long. It now weighs 47.56 kg.	12
Symbols	4	Add up $1 and $2 and $3 and $4 and $5 and $6 and $7 and $8.	12
Punctuation	5	Martha placed her coat hat scarf and boots in the closet	

| 1 | 2 | 3 | 4 | 5 | 6 | 7 | 8 | 9 | 10 | 11 | 12

PREVIEW PRACTICE

Type each line twice as a preview to the 5-minute timings on page 472.

Accuracy	6	quick examine pleasure citizens comprehensive experimenting
Speed	7	local small their with form that make work them the and for

5-MINUTE TIMINGS

Take two 5-minute timings on lines 8–29 on page 472.

■ GOALS
To identify pronouns and their antecedents while typing sentences.
To type 42/5′/4e.
To format and type a news release.

■ FORMAT
Drills: Single spacing 60-space line
5-Minute Timings: Double spacing 5-space tab

LAB 21

Pronouns

Type lines 1–4 once. Then repeat lines 1–4 or take a series of 1-minute timings. (The pronouns are underscored.)

```
1  Nick has placed his tools in the box inside his new garage.   12
2  Rebecca or Roberta has given her term paper to the teacher.   12
3  The contractors hope that they can change the basic design.   12
4  Peter and I have purchased our tickets for a trip to Yalta.   12
   | 1 | 2 | 3 | 4 | 5 | 6 | 7 | 8 | 9 | 10 | 11 | 12
```

PREVIEW PRACTICE

Type each line twice as a preview to the 5-minute timings below.

```
Accuracy  5  quickly complex hundreds calculate computerize step-by-step
Speed     6  language business problem demand world their since such who
```

5-MINUTE TIMINGS

Take two 5-minute timings on lines 7–24.

```
7       Ever since people began to use numbers, they have been    12
8  looking for ways to count and calculate quickly and simply.    24
9  A device such as the abacus, which was invented hundreds of    36
10 years ago, slowly developed into the modern adding machine.    48
11 The rapid growth in business and technology resulted in the    60
12 need for more complex machines--machines that could do more    72
13 than add--a need met by the modern computer.                   81
14      Although a machine can easily process large amounts of    93
15 information, it can't think for itself.  It is the job of a   105
16 computer programmer to supply the machine with the step-by-   117
17 step instructions that are required in computing a problem.   129
18      These machines are becoming a way of life all over the   141
19 world.  More and more companies are starting to computerize   153
20 all their paperwork; professional programmers, who are able   165
21 to translate such data into machine language, are very much   177
22 in demand.  Since computers have a keyboard similar to your   189
23 typewriter, your knowing how to keyboard by touch gives you   201
24 a big advantage when you work with computers.                 210
   | 1 | 2 | 3 | 4 | 5 | 6 | 7 | 8 | 9 | 10 | 11 | 12        SI 1.58
```

3. Amount of difficulty experienced by students as they completes individual activities.
4. Appropriateness of activities which are designated as group and those designated as individual.
5. Logical brakes suggested between activities.
6. Length of time necessary for achievement of stated objective for each activity.
7. Classroom management of course ware.
8. Evaluation of learning during time period.
9. Comments made by students as they work with the courseware.
10. Suggestions for improvement for various segments of courseware.

D. Courseware will be recommended for adoption or returned for revision and re-testing depending on the results of the initial testing.

E. Courseware recommended for adoption will also contain a provision for teacher in-service.

Page 3

If you are using a typewriter, make a carbon copy; if you are using a computer or word processor, print two copies.

CONTENT GUIDELINES FOR ELEMENTARY SCHOOL

The district curriculum committee has established a district wide continuum for the integration of computer materials in the curriculum. The computer use at the elementary level will focus on Computer-Assisted Instruction (C A I). Courseware written for this level will be those materials which are deemed desirable so that students will have a high quality instruction through the use of the computer.

A. Courseware developed at the elementary level should be materials that will enhance existing learning objectives in the basic education curriculum.

B. Courseware will not be developed in place of existing textbooks and supplementary materials previously adopted by the district curriculum committee.

C. Materials developed should have some provisions for both group and individual activities so that students have the opportunity to develop both individual and group activity skills.

D. If the courseware being developed is of the type that will lead to materials being developed at a lower and/or higher grade level, teachers whom will be effected by the continuum should be involved in the planning.

E. Courseware should be written so that they can be easily adapted to different brands of computers.

F. The major focus of the courseware should be enhancement of reading and math skills with emphasis on high levels of thinking.

G. For ease in duplication of materials, follow these formatting guides.

1. Use a 6 inch line since this is a standard line length for many word processing packages.
2. Use a carbon ribbon if the material are prepared on a typewriter. If a computer is used, provision for copying the disk will need to be made.
3. The first page of the courseware should be a title page which contain the purpose, author(s), and content area.
4. The actual pages of the courseware should be neat, free of typographical errors and grammatical errors, and easy to read by elementary students.

Page 4

Use the copy of page 3. Mark the following changes on page 3, and then type page 4 from your corrected copy. Make one carbon copy of this page if you are using a typewriter. Print two copies of this page if you are using a computer or word processor.

1. *Change title to read* CONTENT GUIDELINES FOR MIDDLE SCHOOL.
2. *In the introductory paragraph change* elementary *to* middle school, *change* Computer Assisted Instruction *to* computer literacy, *and at the end of the sentence, add* as a tool for calculating and writing.
3. *Item A should read* Courseware developed at the middle school level should be materials that will assist the student in reaching objectives in the basic education curriculum in a different way.

(Continued on next page)

FORMATTING NEWS RELEASES

Companies often use news releases when they are releasing a new product or introducing a new service. News releases should contain the following information: Who? What? Why? Where? When? and How?

News releases may be typed on a printed form or on plain paper. To format a news release:

1. Set margins for a 6-inch line (60P/70E). Double-space and indent paragraphs 5 spaces.
2. Type the heading fill-ins aligned with the guide words on a printed form (A), or type the data starting on line 9, aligned at the center tab stop on plain paper (B).
3. Center the title in all-capital letters (C). Leave 3 blank lines before and 2 blank lines after the title.
4. Type a dateline: city, abbreviated date, and a dash before the first sentence (D). Include the state (E) only if the city is not well known or could be confused with a city in another state.
5. Type (*END*) at the end of the release.

News Release (A)

RELEASE: On Receipt
FROM: Carmen Ortega

(C) TYPING IS IMPORTANT IN A NEWS RELEASE

(D) DENVER, Feb. 25--If your latest news release never does appear in print, you might be able to blame your typist.

This is what Henry Lee, wire chief of the Journal Press, told 200 members of the Press Service Club meeting here at the Denver Hilton for their el

"Editors get a hundred or
Lee told his audience. "They
extra inch or two to fill, the
easiest to use without change.
to use."

Lee offered five guides f

1. Use a title line that
2. Tell who released the
whom they can turn for confirm
3. Start the story with
is local. It may hit the big
4. So that editors will
pens, double-space and make ma
5. Be sure the typing is
the news release may not be re

Sumter High School
Sumter, South Carolina 29150

N E W S R E L E A S E (B)

Release: At Once

From: Marie Moulin
Acting Principal

(C) NEW TYPING RECORD FOR SUMTER HIGH

(E) SUMTER, S.C., Mar. 3--Ruth Pendergrass, 18, took the typing honors at the annual Sumter Business Skills Competition by writing 76 words a minute for 10 minutes. Ruth set a new record for Sumter High by breaking Carl Edmonton's 8-year-old record of 74 words a minute.

Runners-up in the contest were Al Harmon, 17, a junior, with 70 words a minute; and Ann Dennis, 18, a senior, with 69 words a minute and a record of making no errors at all.

In the 5-minute contest for students in their first year of typing, first place went to Vic Brill, 16, a tenth grader, with 51 words a minute. In second place was Al Pendergrass, 16-year-old sophomore brother of the champion, with 50. Third place went to Stan Hart, 16, with 48 words a minute. (END)

JOB 179 A. NEWS RELEASE

Edit the copy as you type. (Some details are wrong; check with the original copy on page 297.) [**Hint:** Type a speed draft of the copy on plain paper, and mark corrections on your paper. Retype from your edited copy.] Standard format. Workbook 327–328.

(Release) November 1, 19--
(From) Richard Ginallo
Mayor

Mayor's Tour of Switzerland

Des Moines, Nov. 1--Mayor Richard Ginallo has just returned from Switzerland where he spent two weeks studying the major industries of that country. Mayor Ginallo was the guest of the Legal Department and traveled with 32 other mayors of cities in the United States.

"This trip was a great privilege, and I learned many things we can incorporate into our developmental plan for Des Moines," said Mayor Ginallo at a recent press conference.

The group's first stop was Geneva, headquarters of 61 international bodies, including the International Red Cross.

There are 551 watch-assembling plants in Geneva. Production standards are high, according to the Mayor, and the most exacting work is still done by hand.

The next stop was Baden, where small industries flourish. A master machinist with 27 years experience makes about $6,400 a year. In Basel the group visited several steel factories. According to the Mayor, Switzerland is the largest producer of vitamins in the world.

The group traveled to Zurick, where the mayors visited the headquarters of the Swiss Credit Bank. The name of a numbered-account depositor is known to all the bank

St. Moritz, the next stop, is a recreational resort, where skiing is big business. The last stop was Oppenzell, the center of the farm industry.

"I hope I can return to Switzerland someday," indicated the Mayor. "I want to spend more time with the people who were so wonderful to us."

GENERAL GUIDELINES FOR WRITING

I. Teacher Materials

A. The materials will include objectives for each activity and will state what are to be acomplished and the level of acomplishment.

B. Teaching strategies for acheiving each objective will be stated.

C. Examples of possible alternative ways to present each activity will be listed with accompanying sources.

D. Ways to evaluate ~~the~~ each objective will be stated ~~along~~ with examples of evaluat~~ing~~ion materials.

E. A complete list of other materials which can be correlated with the new courseware will be listed, including computer software, text books, and audiovisual materials.

II. STUDENT materials

A. Student Materials will be constructed in small learning segments which is flexible enough in time span to meet variables at the grade level for which the courseware are to be used.

B. Materials will contain clear learning objectives and steps for completing each activity.

C. Materials will contain directions so that Students will know when each activity have been sucessfully completed and at what level.

D. If an activity requires the use of multiple materials, all items will be listed with suggestions for its location within the school district.

E. Suggestions for reproduction ofthe student materials will be made with examples, if necessary.

Page 2

GUIDELINES FOR TESTING, REVISING, AND ADOPTING

Once the courseware have been wirtten, it must be class room-tested before it can be included in the district curriculum materials.

A. Each item of courseware must be reproduced and used by at least three class room teachers.

B. The three class room teachers should not be in the same building if they is elementary or middle school tests, and they should not be in the same unit if they are high school tests.

C. A daily log of the class room activities will be kept while the courseware is being tested. Specific areas for focus is:

1. Clarity of directions of student materials.
2. Interest level of students while they are working with the courseware.

(Continued on next page)

LESSON 180

■ GOALS
To correct pronoun-antecedent agreement while typing sentences.
To type a synopsis (summary) for a magazine article.

■ FORMAT
Single spacing 60-space line

LAB 21

Pronouns

Type lines 1–4 once, correcting pronouns to ensure pronoun-antecedent agreement. Edit your copy as your teacher reads the answers. Then retype lines 1–4 from your edited copy.

1 Vanessa has put (his/her) new car in the garage for expert tests.
2 In January Mr. and Mrs. Quinto bought (his/her/their) home from Zora.
3 All the teachers have rechecked (his/her/their) classrooms and texts.
4 Mayor Joan West submitted (his/her/their) budget to us early last week.

12-SECOND TIMINGS

Type each line three times, or take three 12-second timings on each line. For each timing, type with no more than 1 error.

5 Holly typed three fewer lines than David thought she would.
6 The builder is fitting panels for them and then going home.
7 Jan and Lena got their dishes and silverware for the party.

5 10 15 20 25 30 35 40 45 50 55 60

JOB 180 A. MAGAZINE ARTICLE

Prepare a synopsis (summary) of the trip report for a magazine article of 150 to 200 words. Use the copy of the trip report you made in Job 178 A, and cross out with a pencil or pen the information that can be left out. Title the article "A Businessman's Tour of Switzerland." Standard format (see page 268).

LESSON 181

CLINIC

■ GOAL
To build competency on number and symbol keys.

■ FORMAT
Drills: Single spacing 60-space line
2-Minute Timings: Double spacing

KEYBOARDING SKILLS

Type lines 1–4 once. Then practice using your shift key as you type line 5. Repeat lines 1–4, or take a series of 1-minute timings.

Speed 1 We want to spend our vacation at one of the national parks. 12
Accuracy 2 Paul reviewed the subject before giving Max and Kay a quiz. 12
Numbers 3 The total of 100, 290, 380, 470, and 560 is easy to figure. 12
Symbols 4 I typed receipts for #10, #29, #38, #47, and #56 on Monday. 12
Technique 5 Ruth Mary Zora Paul Rick Kate Dora Jean Ford Lena Alma Kent

| 1 | 2 | 3 | 4 | 5 | 6 | 7 | 8 | 9 | 10 | 11 | 12

PRACTICE

In the chart below find the number of errors you made on the Pretest on page 462. Then type each of the designated drill lines four times.

Pretest errors	0–1	2–3	4+
Drill lines	28–33	27–32	26–31

Accuracy

26 text skills paragraphs personalize statistical manipulating
27 input fill-in difficult documents innumerable transcription
28 keying doesn't revisions processing calculating typesetting
29 expect utilize requires diskettes repetitive correspondence

Speed

30 usually letters office center format major legal those time
31 which firms other place until final since word need you and
32 copy type that form many take from made most goes one is to
33 than code been the are may can few has of in as it if or an

POSTTEST

Take another 5-minute timing on lines 7–25 on page 462 to see how much your skill has improved.

JOB 289/290 A. WRITING GUIDE

Prepare a final draft of a 5-page writing guide for computer courseware. (*Courseware* is the term used for software used in a classroom to teach a course.) All of the pages contain errors in grammar, such as subject-verb agreement, pronoun-antecedent agreement, misuse of confusing words, and so on. Read each page carefully before you type it. Correct all errors as you type—do *not* write in the book. Format: Use a 6-inch line; begin typing on line 7. Single-space each item and double-space between items. Follow the format illustrated below.

GENERAL GUIDELINES FOR WRITING

I. Teacher Materials

A. The materials will include objectives for each activity and will state what is to be accomplished and the level of accomplishment.

B. Teaching strategies for achieving each objective will be stated.

C. Examples of possible alternative ways to present each activity will be listed with accompanying sources.

D. Ways to evaluate each objective will be stated along with examples of evaluation materials.

E. A complete list of other materials which can be correlated with the new courseware will be listed, including computer software, textbooks, and audiovisual materials.

II. Student Materials

A. Student materials will be constructed in small learning segments which are flexible enough in time span to meet the variables at the grade level for which the courseware is to be used.

B. Materials will contain clear learning objectives and steps for completing each activity.

C. Materials will contain directions so that students will know when each activity has been successfully completed and at what level.

D. If an activity requires the use of multiple materials, all items will be listed with suggestions for their location within the school district.

E. Suggestions for reproduction of the student materials will be made with examples, if necessary.

GUIDELINES FOR TESTING, REVISING, AND ADOPTING

Once the courseware has been written, it must be classroom tested before it can be included in the district curriculum materials.

A. Each item of courseware must be reproduced and used by at least three classroom teachers.

B. The three classroom teachers should not be in the same building if they are elementary or middle school tests, and they should not be in the same unit if they are high school tests.

C. A daily log of the classroom activities will be kept while the courseware is being tested. Specific areas for focus are:

1. Clarity of directions of student materials.
2. Interest level of students while they are working with the courseware.
3. Amount of difficulty experienced by students as they complete individual activities.
4. Appropriateness of activities which are designated as group and those designated as individual ones.
5. Logical breaks suggested between activities.
6. Length of time necessary for achievement of stated objective for each activity.
7. Classroom management of courseware.
8. Evaluation of learning during time period.
9. Comments made by students as they work with the courseware.
10. Suggestions for improvement for various segments of courseware.

D. Courseware will be recommended for adoption or returned for revision and retesting depending on the results of the initial testing.

E. Courseware recommended for adoption will also contain a provision for teacher in-service.

PRETEST 1

Take two 2-minute timings on lines 6–9, or type them twice to find out which number keys are the most difficult for you to type. Keep your eyes on your copy as you type. Circle each digit in which an error is made.

```
6  8123 6110 9102 8972 9019 4327 7286 9413 7283 6089 5369 2648  12
7  8968 9481 7068 9065 0914 2541 7395 7045 5923 8162 7951 5316  24
8  1431 7420 0543 7826 1283 4823 5263 7072 1357 9508 8917 5607  36
9  9065 7084 5603 8954 6250 5613 2364 6051 4378 8942 3145 4703  48
   |  1 |  2 |  3 |  4 |  5 |  6 |  7 |  8 |  9 | 10 | 11 | 12
```

PRACTICE 1

Type lines 10–19 three times. Then repeat any of the lines that stress the digit errors you circled in Pretest 1.

*Omit line 10 if your machine does not have a 1 key in the top row.

```
1  10*  que 173 quo 179 qui 178 que 173 quo 179 quip 1780 quit 1785
2  11   wee 233 wit 285 wow 292 two 529 wet 235 weep 2330 writ 2485
3  12   tee 533 err 344 wee 233 ewe 323 eye 363 peep 0330 ewer 3234
4  13   rye 463 roe 493 rip 480 rot 495 rue 473 pert 0345 ripe 4803
5  14   tot 595 top 590 pot 095 pet 035 pit 085 trot 5495 trip 5480

6  15   yet 635 you 697 yep 630 eye 363 try 546 pity 0856 yore 6943
7  16   rue 473 pup 070 rut 475 out 975 our 974 true 5473 putt 0755
8  17   tie 583 rip 480 pit 085 ire 843 tip 580 pipe 0803 riot 4895
9  18   too 599 woo 299 woe 293 toe 593 top 590 toot 5995 your 6974
0  19   pep 030 pip 080 pup 070 pop 090 pot 095 poor 0994 poet 0935
```

POSTTEST 1

Repeat Pretest 1 to see how much your skill has improved.

PRETEST 2

Take two 2-minute timings on lines 20–23, or type them twice to find out which symbol keys are the most difficult for you to type. Keep your eyes on your copy as you type. Circle each symbol in which an error is made.

```
20  Smith & Blake will lend us $500 at 6% interest if you wish.  12
21  Mr. Bilko wants 59# of sugar @ $1.76, which totals $103.84.  24
22  We got 6 orders @ 18¢, and each one now has a 10% discount.  36
23  Can you find #6887, which has a 6% discount for Reb & Neeb?  48
    |  1 |  2 |  3 |  4 |  5 |  6 |  7 |  8 |  9 | 10 | 11 | 12
```

PRACTICE 2

Type lines 24–30 three times. Then repeat any of the lines that stress the symbol errors you circled in Pretest 2.

```
¢ and @  24  Brett quoted us 400 @ 8¢, but we asked for 400 @ 5¢, right?
¢ and @  25  Raymond finally closed the deal at 939 @ 7¢, plus 585 @ 6¢.
      #  26  John claims Order #31 is for 31#, but Order #34 is for 32#.
% and &  27  Hart & Hill offers a 10% discount; H&H offers at least 15%.
% and &  28  Smith & Lerner offers a 2% discount, or is it Thomas & Roe?
      $  29  Jane has $10; Bob has $29; Ida has $38; and Denny has $470.
      $  30  Take $1, $29, $38, $47, and $56; now total all the figures.
```

POSTTEST 2

Repeat Pretest 2 to see how much your skill has improved.

Cover Letter

Dear ________:
I am enclosing a copy of the first draft of the writing guide for preparing computer courseware for the Elk Central School System. this draft is a result of our last series of meetings. Please read each section of the writing guide, checking them for clarity as well as content. a check sheet have been provided to assist you in completing this task. Our target date for completing the final draft is July 1. You Will need to have reviewed that draft by our June 1 meeting so that us can meet that deadline.
Sincerely. Doris J. Juan, Chairperson

Letter and Label Addresses

Elson Schott, elementary principle, Driscoll School; Carol Clark. elementary teacher, Oakhurst school; Marilee Wilson, principle, Tower Heights Middle School; John Novak, teacher, Chenango Middle school; Malcolm Wegley, Principle, Elk Central High School; Ted Balazs, teacher, Elk Central H. S.

■ **GOALS**
To type 50/5′/3e.
To prepare a final draft of a writing guide while correcting all errors in grammar, typing, and format.

■ **FORMAT**
Drills: Single spacing 60-space line
5-Minute Timings: Double spacing 5-space tab

KEYBOARDING SKILLS

Type lines 1–4 once. Then capitalize the appropriate letters in line 5 as you type it. Repeat lines 1–4, or take a series of 1-minute timings.

Speed	1	Andy may pay me for the bicycle if he is paid for the work.	12
Accuracy	2	Have you queried Jack Flagg about his experiment with zinc?	12
Numbers	3	Janice sold 1234 in June, 3456 in July, and 7890 in August.	12
Symbols	4	Type 1 + 2 − 3 + 4 − 5 + 6 − 7 + 8 − 9 + 10 − 11 + 12 − 13.	12
Capitalization	5	ms. owens met ken vance at the sheridan hotel in texarkana.	
		| 1 | 2 | 3 | 4 | 5 | 6 | 7 | 8 | 9 | 10 | 11 | 12	

PRETEST

Take a 5-minute timing on lines 7–25 on page 462. Circle and count your errors. Use the chart on page 468 to determine which lines to type for practice.

LESSON 182

UNIT 30 Formatting Correspondence

UNIT GOAL 42/5'/4e

■ GOALS
To correct pronoun-antecedent agreement while typing sentences.
To format and type letters with inserts.

■ FORMAT
Single spacing   60-space line

LAB 21
Pronouns

Type lines 1–4 once, correcting pronouns to ensure pronoun-antecedent agreement. Edit your copy as your teacher reads the answers. Then retype lines 1–4 from your edited copy.

1 Dr. Orsina-Quinn and Dr. Davenport published (his/her/their) article.
2 Walter cooks (his/her) own meals and cleans (his/her) house every week.
3 Margarita checks (his/her) work carefully in order to be perfect.
4 Jane and Zia eagerly hope (they/them) will complete (his/her/their) program.

FORMATTING INSERTS IN LETTERS

Sometimes the originator of a letter (the person sending the letter) can use the same copy for several letters simply by adding some information in the body of the letter and changing the inside address and salutation.

JOB 182 A. LETTER WITH INSERTS

Format the letter shown below to Addressee No. 1, and insert (at the points indicated in the letter) the name and station call letters of Addressees No. 2 and No. 3. Standard format. Workbook 329–330. Body 154 words.

Addressee No. 1	**Addressee No. 2**	**Addressee No. 3**
Mr. Ramon Santiago	Ms. Georgia Boggs	Ms. Makiko Komoto
Station Manager	News Director	Editorial Director
WTAM-TV	WKAN-TV	WFTL-TV
6100 Dogwood Road	920 Ocean Drive	700 Sunrise Lane
Hollywood, FL 33021	Miami, FL 33139	Ft. Lauderdale, FL 33304

[*Today's date*] / [*Use inside address of Addressee No. 1.*] / Dear [*Insert name.*]:

I am writing to invite you to serve as a judge for a public speaking contest for students from Florida high schools. This meeting of the state finalists, called Florida Speak-Out, will be sponsored by the Miami Daily on Saturday, March 20. We are also inviting [*insert name and station call letters of Addressee No. 2*] and [*insert name and station call letters of Addressee No. 3*] to serve with you.

The contest will be held at Orlando College from 9 a.m. to 4 p.m., and the state winners will go on to the national competition in Washington, D.C., in April.

This activity has been one of the most successful educational projects we have ever sponsored. Last year more than one hundred young people from across the state competed for honors.

Since you have always been interested in public speaking and have a successful career in the field of television broadcasting, we know that you will be a most competent and well-qualified judge. We hope you will be able to accept our invitation. / Sincerely, / Alda Bitterman / Chairperson, Florida Speak-Out / [*Your initials*]

Rule: Some contractions sound like possessive pronouns.

17 It's good to see that the firm is improving its poor image.
18 (You're/Your) lucky that (you're/your) data was not lost during the outage.

Rule: Abbreviations consisting of a single word require a period at the end; abbreviations made up of single initials in lowercase letters or of academic degrees in capital and lowercase letters are written with periods but no spaces.

19 Redy Corp. will only interview those applicants with a Ph.D.
20 (Mr./Mr) William Wylder (Jr./Jr) scheduled a 1:30 (p.m./pm) staff meeting.

Rule: All-capital abbreviations consisting of single initials use no periods and no spaces. **Exceptions:** Geographic names, academic degrees, and a few miscellaneous expressions, such as *A.D., B.C.,* and *P.O.*

21 She used the CRT to complete much of the work for her M.B.A.
22 Did you know that the (UN/U.N.) building is located in the (USA/U.S.A.)?

Rule: Use a hyphen after the prefix *self, great,* and *quasi* and when the root word begins with a capital letter.

23 The group studying pre-American history was self-appointed.
24 My greatgrandmother is going on the transAmerican flight.

Rule: Some compound nouns are hyphenated and some are not; some are expressed as one word and some as two. Consult your dictionary when you're not sure.

25 She did not notice the double entry in her checkbook today.
26 This clerk typist also answered the vice president's phone.

Rule: Compound adjectives are usually hyphenated when they come before the noun and not hyphenated when they come after the noun.

27 Please prepare an up-to-date spreadsheet to show our plans.
28 The owner said that she wants to erect a 10 story building.

Rule: Homonyms are words that sound alike but are spelled differently and have different meanings; other confusing words look and sound similar.

29 Will they change personal items in their personnel records?
30 I will not (accept/except) any excuses (accept/except) those previously read.

JOBS 288 A AND 288 B. FORM LETTERS AND MAILING LABELS

Standard format. Edit the copy as you type. Workbook 693–706.

1. Prepare a final copy of the cover letter on page 467.
2. If you are using a standard typewriter, you will need six copies of the letter; make five carbon copies or five photocopies.
3. Address the six copies to the people listed below the letter. If you are using a microcomputer or a word processor, use the merge function.
4. Prepare a mailing label for each person. Each of the labels should have the name, title, and school of each committee member. The packages will be sent through the interschool mail.

JOB 182 B. LETTER WITH INSERTS

Type the letter in Job 182 A, and address it to Addressee No. 2. At the places indicated, insert the name and station call letters of Addressees No. 1 and No. 3. Standard format. Workbook 331–332.

JOB 182 C. LETTER WITH INSERTS

Type the letter in Job 182 A, and address it to Addressee No. 3. At the places indicated, insert the name and station call letters of Addressees No. 1 and No. 2. Standard format. Workbook 333–334.

LESSON 183

■ **GOALS**
To type 42/3′/3e.
To format and type from handwritten copy letters with special inserts.

■ **FORMAT**
Drills: Single spacing 60-space line Tabs every 14 spaces
3-Minute Timings: Double spacing 5-space tab

KEYBOARDING SKILLS

Type lines 1–4 once. Type line 5 twice using the tab key to go across from column to column. Then repeat lines 1–4 or take a series of 1-minute timings.

Speed 1 When she got to the lake, the girl paid for the oak panels. 12
Accuracy 2 Jack bought five exquisite bronze bowls at Pam's yard sale. 12
Numbers 3 The books 10, 29, 38, 47, and 56 were destroyed by Katrina. 12
Symbols 4 Please order 490# of #17 fertilizer @ $1.99 before June 10. 12
Technique 5 715 260 864 402 398

| 1 | 2 | 3 | 4 | 5 | 6 | 7 | 8 | 9 | 10 | 11 | 12

PRETEST

Take a 3-minute timing on lines 6–16. Circle and count your errors.

6 It is a well-known fact that progress in understanding 12
7 the human race has fallen far behind the quest for advances 24
8 in science and technology. Employees are taken for granted 36
9 in many offices and shops; and often these workers express, 48
10 in many ways, their frustrations by their behavior--staying 60
11 home from work, using drugs, or being lazy on the job. 71
12 These days businesses pay their workers for counseling 83
13 services as stated in their health insurance. Employers in 95
14 the long run will profit because if workers can solve their 107
15 own home problems, they will become more productive and get 119
16 along better with their co-workers. 126

| 1 | 2 | 3 | 4 | 5 | 6 | 7 | 8 | 9 | 10 | 11 | 12 SI 1.54

PRACTICE

In the chart below find the number of errors you made on the Pretest. Then type each of the designated drill lines (page 305) four times.

Pretest errors	0–1	2–3	4+
Drill lines	19–22	18–21	17–20

LESSON 288

UNIT 47 Lab Application Project

UNIT GOAL 50/5′/3e

GOALS
To use confusing words correctly while typing sentences.
To review LABs 17–34: subject-verb agreement, pronouns, contractions, possessives, abbreviations, hyphenated prefixes, compound nouns, compound adjectives, and confusing words.
To type six copies of a cover letter and mailing labels.

FORMAT
Single spacing 60-space line

LAB 34

Confusing Words

Workbook 689–690.

Type lines 1–4 once, selecting the correct words. Edit your copy as your teacher reads the answers. Then retype lines 1–4 from your edited copy.

1 Betty does not have the (patience, patients) to deal with the (patience, patients).
2 Bob needs the (assistance, assistants) of your (assistance, assistants) on the project.
3 To (ensure, insure) getting seats, you should buy your tickets early.
4 We never interfere with (personal, personnel) problems of our (personal, personnel).

LAB REVIEW

Directions: Read each rule carefully, and then type the two sentences below the rule. Note how the rule is applied in the first sentence; you make corrections in the second sentence so that the rule will be applied in the same way as the first sentence.

Rule: A verb must agree with its subject in number and person.

```
5 The managers buy all their supplies from Chung & Chung Inc.
6 Jim want several more high boxes to store all their files.
```

Rule: Irregular verbs *to be, to do,* and *to have* must agree with noun or pronoun in number and person.

```
7 They don't want to lose any of the data stored on the disk.
8 They is quite interested in learning to operate a machine.
```

Rule: Phrases and clauses between subject and verb do not affect their agreement.

```
9 One of the classes did not choose to help with the project.
10 Each of the members are allowed to select one major project.
```

Rule: Two or more subjects require a plural verb.

```
11 Bryant and Darlene are now at a data processing convention.
12 Both Mary and Fred was selected to be the representatives.
```

Rule: Pronouns must agree with their antecedents.

```
13 Next week all of the students hope that they will earn A's.
14 All members must make his own arrangements for this trip.
```

Rule: A contraction is a shortened form of a phrase in which an apostrophe indicates omitted letters.

```
15 He's going to be the first teacher chosen to orbit in space.
16 It is his dream to develop a classroom in space for everyone.
```

(Continued on next page)

Accuracy

17 human science express benefits advances services co-workers
18 lazy behavior productive businesses counseling frustrations
19 quest because employers technology well-known understanding

Speed

20 productive workers using today that they with for and it by
21 problems, benefits taken part work well gain the end own is
22 progress health being their these more for pay can if or in

POSTTEST Take another 3-minute timing on lines 6–16 on page 304 to see how much your skill has improved.

FORMATTING LISTS/TABLES IN LETTERS

To format a list or a table in the body of a letter, follow these steps:

1. Block-center a list. Horizontally center a table following standard placement rules. Reduce space between columns to keep the table within the margins of the letter.
2. Double-space before and after the list or table.
3. Add 20 words to the body count for the special display.

JOB 183 A. LETTER WITH LIST

Standard format. Workbook 335–336. Body 103 words.

[Today's date] Mr. T. G. Skaff, 11
Jr., 373 West Shore Drive, 16
Wantagh, NY 11793, Dear Mr. 22
Skaff: For under $6—less 29
than an advertisement in your 35
local newspaper—you can 40
reach over 1 million readers 46
in New York City and the 51
surrounding areas to sell 56
numerous items you no 60
longer need or want, such 65
as an automobile or electric 71
appliance. 74
If you're trying to sell 80
your house, you certainly will 86
want to take advantage of the 92
opportunity to reach as many 98
prospective buyers as possible. 104
The Sunday New York Press 116
has classified advertisements 122
that get results. For a real 128
time-saver, call one of 133
these locations: 137

New York	212-555-9300	151
Nassau	516-555-5000	157
Suffolk	516-555-8100	163

Why not telephone us 168
today while you are thinking 174
about it? Yours truly, Suzanne 186
Regina, Director of Advertising, 195
[Your initials] 196

JOB 183 B. LETTER WITH LIST

Standard format. Workbook 337–338. Retype Job 183 A, making the following changes.

Addressee: Mr. and Mrs. Francis Blackwood, 3535 Garden Street, White Plains, NY 10607.

New Jersey	201-555-3090
Westchester	914-555-3600
Connecticut	203-555-7700

Dashes

```
5 Ann's word processor--the CRT--is easy to learn to operate.   12 60
6 I ordered a new word processor--a special standalone model.   24 72
7 Making major changes--text editing--is very quick on a CRT.   36 84
8 Please format this copy--a rough draft--for me before noon.   48 96
  | 1 | 2 | 3 | 4 | 5 | 6 | 7 | 8 | 9 | 10 | 11 | 12
```

PRACTICE 1

In which timing did you make more errors? If in the first one (lines 1–4 on page 463), type lines 9–12 six times and lines 13–16 three times. If most of your errors were in the second timing (lines 5–8), reverse the procedure.

Quotation Marks

```
9  "the" "hay" "and" "men" "for" "pan" "but" "own" "fix" "may"
10 "mat" "vat" "ham" "pat" "tab" "van" "war" "add" "bag" "cab"
11 "palm" "past" "load" "leap" "name" "mark" "hot" "sea" "fad"
12 "loan" "feel" "bale" "dart" "gaze" "bake" "pal" "act" "cat"
```

Dashes

```
13 the--now--for--and--for--but--may--too--was--had--its--will
14 text--very--easy--word--part--name--gaze--jump--time--vines
15 major--order--makes--blind--learn--asked--drive--such--call
16 check--lives--finds--while--yours--dates--keyed--week--when
```

POSTTEST 1

Repeat Pretest 1 on page 463 and above to see how much your skill has improved.

PRETEST 2

Take a 2-minute timing on lines 17–20; then take a 2-minute timing on lines 21–24. Circle and count your errors on each.

Periods

```
17 Jamie Tymes is very busy.  She works for a big health firm.   12
18 Robert paid for the audit and for a map.  He paid the city.   24
19 Lois bought a membership.  She likes to go to the new spas.   36
20 Ben is at the store.  He is paying for groceries they sent.   48
```

Question Marks

```
21 Did they blame the cat?  Did they blame her for the attack?   12
22 Why did he give away that money?  Did he owe it to someone?   24
23 What is the theme?  Is it apt to irk the ones on the panel?   36
24 When did the salesperson come?  Did she explain the design?   48
   | 1 | 2 | 3 | 4 | 5 | 6 | 7 | 8 | 9 | 10 | 11 | 12
```

PRACTICE 2

In which timing did you make more errors? If in the first one (lines 17–20), type lines 25–28 six times and lines 29–32 three times. If most of your errors were in the second timing (lines 21–24), reverse the procedure.

Periods

```
25 goal.   pale.   rush.   theme.   usual.   visit.   world.   theme.
26 gown.   name.   form.   eight.   dozen.   audit.   chair.   black.
27 gave.   give.   gull.   seven.   nurse.   claim.   bored.   table.
28 ride.   step.   play.   drill.   third.   giant.   finds.   basic.
```

Question Marks

```
29 rush?   rich?   push?   claim?   dials?   angle?   panel?   doors?
30 worn?   burn?   coin?   shell?   onion?   rifle?   hopes?   score?
31 clue?   noun?   blue?   milky?   fight?   ivory?   giant?   forms?
32 honk?   torn?   hymn?   pupil?   towns?   shake?   garbs?   nylon?
```

POSTTEST 2

Repeat Pretest 2 to see how much your skill has improved.

■ GOALS
To recognize the correct use of pronouns while typing sentences.
To format and type form letters with inserts.

■ FORMAT
Single spacing 60-space line

Pronouns

Type lines 1–4 once. Then repeat lines 1–4 or take a series of 1-minute timings.

```
1  Our teacher said that you can learn geometry easier than I.   12
2  It is very important to us, Maria and me, to pass the test.   12
3  We students must make every effort to become good citizens.   12
4  The member of whom I am speaking will resign from the club.   12
   | 1 | 2 | 3 | 4 | 5 | 6 | 7 | 8 | 9 | 10 | 11 | 12
```

Pronouns, like nouns, can be used as subjects (nominative case), as objects (objective case), or to show possession (possessive case).

Nominative case: I, you, he, she, it, who, we, they
Objective case: me, you, him, her, it, whom, us, them
Possessive case: my/mine, your/yours, his, her/hers, its, our/ours, their/theirs, whose

When a pronoun identifies a noun or another pronoun, it can be in the nominative, objective, or possessive case, depending on how the antecedent is used.

The last people to get to the party were Pat and I. (Pat and I were)
The books belonged to us, Tim and me. (*us* is objective; therefore, *me* is objective)
The computers were ours, Alice's and mine. (possessive)

When a pronoun follows the word *than* or *as* in a comparison, you can determine the correct case if you think about the missing words.

You want to go to the library more than she. (than she wants to go)
I want you to bowl with us rather than her. (than I want her to bowl)
She cannot sing as high as I. (as high as I can sing)

12-SECOND TIMINGS

Type each line three times, or take three 12-second timings on each line. For each timing, type with no more than 1 error.

```
5  Mitchell can type a lot faster on these sentences than she.
6  Sue says that she can fix the vase that fell from her desk.
7  The four of them had to get to the bus by the time it left.
```

FORMATTING FORM LETTERS

When one message is to be sent to many people, form letters are very effective. The form letter can be typed without the date, inside address, and salutation, and copies can then be printed. The typist can then add the date, inside address, and salutation to each letter.

Word processing equipment, often called *text-editing* or *automatic* typewriters, can be used for form letters. The letter is recorded while it is keyboarded, and then the equipment "plays back" the recording at high speeds. Codes at key places allow the typist to insert the date,

(Continued on next page)

REQUESTS FOR MEDICARE PAYMENT

This form was designed by the Social Security Administration for services covered by Medicare.

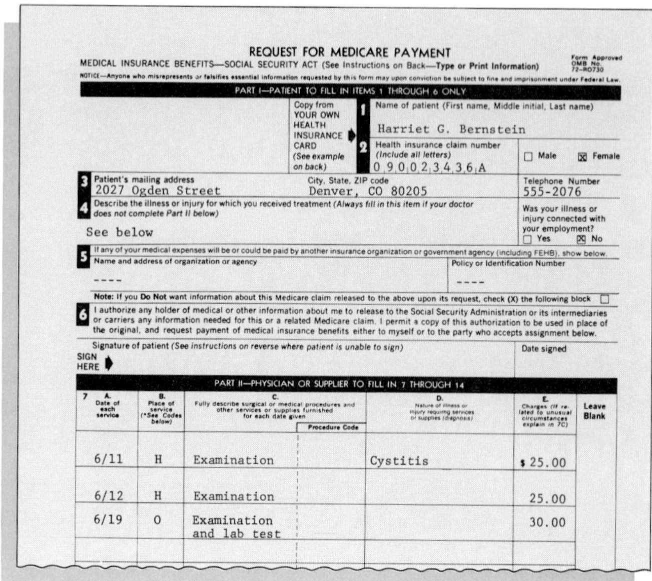

REQUEST FOR MEDICARE PAYMENT

MEDICAL INSURANCE BENEFITS—SOCIAL SECURITY ACT (See Instructions on Back—**Type or Print Information**)

Form Approved OMB No. 72-RO730

NOTICE—Anyone who misrepresents or falsifies essential information requested by this form may upon conviction be subject to fine and imprisonment under Federal Law.

PART I—PATIENT TO FILL IN ITEMS 1 THROUGH 6 ONLY

Copy from YOUR OWN HEALTH INSURANCE CARD (See example on back)

1 Name of patient (First name, Middle initial, Last name): Harriet G. Bernstein

2 Health insurance claim number (Include all letters): 0 9 0 0 2 3 4 3 6 A — ☐ Male ☒ Female

3 Patient's mailing address: 2027 Ogden Street — City, State, ZIP code: Denver, CO 80205 — Telephone Number: 555-2076

4 Describe the illness or injury for which you received treatment (*Always fill in this item if your doctor does not complete Part II below*): See below — Was your illness or injury connected with your employment? ☐ Yes ☒ No

5 If any of your medical expenses will be or could be paid by another insurance organization or government agency (including FEHB), show below.
Name and address of organization or agency: ---- — Policy or Identification Number: ----

Note: If you **Do Not** want information about this Medicare claim released to the above upon its request, check (X) the following block ☐

6 I authorize any holder of medical or other information about me to release to the Social Security Administration or its intermediaries or carriers any information needed for this or a related Medicare claim. I permit a copy of this authorization to be used in place of the original, and request payment of medical insurance benefits either to myself or to the party who accepts assignment below.

Signature of patient (*See instructions on reverse where patient is unable to sign*) SIGN HERE — Date signed

PART II—PHYSICIAN OR SUPPLIER TO FILL IN 7 THROUGH 14

7 A. Date of each service	B. Place of service (*See Codes below)	C. Fully describe surgical or medical procedures and other services or supplies furnished for each date given	Procedure Code	D. Nature of illness or injury requiring services or supplies (diagnosis)	E. Charges (If related to unusual circumstances explain in 7C)	Leave Blank
6/11	H	Examination		Cystitis	$ 25.00	
6/12	H	Examination			25.00	
6/19	O	Examination and lab test			30.00	

JOBS 286 A TO 286 C. REQUESTS FOR MEDICARE PAYMENT

Complete a form for each of the following three patients. Use the illustration above as a guide. Workbook 683–688.

A. Ron Erimore, 78 Canyon Rd., Denver 80237, Medicare claim number 072-34-9873A, received special diet for diabetes mellitus on June 3, (O). The doctor's charge was $65. The patient paid $5, and the unpaid balance is $60. The physician is Dr. Martino [*clinic address: Trail Ridge Clinic, 83 Skyline Drive, Denver, CO 80215*].

B. Linda Wick, Apartment 4, 31 Rawlins Rd., Denver 80219, Medicare claim number 839-29-72859B, received treatment for pneumonia from June 1 through June 14, (H). The doctor's charge was $450. The patient paid $25, and the unpaid balance is $425. The physician is Dr. Oakley [*use clinic address*].

C. Donna Courtney, 45 Sunshine Court, Denver 80212, Medicare claim number 084-94-8293B, received treatment for arthritis on May 4, (O). The doctor's charge was $73, and the patient paid $5. The unpaid balance is $68. The physician is Dr. Ulrich [*use clinic address*].

LESSON 287

CLINIC

■ GOAL
To improve technique in typing quotation marks, dashes, periods, and question marks.

■ FORMAT
Drills: Single spacing 60-space line
2-Minute Timings: Double spacing

KEYBOARDING SKILLS Type lines 1–4 on page 457 three times each.

PRETEST 1 Take a 2-minute timing on lines 1–4; then take a 2-minute timing on lines 5–8 on page 464. Circle and count your errors on each.

Quotation Marks

```
1  The so-called "expert" on finance is our manager, Mr. Lang.   12  60
2  Ellen gave a firm "no" when asked if she planned to retire.   24  72
3  Read the third chapter, "Planning," when you have time, Al.   36  84
4  Rejecting the offer was, as he pointed out, "discourteous."   48  96
   | 1 | 2 | 3 | 4 | 5 | 6 | 7 | 8 | 9 | 10 | 11 | 12
```

(*Continued on next page*)

inside address, salutation, and any other "personalized" information.

To format the form letter, allow space for the date, inside address, and salutation. Begin the body of the letter on line 26.

JOB 184 A. FORM LETTER

Standard format. Make four carbon copies for use in Job 184 B. Workbook 339–348. Body 138 words.

Congradulations! You are a winner in the Bold journey contest 13
sponsored by Outdoor Magazine. As you know, you have quali- 31
fied for to attend the outdoor Adventure camp this summer at 43
at Big Brnach, Uah. 47

Outdoor magazine is proud to ward you this all-expenses-paid 67
vacation and we hope that you looking foreward to joining the 80
other 75 students a cross the country who were also winners. 94
You have been assinged to attend during the week of (*allow 14* 105
blank spaces here to insert the date). Later we will send you 113
all the detials consserning you travel plans, equipment and the 126
type of clothing you shuld 130
should bring. the group leaders at big Branch have planned 142
for you an exciting shedule of mountain climing, horse back 155
riding, and white water rafting. in the meantime, we hopeyou 167
will read the articles which will appear monthly in Outdoor 186
Magazine. / Sincerly, / Bruno T. Di Sibio / editor in chief / 207
[*Your initials*] 208

Computers and word processors have a "merge" function. An operator can code two documents such as a mailing list and a form letter. The computer will automatically address the letters to the names on the mailing list.

FORMATTING INSERTS ON FORM LETTERS

To fill in the date, inside address, and salutation on a form letter, follow these steps:

1. Type the date at the center, using standard format.
2. Space down to the first line of text, and align the copy vertically and horizontally.
3. Count the total lines—usually 6—that you will need for the inside address (3 lines plus 1 blank) and the salutation (1 line plus 1 blank).
4. Roll the copy back the number of lines you counted in Step 3, and type the information. If you have a machine with vertical half spacing, make sure you roll back 2 clicks for every line determined in Step 3.

JOB 184 B. FORM LETTER INSERTS

Address the letters you prepared in Job 184 A to the people listed below. Add a personalized salutation to each letter, and insert the date in paragraph 2.

1. Harvey Cepekski, 100 Coconut Creek Boulevard, Pompano Beach, FL 33066 [*Insert*] July 1–7.
2. Victoria Johnson, 2400 Canal Street, New Orleans, LA 70119 [*Insert*] July 8–14.
3. Peter Schmitt, 12 Iron Way, Marlborough, MA 01752 [*Insert*] July 15–21.
4. Sally Ramando, 290 Main Street, East Greenwich, RI 02818 [*Insert*] July 22–28.
5. Clifford Griffith, 4200 Dickinson Street, Charleston, WV 25301 [*Insert*] July 22–28.

LESSON 286

■ **GOALS**
To use confusing words correctly while typing sentences.
To type 50/5′/3e.
To type requests for Medicare payments.

■ **FORMAT**
Drills: Single spacing 60-space line
5-Minute Timings: Double spacing 5-space tab

LAB 34

Confusing Words

Type lines 1–4 once, selecting the correct words. Edit your copy as your teacher reads the answers. Then retype lines 1–4 from your edited copy.

1 Please be sure you have (patience, patients) when training a new puppy.
2 Since I was not sure, I asked Jennifer for some (assistance, assistants).
3 It's certainly a good idea to (ensure, insure) all of your valuables.
4 The (personal, personnel) department asked for two (personal, personnel) references.

PREVIEW PRACTICE

Type each line twice as a preview to the 5-minute timings below.

Accuracy 5 `expect utilize require statistical personalize manipulating`
Speed 6 `which firms other those major final since word form may the`

5-MINUTE TIMINGS

Take two 5-minute timings on lines 7–25.

7 If you accept a position as a word processing operator in a center or in an 16
8 office, you can expect input to arrive in different ways. Standard transcrip- 32
9 tion of documents and correspondence which doesn't need revision usually 46
10 requires extra time. Another type of input is correspondence that's primar- 61
11 ily repetitive in content. Insurance firms and legal offices utilize form 76
12 letters, fill-in forms, and many other documents that are repetitive in con- 91
13 tent. 92
14 Multiple revision documents are those which undergo an enormous 106
15 amount of text editing. Innumerable revisions may take place from the time 121
16 the original copy is keyed until a final copy is keyed. Format and content 136
17 which receive many major changes require more skills in keying. Docu- 150
18 ments can be composed from standard paragraphs stored on diskettes to be 165
19 recalled later. Very few changes are made since each of the paragraphs has 180
20 been heavily edited before. The changes which are made are those made to 195
21 personalize the documents. 200
22 The most difficult keying is that of statistical documents and typesetting 216
23 related skills. Skill in calculating the placement and skill in manipulating 232
24 the data as it goes on the screen are needed. Other records may need more 247
25 than one code. 250

| 1 | 2 | 3 | 4 | 5 | 6 | 7 | 8 | 9 | 10 | 11 | 12 | 13 | 14 | 15 SI 1.74

■ GOALS
To identify the correct use of pronouns while typing sentences.
To format and type form letters from programmed paragraphs.

■ FORMAT
Single spacing   60-space line

LAB 22

Pronouns

Type lines 1–4 once. Then repeat lines 1–4 or take a series of 1-minute timings. (The pronouns are underscored.)

1 Sue is a super person; she can do everything better than I. 12
2 Pete asked us, you and me, to go to the ball game with him. 12
3 I asked Jerry if he knew who was going to the band concert. 12
4 I asked Alice for whom had she bought band concert tickets. 12

| 1 | 2 | 3 | 4 | 5 | 6 | 7 | 8 | 9 | 10 | 11 | 12

30-SECOND "OK" TIMINGS

Type as many 30-second "OK" (errorless) timings as possible out of three attempts on lines 5–7.

5 Quite by chance you may have seen a person of the other sex 12
6 do a crazy thing. You want to explode in laughter, but you 24
7 just smile. The other person smiles back. You feel great. 36

| 1 | 2 | 3 | 4 | 5 | 6 | 7 | 8 | 9 | 10 | 11 | 12

FORMATTING PROGRAMMED PARAGRAPHS FOR FORM LETTERS

To give form letters greater personalization and variety, and at the same time to prepare letters quickly, many companies develop a variety of opening, middle, and closing paragraphs for each type of form letter. The originator or writer merely chooses the appropriate paragraphs and gives this information to the typist along with the name and address of each person who is to receive that letter.

JOBS 185 A TO 185 D. FORM LETTERS

Prepare four form letters from standard paragraphs. Closing: *Sincerely, Amanda T. Brown, Personnel Director.* Standard format. Workbook 349–356. Body varies.

A. Address a letter to Ms. Tina Parker, 2 Crescent Place, Oceanport, NJ 07757. Use paragraphs 2, 6, and 8. (81 words)

B. Address a letter to Mr. Abraham C. Clark, 183 Union Avenue, Memphis, TN 38103. Use paragraphs 1, 4, and 7. (103 words)

C. Address a letter to Ms. Doris Davella, P.O. Box 600, Phoenix, AZ 85001. Use paragraphs 3, 5, and 8. (73 words)

D. Address a letter to Dr. Marshall Oliver, 737 29th Street, Boulder, CO 80303. Use paragraphs 1, 6, and 9. (74 words)

Opening Paragraphs

1. Thank you for thinking of Lively Arts as a magazine for which you would be interested in working. There are many exciting careers in the publishing business for people with talent and ambition.

2. We have received your letter of application, and we thank you for thinking of Lively Arts as the magazine with which you would like to begin your publishing career.

3. Your letter of application has been reviewed by our editorial staff and by our graphic arts staff.

(Continued on next page)

12-SECOND TIMINGS

Type each line three times, or take three 12-second timings on each line. For each timing, type without error.

5 We do not know yet all that we would like to know about it.

6 He could go if he wanted to, but he wished to stay at home.

7 I can drive the new car to the field and meet their flight.

5 10 15 20 25 30 35 40 45 50 55 60

GROUP HOSPITAL INSURANCE FORMS

Insurance forms are prepared by medical typists and sent to insurance companies for charges incurred by policyholders or by members of their families.

GROUP HOSPITAL INSURANCE FORM

To Trail Ridge Clinic Hospital. This certifies that Betty O'Brien is insured for the following Group Hospital Benefits (in behalf of his or her dependent Self (Name) ---- (Relationship)) By Colorado Security Insurance Company (Name of Insurer)

BENEFITS FOR MATERNITY CASES	BENEFITS FOR OTHER THAN MATERNITY CASES
HOSPITAL ROOM AND BOARD (INCLUDING GENERAL NURSING SERVICE) AND OTHER HOSPITAL SERVICES . . . ACTUAL CHARGES UP TO $ ______ OR 1. HOSPITAL ROOM AND BOARD (INCLUDING GENERAL NURSING SERVICES) $______ FOR EACH DAY OF HOSPITALIZATION UP TO ______ DAYS 2. OTHER HOSPITAL CHARGES FOR HOSPITAL CARE AND TREATMENT (EXCLUDING CHARGES FOR NURSES' AND PHYSICIANS' SERVICES AND TAKE-HOME DRUGS) $______	A. HOSPITAL ROOM AND BOARD (INCLUDING GENERAL NURSING SERVICES) ACTUAL HOSPITAL CHARGES UP TO $ 90.00 FOR EACH DAY OF HOSPITALIZATION UP TO 90 DAYS. B. OTHER HOSPITAL CHARGES FOR HOSPITAL CARE AND TREATMENT (EXCLUDING CHARGES FOR NURSES' AND PHYSICIANS' SERVICES AND TAKE-HOME DRUGS) $ No limit

GROUP POLICYHOLDER	ADDRESS	PHONE
Adams Department Store	1496 Broadway Street, Denver, CO 80203	555-0214
BY (Name and Title) ----	ABOVE CERTIFICATION VALID FOR ONLY SEVEN DAYS FROM THIS DATE (Exception—Maternity Cases)	DATE ----

HOSPITAL COMPLETE FOLLOWING AND FURNISH COPY TO Adams Department Store — ADDRESS See above

NAME OF PATIENT	AGE	DATE ADMITTED	TIME ADMITTED	DATE DISCHARGED	TIME DISCHARGED
Betty O'Brien	60	6/12/--	2:30 PM	6/30/--	11:15 AM

DIAGNOSIS FROM RECORDS (If Injury, Give Date and Place of Accident)
Cerebrovascular spasm and generalized arteriosclerosis

OPERATIONS OR OBSTETRICAL PROCEDURES PERFORMED (Nature and Date)
None

HOSPITAL CHARGES (Complete This Section or Attach Copy of Itemized Bill Showing Information Below)

ROOM AND BOARD	☐ WARD DAYS AT $ TOTAL	$	TOTAL CHARGES	$1,546.50
	☒ SEMIPRIVATE 18 DAYS AT $ 75.00 TOTAL	$1,350.00	Patient Credit	$ 36.00
	☐ PRIVATE DAYS AT $ TOTAL	$		$
	☐ OTHERS	$	Balance Due	$1,510.50
OTHER CHARGES	OPERATING OR DELIVERY ROOM			
	ANESTHESIA			
	X-RAY	50.00		
	LABORATORY			
	EKG BMR	35.00		
	PHYSICAL THERAPY			
	AMBULANCE			
	MEDICAL AND SURGICAL SUPPLIES			
	PHARMACY (Except Take-Home Drugs)	75.50		
	INHALATION THERAPY			
	INTRAVENOUS SOLUTIONS			
	Television	36.00		
	TOTAL	$1,546.50		

HOSPITAL Trail Ridge Clinic — ADDRESS 83 Skyline Drive, Denver, CO 80215

TAKEN FROM RECORDS ON (Current date) 19-- — SIGNED BY

AUTHORIZATION TO RELEASE INFORMATION: I hereby authorize the above-named hospital to release the information requested on this form.

Date ______, 19____ Signed ______________ Patient (Parent if a Minor)

AUTHORIZATION TO PAY INSURANCE BENEFITS: I hereby authorize payment directly to the above-named hospital of the Group Hospital Benefits herein specified and otherwise payable to me but not to exceed the hospital's regular charges for this period of hospitalization. I understand I am financially responsible to the hospital for charges not covered by this authorization.

Date ______, 19____ Signed ______________ (Insured)

JOBS 285 A TO 285 C. GROUP HOSPITAL INSURANCE FORMS

Using the data provided for the three patients listed in the next column, complete a form for each patient. Use the illustration above as a guide. Workbook 677–682.

A. Dennis Dieterlie's son, Joe, who is 9 years old, fell off the swing at school on May 10 and was admitted to Trail Ridge Clinic, Denver, CO, at 11 a.m. Joe broke his left ankle. Mr. Dieterlie's insurance provides coverage of $85 a day for 70 days. He works at Mountain Electric on 3894 Aspen Lane in Denver, CO 80204. Joe was discharged on May 11 at 10 a.m. with charges of $90 for a semiprivate room, $100 for surgical costs, and $75 for lab costs. *Insurance company:* Health Plan of America; *clinic address:* 83 Skyline Drive, Denver 80215.

B. Paula Ruppert, who is 40, was in an automobile accident on May 12 and was admitted to the clinic at 8:45 p.m. with facial lacerations. Insurance provides for $85 a day for 70 days. She works as a counselor at Denver High School on 2625 Main Street in Denver, CO 80208. Paula was discharged on May 13 at 9:30 a.m. with charges of $90 for a semiprivate room; $100 for the doctor's fee, and $40 for medical and surgical supplies. *Insurance company:* AllCo Insurance.

C. Yolanda Padilla, who is 18, was burned while grilling meat on May 15 and was admitted to the clinic at 7:30 p.m. Insurance provides $95 a day for 60 days. She is a homemaker, and her husband, John, works at the Giant Warehouse at 75 Hoke Road, Denver, CO 80207. Yolanda was discharged on May 17 at 10 a.m. with charges of $125 a day for a private room and $200 for medical and surgical supplies. The doctor's fee was $100. *Insurance company:* Union Health and Life.

Middle Paragraphs

4. There are no openings for writers at the present time. However, we will keep your letter of application in our active files; if an opening occurs in the next few months, we will certainly contact you.
5. We do not have a need for new writers now. We hope, however, to expand our Advertising Department in a few months if our sales continue to grow.
6. At the present time we have no openings for staff writers. We are, however, impressed with your résumé, and we hope that you will not be discouraged.

Closing Paragraphs

7. We hope that you will continue to pursue your ambition to be a magazine writer. You have excellent credentials, which will be a great asset to you as you search for a promising position.
8. Why not give us a call in three or four months if you are still interested in seeking employment in our Advertising or Creative Arts Department?
9. Our best wishes to you for success in locating a job that meets your expectations.

LESSON 186

- GOALS
  To use pronouns correctly while typing sentences.
  To type 42/5'/4e.
  To compose form letters.
- FORMAT
  Drills: Single spacing 60-space line
  5-Minute Timings: Double spacing 5-space tab

LAB 22

Pronouns

Type lines 1–4 once, selecting the pronoun to ensure pronoun-case agreement.

```
1 It is up to (we/us) students to determine the assembly programs.
2 Peter said that you and (he/him) were going to the football game.
3 It is essential that we, Mark and (I/me), get to school on time.
4 I cannot believe that he was the one (who/whom) won the big prize.
```

PREVIEW PRACTICE

Type lines 5 and 6 on page 299 as a preview to the 5-minute timings on page 299.

5-MINUTE TIMINGS

Take two 5-minute timings on lines 7–24 on page 299.

JOBS 186 A AND 186 B. LETTERS FROM INCOMPLETE COPY

Use the programmed paragraphs on page 308 and above. Change as many words as you can in the paragraphs so that you are composing some of the letters. If possible, add a paragraph that you compose entirely. Complimentary closing: *Cordially yours.* Use your own name as writer. Your title: *Assistant to the Editor.* Standard format with indented paragraphs. Workbook 357–360.

A. Address a letter to Mrs. Anna Verdi, 745 Washington Street, Marblehead, MA 01945. Use paragraphs 1, 6, and 9.

B. Address a letter to Mr. Pierre Dutou, 140 Barclay Lane, Cherry Hill, NJ 08034. Use paragraphs 3, 4, and 7.

OUTPATIENT RECORD

A record of patients treated at a clinic or hospital but not required to stay overnight is kept on a card. Each subsequent visit is also recorded.

OUTPATIENT RECORD

Family Name	First Name	Middle Initial	Sex	Marital Status (M S W D Sep.)	Age—Yrs.	Birth Date (Mo. Day Yr.)	Home Phone
Budich	Larry		M F	M S W D Sep.	74	5 9 08	555-3857

Address	Nationality	Occupation
18 Glencoe Street, Denver, CO 80220		Retired

Employer or Employer of Spouse	Address of Employer—Phone

Personal History

Patient has acute allergy to bee stings.

Present Illness

Stung by bee while working in yard.

Physical Examination

Patient exhibited some reaction to sting when brought to clinic, but first aid administered at scene kept allergy under control.

Remarks

DATE	TREATMENT	PHYSICIAN
8/21/--	First aid administered at scene. Patient was checked for further complications and released.	Dr. Oakley

JOBS 284 A AND 284 B. OUTPATIENT RECORDS

Using the data for the two patients listed below, complete a form for each patient. Use the illustrations on the left as a guide. Workbook 675–676.

A. Marie Belpalsi; Phone 555-6403; Age 36; Birthdate 2/8/53. Lives at 45 Evergreen, Denver, CO 80204, and is a nurse. Personal History: Patient is a healthy female. Present Illness: Lacerated left thumb from broken test tube in lab at Trail Ridge Clinic, on May 19. Physical Examination: Patient showed a wound about 2 inches long and almost ¼ inch deep. Wound was disinfected, sutured, and bandaged. Dr. Chuang.

B. Fred Caton; Phone 555-9385; Age 30; Birthdate 2/9/57. Lives at Route 1, Fort Collins, CO 80521, and is a flagman. Personal History: Patient is a healthy male. Present Illness: Snakebite on left ankle occurred on Trail Ridge Road on afternoon of May 19. Physical Examination: Patient showed a bite about ¼ inch deep. Venom was extracted from wound and injection was given immediately to counteract poison. Wound was bandaged. Dr. Ulrich.

- GOALS
  To identify the correct use of confusing words while typing sentences.
  To type group hospital insurance forms.
- FORMAT
  Single spacing 60-space line

LAB 34

Confusing Words

Type lines 1–4 once. Then repeat lines 1–4 or take a series of 1-minute timings.

```
1 We do not have enough beds to accommodate the new patients.  12
2 My two medical assistants are qualified to give assistance.  12
3 Donald has no idea how much it costs to insure his new car.  12
4 The personnel records could contain several personal items.  12
  | 1 | 2 | 3 | 4 | 5 | 6 | 7 | 8 | 9 | 10 | 11 | 12
```

LESSON

187

CLINIC

■ GOALS
To type copy that reinforces skill in using the space bar, tabulator, shift key, and margin release.
To type 42/3′/3e.

■ FORMAT
Drills: Single spacing 60-space line
3-Minute Timings: Double spacing 5-space tab

KEYBOARDING SKILLS

Type lines 1–4 once. Then practice using your space bar as you type line 5. Repeat lines 1–4, or take a series of 1-minute timings.

```
Speed       1 The man got a snap of a very large whale by the big island.   12
Accuracy    2 Six jumbo elephants quickly moved the wagon from the blaze.   12
Numbers     3 He has 10 or 29.  She has 38 or 47.  I have 10 or maybe 56.   12
Symbols     4 Do you know whether the B/L (bill of lading) has been sent?   12
Technique   5 a b c d e f g h i j k l m n o p q r s t u v w x y z . , / ?
              | 1 | 2 | 3 | 4 | 5 | 6 | 7 | 8 | 9 | 10 | 11 | 12
```

PRETEST

Type lines 6–11 twice. To force the use of the margin release key at the end of each line, set margins (**M**) for a 60-space line exactly (do not add 5). Keep your eyes on the copy.

```
                                                          ↓
                                                       Reset M
 6      We are fortunate today that Beth Mason, the famous inventor
 7 of ERASE-EZ paper, is scheduled to speak at our fall conference.
 8      Welcome, Dr. Mason, to Washington, D.C., our great capital!
 9      We all hope Dr. Mason will tell us how she created ERASE-EZ
10 and what it will do to make our typing jobs easier--yes, easier.
11      Ladies and Gentlemen, Dr. Beth Mason, and her new ERASE-EZ.
```

PRACTICE

Set a tab (**T**) every tenth space; then type lines 12–14 twice, tabbing and backspacing to make each column of decimals align at the decimal point, as shown here.

Tabulator

```
   M       T         T         T         T         T
12 1     101.0      20.2     101.1      10.0       0.6
13 2      20.1     101.18      2.0       2.21     22.22
14 3       3.6      30.2     203.19    334.0       1.31
```

Shift Key

Type lines 15–17 twice.

```
15 A An Ann B Bo Bob C Ca Cal D Da Dan E Ev Eve F Fa Fay G Gus
16 H Ha Hal I Id Ida J Ji Jim K Ka Kay L Li Liz M Ma Mat N Ned
17 O Ol Oli P Pa Pat R Ra Rae S Sa Sam T Te Ted V Va Val W Wes
```

Margin Release

Set margins for an exact 55-space line. Then type lines 18–21 twice.

```
                                                      ↓
                                                   Reset M
18      I hope to get on the bus by two o'clock.  If I miss my
19 ride, I must take the next bus.  It may not be here by two,
20 and that means that I will have to take my car for the day.
21 Do you think we'll find a place to leave your auto in town?
```

POSTTEST

Repeat the Pretest to see how much your skill has improved.

TIMINGS

Repeat the 3-minute Pretest/Practice/Posttest routine on pages 304 and 305.

■ **GOALS**
To recognize the correct use of confusing words while typing sentences.
To improve technique in typing parentheses and hyphens.
To type outpatient records.

■ **FORMAT**
Drills: Single spacing 60-space line
2-Minute Timings: Double spacing

LAB 34

Confusing Words

Type lines 1–4 once. Then repeat lines 1–4 or take a series of 1-minute timings.

```
1  If you need further assistance, my assistants will be here.  12
2  To ensure your family's safety, you must insure your house.  12
3  Dealing with the many patients in hospitals takes patience.  12
4  The personnel department has all employees' personal files.  12
   | 1 | 2 | 3 | 4 | 5 | 6 | 7 | 8 | 9 | 10 | 11 | 12
```

assistance: help, aid
assistants: those who help

ensure: to make certain
insure: to protect against loss

patience: composure, endurance
patients: sick people

personal: private
personnel: the staff

PRETEST

Take a 2-minute timing on lines 5–8; then take a 2-minute timing on lines 9–12. Circle and count your errors on each.

Parentheses

```
5  All classes meet two days a week (Tuesdays and Wednesdays).  12 60
6  At the time of the merger (1980), they needed more support.  24 72
7  Send the following:  (1) sweater, (2) pants, and (3) socks.  36 84
8  Your paper needs several revisions (see attached comments).  48 96
```

Hyphens

```
9  Her brother-in-law has written a first-class mystery novel.  12 60
10 Shawn is a well-qualified candidate for the director's job.  24 72
11 The question-and-answer period on Tuesday was very popular.  36 84
12 We purchased several 3- by 4-meter rugs for our main house.  48 96
   | 1 | 2 | 3 | 4 | 5 | 6 | 7 | 8 | 9 | 10 | 11 | 12
```

PRACTICE

In which timing did you make more errors? If in the first one (lines 5–8), type lines 13–16 six times and lines 17–20 three times. If most of your errors were in the second timing (lines 9–12), reverse the procedure.

Parentheses

```
13 (0) (1) (2) (3) (4) (5) (6) (7) (8) (9) (10) (11) (12) (13)
14 (and) (for) (the) (cot) (let) (sit) (tie) (tow) (jam) (ham)
15 (for it is) (and it is) (is it for) (is it the) (let it be)
16 (how it is) (if it was) (can it be) (is it one) (yes or no)
```

Hyphens

```
17 question-and-answer black-out snow-covered ice-clad up-down
18 wind-swept antique-like small-sized for-against well-marked
19 well-qualified paper-and-pencil up-to-date on-off down-hill
20 mothers-in-law fathers-in-law sisters-in-law brother-in-law
```

POSTTEST

Repeat the Pretest to see how much your skill has improved.

LESSON 188

UNIT 31 Formatting Tables

UNIT GOAL 42/5'/4e

■ GOALS
To use pronouns correctly while typing sentences.
To format and type two-page tables.

■ FORMAT
Single spacing   60-space line

LAB 22

Pronouns

Workbook 361–362.

Type lines 1–4 once, selecting the pronoun to ensure pronoun-case agreement.

```
1  It is important for us, Sally and (I/me), to get there on time.
2  (Who/Whom) did they say was going to be this year's valedictorian?
3  Those teams did not score as many points in the game as (we/us).
4  We will win, Marcia and (I/me), if we can manage the assignment.
```

30-SECOND SPEED TIMINGS

Take two 30-second speed timings on lines 5 and 6. Then take two 30-second speed timings on lines 7 and 8. Or type each sentence twice.

```
5  I quickly explained that few big jobs involve many hazards,    12
6  but the directors felt that we needed more safety measures.    24
7  Peter reviewed the subject before giving Kay and Max a quiz    12
8  on the computer; they like using the machine to take tests.    24
   | 1 | 2 | 3 | 4 | 5 | 6 | 7 | 8 | 9 | 10 | 11 | 12
```

FORMATTING TWO-PAGE TABLES

A table too wide to fit on one page must be split as follows:

1. Type half on one page and half on a second page; then tape both pages together. Carefully position the table so that the two halves will line up.
2. Type ruled lines as close to the center edges of the paper as possible if ruled format is used.
3. Use no more than 2 spaces to separate words in the title.
4. Split the table and title as close to the middle as possible, but make the break between columns.

To format the left-hand page:

1. Backspace half the title from the right edge of the paper.
2. Backspace the key line from the right edge of the paper; set the margin and tab stops.
3. Type rules from the left margin to the right edge of the paper if ruled format is used.

To format the right-hand page:

1. Begin the other half of the title as close to the left edge as possible. Make sure that at least 1 space (no more than 2 spaces) separates it from the end of the title on the left-hand page.
2. Reset the tab stops and the left margin.
3. Type rules from the left edge of the paper to the end of the table if ruled format is used.
4. Begin the first column entry as close to the left edge as possible.

Left-Hand Page   ***Right-Hand Page***

ADMISSION RECORDS

An admission record is typed by the receptionist at the time a patient is admitted to a clinic or hospital.

ADMISSION RECORD

Family Name: Rossi | First Name: Mario | Middle Name: J. | Social Security Number: ----

Address: 7039 Pearl Street | City: Denver | State: CO | ZIP Code: 80229 | Home Phone: 555-5462 | Sex: (M) F | Marital Status: M (S) W D Sep.

Age—Yrs.: 8 | Birth Date: Mo. 8 Day 22 Year -- | Birthplace: Denver, CO | Nationality | Religion

Occupation: Third grade student | Employer or Employer of Spouse: ---- | Address of Employer—Phone: ----

Name of Husband or Maiden Name of Wife: ---- | Address if Other Than Above: ---- | Birthplace: ----

Notify in Case of Emergency: Mr. Joseph Rossi | Relationship: Father | Address: Same as above | Phone: Same

Name of Father: Joseph | Birthplace: Chicago, IL | Maiden Name of Mother: Marie Martin | Birthplace: Chicago, IL

Name of Blue Cross and/or Blue Shield Plan: Local Blue Cross and Blue Shield | Group No.: 023-8567 | Contract No.: B85291 | Effective Date: 6/15/72 | Subscriber ☐ Dependent ☒ | Family Member ☐ Comprehensive Coverage ☐

Other Hospitalization Insurance: ---- | Name | Address | Cert. or Policy No.: ---- | Group No.: ---- | Effective Date: ----

Attending Physician: Dr. Chuang | Admission Date: September 15, 19-- A.M. XX | Discharge Date: September 22, 19-- XX P.M.

Provisional Diagnosis (to be completed within 24 hours after admission): Pneumonia

On admission, patient or qualified person must sign Authorization for Medical and/or Surgical Treatment on reverse side.

Final Diagnosis: Lobar pneumonia

Code No.

Secondary Diagnosis or Complications:

Operation:

Signed ________________ **Attending Physician**

AUTHORIZATION FOR MEDICAL AND/OR SURGICAL TREATMENT

I, the undersigned, a patient in Trail Ridge Clinic Hospital, hereby authorize Dr. Chuang (and whomever he may designate as his assistants) to administer such treatment as is necessary, and to perform the following operation ---- (NAME OF OPERATION), and such additional operations or procedures as are considered therapeutically necessary on the basis of findings during the course of said operation.

I also consent to the administration of such anesthetics as are necessary, with the exception of ---- (NONE, SPINAL ANESTHESIA, OR OTHER).

Any tissues or parts surgically removed may be disposed of by the hospital in accordance with accustomed practice.

I hereby certify that I have read and fully understand the above Authorization for Medical and/or Surgical Treatment, the reasons why the above named surgery is considered necessary, its advantages and possible complications, if any, as well as possible alternative modes of treatment, which were explained to me by Dr. Chuang. I also certify that no guarantee or assurance has been made as to the results that may be obtained.

Date ________ Signed ________ PATIENT

Witness ________ Or ________ NEAREST RELATIVE

Relationship to Patient ________

Both authorizations must be signed by the patient, or by the nearest relative in the case of a minor or when patient is physically or mentally incompetent.

AUTHORIZATION FOR RELEASE OF INFORMATION

Authorization is hereby granted to release to the Local Blue Cross and Blue Shield (NAME OF INSURANCE COMPANY OR COMPANIES) such information as may be necessary for the completion of my hospitalization claims.

Date ________ Signed ________ PATIENT

Or ________ NEAREST RELATIVE

Relationship to Patient ________

JOBS 283 A TO 283 C. ADMISSION RECORDS

Using the data for the three patients provided below, complete a form for each patient. Use the illustrations on the left as a guide. Workbook 669–674.

A. Belinda Elliott, Route 4, Denver, CO 80208. Phone 555-7384. Age 12; Birthdate 2/11/75. Birthplace: Tucson, Arizona. S.S. No. 425-16-7839. Occupation: Student. Notify Betty Elliott in case of emergency. Mother is Betty Elliott; Birthplace is Tucson, Arizona. Father is deceased. Local Blue Cross and Blue Shield Plan and no other insurance; Group No. is 080-9785; Contract No. is B086374; Effective Date is 5/8/85. Admitted 7/12/— at 2:15 p.m. Provisional and final diagnosis: acute appendicitis. Operation: emergency appendectomy. Doctor is Matthew Chuang, M.D.

B. Andrew Anspach, Evergreen Drive, Denver, CO 80204. Phone 555-6921. Age 18; Birthdate 6/25/69. Birthplace: Greeley, CO. S.S. No. 384-22-8493. Occupation: Student. Notify Gene Anspach in case of emergency. Father is Gene Anspach; Birthplace is Dayton, Ohio. Mother is Linda Anspach; Birthplace is Lubbock, Texas. Local Blue Cross and Blue Shield Plan and no other insurance; Group No. is 094-9473; Contract No. is B87983; Effective Date is 4/8/70. Admitted 7/14/— at 1:30 p.m. Provisional diagnosis is broken right leg and so is final diagnosis. No surgery required. Doctor is Kevin Lia, M.D.

C. Jane Michener, North Trail, Fort Collins, CO 80522. Phone 555-8392. Age 35; Birthdate 9/18/52. Birthplace: Fort Collins, CO. S.S. No. 382-59-4792. Occupation: Secretary at Colorado State, Fort Collins. Notify husband, Paul Michener, in case of emergency at same address and phone number. Local Blue Cross and Blue Shield Plan and no other insurance; Group No. is 184-8392; Contract No. is B89043; Effective Date is 4/15/70. Admitted 8/3/— at 4:30 p.m. Provisional diagnosis is snakebite and so is final diagnosis. Surgery required to remove venom. Doctor is Kevin Lia, M.D.

JOB 188 A. TWO-PAGE RULED TABLE

Standard format with triple spacing.

Periods (or hyphens) in a table tell readers that information is not available or does not apply. Use as few as three periods centered on the column width or fill the column width. Placement of the *X* follows standard placement rules (centered under column heads).

Some word processors have a right-scroll feature that makes it possible to type documents wider than the display screen. The screen shifts to the right as soon as more space is needed. Of course, when the right screen is displayed, the left screen cannot be seen.

AIRLINES SERVING PRINCIPAL TRAFFIC CENTERS IN THE WORLD

AIRLINE	FRANCE	GERMANY	U.S.S.R.	CHINA	JAPAN	HAWAII	BRAZIL	MEXICO	CANADA	ENGLAND
ATLAS AIR	X	X	X	...	...	...	X	...	...	...
GLOBAL AIR	X	X	...	X	X	X	...	...	X	X
PANOWAY AIR	...	...	...	...	...	X	X	X	X	...
WORLDWIDE AIR	X	X	X	X	X	X	...	X	X	X
ZENITH AIR	...	...	...	X	X	X	...	X	X	...

LESSON 189

■ **GOALS**
To type 43/5′/4e.
To format and type a boxed table with footnote.

■ **FORMAT**
Drills: Single spacing 60-space line
5-Minute Timings: Double spacing 5-space tab

KEYBOARDING SKILLS

Type lines 1–4 once. Then practice making dashes as you type line 5. Repeat lines 1–4, or take a series of 1-minute timings.

Speed	1	The man and his two sons liked to play with the little pup.	12
Accuracy	2	Spot was freezing until Jack quietly put him in a warm box.	12
Numbers	3	we 23 wet 235 234 233 rio 489 488 487 486 our 974 973 9722.	12
Symbols	4	"He will come," he said. "Yes," she replied. "Good luck!"	12
Technique	5	A puppy--a lot of fun--a good friend--a pleasure--cute pup.	

| 1 | 2 | 3 | 4 | 5 | 6 | 7 | 8 | 9 | 10 | 11 | 12 |

FORMATTING MONTHLY STATEMENTS

The monthly statement for a doctor or medical facility is prepared following the basic formatting rules (page 353). However, the description column indicates the type of professional service provided. Codes for the various services appear at the bottom of the form.

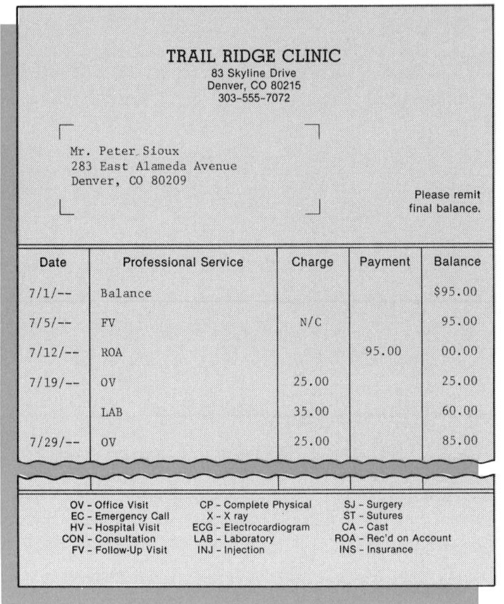

TRAIL RIDGE CLINIC
83 Skyline Drive
Denver, CO 80215
303-555-7072

Mr. Peter Sioux
283 East Alameda Avenue
Denver, CO 80209

Please remit final balance.

Date	Professional Service	Charge	Payment	Balance
7/1/--	Balance			$95.00
7/5/--	FV	N/C		95.00
7/12/--	ROA		95.00	00.00
7/19/--	OV	25.00		25.00
	LAB	35.00		60.00
7/29/--	OV	25.00		85.00

OV - Office Visit
EC - Emergency Call
HV - Hospital Visit
CON - Consultation
FV - Follow-Up Visit
CP - Complete Physical
X - X ray
ECG - Electrocardiogram
LAB - Laboratory
INJ - Injection
SJ - Surgery
ST - Sutures
CA - Cast
ROA - Rec'd on Account
INS - Insurance

JOBS 282 A AND 282 B. MONTHLY STATEMENTS

Using the data below, prepare two monthly statements. Use the illustration on the left as a guide. Standard format. Workbook 667–668.

A. Mr. Carlos Ramirez, 11109 East Sixth Avenue, Aurora, CO 80010, fell and cut himself on a hiking trail. During an office visit ($25) on 7/6/—, the wound was cleaned and sutured ($15), and Mr. Ramirez was given a tetanus shot ($15). He returned for a follow-up visit on 7/27/— to have two sutures removed (no charge—N/C) and was given a tetanus booster ($15). No payment has been made.

B. Mrs. Jean Featherstone, 3454 Brighton Boulevard, Denver, CO 80216, had a balance due from last month of $175. She came to the Clinic on 7/13/— because she was having chest pains. She was charged for an office visit ($25) and an ECG ($30). We received a check for $100 from the insurance company on 7/21/— and a check for $50 from Mrs. Featherstone on 7/28/—.

- **GOAL**
  To type admission records.
- **FORMAT**
  Single spacing 60-space line

KEYBOARDING SKILLS

Type lines 1–4 once. Then spell out the numbers in line 5 as you type it. Repeat lines 1–4, or take a series of 1-minute timings.

Speed	1	She is busy with the work but is to go to town for the pen.	12
Accuracy	2	Wolf gave Jake an extra dozen quarts, but he can't pay him.	12
Numbers	3	Tammy read pages 10 through 29, 38 through 47, and page 56.	12
Symbols	4	Add 1 + 2 + 3 + 4 + 5 + 6 + 7 + 8 + 9 + 10 + 11 + 12 + 130.	12
Number usage	5	Walt needs 3 typists and 8 editors on duty at 5.	

| 1 | 2 | 3 | 4 | 5 | 6 | 7 | 8 | 9 | 10 | 11 | 12

30-SECOND "OK" TIMINGS

Type as many 30-second "OK" (errorless) timings as possible out of three attempts on lines 6–8.

6 The sudden revocation of these policies has upset our plans 12
7 for developing that part of our program. We must negotiate 24
8 a new contract or seek some good alternative consideration. 36

| 1 | 2 | 3 | 4 | 5 | 6 | 7 | 8 | 9 | 10 | 11 | 12

PRETEST

Take a 5-minute timing on lines 6–25. Circle and count your errors.

```
6       All city councils play an important role in each local     12
7  government they serve.  They are elected officials who must     24
8  make the day-to-day decisions that run a city.  A very wide     36
9  assortment of issues comes before the council, and it's the     48
10 responsibility of all members to recognize the implications     60
11 of their stands on the issues.                                  66
12      Every time a new building is designed for the city, it     78
13 must be approved by the city council.  Local monies must be     90
14 allocated through the council, and projects needing funding    102
15 from the city must be justified by experts who must testify    114
16 before the council.  Contracts for businesses that work for    126
17 the city, such as road building, are granted by the vote of    138
18 city council members.  Even a cable television company must    150
19 get the permission of the council if it wants to operate in    162
20 the city.                                                      164
21      City council members must be quite well informed about    176
22 a variety of subjects, both ordinary and unique.  They have    188
23 many advisers who help them stay up to date.  Yet it can be    200
24 difficult for people to be responsible for so much.  Who is    212
25 on your council?                                               215
   | 1 | 2 | 3 | 4 | 5 | 6 | 7 | 8 | 9 | 10 | 11 | 12       SI 1.56
```

PRACTICE

In the chart below find the number of errors you made on the Pretest. Then type each of the designated drill lines four times.

Pretest errors	0–1	2–3	4–5	6+
Drill lines	29–35	28–34	27–33	26–32

Accuracy

```
26 people council experts advisers building projects allocated
27 monies issues before approved designed decisions television
28 it's unique variety awarded recognize government businesses
29 stand elected contracts important assortment responsibility
30 quite subjects testimony justified responsible implications
```

Speed

```
31 permission through quite each must can do by it if an so is
32 officials difficult issue role even much all day yet run up
33 ordinary giving comes from have many they such them who and
34 members funding city make help wide both work road vote for
35 every cable about play well date time that your the new are
```

POSTTEST

Take another 5-minute timing on lines 6–25 to see how much your skill has improved.

PRETEST

Take a 5-minute timing on lines 5–26. Circle and count your errors.

```
     Thousands of documents are handled daily through banks   12
of data linked to hospitals and clinics.  Personnel keep on   24
hand inventories of patient diagnoses as well as other data   36
needed.  Forms are utilized whenever possible to save time.   48
While current patient information is being processed, other   60
patient information is being adjusted electronically.  Data   72
is compiled quickly and exactly for individual therapy.       83
     Using the computer not only keeps medical records more   95
efficiently, but it also enables the physicians to see that  107
patients live more convenient lives.  The patient who wears  119
a heart monitor can have the monitor evaluated by calling a  131
special telephone number; the evaluation takes place within  143
minutes of the patient's call.                               149
     If one believes in miracles, the computer will be seen  161
as a miracle according to the patients who've been trying a  173
new way to learn to control their muscles in their arms and  185
their legs in order to move again.  Persons who haven't had  197
control of their muscles for an extended period of time are  209
suddenly able to maneuver the muscles by using the computer  221
to send signals to various parts of the body.                230
     Computers are excellent--for keeping patients' records  242
and helping patients to help themselves.                     250
| 1 | 2 | 3 | 4 | 5 | 6 | 7 | 8 | 9 | 10 | 11 | 12           SI 1.74
```

PRACTICE

In the chart below find the number of errors you made on the Pretest. Then type each of the designated drill lines six times.

Pretest errors	0–1	2–3	4+
Drill lines	29–32	28–31	27–30

Accuracy

```
quickly monitor exactly miracles utilized suddenly computer
documents hospitals personnel diagnoses telephone patient's
thousands individual information inventories electronically
```

Speed

```
banks being keeps order learn their forms other place while
hand data save time only more also will live have take seen
that arms legs if way to move one able takes send well call
```

POSTTEST

Take another 5-minute timing on lines 5–26 to see how much your skill has improved.

FORMATTING BOXED TABLES

Use the standard format for ruled tables with this change: Vertical lines between columns are penned in after the table is completed. (Use a ruler to pen in the lines.)

Dollar signs in tables are shown only on the first line and on total lines. Percent signs are repeated on every line of a table if the heading does not clearly indicate that the data is a percentage.

JOB 189 A. BOXED TABLE WITH FOOTNOTE

Standard format. Full sheet of paper turned lengthwise. In the subtitle, use last Friday's date.

center column heads

NATURAL FOODS STORES

Food Prices for the Week Ending (insert date)

Food Group	Previous Week	Current Week	Percent change	Index Value*
Eggs and Dairy	$ 5.65	$ 5.66	+ 0.18	158%
Fats and Oils	8.37	7.903	- 5.62	180%
Sugar and Sweets	4.78	4.99	+ 4.39	241%
Beverages	7.37	7.24	- 1.76	208%
Meats	18.04	17.68	- 2.00	137%
Dry and bakery	4.57	4.48	~~3.72~~ -1.97	170%
Vegetables	8.76	8.56	~~+10.31~~ -2.28	186%
TOTAL	$57.54	$56.54	-1.74	183%

*The index value is the current price expressed as a percentage of the prices during the index period, September 1975.

Summary words like *Total* are blocked. They may be typed in all-capital letters or in initial caps.

LESSON 190

GOALS

To recognize the correct use of contractions while typing sentences.
To format and type boxed tables with braced headings.

FORMAT

Single spacing   60-space line

LAB 23

Contractions

Type lines 1–4 once. Then repeat lines 1–4 or take a series of 1-minute timings.

1 Let's quickly get a dozen people together at the local gym. 12
2 I'm sure that they won't miss your excellent speeches, Don. 12
3 Did you know that she'll be the first woman president here? 12
4 Jan isn't a member of the class, but she's very well known. 12

| 1 | 2 | 3 | 4 | 5 | 6 | 7 | 8 | 9 | 10 | 11 | 12

A contraction is a shortened form of a phrase in which an apostrophe indicates omitted letters.

we have	we've	who will	who'll	I am	I'm
are not	aren't	I have	I've	he is	he's
they are	they're	do not	don't	you would	you'd

Semicolons

13 down; jamb; wish; name; them; hard; such; paid; form; make;
14 city; paid; fish; maps; they; land; also; kept; coal; lame;
15 slay; idle; melt; fight; turns; girls; panel; slept; ivory;
16 time; them; they; prize; voted; signs; firms; audit; field;

POSTTEST 1 Repeat Pretest 1 on page 454 to see how much your skill has improved.

PRETEST 2 Take a 2-minute timing on lines 17–20; then take a 2-minute timing on lines 21–24. Circle and count your errors on each.

Apostrophes

17 It's their turn to cut the neighbor's field of corn or hay. 12 60
18 Lena's firm may make a big profit with the auditor's forms. 24 72
19 Bob's profit with the corn may go to aid the widow's girls. 36 84
20 My town's citizens voted not to approve the firm's invoice. 48 96

Colons

21 Here is my problem: I must complete the project by June 1. 12 60
22 They visited these cities: Des Plains, Chicago, and Wayne. 24 72
23 Remember: Always wear your safety mask in this laboratory. 36 84
24 The committee nominated two people: Mona Webb and Hal Loo. 48 96

| 1 | 2 | 3 | 4 | 5 | 6 | 7 | 8 | 9 | 10 | 11 | 12

PRACTICE 2 In which timing did you make more errors? If in the first one (lines 17–20), type lines 25–28 six times and lines 29–32 three times. If most of your errors were in the second timing (lines 21–24), reverse the procedure.

Apostrophes

25 giant's lemon's widow's panel's title's problem's visitor's
26 whale's audit's field's ivory's shelf's memento's auditor's
27 right's badge's juror's proof's graph's element's antique's
28 stage's grape's zebra's habit's wagon's luggage's speaker's

Colons

29 than: height: formal: handle: chapel: island: signal:
30 tank: thanks: candid: tables: ethics: scores: drinks:
31 that: topics: vacant: inland: enable: habits: basics:
32 cope: source: intent: mother: events: employ: almost:

POSTTEST 2 Repeat Pretest 2 to see how much your skill has improved.

LESSON 282

UNIT 46 Processing Medical Forms

UNIT GOAL 50/5′/3e

- GOALS
  To use confusing words correctly while typing sentences.
  To type 50/5′/3e.
  To format and type monthly statements.
- FORMAT
  Drills: Single spacing 60-space line
  5-Minute Timings: Double spacing 5-space tab

LAB 33

Confusing Words

Type lines 1–4 once, selecting the correct words. Edit your copy as your teacher reads the answers. Then retype lines 1–4 from your edited copy.

1 I took her (advice, advise) because she is a very intelligent person.
2 The (council, counsel) hired a local attorney to act as their (council, counsel).
3 I (disbursed, dispersed) a lot of money in connection with this lawsuit.
4 I'm unaware of any (precedence, precedents) for planning task (precedence, precedents).

12-SECOND TIMINGS

Type each line three times, or take three 12-second timings on each line. For each timing, type with no more than 1 error.

5 They'll wish to fight to the very end to solve the problem.
6 The plane took off with a gust of wind and a whine of jets.
7 A big fire is one in which the smoke curls high in the sky.

5 10 15 20 25 30 35 40 45 50 55 60

FORMATTING TABLES WITH BRACED HEADINGS

A "braced" heading is one that centers over (or *embraces*) two or more columns, such as the heading *Passengers (000)* in Job 190 A below. To format braced headings:

1. Begin by typing the column headings below the braced heading. Leave room for the braced heading.
2. Count the number of spaces in the braced heading. In Job 190 A the heading is 16 spaces.
3. Count the number of spaces in the longest items in the columns to be braced—remember to include the spaces between columns. In Job 190 A the number of spaces is 20 (*20,568* + 6 spaces + *Domestic*).
4. Subtract the number of spaces determined in Step 2 from those in Step 3; divide the difference by 2; drop any fraction. (20 − 16 = 4 ÷ 2 = 2)
5. Roll the paper back, and indent the braced heading the number of spaces you determined in Step 4.
6. Begin the underscore a single space below the braced heading, 3 spaces to the left of the beginning of the left column.

Note: Column headings align at the bottom.

JOB 190 A. TABLE WITH BRACED HEADING

Standard format.

In tables, long words may be contracted: *Int'l* for *International*, for example. Because all the figures for passengers are in the millions (for example, *London 20,568,000*), the final three digits are shown in the heading to save column space.

ESTIMATED PASSENGER TRAFFIC AT WORLD AIRPORTS

		Passengers (000)	
Airport	City	Int'l	Domestic
Heathrow	London	20,568	2,822
J. F. Kennedy	New York	11,490	11,056
Frankfurt-Main	Frankfurt	9,634	4,329
Schiphol	Amsterdam	8,444	147
DeGaulle	Paris	7,550	853
Orly	Paris	7,543	5,017
Kastrup	Copenhagen	6,795	1,680

JOB 190 B. TABLE WITH BRACED HEADING

Standard format. Arrange branches in alphabetic order.

A computer can calculate figures in total columns. A change in one column will automatically result in a change in the total column.

ANALYSIS OF FIRST QUARTER SALES

	Type of Product		
Branch	Computers	Word Processors	Total
Boston	186	58	244
Houston	843	429	1272
Milwaukee	1107	967	2074
Seattle	639	240	879
Oklahoma City	908	624	1532
San Francisco	927	597	1524
St. Louis	584	342	926
Detroit	736	517	1253

JOB 280 A. FINAL DECREE

Standard legal format. Follow the heading illustration on page 453. Workbook 663–666.

IN THE PROBATE COURT OF RICHLAND COUNTY / IN THE MATTER OF THE / ADOPTION OF / PEGGY LYNN JONES / NO. 618342 / FINAL DECREE OF ADOPTION

This day, this cause came on for a full hearing before the Court upon the petition of John Jones and Linda Jones, and the proceedings held thereafter for the adoption of Peggy Lynn, who prior to the interlocutory decree herein was known as Infant Girl Johnson, and who was born on April 12, 19—, at Mansfield, Ohio. ¶ It appearing to the Court that more than six months have expired from the date on which the Court entered the interlocutory decree of adoption herein, and that said interlocutory decree has not been revoked, and it further appearing that the next friend heretofore appointed by the Court has submitted to the Court a further report of their findings relative to the suitability of this adoption, the Court therefore finds that adoption will be to the best interests of said child. ¶ It is therefore ordered and adjudged by the Court that a final decree of adoption be and is hereby entered in this adoption and that henceforth said child shall have the status of an adopted child of said petitioners.

____
Judge
↓ 2

Approved:

____
F. J. Stockwell
Attorney for Petitioners

CLINIC

GOAL
To improve technique in typing commas, semicolons, apostrophes, and colons.

FORMAT
Drills: Single spacing 60-space line
2-Minute Timings: Double spacing

KEYBOARDING SKILLS

Type lines 1–4 on page 447 three times each.

PRETEST 1

Take a 2-minute timing on lines 1–4; then take a 2-minute timing on lines 5–8. Circle and count your errors on each.

Commas

1 They paid the city, town, and county for the right to fish. 12 60
2 They may make a big profit with the corn, hay, and turkeys. 24 72
3 Janice may own title to the land, lake, and island by June. 36 84
4 I think we should have meat, potatoes, and milk for dinner. 48 96

Semicolons

5 The secretary got the audit form; the city auditor sent it. 12 60
6 Their big problems may end; their firm is busy with panels. 24 72
7 Robert pays for the land work; they pay for the audit work. 36 84
8 It is now time for us to go; it is not time for them to go. 48 96

| 1 | 2 | 3 | 4 | 5 | 6 | 7 | 8 | 9 | 10 | 11 | 12

PRACTICE 1

In which timing did you make more errors? If in the first one (lines 1–4), type lines 9–12 six times and lines 13–16 three times (page 455). If most of your errors were in the second timing (lines 5–8), reverse the procedure.

Commas

9 maps, girl, make, firm, kept, busy, half, part, held, when,
10 pens, turn, odor, worn, name, they, pays, them, kept, such,
11 have, paid, wish, form, land, lake, duty, down, oaks, gown,
12 held, busy, with, envy, they, kept, snap, form, sign, town,

(Continued on next page)

LESSON 191

■ GOALS
To identify the correct use of contractions while typing sentences.
To type one- and two-page tables with braced headings.

■ FORMAT
Single spacing   60-space line

LAB 23

Contractions

Type lines 1–4 once. Then repeat lines 1–4 or take a series of 1-minute timings.

```
1  It doesn't seem possible that Joe Rexon is ready to retire.   12
2  Here's the quickest way to go to my warehouse in Kalamazoo.   12
3  What's the reason for sending all your cartons to Veronica?   12
4  It wouldn't be fair to let your customers pay for shipping.   12
   | 1 | 2 | 3 | 4 | 5 | 6 | 7 | 8 | 9 | 10 | 11 | 12
```

30-SECOND "OK" TIMINGS

Type as many 30-second "OK" (errorless) timings as possible out of three attempts on lines 5–7.

```
5  We acquire jerky habits from having typed exercises lazily;   12
6  but we can overcome such bad habits by practice that forces   24
7  us to concentrate on typing smoothly, as we've been taught.   36
   | 1 | 2 | 3 | 4 | 5 | 6 | 7 | 8 | 9 | 10 | 11 | 12
```

JOB 191 A. BOXED TABLE WITH BRACED HEADING

Standard format. Full sheet of paper.

International Oil
Current Recommendations

Company	Net Earnings Per Share			Percent Yield
	Last Year	This Year	Next Year*	
Axion Corp.	$4.13	$4.50	$5.25	0.3
Global Corp.	2.25	2.85	3.15	2.7
Motoron Corp.	2.37	3.61	4.20	2.5
Royal Petroleum	9.38	11.07	12.12	1.4
Sestor, Inc.	3.37	3.65	4.05	1.8
Textrons, Inc.	6.15	6.70	7.20	2.6
United Int'l	2.37	3.28	4.10	0.6

* Anticipated.

PREVIEW PRACTICE

Type each line twice as a preview to the 5-minute timings below.

Accuracy
5 text realize acquires customized requirement electronically

Speed
6 figure paper their forms them with also the key for but own

5-MINUTE TIMINGS

Take two 5-minute timings on lines 7–28.

7 There are numerous varieties of word processors on the 12
8 market. Some have screens and are called CRTs. Others are 24
9 blind processors, which do not have screens; operators must 36
10 key documents without viewing what they're recording on the 48
11 diskettes or magnetic tape. Some are standalones because a 60
12 central processing unit is not connected to them. Some are 72
13 connected to CPUs and operate in conjunction with terminals 84
14 handling similar or different text. 91
15 Combining the newest types of word processors and data 103
16 processors has helped businesses realize the requirement of 115
17 heavy paper flow. Businesses can merge information in word 127
18 and figure forms by manipulating and changing formats elec– 139
19 tronically to speed up information flow. 147
20 The practicality for this merger between word and data 159
21 processing has led the producers of hardware to develop the 171
22 microcomputer which has the capacity to run any software on 183
23 any operating system that programmers and engineers will be 195
24 able to create. The microcomputer allows users to run some 207
25 commercial software, but it also allows users who know some 219
26 programming to write their own customized software. As the 231
27 users acquire more skill at operating their microcomputers, 243
28 a demand for more power will grow. 250

| 1 | 2 | 3 | 4 | 5 | 6 | 7 | 8 | 9 | 10 | 11 | 12 SI 1.73

FORMATTING COURT HEADINGS

Some legal documents are papers used in court. These documents need a court heading in addition to the title of the document. Format court headings as follows when typing these documents:

1. Center the name of the court in all-capital letters on line 13.
2. Display the title of the court action. See the illustration at the right for one such display.
3. Type the number of the court action in the right half of the page, on the middle line of the displayed court action title.

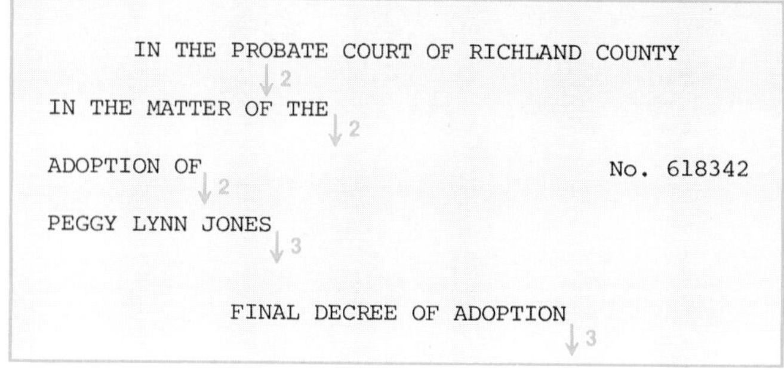

IN THE PROBATE COURT OF RICHLAND COUNTY
↓2
IN THE MATTER OF THE ↓2
ADOPTION OF ↓2 No. 618342
PEGGY LYNN JONES ↓3
FINAL DECREE OF ADOPTION ↓3

4. Begin the title of the document a triple space below the court action title.

A spreadsheet is used by accountants to lay out columns of figures to forecast budgets and production costs.

A spreadsheet on a computer may be larger than what can be seen on the screen at one time. You can scroll left, right, up, and down to see the various sections of the spreadsheet.

JOB 191 B. TWO-PAGE BOXED TABLE WITH BRACED HEADINGS

Standard format. Title: FOUR-YEAR SALES ANALYSIS

	------------------SALES UNITS------------------				------------------SALES DOLLARS------------------			
COLOR TV MODELS	CURRENT YEAR	FIRST PRIOR	SECOND PRIOR	THIRD PRIOR	CURRENT YEAR	FIRST PRIOR	SECOND PRIOR	THIRD PRIOR
09--925AD	27,160	14,862			9,777,600	5,944,800		
13--373P	48,452	52,261	43,906	25,071	8,479,100	9,929,590	9,659,320	5,139,555
13--373PR	55,822	47,370	28,651		10,885,290	10,184,550	7,019,495	
15--562P		41,006	67,719	95,326		8,201,200	16,252,560	21,448,350
15--562PR	235,359	210,901	182,606	147,963	50,602,185	47,452,725	48,390,590	36,990,750
19--922P	220,864	234,072	240,193	255,668	61,841,920	70,051,240	78,062,725	72,865,380
19--922PR	225,436	217,167	202,944	200,174	74,393,880	74,922,615	76,104,000	68,060,030
25--293T	168,381	150,905	122,833		90,925,740	84,506,800	73,699,800	
25--293TR	178,557	150,722	119,196		105,348,630	91,940,420	77,477,400	

JOB 279 B. INTERLOCUTORY AGREEMENT

Standard legal format. Workbook 659–662.

INTERLOCUTORY AGREEMENT 14

THAT WHEREAS Buckeye Children's 24
Agency is a corporation organized for the care of 34
children, and 37
WHEREAS Buckeye Children's Agency 46
has on occasion children placed with it for the 56
purpose of adoption, and 61
WHEREAS John Jones and Linda Jones are 70
desirous of having placed with them a child for 80
adoption, 82
BE IT THEREFORE agreed by and be- 90
tween said parties as follows: that in considera- 100
tion of Buckeye Children's Agency's placing 109
with them Infant Girl Johnson to be known as 118
Peggy Lynn, a child to which Buckeye 125
Children's Agency has for the purpose of adop- 134
tion, 136
John Jones and Linda Jones hereby agree to 146
accept said child, to maintain and support it, to 156
assume all responsibility for said child from the 166
time it is placed in their possession; that they 176
will obtain the services of an attorney and pre- 185
pare and file a petition for the adoption of said 195
child with Richland County Probate Court 204
within 30 days after written approval for adop- 213
tion has been given by the physician of their 222
choice. 224
SAID John Jones and Linda Jones further 234
say that in accepting said child, it is their intent 244
within a time specified herein, to make applica- 254
tion to the Richland County Probate Court for 263
the purpose of adoption of said child. 271
SAID John Jones and Linda Jones further 281
agree to pay the placement fee in full at the time 291
the medical approval of the aforesaid child is 301
filed with Buckeye Children's Agency. 315
IN WITNESS WHEREOF, said parties 324
have hereunto set their hands and seal this tenth 334
day of May, 19—. 338

______________________ 351
John Jones 361

______________________ 373
Linda Jones 384

WITNESSETH THAT the above-men- 392
tioned parties appeared before me this tenth day 402
of May, 19—, and acknowledged the signing of 411
the foregoing instrument to be their voluntary act 421
and deed. 423
IN TESTIMONY WHEREOF, I have here- 432
unto set my hand and seal on the day and year 441
last aforesaid. 444

______________________ 458
Jane Casady, Notary Public 484

■ GOALS
To use confusing words correctly while typing sentences.
To type 50/5′/3e.
To format and type court headings.

■ FORMAT
Drills: Single spacing 60-space line
5-Minute Timings: Double spacing 5-space tab

LAB 33

Confusing Words

Type lines 1–4 once, selecting the correct words. Edit your copy as your teacher reads the answers. Then retype lines 1–4 from your edited copy.

1 The president asked us to (advice, advise) him; he wanted our (advice, advise).
2 The (council's, counsel's) actions forced the taxpayers to hire (council, counsel).
3 It was impossible to (disburse, disperse) the crowd after that concert.
4 His attorney cited a number of (precedence, precedents) during the trial.

■ GOALS
To provide appropriate contractions for certain words while typing sentences.
To type 43/5′/4e.
To type a ruled table and a boxed table.

■ FORMAT
Drills: Single spacing 60-space line
5-Minute Timings: Double spacing 5-space tab

LAB 23
Contractions

Type lines 1–4 once, providing appropriate contractions for the underscored words. Edit your copy as your teacher reads the answers. Then retype lines 1–4 from your edited copy.

```
Al Juarez does not believe that Ken will deliver it on time.
When do you think we will be told about that proposed merger?
What is the quickest way to order more of this great polish?
I have received only five or six suggestions from Mr. Truman.
```

PREVIEW PRACTICE

Type each line twice as a preview to the 5-minute timings below.

Accuracy
```
fact test only year state detente testees foreign determine
```
Speed
```
choice civics third their high know half when they vote how
```

5-MINUTE TIMINGS

Take two 5-minute timings on lines 7–21.

Last year a group of high school students participated in a citizenship 15
test conducted to determine how much young people know about our sys- 29
tem of government and about how to split their ballot when they vote. 43
The results of the test were shocking. Only one-third of the students 58
participating in the program recognized the fact that a voter could split his 74
or her party choice. The majority were ignorant of politics. 86
Barely half of the students in the survey knew that we base the number 101
of representatives on population and that a state has only two U.S. sena- 115
tors. Many students believed a member of the House was appointed. 129
On the questions relating to foreign policy, the tests revealed that the 144
students were equally uninformed. Around half the testees did not know 159
what NATO is; only a few knew the meaning of the word "detente." 171
The failing marks of these future voters were not much of a surprise to 187
high school teachers because students show scant interest in history, civics, 202
or political science; so they don't learn about government. 214

| 1 | 2 | 3 | 4 | 5 | 6 | 7 | 8 | 9 | 10 | 11 | 12 | 13 | 14 | 15 | SI 1.56

LESSON 279

■ GOALS
To identify the correct use of confusing words while typing sentences.
To format legal documents on a form.
To type a bill of sale on a form and an interlocutory agreement.

■ FORMAT
Single spacing   60-space line

LAB 33

Confusing Words

Type lines 1–4 once. Then repeat lines 1–4 or take a series of 1-minute timings.

```
1  Can he advise me as to where I can get professional advice?  12
2  Who will counsel her about the candidates for city council?  12
3  I must pay my lawyer for the fees she disbursed on my case.  12
4  I have precedence in selecting vacation based on seniority.  12
   | 1 | 2 | 3 | 4 | 5 | 6 | 7 | 8 | 9 | 10 | 11 | 12
```

30-SECOND "OK" TIMINGS

Type as many 30-second "OK" (errorless) timings as possible out of three attempts on lines 5–7.

```
5  Our school day ends at three.  I hope that they will take a  12
6  plane that will get here at four or five.  If they do, then  24
7  I can drive the new car to the field and meet their flight.  36
   | 1 | 2 | 3 | 4 | 5 | 6 | 7 | 8 | 9 | 10 | 11 | 12
```

FORMATTING LEGAL FILL-IN FORMS

When typing legal documents on a form, you are required to insert the necessary information. Follow these guidelines and study the illustration to the right when typing on a preprinted legal form:

1. Align the insertions with the preprinted words.
2. Treat any blank areas on the form as follows:
   Ⓐ Fill in any blank spaces within individual lines of the form with *leaders* (a series of hyphens).
   Ⓑ Fill in any blank areas that occupy several blank lines with two horizontal underscores joined by a solid diagonal line. This is called a *Z rule.*
3. Leave 1 blank space between the preprinted word and the typed insertion.
4. Align margins with those of the form. **Note:** In some states erasing is not permitted on dates, addresses, amounts of money, and names.

Bill of Sale

Know all Men by these Presents,

That I, Sharon Kaye Edmunds, of 534 Juniper Drive, Billings, Yellowstone County, State of Montana,----------------------(Seller),

for and in consideration of the sum of One Thousand Seventy-five-------------- --Dollars ($1075--------), lawful money of the United States, to the Seller in hand paid, the receipt of which is hereby acknowledged, does by these presents grant, bargain, sell, and convey unto Donald E. Garcia, of 283 Pine Tree Road, Hardin, Big Horn County, State of Montana,--- ---(Buyer), the following described personal property One 1980 Ford Fairmont four-door sedan, white in color, serial number AF778-3492-165H.

To Have and to Hold the same unto the said Buyer, the heirs, executors, and assigns thereof forever. The Seller herein covenants and agrees to warrant and defend the sale of said property hereby sold to the Buyer against all and every person or persons whomsoever, lawfully claiming the same or any part thereof.

In Witness Whereof, the Seller has hereunto set hand and seal this first-----day of December----- 19--

JOB 279 A. BILL OF SALE ON A FORM

Standard format. Workbook 657–658. Use the information in Job 278 B on page 450 to fill in the workbook form for a bill of sale.

JOB 192 A. RULED TABLE

Standard format with leaders (see page 288). Half sheet of paper. 14 spaces between columns.

Contico Corporation

Foreign Investment	Market Value
Australia	9,255,190
Belgium	3,425,293
France	13,261,141
Hong#Kong	5,383,260
Japan	465,891,8889
Netherlnads	4,248,516
Spain	3,238,357
Switzerlandd	11,130,281

Please add: United Kingdom 30,486,355

JOB 192 B. BOXED TABLE

Standard format. Full sheet of paper, lengthwise.

Firsts by U.S. Women

Career	Name	Year	Place
Newspaper Editor	Ann Franklin	1762	Newport, RI
Doctor	Elizabeth Blackwell	1849	New York State
College Professor	Rebecca Mann Pannell	1852	Antioch College, OH
Minister	Antoinette Brown	1852	South Butler, NY
Lawyer	Carrie Brunham Kilgore	1884	Delaware County, PA
Mayor	Susanna Medora	1887	Argonia, KS
Congresswoman	Jeanette Rankin	1917	Montana
U.S. Senator	Rebecca Felton	1922	Georgia
Governor	Nellie Taylor Ross	1924	Wyoming
Cabinet Member	Frances Perkins	1933	Washington, DC
Supreme Court Justice	Sandra Day O'Connor	1981	Washington, DC

advice: information, recommendation
advise: to recommend, inform

council: an assembly
counsel: (n.) an attorney
(v.) to give advice

disburse: to pay out
disperse: to scatter, distribute

precedence: priority
precedents: established rules

FORMATTING RECIPROCAL DOCUMENTS

In law offices many documents such as wills and powers of attorney are prepared simultaneously for both husband and wife. If the clauses in the documents are identical except for the reversal of the names, they are called *reciprocal* documents.

When typing a reciprocal document, you must remember to change all the names, pronouns, and other identifying nouns. For example, in the will for Job 276 A on pages 446–447, the testator (maker) of the will is Earl Sizemore. He has named his wife, Barbara Sizemore, as executrix. In a reciprocal will, Barbara Sizemore is the testatrix, and she will name her husband, Earl Sizemore, as the executor.

Computers and word processors have a feature called global search and replace. *If you want to change a word or correct an error throughout a document, the computer or word processor will* search for *each use of that word and replace it with the substitute word. You only have to type the correction once.*

JOB 278 A. RECIPROCAL WILL

Standard legal format. Workbook 647–650.

Type a reciprocal will for Barbara Sizemore. Make appropriate changes in names. Her will is made out to Earl Sizemore, and he is the executor if living. Her daughter is the executrix if he is not living.

OPTIONAL JOB. PROPERTY DEED

Standard legal format. Workbook 651–654.

Prepare a second deed for property to be transferred from the Williamsons to Carolyn and Jerry Basford of Paintsville, Kentucky. Use lot number 27 in the same area and record book for the county. Date this deed June 29, 19—.

BILL OF SALE

A bill of sale is an agreement by which one person agrees to sell a piece of personal property to another.

JOB 278 B. BILL OF SALE

Standard legal format. Workbook 655–656.

B I L L   O F   S A L E ↓3 14

KNOW ALL MEN BY THESE PRESENTS 24
that I, Grace Ann Roth, of 548 Blue Jay Drive, 34
Flint, Genesee County, State of Michigan, party 43
of the first part, for the sum of Six Thousand 53
Dollars ($6000), to me in hand paid, at or before 63
the ensealing and delivery of these presents by 72
James Earl Grant, of 247 Cedar Street, Ingham 81
County, State of Michigan, party of the second 91
part, do sell and grant and convey unto the said 101
party of the second part my 1986 Buick Regal, 110
serial number KT1038-56-47-29S. 116

TO HAVE AND TO HOLD the same unto the 126
said party of the second part forever. And I do 136
covenant and agree to defend the sale of the said 146
automobile against all and every person. 154

IN WITNESS WHEREOF, I have hereunto 163
set my hand and my seal on the sixth day of June 173
in the year of one thousand nine hundred and 185
↓3
______________________ 196
↓2
Sealed and delivered in the presence of ↓3 204

______________________ 214

UNIT 32 In-Baskets

UNIT GOAL 43/5′/4e

GOALS

To provide appropriate contractions for certain words while typing sentences.
To type 43/5′/4e.
To prioritize and format related office communications with speed and accuracy.

FORMAT

Drills: Single spacing 60-space line
5-Minute Timings: Double spacing 5-space tab

LAB 23 Contractions

Workbook 363–364.

Type lines 1–4 once, providing appropriate contractions for the underscored words. Edit your copy as your teacher reads the answers. Then retype lines 1–4 from your edited copy.

1 Terri Saxon said that she is going to promote her assistant.
2 Judd Bertram will not be able to attend tomorrow's conference.
3 They will need two dozen more copies, according to Ms. Klein.
4 I would prefer having you and her quickly review these figures.

PREVIEW PRACTICE

Type each line twice as a preview to the 5-minute timings below.

Accuracy 5 Zion extra require analyze full-time restaurant Yellowstone
Speed 6 visitors worker owned duties spend with when also they make

5-MINUTE TIMINGS

Take two 5-minute timings on lines 7–24.

Would you like to spend a summer working in one of our national parks? The National Park Service, one division of the Department of the Interior, maintains a full-time staff of employees at every park all over the country; also, when the number of visitors increases in summer, extra employees are required to keep the parks clean and safe from vandals.

National parks are owned by the people of America, and they are preserves for wildlife and timber. They are cared for by our government to make sure parks stay protected and guarded resources. Rangers check forest fires, analyze the weather conditions, and keep close tabs on the wild animals to make certain they're not hunted, infected, or injured in any way. Rangers also assist the backpackers so they don't get lost in the wilderness or hurt climbing mountains. The summer employees should help the rangers with these duties.

Many parks have campgrounds so visitors can enjoy time out of doors, because hotels and restaurants are restricted in many parks. Next summer, visit Yellowstone or Zion.

| 1 | 2 | 3 | 4 | 5 | 6 | 7 | 8 | 9 | 10 | 11 | 12 | SI 1.56

and State of Kentucky, and being Lot numbered twenty-three (23) of 128
Second Addition to Clintwood Subdivision, Section Two (2), Town 141
Two (2), Page 42 of the Plat Records of Floyd County, Kentucky. 154
The said Frank E. Williamson and Reda F. Williamson do hereby 166
covenant and warrant that the title so conveyed is clear, free, 179
and unencumbered, and that they will defend the same against all 192
lawful claims of all persons whomsoever. 201

In witness whereof, the said Frank E. Williamson and 212
Reda F. Williamson have hereunto set their hands this twenty-fifth day 226
of June in the year A.D. nineteen hundred and (fill in year). 238
Signed in the presence of: 248

↓4

____________________ ____________________ 265

____________________ ____________________ 288

↓4

State of Kentucky, County of Floyd: On this twenty-fifth day of 301
June, 19--, before me a notary public and for said County, 313
personally came Frank E. Williamson and Reda F. Williamson the grantors in 328
the foregoing deed, and acknowledged signing thereof to be their 341
voluntary act and deed. Witnesseth my official signature and seal 354
on the day last above mentioned. 361

↓4

____________________ ____________________ 378

Notary Attorney 413

■ GOALS

To recognize the correct use of confusing words while typing sentences.
To format and type a reciprocal will.
To type a bill of sale.

■ FORMAT

Single spacing 60-space line

LAB 33

Confusing Words

Type lines 1–4 once. Then repeat lines 1–4 or take a series of 1-minute timings.

1 I would advise you to get some legal advice in this matter. 12
2 The counsel hired by the council was not present yesterday. 12
3 The meeting will disperse only when all fees are disbursed. 12
4 All precedents in this manual clearly state job precedence. 12

| 1 | 2 | 3 | 4 | 5 | 6 | 7 | 8 | 9 | 10 | 11 | 12

(Continued on next page)

IN-BASKET A:

Working for a Government Agency

An in-basket is a group of production typing jobs related to a particular workstation.

Workbook—Priority Learning Guide 365–366.

You are a member of the Youth Conservation Corps, which is a government-sponsored program for young people in high school who want to work summers in the national forests. You are scheduled to work at the Smithport Ranger Station, Chicora National Forest. Because of your business training, the district ranger, Albert Fruhauf, has asked you to help in the office. Use letterheads and forms where appropriate. Workbook 367–382.

PRIORITY RECORDING SHEET

Today is June 2, 19—. You have reported for work at the ranger station. In your in-basket are the jobs shown on pages 321–323. Before starting to type, you should read through all the jobs to be done and decide which ones (1) are RUSH, to be done immediately; (2) are to be done promptly; or (3) may be completed when time permits. Using a priority recording sheet, list next to each job the priority that you think it should be given.

WORK LOG

Ranger Fruhauf has asked you to keep a work log of the various jobs as you complete them. The log contains a place for you to write in the time started, the time completed, the total minutes taken to complete the job, and the number of lines typed. Many businesses use work logs to evaluate an employee's productivity (the quantity of work produced) and to allocate costs.

Government memos use this order in the heading: (1) *Reply to,* (2) *Subject,* and (3) *To.* The date is backspaced from the right margin on the same line as *Reply to.*

GOVERNMENT MEMO WITH TABLE

Standard format. This document should be done within the first or second day of the next month.

[*Reply to*] 7120 Fleet Equipment, [*Subject*] Mileage and Gasoline Use, [*To*] Forest Supervisor

The following shows our vehicle and gasoline use for the YCC recruitment program for the months of March, April, and May:

Vehicle	Mileage	Gasoline (gallons)
YCC Rental	482	17
Privately Owned Vehicles	1,322	84
Forest Service Vehicle	8,383	552
Total	10,187	653

[*Signed*] Albert R. Fruhauf, District Ranger

Mail to the Forest Supervisor is picked up by interoffice delivery.

MEMO WITH TABLE FROM HANDWRITTEN COPY

Format as a four-column table the names, job titles, government service classifications, and YCC group assignments for the four employees listed. Standard format. Body 50 words.

[Reply to] 6150 Uniforms [Date]
[Subject] Designation of Positions
Requiring a Uniform
[To] Forest Supervisor
The following employee positions fall into the "other" category for designation for wearing the

(Continued on next page)

Information processing popularity continues to explode as the service 15
businesses continue to grow. At the present time, law offices, insurance 30
companies, hospitals, and some sales offices are using terminals to boost 45
their productivity rates. 50

All legal firms produce a good deal of long agreements and wills in a 15
short period. Some records will quite often show great similarities in 29
their contents. Thus previously keyed documents can be edited for other 44
situations and save much time. 50

Insurance companies send a number of communications to clients con- 14
cerning their policies. The repetitiveness that insurance companies encoun- 29
ter as they correspond with their clients makes them good prospects for 44
using word processing equipment. 50

The sales office that does a great deal of work in its branch office 15
benefits from having terminals at each office for the staff to communicate 30
with each other quickly. They can keep records of all styles and communi- 44
cate the data via terminals. 50

Hospitals always need to keep patient files current to diagnose illnesses 15
and save lives. Communicating terminals increase the performance of most 31
operations a good deal. A form is handled quickly so that a patient is 45
cared for in a short time. 50

| 1 | 2 | 3 | 4 | 5 | 6 | 7 | 8 | 9 | 10 | 11 | 12 | 13 | 14 | 15   SI 1.72

DEED

A deed is a legal document that provides proof of ownership of real property and is used to transfer ownership to another party.

JOB 277 A. PROPERTY DEED

Standard legal format. Workbook 643–646.

PROPERTY DEED 8

10 Know all men by these presents: that Frank E. Williamson and 24
Reva F. Williamson of Floyd County, Kentucky, in consideration 36
of one dollar ($1.00) and other valuable consideration to them in hand 50
paid by Wallace R. Herald and William G. Herald, whose address is 64
Route 3, Wheelright, Kentucky, do hereby grant, bargain, sell, 76
and convey to the said Wallace R. Herald and William G. Herald 89
their heirs and assigns forever, the following described real 101
estate, (1) situated in the Township of Wheelright, County of Floyd 115

(Continued on next page)

448

Forest Service uniform during YCC camp:
(1) Daniel Miller, Forestry Technician, GS-8, Group 3
(2) William Walters, Geologist, GS-8, Group 5
(3) Donna Clow, Forester, GS-9, Group 9
(4) W. M. Harper, Biologist, GS-9, Group 12
Albert R. Fruhauf, District Ranger

Arrange as a 4-column table. Omit numbers before employees' names. Use column headings.

DISPLAY NOTICE FOR HIGH SCHOOL BULLETIN BOARDS

Format attractively on a full sheet of paper. Double-space bulletin board display.

The ranger wants to post this at the local high school tomorrow afternoon.

YOU CAN EARN AND LEARN IN THE YOUTH CONSERVATION CORPS THIS SUMMER IF YOU ACT NOW [*Subtitle*] Only Five Openings Left
The YCC is a program sponsored by the U.S. Department of Agriculture Forest Service. To qualify, you must (1) be between the ages of 15 and 18, (2) provide your own transportation to and from the camp, (3) work from 8 a.m. to 4:30 p.m., (4) wear hard hats and gloves on all outdoor jobs. MAJOR WORK: Deer fencing, trail maintenance, stream improvement, and soil stabilization. PAY: Minimum wage for eight weeks. Get an application from your school guidance counselor.

ENUMERATION

Format attractively on a full sheet of paper as a handout for the students in YCC who will report for their first day on June 23.

The proofreaders' mark ⌐—— as in /VEHICLES means all letters are lowercase.

```
CHICORA NATIONAL FOREST, [Subtitle] Smithport Ranger Station,
[Subtitle] YCC Work Rules
1.  No drugs, narctics, or alcholic bevreages are permitted in gov-
    ernmeпt VEHICLES OR on the word sights. [sites]
2.  Enrolees will report all accidents, irregardless of there [their] seri-
ousness, to their crew leader.
3.  No fire arms are permitted in government vehicles or [on] the work [sites].
4.  All smoking at the work [sites] will be done at "safe" locations.
(5) Cigarettes and matches will be crushed "deadout" and mixed with
    soil--not tossed on theground.
56. Enrolles are expected to do the jobs there [their] crew leaders assign [to]
them. Crew leaders will rotate assignments so that each enrollee [will]
    have variety.
6.  Workhours are from 8 AM [a.m.] to 4:30 PM [p.m.] with one-half hour for lunch.
    All enrollees are expeected to repotrn tothe Forest service wear- [ware-]
    hourse on time each morning.
7.  Since the ycc progrm is of such a short duration [this summer], all enrollees
    are expected to attend eachday.
```

In Witness WHEREOF I have hereunto set my hand at Lebanon, Tennessee, this fourteenth day of April, 19—. ↓4

____

SUBSCRIBED, Sealed, Published, and Declared by the Testator, Earl Sizemore, on the date above written, as and for his Last Will and Testament in the presence of each of us, who, at his request, in his presence and in the presence of each other, have hereunto subscribed our names as witnesses.

↓4

________________________ residing at ________________ ↓2
________________ ↓2

________________________ residing at ________________
____

________________________ residing at ________________
____

LESSON 277

GOALS
To type 50/5'/3e.
To type a deed.

FORMAT
Drills: Single spacing 60-space line
5-Minute Timings: Double spacing 5-space tab

KEYBOARDING SKILLS

Type lines 1–4 once. Then punctuate line 5 as you type it. Repeat lines 1–4, or take a series of 1-minute timings.

Speed	1	We had a chance to try on the suits before he had to leave.	12
Accuracy	2	Pat quickly froze the gold mixtures in five old brown jars.	12
Numbers	3	Just order 1 or 2 or 3 or 4 or 5 or 6 or 7 or 8 or 9 or 10.	12
Symbols	4	Report Friday on Sections (10), (29), (38), (47), and (56).	12
Punctuation	5	Ann our manager ordered paper erasers carbons and rulers	

| 1 | 2 | 3 | 4 | 5 | 6 | 7 | 8 | 9 | 10 | 11 | 12

PRETEST Take a 5-minute timing on lines 6–25 on page 448.

PRACTICE Take a 1-minute timing on each paragraph of the Pretest on page 448.

POSTTEST Take another 5-minute timing on lines 6–25 on page 448 to see how much your skill has improved.

FORM LETTER

Standard format. Make four carbon copies. Use letterhead for each copy.

Open House programs have been scheduled by the Chicora National Forest at its ranger station at Smithport on Sunday, June 8, from noon to 5 p.m. Rangers will be on hand at the station to explain the YCC program to interested students and their parents, teachers, and counselors.

Since you have been active in supporting the YCC program, I especially want to invite you to attend and hope that you will be able to help us welcome our guests. Sincerely, Albert R. Fruhauf, District Ranger

ADDRESSING FORM LETTERS AND ENVELOPES

Address the five Open House form letters, using the addresses below. Address five envelopes.

1. Mrs. Betty Myer Birson, President, A.A.U.W., P.O. Box 26, Helena, MT 59601.
2. Ms. Madeline B. Kerr, President, Volunteer Fire Fighters, Butte, MT 59701.
3. Mr. Homer Neff, President, P.T.A., Helena Public Schools, Helena, MT 59601.
4. Mr. Stanley T. Scott, President, Chamber of Commerce, Butte, MT 59701.
5. Ms. Shirley A. Weyrauch, President, Civic Association, Helena, MT 59601.

NEWSLETTER

Standard format. Edit the copy as you type it. Needed for Forest Service Newsletter that goes to press on June 5. Must be hand-delivered to local printer the day before.

YCC AT BLUE KNOLL by Tom Yusi, Chicora High School

48 young people will be at work this summer at Game Lands in northern Sheffield county. They are involved in the second year of work with the game commission's in cooperation with the Youth Conservation Corps. Camp at Blue Knoll state park.

Last summer corps. members developed wildlife management plans for both game and nongame species in various areas, constructed a wooden bridge to gain access to a section of Game Lands where they helped plow and plant food plots for wildlife, and also laid out and marked a hikeing and nature trail.

YCC members are paid for their labor, but their is much more to the interprise than providing summer jobs. The corps. aims to make conservation and envirnment science more significant than textbook abstractions by involving YCC members in actual field situations.

YCY participants work in coed crews of six, including a group leader who is usually a college student. Each year a new group of participants is selected from thousandes of applicants. The program sharpens their awareness of environmental concepts.

COMPOSE A LETTER

Jerome Moneta, Forest Supervisor, Bitterroot National Forest, Missoula, Montana 59801, wants a copy of the display notice. Make a carbon copy for him, and compose a brief letter explaining that you are enclosing the display notice.

LAST WILL AND TESTAMENT

A last will and testament is a document that enables people to ensure that their belongings are distributed as they wish after they die.

JOB 276 A. WILL

Standard legal format. Workbook 639–642.

Last Will and Testament

I, EARL SIZEMORE, of 1729 Marbough Court, Lebanon, Tennessee, being of full age, sound mind and memory, and under no restraint, do make, publish, and declare this to be my Last Will and Testament, hereby revoking and making null and void any and all last wills and testaments and any codicils thereto by me heretofore made.

ITEM I: I direct that my legal debts, including the expense of my last illness and funeral, be first paid out of my estate as soon as practicable after the time of my decease. I further direct that all my inheritance, estate, succession and other taxes of similar nature levied or imposed by reason of my death, together with interest and penalties thereon, if any, regardless of against whom the same may be assessed, shall be paid by my Executor from the residue of my estate, and my Executor shall not request or obtain reimbursement or contribution from any person.

ITEM II: I give, bequeath, and devise all my property, real, personal, and mixed, of every kind and description, wheresoever situated, which I may own or have the right to dispose of at the time of my death, to my beloved wife, Barbara Sizemore.

ITEM III: I make, nominate, and appoint my wife, Barbara Sizemore, to be the Executrix of my estate if she is living at the time of my death. In the event that said wife is not living or for any reason is unable to serve, then I make, nominate, and appoint my daughter, Aleen, to be the Executrix.

(Continued on next page)

■ **GOALS**
To type 43/5'/4e.
To prioritize and format related office communications with speed and accuracy.

■ **FORMAT**
Drills: Single spacing 60-space line
5-Minute Timings: Double spacing 5-space tab

KEYBOARDING SKILLS

Type lines 1–4 once. Then practice using your shift key by typing line 5—do not use your shift lock. Repeat lines 1–4, or take a series of 1-minute timings.

Speed	He and I did work the eighth problem also, and it is right.	12
Accuracy	Jacqueline was very glad because her film took sixth prize.	12
Numbers	The winning bulletins were numbered 10, 29, 38, 47, and 56.	12
Symbols	The asterisk, *, is used to indicate a footnote* reference.	12
Technique	Three CPAs with IBM used to work for RCA, ABC, and NBC too.	

| 1 | 2 | 3 | 4 | 5 | 6 | 7 | 8 | 9 | 10 | 11 | 12

PRETEST

Take a 5-minute timing on lines 6–25. Circle and count your errors.

Backpacking through Europe is an economical as well as 12
an exciting way to see many countries. In summer, students 24
and young working people who have saved money for this kind 36
of experience roam all over Europe. 43

The inconveniences that a wealthier tourist pays money 12
to shun are what makes backpacking fun, cheap, and so often 24
more worthwhile. These travelers carry their gear on their 36
backs; moving about is quite easy. 43

Many backpackers travel by train because Europe has an 12
efficient rail system, and long-distance travel is not very 24
costly. Others ride bikes or rent cars. Youth hostels and 36
local homes provide places to rest. 43

Food prices can be kept to a minimum by buying cheese, 12
juices, bread, and other basics in the markets. Fast foods 24
are offered by sidewalk cafes and restaurants. Many cities 36
have cafeterias just for students. 43

Since backpackers travel like ordinary people, they do 12
come in contact with many kinds of citizens. They can make 24
many lasting friendships through shared experiences—a real 36
souvenir of a trek through Europe. 43

| 1 | 2 | 3 | 4 | 5 | 6 | 7 | 8 | 9 | 10 | 11 | 12 SI 1.58

PRACTICE

Take a 1-minute timing on each paragraph of the Pretest.

POSTTEST

Take another 5-minute timing on lines 6–25 to see how much your skill has improved.

LESSON 276

UNIT 45 Processing Legal Documents

UNIT GOAL 50/5'/3e

■ **GOALS**
To format legal documents.
To type a will.

■ **FORMAT**
Single spacing   60-space line

KEYBOARDING SKILLS

Type lines 1–4 once. Then punctuate line 5 as you type it. Repeat lines 1–4, or take a series of 1-minute timings.

Speed	1	As soon as we had tried on the blue suits, we had to leave.	12
Accuracy	2	Brown jars prevented the mixture from freezing too quickly.	12
Numbers	3	No. 101 is 29 mm wide, 38 cm long. It now weighs 47.56 kg.	12
Symbols	4	Add up $1 and $2 and $3 and $4 and $5 and $6 and $7 and $8.	12
Punctuation	5	Martha placed my coat hat scarf and boots in the closet	

| 1 | 2 | 3 | 4 | 5 | 6 | 7 | 8 | 9 | 10 | 11 | 12

12-SECOND TIMINGS

Type each line three times, or take three 12-second timings on each line. For each timing, type without error.

6 Please stop at the store and pay the man for the new shoes.
7 We hope that the eight of them will visit the lake with us.
8 Ask her to run over to the bank and ask for some new dimes.

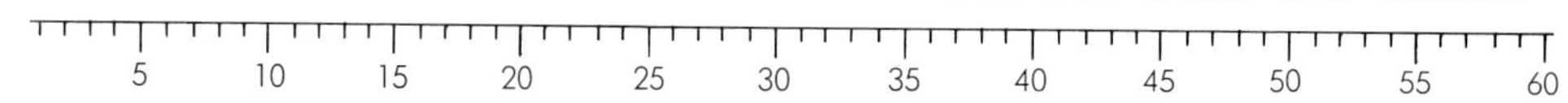

PRODUCTION LOG

As you learned in the In-Baskets, some word processing centers measure an operator's work by the number of correct lines he or she can produce in a given amount of time. In Level 12 you should log *all* your production work according to the number of lines you can produce in a given amount of time. Use the logs on Workbook page 635 top.

FORMATTING LEGAL PAPERS

Workbook 637–638.

Legal paper has a double vertical line ruled 14P/17E spaces from the left edge and a single vertical line 4P/5E spaces from the right edge. To format copy on legal paper:

1. Set margin stops 2 spaces inside the vertical ruled lines.
2. Center the title of the document between the margins.
3. Indent paragraphs 10 spaces.
4. Double-space unless directed to do otherwise.
5. Type a signature line starting at the center and ending at the right margin. If there are two signature (or address) lines on the same line of writing, they should be of equal length and separated by a minimum of 2 spaces.

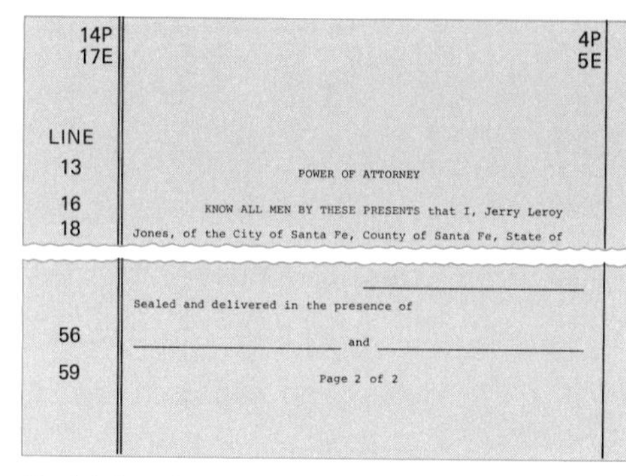

6. Maintain a top margin of 12 blank lines on the first page, 9 blank lines on others.
7. Center page numbers between the margins about 6 lines from the bottom of the page. The phrase to use is "Page 1 of 3," "Page 2 of 3," and so on. Omit the page number from a one-page document.

IN-BASKET B:

Working for a Travel Agency

You are working for Worldwide Travel Agency, located at 1200 East Sixth Street, Cleveland, OH 44114. The owner-manager is Ms. Holly Allen-Sloan. Today is July 25, 19—. Use letterheads and forms where appropriate. Workbook 383–387.

PRIORITY SHEET AND WORK LOG

Read through the entire in-basket, and then complete the priority sheet. Keep an accurate work log as you complete each job.

ITINERARY

Standard format.

ITINERARY FOR MR. AND MRS. GRAY

MR. GRAY WILL PICK THIS UP BY THE FIRST.

DAY	DATE	TIME	EVENT
SUNDAY	8/8	8:00 a.m.	BUS FROM CLEVELAND TO TORONTO
		2.00 p.m.	TOUR TORONTO
			FRIARS' INN
MONDAY	8/9	8:00 a.m.	TORONTO TO OTTAWA
		1:30 p.m.	TOUR OTTAWA
			VICTORIA PLAZA
TUESDAY	8/10	8:30 a.m.	OTTAWA TO QUEBEC CITY
			CHELSEA HOTEL
WEDNESDAY	8/11	9:00 a.m.	TOUR CITY; VISIT ST. ANNE-DE-BEAUPRE
			CHELSEA HOTEL
THURSDAY	8/12	8:00 a.m.	QUEBEC CITY TO MONTREAL
		2:00 p.m.	TOUR THE CITY
			ROYAL HOTEL
FRIDAY	8/13	8:30 a.m.	MONTREAL TO GANANOQUE
		10:30 a.m.	CRUISE THROUGH ISLANDS
		4:15 p.m.	BUS TO KINGSTON
			KINGSTON INN
SATURDAY	8/14	8:30 a.m.	TOUR FORT HENRY
		2:00 p.m.	BUS TO NIAGARA FALLS
			HAMILTON HOUSE
SUNDAY	8/15	9:00 a.m.	TOUR THE FALLS
		5:00 p.m.	BUS TO CLEVELAND

LEVEL 12

GOALS

1. Demonstrate keyboarding speed and accuracy on straight copy with a goal of 50 words a minute for 5 minutes with 3 or fewer errors.
2. Correctly proofread copy for errors and edit copy for revision.
3. Apply advanced production skills in keyboarding and formatting copy for business documents from a variety of input modes.
4. Apply rules for correct use of homonyms and confusing words, review all language arts rules presented in Levels 7 through 12.
5. Determine format and placement of documents while completing a word processing manual in-basket.

PROGRAM BULLETIN

Format an attractive bulletin to advertise the agency's fall travelogue series. The agency sponsors the series of programs to promote travel and to advertise its services.

TRAVELOGUE SERIES, FALL 19—, Sponsored by Worldwide Travel Agency

Thursday, September 18

Exploring Norway—Jonathan Forshee

The travelogue takes viewers to Norway's famous fjords; to Bergen, Norway's second largest city, which gives the appearance of a quaint eleventh-century Viking seaport; to the ski and resort countryside of rural Norway; and to Oslo, the capital city and chief seaport.

Thursday, October 23

Alaska Adventure—Betty Ebbert

Magnificent coverage of the wonders to be found along the great north highways that lead to the innermost points of northern Canada and Alaska. Popular spots, as well as those seldom visited by tourists, are covered. Daring close-ups of wildlife, trips to exciting fishing streams, and mountain climbing are featured.

Tuesday, November 11

Bermuda, Isle of Rest—Thomas O'Reilly

In Bermuda viewers will visit the U.S. Naval Base, tour the Cathedral, explore for sunken treasure, and learn of the island's role in our War of Independence.

Tickets are free at Worldwide Travel Agency. Programs will be held at the Downtown Chamber of Commerce Building, Century III Shopping Mall, Cleveland, OH 44114, at 10 a.m. and again at 7:30 p.m.

NEWS RELEASE

Compose a news release about the fall travelogue series. The release is from Holly Allen-Sloan; date the release August 1.

NEWSPAPER ADVERTISEMENT

Format attractively on a half sheet of paper. Final copy should be about 5 by 3 inches in size.

ADVERTISEMENT
MUST BE AT
NEWSPAPER
OFFICE BY
5 P.M. TODAY

LAS VEGAS—Group or Individual Tours

5 days, 4 nights

Price includes airfare for round-trip nonstop flights, shows, top hotels, transportation to/from airport, baggage handling, some meals. From $405 and up per person with double occupancy.

Worldwide Travel Agency.

Phone 555-8900.

Act now!

Space is limited.

JOB 274/275 B. LETTER

Standard format. Workbook 633–634.

(Current date) Dr. John Williams, University of Dayton, Dayton, OH 45469, Dear Dr. Williams: The students in ~~our~~ my computer programming class are very much interested in viewing your new high-technology laboratory. ~~which was recently installed.~~

Congratulations on the installation of your new computer laboratory. I am sure you are very proud of it.

About half of the class ~~plans on~~ wants to attend~~ing~~ a university and major in systems analysis or computer programming. The other members of the class are planning careers in the high-tech area immediately after high school.

Please let ~~us~~ me know whether it will be possible for the class to visit the new installation and talk with the instructors who are in charge of the installation. Sincerely, Janette Wallace, Instructor

JOB 274/275 C. CREATE A FORM

Standard format. Use a half sheet of paper to create a student schedule form.

Name ____________ Grade ________ Phone ________
Address ______________________ Homeroom ________

Quarter 1	Quarter 2	Quarter 3	Quarter 4
1			
2			
3			
4			
5			
6			

JOB 274/275 D. FORMAT AN ORGANIZATIONAL CHART

Standard format. Use a full sheet of paper turned sideways.

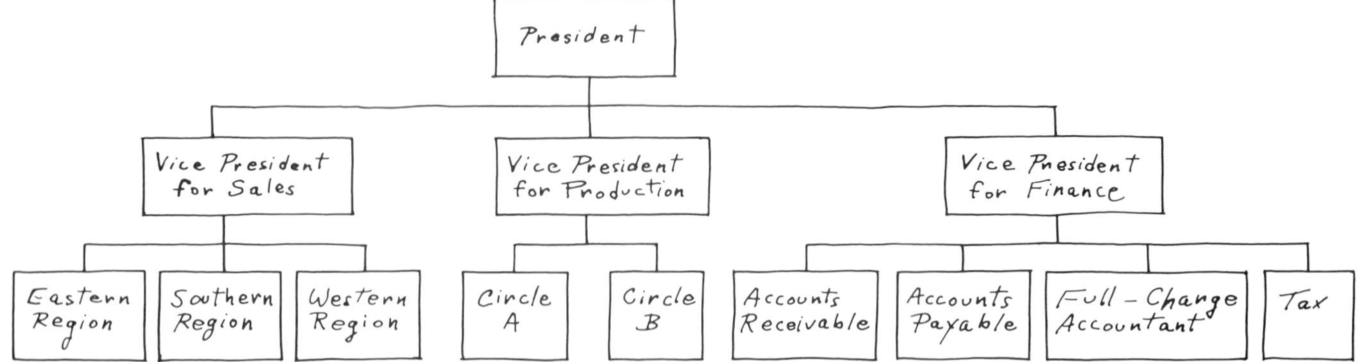

NEWSPAPER ARTICLE

Ms. Allen-Sloan wants you to prepare a correct copy for publication in the *Cleveland News,* Sunday edition, July 29. Standard format.

(Title) Jamaica PUT MANAGER'S NAME AND AGENCY AS BYLINE.

Jamaica is a island in the Caribbean, rich in beauty and culture. it has a long history thatdates before the days of explseers. Its many different peoples are testimony to it's varied past, and they live in harmony under under a government that maintains friendly contact with all nations on earth.

Tourists love jamaica for its beautful white-sand beaches and cristal-clear waters, the lush jungles that dot thehillsides, and the exciting night life that features steel-drum bands and reggae music.

The food of Jamica is healthy and natrual because most of it comes from the island. Fresh sea food and delicious fruits are important that the natives cook in a variety of dishes.

Visitors to the island may stay in the big on the beaches, rent homes, or campout in the country side. The unique aspects of Jamaica is that it is an entire country, not just a resort, so vacationing there becomes a total experience.

Relaxing as a visit maybe, it is, also, educational. The daily life of Jamaicans goes on undisturbed by tourists, and this gives visitors a chance to observe a different culture first hand. Although Jamaica is close to florida, it is far enough awya to provide visitors withthe feeling of being in a strange land!

ALMOST — STAPLES — HOTELS — FROM — OR

ARTICLE MUST BE AT NEWSPAPER OFFICE THREE DAYS BEFORE PUBLICATION.

NO #

FORM LETTER

Standard format. Edit the copy as you type it.

variety is the spice of life! whether you'd like exploring americas favorite resort destenations or cruising the blue caribbean...its up to you. this year the chamber of commerce has arranged not one but two greast vacations. you have a choice of:

americas own san francisco, hawaii, and las vegas

or

a caribbean cruise aboard the ss princess grace

we would like to point out that the price of each trip (including round-trip jet transportation accommodations all transfers baggage handling plus most taxes and tips) is only $690 less than you would pay to plan the trip yourself. besides, if you traveled on your own, you would miss out on the convience and companion ship you'll get when traveling with members of the chamber.

all the excellent features of these too outstanding vacations are discribed in detail in the enclosed brosures. look them over, and then join the chanber for a vacation to remember. sincerely, holly allen-sloan.

JOB 274/275 A. FOUR-PAGE BROCHURE

Design a course description brochure. Put the descriptions on pages 2, 3, and 4, and make an attractive front cover of your own design.

Typewriting I and Computer Literacy—Page 2

This course provides an integration of computer skills and typewriting skills. During the first semester, students will learn computer terminology, history, and impact on society while they are developing keyboarding skills and basic formatting skills on an electric typewriter. Spelling, punctuation, and grammar are also integrated.

During the second semester, students will use a microcomputer for one nine-week period to apply computer concepts learned during the first semester and learn basic word processing skills necessary for preparing personal and business reports. A variety of software packages will be used for classroom instruction. (Workbook and lab fees) (Year course—1 credit)

Typewriting II and Word Processing

Students who enroll in this course will spend one semester using the microcomputer to prepare letters, tables, and reports. Specific instruction will be given for Wordwrite, Wordmerge, and Spellright. The other semester will be spent using an electric typewriter to prepare a variety of business forms that are more easily prepared using a typewriter. Spelling, punctuation, and grammar are also integrated with the machine skills. (Workbook and lab fees) (Year course—1 credit)

Introduction to Computer Programming—Page 3

This class is for those students who have completed Typewriting I and Computer Literacy and who want to learn more about computer systems. Students will learn to use the computer as a tool for information processing. Computer programming will be studied using at least two different programming languages. Completion of Typewriting I and Computer Literacy is a prerequisite (or permission of the instructor). (Lab fee) (Semester course—1/2 credit)

Advanced Computer Programming

Students of this class will concentrate on programming of microcomputers. They will receive additional experience with concepts learned in previous computer classes. Program design and structure are stressed. Topics will include graphics and machine language. Student independent projects are possible with instructor approval. Introduction to Computer Programming is a prerequisite, and permission of the instructor is required. This course may be repeated with instructor permission. (Lab fee) (Semester course—1/2 credit)

Accounting I With Spreadsheets—Page 4

Accounting I prepares students to handle the daily recording and financial activities of the modern business office and provides them with vocational skills and business knowledge that will contribute to success in entry-level jobs. It develops an understanding of basic accounting concepts and procedures and an understanding of the work flow through the complete accounting cycle in a modern accounting system. It also acquaints students with general accounting and spreadsheet applications on the microcomputer.

Accounting I develops an understanding of how accounting relates to all aspects of business both economically and in terms of decision making and reasoning. It helps to develop good work habits, business competency, and a modern business vocabulary. It also provides students with the necessary background for future study in accounting and business data processing. (Workbook and lab fees) (Year course—1 credit)

Accounting II With Spreadsheets

Accounting II is an advanced accounting class. The first semester introduces managerial accounting for merchandising and manufacturing businesses, with some emphasis on installment and credit card sales and cost accounting. During the second semester, the students learn about financial accounting for partnerships and corporations.

The computer is used to develop spreadsheets and some financial statements. (Workbook and lab fees) (Year course—1 credit)

LESSONS 199/200

TEST

- **GOALS**
  To type 43/5′/4e.
  To format and type correctly a form letter with inserts, a news release, a report, and a boxed table.
- **FORMAT**
  Double spacing 60-space line 5-space tab

PREVIEW PRACTICE

Type each line twice as a preview to the 5-minute timings below.

Accuracy `views unique active citizens qualified criticize excitement`

Speed `elements voting right blame their city held them the pay of`

5-MINUTE TIMINGS

Take two 5-minute timings on lines 3–18.

One of the many unique elements of a democracy is that everyone of 14
legal age has the right to vote. Voting should be taken very seriously 29
because it is a responsibility. It is apparent that a government will not be 45
representative if citizens don't take active roles in choosing the people who 60
represent them. It is easy to criticize our leaders, but a part of the blame 76
rests with those citizens who do not care enough for our country to vote. 91

Voting is done at many levels of government. Federal, state, county, and 107
city elections must be planned for every year in which the terms of officials 123
are ending. Primaries are held in the spring to narrow the number of per- 138
sons running. Although the year a president is chosen can create a lot of 151
excitement, people should be interested and vote for their choice at each 166
election. 168

A good voter should pay close attention to significant issues and the 183
candidates. Newspapers, public debates, and interviews are good sources 198
of information. Choose the one who shares your views and is qualified to 213
do the job. 215

| 1 | 2 | 3 | 4 | 5 | 6 | 7 | 8 | 9 | 10 | 11 | 12 | 13 | 14 | 15 SI 1.54

JOB 199/200 A. FORM LETTER WITH LIST

Standard format. Make two carbon copies. Workbook 389–394. Body 122 words.

Yes! That's all you have to say in order to beat the upcoming price increase. Renew your subscription to USA TECHNOLOGY now at bargain rates available this month only. ¶ We know you'll enjoy USA TECHNOLOGY more than ever before because it is completely new. There is wider coverage of activities within each state, more information from the government concerning the uses of technology, and more in-depth coverage of equipment and procedures. ¶ Select the number of issues you would like to receive by checking your choice:

_____ 52 weeks for only $52—save $26
_____ 26 weeks for only $27—save $12
_____ 12 weeks for only $13—save $5

Then return this letter in the enclosed reply envelope, and we will bill your account number [*leave space to insert account number*]. Cordially yours, A. J. Ouchi, Circulation Manager

TEST

■ **GOALS**
To type 49/5′/3e.
To demonstrate competency in typing a brochure, a letter, and a chart and in creating a form.

■ **FORMAT**
Double spacing   60-space line   5-space tab

PREVIEW PRACTICE

Type each line twice as a preview to the 5-minute timings below.

```
Accuracy  1  facsimile equipment components communication administrative
Speed     2  provide length demand visual market audio entry other which
```

5-MINUTE TIMINGS

Take two 5-minute timings on lines 3–23.

```
3       Electronic mail is defined as the delivery of messages   12
4   electronically.  There are numerous differences among audio  24
5   and hard-copy delivery systems.  But more similarities than  36
6   differences can be found.  Therefore, market analyses often  48
7   include the telephone and other audio communication devices  60
8   in the category of electronic mail.                          67
9       The telephone is used in business these days as a gen-   79
10  eral message delivery system, as a sales tool, as an order-  91
11  entry device, and as an administrative message system.  One 103
12  limitation is that there is no hard copy, or any other form 115
13  of visual record, available.  When the telephone is used in 127
14  the transmission of long messages, the possibility of error 139
15  increases greatly with the length of the message.           149
16      The demand for electronic mail message systems and the  161
17  services which accompany them continues to grow.  The major 173
18  components of these systems are facsimile equipment, commu- 185
19  nicating word processors, and telex service.  Other message 197
20  services are continuing to grow as the communication demand 209
21  moves ahead and as technology provides more efficient tools 221
22  to implement faster communication flow.  As quick decisions 233
23  are demanded, even quicker communications must be realized. 245
    | 1 | 2 | 3 | 4 | 5 | 6 | 7 | 8 | 9 | 10 | 11 | 12        SI 1.92
```

JOB 199/200 B. FILL-IN FORM LETTERS

Use the information below to complete the three form letters you prepared in Job 199/200 A.

1. Thomas Jakimer, 346 Windsor St., Hartford, CT 06120-8071, Acct. 030-861-050
2. Prof. Margaret Hirsch, 519 Broussard Ave., Baton Rouge, LA 70808-2265, Acct. 361-090-012
3. Clay Whitewater, 1022 Mountain Rd., NE, Albuquerque, NM 87106-4396, Acct. 911-253-346

JOB 199/200 C. NEWS RELEASE

Standard format. Workbook 395–396.

Release: At Once 2
From: Tammy Colton 6
Manager 10

NEW EXERCISE PROGRAM 25
Palo Alto, Calif., Apr. 11--The 34
an exciting
A-1 Health Spa is introducing a new 44
exercise program that will begin on 51
Monday, April 24th. ¶ Ms. Mia Creasman 59
and Mr. Mike Dean will demonstrate the 67
TUESDAY,
new program (3) times Next week: April 77
WEDNESDAY, THURSDAY,
18; April 19; and April 20. 87
NO ¶ Each demonstration, will begin at 102
(especially designed for weight reduction,)
10:00 a.m. and will last about (1) hour. 110

Persons who are interested in 116
attending one of Ms. Creasman and Mr. 123
Dean's sessions should call the spa at 131
MONDAY,
555-4729 by noon on April 17. 139
Additional programs in exercise 146
are also offered at A-1 Health Spa. 153
Brochures on the entire offerings are 161
available on request. (END) 167

JOB 199/200 D. UNEDITED REPORT

Standard format. Edit copy. Compose a title.

Now the computer can become your nutrisional adviser. Today nutrisional information is printed on the package of all foods. But how nutricious is your favorite quiche receipe or grandmother's upside-down cake? When it comes to fresh foods or receipes that you prepare, analysing the nutrisional information—calories, carbohydrates, fat, and protein—can be complicated. ¶ Now there is a soft ware program that can give you nutrisional information about the foods you prepare. The program prompts you to list the receipe's ingredents one at a time. Then the program asks you to specify the quantity used. For example, after you type "milk," the computer asks, "How many cups are used?" ¶ After you have typed in all the ingredients, the program then asks how many servings the receipe makes. Finally, the program gives you a nutrisional analysis of a topical serving.

JOB 199/200 E. TABLE WITH BRACED HEADING

Standard format.

SEPTEMBER SALES ANALYSIS

Budgeted vs. Actual

Branch	Last Year		This Year	
	Budgeted	Actual	Budgeted	Actual
Boston			$ 15,000	$ 17,500
Detroit	$ 25,000	$ 24,500	26,500	25,950
Houston	35,000	36,000	39,000	39,500
Jacksonville	45,000	50,000	50,000	49,000
Milwaukee	90,000	93,000	94,000	92,250
St. Louis	50,000	35,000		
San Francisco	70,000	68,500	71,000	70,250
Seattle	20,000	18,000	19,500	20,500
Total	$335,000	$325,000	$315,000	$314,950

BROCHURE

Place the following information on the front cover of the brochure.

THE FRANKLIN AREA HISTORICAL SOCIETY PRESENTS
"A Walk Through the Past"
Sunday, July 9, Through Saturday, July 15

Place the following list on the two inside pages. Divide the list evenly, half on each page. Each item should be numbered so that the numbers can be placed on the map that will be prepared later.

1. Begin at the Harding Museum at 320 Park Avenue. The museum was donated by the late Mrs. William Harding along with the items that are displayed on the first floor of the museum. The rooms on the second floor have pieces donated by members of the Franklin community and surrounding area.
2. Mr. and Mrs. James Roberts, 230 Park Avenue. This home was built in 1891 by David Carpenter. The architecture is Victorian and Queen Anne.
3. Mr. and Mrs. Dan Neal, 221 Elm Street. This home was built in 1906. Mr. and Mrs. Roy Eldridge lived in it for 50 years. Their daughter, Joyce, was married to Clarence Brown (now congressman) in the formal garden at the rear of the home.
4. Mr. and Mrs. Thomas Shera, 303 Elm Street. This home of Queen Anne architecture was built in 1893 by Will Vail, a farmer. He lived in the home for 20 years. Adam Bridge then bought the home. The original structure of the home has never been changed.
5. Mr. and Mrs. Seth Adkins, 301 Oxford Road. Built in 1927, this home shows Georgian influence in its architectural design. The home was built by S. S. Tibbals, publisher, business executive, and editor of the Franklin Chronicle.
6. Mr. and Mrs. Jack Rhude, 227 Oxford Road. The oldest home in the district is a fine example of Greek architecture and originally included 1000 acres. It was built in 1847.
7. Mr. and Mrs. Frank Neal, 123 Miami Avenue. This home was built in 1922 on the old Baptist parsonage site by Harry C. Eldridge, founder of the Eldridge Entertainment House. The home was later owned by Paul Logan of Logan-Long Paper Company.
8. Mr. and Mrs. Seth Howard, 117 Miami Avenue. Built in 1890, this example of Queen Anne architecture has Eastern Stick influence. At one time it was sold for as little as $700.
9. Mr. and Mrs. Thomas Burns, 321 Park Avenue. This home was originally located on the Harding Museum plot and was moved to the present location in 1896. It was built in 1882 and is an example of Victorian architecture.
10. Mr. and Mrs. Robert Morton, 103 Miami Avenue. This home was built in 1880 by Derrick B. Anderson, assessor for Franklin Township. The architecture is Italian with Greek Revival influence.

INVITATION

Half sheet of plain paper.

You are cordially invited
to attend the
dedication ceremony
and
walking tour
sponsored by
The Franklin Area Historical Society
Sunday, July 9, 19__

MEMBERSHIP CARDS

We just ran out of membership cards. New ones are on order, but they may not arrive in time for the walking tour. Prepare six temporary cards.

____
is a member in good standing of
THE FRANKLIN AREA HISTORICAL SOCIETY
for the year
19__ to 19__

____________ ____________
President Treasurer

LEVEL 9

GOALS

1. Demonstrate keyboarding speed and accuracy on straight copy with a goal of 45 words a minute for 5 minutes with 4 or fewer errors.
2. Correctly proofread copy for errors and edit copy for revision.
3. Apply production skills in keyboarding and formatting copy for business documents from a variety of input modes.
4. Apply rules for correct use of contractions, possessive pronouns, and abbreviations in written communications.
5. Prioritize and make appropriate formatting decisions while completing two in-baskets.

"We're trying to encourage outside fixup," said Brenda Litsch, current president of the area historical society. "The organization wants people to see the possibilities of the homes." Mrs. Litsch lives at 832 Park Avenue and owns two rentals in the district. "Over the past 10 to 20 years many of the houses owned by absentee landlords suffered from neglect, and the area received the stigma of being a slum and high-crime area," she said. Now residents say they have no fear about living in the area.

"We are doing things we never knew we could do," Mrs. Newland said, "We read books and learn how to do them--strip woodwork, strip floors, refinish furniture." "Everything that has to be replaced has to be made special, say many of the residents. "Screen doors just aren't made or such high doorways. Drapes and curtains aren't long enough either."

Not all the houses are in such poor repair. The Cases of 131 Oxford State Road were "lucky." They replaced some of the plumbing and most of the wiring, but otherwise their Colonial Revival home was livable when they moved in four years ago. The house has 12 rooms with 9-feet ceilings. Specail features of the house include double glass interior and exterior door and windows and some stained glass in the dining room.

House tours are being arranged for the week of July 9. All the owners of homes in the restoration district who wish to participate will have their homes open for the public to enjoy.

LETTER

Mr. Frank Neal, 123 Miami Avenue, Franklin, OH 45005, Dear Mr. Neal: Thank you very much for the beautiful Victorian chest that you recently donated to the Harding Museum. Mrs. Rousch is especially pleased with the way it blends with her newest arrangement on the second floor. ¶ A plaque is now being engraved and should be in place within the next few weeks. The plaque will have your name and a short history of the Victorian chest. ¶ Please stop in and see our newest display when you have an opportunity. Thank you again for your contribution to the Harding Museum. Cordially, Brenda Litsch, President

LETTER

Mrs. Sally Cheney donated some china dolls recently. She lives at 307 Park Avenue in Franklin. The dolls are historically significant to our area because they belonged to Juanita Anderson, a well-known music teacher in the area. Please write Mrs. Cheney a thank-you letter similar to the one written to Mr. Neal.

LESSON 201

UNIT 33 Formatting Reports

UNIT GOAL 44/5′/4e

■ **GOALS**
To type 44/5′/4e.
To format and type an agenda.

■ **FORMAT**
Drills: Single spacing 60-space line
5-Minute Timings: Double spacing 5-space tab

KEYBOARDING SKILLS

Type lines 1–4 once. Then practice using your space bar by typing line 5. Repeat lines 1–4, or take a series of 1-minute timings.

Speed 1 Sue is to pay that man to fix the bike for the eight girls. 12
Accuracy 2 Squad sixteen was puzzled by the vigor of the major attack. 12
Numbers 3 The 10 men lived 29 days at 3847 North Buff Street for $56. 12
Symbols 4 These test scores ranged from 10% to 56%; my score was 47%. 12
Technique 5 Then . . . . Well, I tried . . . and tried . . . and I won.

| 1 | 2 | 3 | 4 | 5 | 6 | 7 | 8 | 9 | 10 | 11 | 12

PRETEST

Take a 5-minute timing on lines 6–25. Circle and count your errors. Use the chart on page 332 to determine which lines to type for practice.

6 When people travel, they do not consider just how many 12
7 different businesses are involved in making their journey a 24
8 success. Several modes of transportation, hotels, resorts, 36
9 and restaurants will profit; and each of these services for 48
10 the traveler adds mainly to the quality and, in the end, to 60
11 the pleasure of the trip. 65
12 Most travel agencies offer a range of prices to accom- 77
13 modate almost any travel budget. They also try to offer an 89
14 assortment of pleasant places to visit. Some tourists seem 101
15 undeterred today by distance or high costs. For example, a 113
16 ship to Antarctica is always sold out, even though it's one 125
17 of the most unreachable places in the world--and one of the 137
18 coldest. And as a result of this increasing tourism, there 149
19 are plans for permanent clusters of tourists' cabins there, 161
20 complete with an airstrip. 166
21 Several years ago the demand to see Antarctica quickly 178
22 and cheaply led to charter-jet flights from New Zealand. A 190
23 flight gave tourists, gawking through windows of the plane, 202
24 a panorama of spectacular scenery. Remarkably, this market 214
25 soared, in spite of hazards. 220

| 1 | 2 | 3 | 4 | 5 | 6 | 7 | 8 | 9 | 10 | 11 | 12 SI 1.59

IN-BASKET H:

Historical Society

You have been employed to work in your home for the newly formed historical society in your community. The major thrust of the organization presently is to gain publicity for the restoration district recently approved by the federal government. The documents about the dedication and walking tour are the most important. Today is May 25. Use letterheads and forms where appropriate. Workbook 617 bottom–632.

PRIORITY SHEET AND TIME LOG

Read through the entire in-basket, and then complete the priority sheet. Be sure to keep an accurate time log as you complete each job.

DICTATED LETTER

mr and mrs seth adkins 301 oxford road franklin ohio 45005 dear mr and mrs adkins congratulations on having your home placed in the national register of historic homes the franklin area historical society is extremely proud to include your home in its restoration district during the next month our organization will be planning our summer activities the main event will be a tour of the historical homes in the restoration district of course you will want to have your home included in the tour a brochure is being prepared with a brief description of each home in the district and an accompanying historical reference would you please prepare both of these items for us within the next two weeks so that we may properly identify your home in the brochure cordially brenda litsch president

DICTATED LETTER

mrs josephine rousch 319 park avenue franklin ohio 45005 dear josephine i have just returned from the museum and was most impressed with the new display in the harding room you certainly have spent a great deal of time searching for the unusual pieces that are displayed i was especially impressed with the number of victorian pieces of furniture you were able to locate the plaques that you have requested for each of the pieces will take about three weeks to be engraved this will be in plenty of time for our special events this summer i will notify you when the plaques are finished so that you can personally see that they are attached to the proper pieces thank you so much for the marvelous display cordially brenda litsch president

NEWS RELEASE

Get ready for the local paper immediately.

RESTORATION DISTRICT TAKES SHAPE

Area residents are quietly admiring their finished and parially [t inserted] finished ~~products~~ buildings in preparation for the first annual tour of homes in the newest restoration district in Ohio. "Two things sold me on the house," Mrs. Greene said, "the ~~stairs~~ stairway with a winding cherry banister and the arch [sway inserted] door beteen [w inserted] the dinning [n deleted] room and library."

One of the homes on this tour, the Bookwalter-Brewster house at 311 Park Avenue, is considered an outstanding example of french second empire style from the 1870s. It was listed in the National Register this spring. Being listed ~~on~~ in the national register puts restrictions on the architecture [e changed to al] alterrations [r deleted] that can be made to a house, but it also qualified [d changed to s] the owner for federal loans and grants.

(Continued on next page)

PRACTICE

In the chart below find the number of errors you made on the Pretest. Then type each of the designated drill lines four times.

Pretest errors	0–1	2–3	4–5	6+
Drill lines	29–35	28–34	27–33	26–32

Accuracy

```
26 budget example involved permanent assortment transportation
27 out years windows cluster increasing undeterred spectacular
28 are gave traveler agencies Antarctica businesses remarkably
29 result hazards pleasure unreachable restaurants accommodate
30 try travel success quickly journey several quality services
```

Speed

```
31 people hotels plane when they trip high also and the one to
32 benefit prices though market their sold some all how led of
33 tourist flights world spite visit most this end for ago jet
34 permanent consider demand these seem with just many even an
35 distance tourism through always seldom today range also any
```

POSTTEST

Take another 5-minute timing on lines 6–25 on page 331 to see how much your skill has improved.

FORMATTING AGENDAS

An agenda may be a list of topics to be discussed at a meeting, or it may be a formal program of a meeting. To format an agenda that is a list of topics:

1. Use the hanging-indented format for enumerations.
2. Arrange the topics in a logical sequence.

To format an agenda that is a formal program:

1. Use a columnar format (like the format for itineraries).
2. Arrange the time information in the first column.
3. Leave 3 to 6 spaces between columns.
4. Arrange the descriptive information in the second column. Begin individual entries (topic, speaker's name, room number) at the tab stop.
5. Indent any lines that turn over.
6. Use a 5-inch line. If the descriptive information is short and will not fill a 5-inch line, center the program horizontally as you would a table.

JOB 201 A. AGENDA

Standard format for program. Center horizontally.

SOFTWARE FOR THE LAW OFFICE
ABA Seminar III
Santiago Beach Resort--Puerto Rico
June 23, 19--

8:30 <u>Computerizing Your Practice</u>
Hazel Nagamatsu / Ballroom A
9:30 Coffee
10:00 <u>Accounting Programs</u>
Client Billing and Telephones
Terence Mendelssohn / Room 7
11:30 <u>Management Systems</u>
Repetitive Documents and Calendars
Alexis Halliman / Ballroom A

(Continued on next page)

■ GOALS
To type 49/5′/3e.
To prioritize and format related business documents.

■ FORMAT
Drills: Single spacing 60-space line
5-Minute Timings: Double spacing 5-space tab

KEYBOARDING SKILLS

Type lines 1–4 once. Then do what line 5 tells you to do. Repeat lines 1–4, or take a series of 1-minute timings.

```
Speed       1  If the eight men do the work right, they may make a profit.  12
Accuracy    2  Jebb gave my excited dog quite a prize for his clever work.  12
Numbers     3  Que Company ordered 10, 29, and 38; we asked for 47 and 56.  12
Symbols     4  Mello (the fluffy one) won't win the prize--she's too slow!  12
Technique   5  Underscore each of the words immediately after you type it.
               | 1 | 2 | 3 | 4 | 5 | 6 | 7 | 8 | 9 | 10 | 11 | 12
```

PREVIEW PRACTICE

Type each line twice as a preview to the 5-minute timings below.

```
Accuracy    6  request activity someone's attention excitement restoration
Speed       7  many them that they have been will take this more item each
```

5-MINUTE TIMINGS

Take two 5-minute timings on lines 8–24.

8 Many people enjoy maintaining accurate historical data of homes and 15
9 communities. The enthusiasm is often enhanced through group efforts. 29
10 Citizens usually pick structures to restore and request grants to provide 44
11 money to return these buildings to their original status and keep them like 59
12 that. They generate community interest in various activities. 71
13 Organizing a tour of the areas where the buildings are to be restored and 87
14 where they have already been restored is one activity that always creates 102
15 public curiosity. Who can resist the chance to take a peek at someone's 116
16 new creations or designs and styles of the past? 126
17 Although this restoration of old buildings is probably more exciting than 142
18 collecting artifacts and relics portraying an earlier life-style, there are many 158
19 who enjoy working with such historical articles. A photograph stored away 173
20 in an old trunk or a letter hidden between the pages of an old book attracts 189
21 the attention of a real history buff for many long hours. 200
22 Tracing one's personal history is also another way for people to find a 215
23 common interest in a community. Histories of families can be researched, 230
24 and the source of mutual interest can be shared as each item is located. 245

| 1 | 2 | 3 | 4 | 5 | 6 | 7 | 8 | 9 | 10 | 11 | 12 | 13 | 14 | 15 SI 1.68

12:30 Lunch on the Patio
2:00 Communications
Legal Libraries and Electronic Mail
Juan Carrona / Oceanside Solarium
3:00 Coffee
3:30 Data-Base Management
Litigation Support Systems
Martha Immel / Auditorium

■ **GOALS**
To type agendas.
To justify right margins.

■ **FORMAT**
Single spacing 60-space line

KEYBOARDING SKILLS

Type lines 1–4 once. Then practice using your backspace and underscore keys by typing line 5 twice. Repeat lines 1–4, or take a series of 1-minute timings.

Speed	1	My neighbors kept five or six keys for their downtown shop.	12
Accuracy	2	The amazing jackals quickly exited from the blue wire cage.	12
Numbers	3	James moved from 596 East 87 Street to 403 North 21 Avenue.	12
Symbols	4	Employee business expenses* include: (1) travel, (2) food.	12
Technique	5	Kay and Alan and Max and Pam and Anne and Zoe went to Iowa.	

| 1 | 2 | 3 | 4 | 5 | 6 | 7 | 8 | 9 | 10 | 11 | 12

12-SECOND TIMINGS

Type each line three times, or take three 12-second timings on each line. For each timing, type with no more than 1 error.

6 Sue said the five girls can swim across the lake with ease.
7 Please take two of these big boxes down to the post office.
8 Maybe he's going home with you, or do you have other plans?

5 10 15 20 25 30 35 40 45 50 55 60

JOB 202 A. AGENDA

Standard format for list of topics.

OFFICE TECHNOLOGY COMMITTEE 16
Meeting Agenda 28
September 12, 19— 42

1. Approval of minutes of August 10 meeting. 53
2. Report of meeting with all employees in the word processing center on the 18th floor. 64 74

(Continued on next page)

GIVE TO MANAGER BEFORE YOU LEAVE TODAY.

CHECKS

Send two commission checks to the following two salespersons: Sandra J. Henkel for $450 and James L. Hustad for $730.

TABLE

Use an attractive, easy-to-read format.

STOCK OWNERSHIP IN SOS, INC.

	DECEMBER 31, 1985		LAST YEAR	
	HOLDERS	PERCENT	HOLDERS	PERCENT
INDIVIDUALS:				
MEN	4,500	25.7	4,950	25.1
WOMEN	4,200	24.0	4,600	23.3
JOINT OWNERS	5,000	28.6	5,555	28.2
STOCKBROKERS, SECURITY DEALERS . . .	950	5.4	890	4.5
NOMINEES	350	2.0	530	2.7
FOREIGN HOLDERS	400	2.3	600	3.0
INSTITUTIONS AND MUTUAL FUNDS	1,900	10.9	2,280	11.6
ALL OTHERS	200	1.1	310	1.6
TOTALS	17,500	100.0	19,715	100.0

ORGANIZATIONAL CHART

This regional sales office has been given new territories and new personnel. Please make a new chart using the names written in. Type the names in all capitals and their titles in capitals and lowercase.

DO WHEN YOU HAVE TIME.

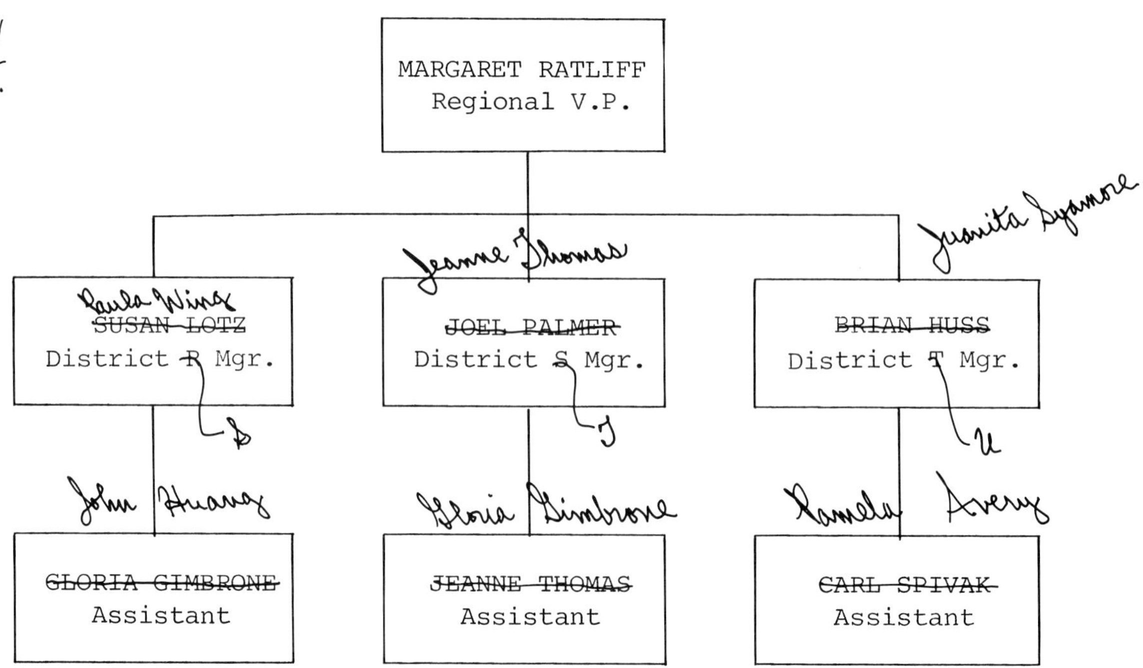

3. Discussion of trial use of CTI equipment last 85
month and operators' evaluations. 93
4. Report from ad hoc committee to study the 103
available software for CTI system. 111
5. Discussion of BioTech proposal. 119
6. Discussion of operators' evaluations of the 130
BioTech equipment and software. 138
7. Graphic comparison of CTI and BioTech by 148
Alice Davis, manager, Office Technology. 157

FORMATTING PROGRAMS WITH JUSTIFIED RIGHT MARGINS

If the speaker's name or the room number is typed in a third column, the program will look more attractive if the right margin is justified (ends evenly). To format programs with the right margin justified:

1. Arrange the time and descriptive material in columns 1 and 2 as in programs that are not justified.
2. Backspace each item in the third column from the right margin.
3. When the space between columns is wide, use leaders to fill in the space. Also use leaders if items in the description column are very different in length (as in Job 202 B below). Leave 1 space after the last word in column 2 and 1 space before the first word in column 3.

Production Practice. Set your left margin at 10 and your right margin at 80. Set a tab 9 spaces in from the left margin. Single spacing. Clean sheet of paper. Use Job 202 B below.

Space down to line 7. Be sure the printing point is positioned at the left margin. Tap the space bar once. Type *9:00.* Tab. Type *Vendor Demonstration of BioTech System.* Move the printing point to the right margin (80). Backspace for every letter and space in the words *Computer Room.* Type the words *Computer Room.* Position the printing point at the space after the word *System.* Space once and type leaders to fill the line, leaving 1 space blank before the word *Computer.* Return twice. Type *10:15.* Tab and type the word *Coffee.* Position the printing point at the right margin. Backspace for the word *Lobby.* Type the word *Lobby.* Move the printing point to the space after the word *Coffee.* Fill in the line with leaders as before.

Check your work. Did you type 8 leaders in line 1? Do the colons line up in column 1?

JOB 202 B. AGENDA

Standard format for program. Justify the right margin.

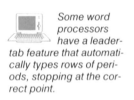

Many word processors have a right-justify feature that automatically justifies the right margin.

Some word processors have a leader-tab feature that automatically types rows of periods, stopping at the correct point.

```
            OFFICE TECHNOLOGY CONFERENCE
                  August 79, 19--
 8:30   Registration ................................ Lobby
 9:00   Vendor Demonstration of Biotech System .... Computer Room

10:15   Coffee .......................................... Lobby

11:30   Displaly of BioTeck Software ................... Gallery

12:00   Lunch ...................................... Dining Room

 1:30   Records Managment and the Computer
        Speaker:  Jack Bellari, Systems Analyst .... Conference A

 2:30   Poffee .......................................... Lobby

 2:45   Networking  Marilyn Gowdy       Coordinator
        Speaker:  Alice Davis, WP Supervisor ...... Computer Room

 4:00   Questions and Answers
        Leader: Speaker:  Joseph Ogarkov, Programmer ....... Conference C

 4:30   Discussion and evaluation ................. Conference C
```

INVOICES

Send two invoices. (1) To Info Systems, 9025 South Broadway, Westboro, NJ 07701, for 3 boxes of minidiskettes @ $90 a box, 6 dozen polyfilm ribbons @ $29.95 a dozen. (2) To Montgomery County Joint Vocational School, 191 Hoke Road, Westboro, NJ 07701, for cleaning circuits and repairing the alternating component on the SOS-80 Word Processor—$45 for labor and $15 for the part.

CONFERENCE REPORT

TYPE THIS WHEN YOU HAVE THE TIME.

WATCH FOR ERRORS—I MARKED MOST OF THEM.

MAKE A CARBON COPY OF THIS FOR MY FILE.

TITLE

Over 1,400 exhibits, 95 sessions, a personal computing festival, and special conference on minicomputers ~~was~~ WERE featured at the national computer confernece, December 28-29, at the Anaheim California convention center. ~~A presentation of~~ the American federation of Information Processing Societies, Inc. had as its theme "New directions for new decate Pam Rizzo of Moorpark College was the program chairperson.

Beginning the first session was Paula Wing, who presented a seminar on A Pragmatic View of Distributed Procesing Systems moderated by Susan Lotz. Full-day seminars included Performance measurement in systems and programming by Pam Avery, Quality control for software by Mark Monk, "Structuring the Data Base System by Natalie Caskey, "Software Design Techniques" by Julie Schaefer, "Computer Security" by Lori Robins, "Software Tools" by Gloria Gimbrone. Half-day seminars were conducted by Julie Scheper on "Design by Objectives," Kelly Maxton on "Packaging Your Image for Success," Tammy Colton on "How to Develop a Long-Range Plan," Dixie Wiseman on "Contract Negotiations," and Jeannie Thomas on "An Overview of Distributed Processing."

A complete file of the literature from the conference is available for anyone who is interested in reviewing materials from any of the sessions. Cassette tapes are also available ~~from~~ OF the sessions that I attended.

DICTATED MEMO

IMMEDIATELY! EDIT CAREFULLY.

to all sales personnel from margaret ratliff vice president for marketing subject open house the letters for the open house will be mailed next week to all sales prospects in the westboro area please check the computer printout in the next two days and let my secretary know if you have additional prospects this open house is going to be an excellent opportunity for us to show our new products and familiarize clients with our complete line of services please review your sales

LESSON 203

■ GOALS
To recognize contractions and possessive pronouns while typing sentences.
To format and type minutes of a meeting.

■ FORMAT
Single spacing 60-space line

LAB 24

Contractions and Possessive Pronouns

Type lines 1–4 once. Then repeat lines 1–4 or take a series of 1-minute timings.

```
1  You're working quickly with James to complete your reports.  12
2  They're planning to itemize all taxes before their meeting.  12
3  It's good to see that the firm is improving its poor image.  12
4  Tony and I will decide who's going to present whose awards.  12
   | 1 | 2 | 3 | 4 | 5 | 6 | 7 | 8 | 9 | 10 | 11 | 12
```

Contractions such as *it's, they're,* and *you're* sound like the possessive pronouns *its, their,* and *your.* To avoid mistakes, say "it is" whenever you see *it's;* say "they are" whenever you see *they're;* and so on. By doing so, you will always know if the contraction is correct.

I know *you're* pleased with *your* results. ("You are pleased." Okay. "You are results." Not okay, so *your results* is correct.)

30-SECOND "OK" TIMINGS

Type as many 30-second "OK" (errorless) timings as possible out of three attempts on lines 5–7.

```
5  Our nation grows its own food; so it's farmers who have the  12
6  most significant job in the country.  If we had no food, we  24
7  would have no use for the many other things we enjoy today.  36
   | 1 | 2 | 3 | 4 | 5 | 6 | 7 | 8 | 9 | 10 | 11 | 12
```

MINUTES OF A MEETING, ALTERNATE FORMAT

1. Headings such as *Attendance, Unfinished Business,* and *New Business* are not used. Other appropriate headings are used.
2. Headings "hang" in the margin. Type headings at the left margin. The copy that follows a heading begins on the same line as the heading. Set a tab 2 spaces after the longest heading. (See the illustration at the right.) Very long headings may be divided on two lines.
3. Do not indent paragraphs. Double-space between paragraphs.
4. All other standard rules apply.

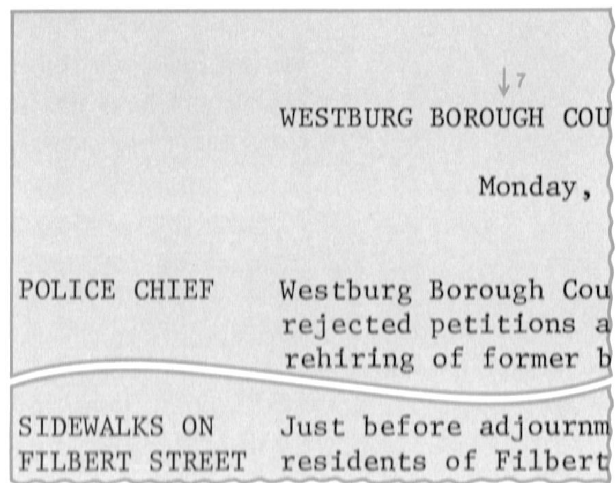

↓7
WESTBURG BOROUGH COU
Monday,
POLICE CHIEF
Westburg Borough Cou
rejected petitions a
rehiring of former b
SIDEWALKS ON
FILBERT STREET
Just before adjournm
residents of Filbert

Remember:

Some computer software programs allow you to set a temporary left margin that automatically indents the turnover lines when you use the word wrap feature. Hitting the return key returns you to the original margin.

PRACTICE

In the chart below find the number of errors you made on the Pretest. Then type each of the designated drill lines four times.

Pretest errors	0–1	2–3	4+
Drill lines	28–31	27–30	26–29

Accuracy

```
26 accent amazing software characters keystrokes breakthroughs
27 screen quickly adapting printwheel manuscript automatically
28 required processing accomplishes transferring communicating
```

Speed

```
29 enables display system permit proper major disks types been
30 entire marks these while over that hold same time copy what
31 print word from disk with each done this more than will has
```

POSTTEST

Take another 5-minute timing on lines 5–25 on page 433 to see how much your skill has improved.

IN-BASKET G:

Sales Office

You are a secretary for the regional sales office for SOS, Inc., an information processing equipment distributor. Your boss is Margaret Ratliff, vice president for marketing. Today is January 5; Ms. Ratliff has left the office for one week and given directions for you to complete the following jobs. *Remember to prioritize your work before you begin.* Record documents in the order in which you complete them. Record the amount of time you used to complete each job. Workbook 611–617 top.

PRIORITY SHEET AND TIME LOG

Read through the entire in-basket, and then complete the priority sheet. Be sure to keep an accurate time log as you complete each job.

FORM LETTER

GET THIS TO THE GRAPHIC ARTS DEPARTMENT BY NOON TOMORROW.

Plain paper.

I would like to take this opportunity to invite you to the Westboro Regional Center Open House, which will be held on Wednesday, January 28, 19—. The hours will be 3 p.m. to 8 p.m. This event will be a gala new-product introduction featuring many exciting innovations!

Every 15 minutes there will be a miniseminar on one of several topics of interest, such as the Model SOS-90, the SOS-12 Pocket Computer, and the SOS-80 Word Processor. Refreshments will be served, and for each attendee there will be a coupon worth $20 toward any of our educational classes.

You will have the opportunity to meet with all our trained sales personnel as well as with other company representatives. This promises to be the most fascinating event in our area for some time to come. If you will be able to attend, please mail the enclosed postcard today. Please feel free to invite any of your colleagues who would enjoy this experience. Best regards,

POSTCARD

Yes! I will attend the Westboro Regional Center Open House on January 28, 19—. I will bring ____ guests with me.

Name ________________________ Company/School ________________________

JOB 203 A. MINUTES OF A COUNCIL MEETING

Alternate format.

WESTBURG BOROUGH COUNCIL MEETING 19
Monday, June 20, 19— 35

Police Chief—Westburg Borough Council Mon- 47
day night rejected petitions attempting to force 57
the rehiring of former borough police chief Rex 67
Sill. A brief statement read by Mayor Gail Burns 77
said borough manager Ben Strange had acted 85
within the guidelines of his office to accept Sill's 96
resignation on May 12. 101

Sewage System—Council spent a good part of 112
its three-hour meeting discussing the storm and 122
sewage systems in the borough and the ban on 131
new hookups imposed by the state's Department 140
of Environmental Resources. 146

Councilman Thomas Hessburg, referring to the 156
hydrogen sulfide that Corr Refining released into 166
the system recently, said he had been checking 175
ordinances to determine what can be dumped. 184
He found that the fine for offenders was low, 194
ranging from $10 to $100. Hessburg then of- 202
fered a motion for three amendments to protect 212
the borough: 214

1. Increase the fine for dumping, with no limit 226
to the amount that can be charged offenders. 236
Charge a million dollars if necessary. 245
2. Expand the list of substances that are prohib- 257
ited from being dumped in the lake. 265
3. Establish a date by which downspouts on all 276
structures must be disconnected from the 285
sanitary sewage system. Hessburg indicated 295
that borough engineer Art Sears said that a 304
rapid 1-inch rainfall would produce over 1 314
million gallons of water. This water empties 324
into the street sewers, causing them to over- 334
flow. 335

Hessburg, Olson, and Segel voted for the 344
amendments; Council member Lew Smyth was 352
absent. The motion passed. 358

Council member Tony Lomassoni cast the only 368
negative vote on the motion to begin work on the 378
amendments—he argued that it would be hard to 387
force people to take out downspouts. 395

Plant Odor—Lomassoni conveyed East Side 406
residents' complaints about the sewage plant 415
odor. Mr. Strangis, manager at the firm, re- 424
ported that a new disposal site had been selected, 434
but he did not promise that dumping at a new site 444
would take care of the odor. 450

Ben Strange, the borough manager, said he had 460
written to three consulting engineers asking for 470
help in solving the problem. He stressed that the 480
borough needs expertise. He pointed out that 489
there was no panic yet. Lomassoni countered 498
that action should be taken because the problem 508
was critical. No action was taken, however. 517

Sidewalks on Filbert Street—Just before ad- 525
journment, Lomassoni said that residents of Fil- 540
bert Street had received letters from the borough 550
directing them to repair their sidewalks as a re- 559
sult of a program approved by Council last 568
month and that many homeowners could not pay 577
for this work. 580

Borough manager Ben Strange noted that some 590
persons on Filbert Street might apply for grants 600
through the HUD small-cities program to repair 609
their sidewalks. Since the notification letters set 620
an October 15 deadline for repairs to be made, 629
Lomassoni made a motion that Council recall the 639
ordinance for further study. Neither Hessburg 648
nor Segel would provide a second to the motion. 658

Second Avenue Traffic—Council approved a 668
90-day parking and traffic change for the inter- 681
section of Second Avenue and South Street. The 690
change calls for installing stop signs on South 700
Street, making Second Avenue a through street 709
with the traffic signal flashing yellow, reducing 719
the speed limit from 35 mph to 25 mph on Sec- 728
ond Avenue from Main Street to Lang Avenue, 737
and prohibiting parking on Second Avenue. 745

(Continued on next page)

UNIT 44 In-Baskets

UNIT GOAL 49/5′/3e

■ **GOALS**
To use confusing words correctly while typing sentences.
To type 49/5′/3e.
To prioritize and format related office communications.

■ **FORMAT**
Drills: Single spacing 60-space line
5-Minute Timings: Double spacing 5-space tab

Type lines 1–4 once, selecting the appropriate word from those enclosed in parentheses. Edit your copy as your teacher reads the answers. Then retype lines 1–4 from your edited copy.

LAB 32
Confusing Words

1 They were able to quickly (access, assess) which employee had (access, assess).
2 The (affect, effect) of the testing program will (affect, effect) our decision.
3 Ms. Angert spent the day catching up on her (correspondence, correspondents).
4 Yes, some research will always (precede, proceed) approval to (precede, proceed).

PRETEST

Take a 5-minute timing on lines 5–25. Circle and count your errors.

```
 5      It is amazing what major breakthroughs word processing   12
 6 enjoys.  Software has been developed to permit operators to   24
 7 input text in over 15 different languages without knowledge   36
 8 of the language that is input.  Two disks hold the required   48
 9 software that enables the units to use two languages at the   60
10 same time.  An operator types copy from foreign manuscript,   72
11 inserting proper accent marks.  The table disk converts the   84
12 keystrokes on the keyboard to the designated characters for   96
13 the particular language on the display screen; and with the  108
14 proper printwheel inserted, it coordinates the keyboard and  120
15 the rotary printer.  The message disk converts these system  132
16 messages to each language.                                   137
17      The entire procedure for adapting a word processor for  149
18 another language can be done quickly.  The machine operator  161
19 accomplishes this with a few keystrokes by transferring the  173
20 tables of the desired language from one disk to another one  185
21 while the word processor automatically adapts to the desig-  197
22 nated language.  The word processor is actually communicat-  209
23 ing in more than one language at a time.  A German operator  221
24 can key and print in French; however, the machine will dis-  233
25 play the text in German to allow the operator to proofread.  245
   | 1 | 2 | 3 | 4 | 5 | 6 | 7 | 8 | 9 | 10 | 11 | 12        SI 1.68
```

Other Business—In other business, Council: 757

Approved advertising of bids for the storm sewer 768
projects on Elm, Cherry, and Birch Streets. 777

Heard a protest to its parking ban on Lang Ave- 787
nue near the Third Avenue intersection but de- 796
cided not to change the present law. 803

Agreed to hire a labor negotiator at $55 per hour, 815
plus expenses, to conduct contract talks for the 824
borough with the police, who are members of 833
the IMAW union. 836

The meeting was adjourned at 11:15 p.m. 845

Osvaldo Medici, 853
Borough Secretary 859

■ GOALS
To identify contractions and possessive pronouns while typing sentences.
To format and type special types of reports.

■ FORMAT
Single spacing 60-space line Tabs as needed

Contractions and Possessive Pronouns

Type lines 1–4 once. Then repeat lines 1–4 or take a series of 1-minute timings.

```
1 You're well prepared to give all your six speeches, Alonzo.   12
2 Their letters must be signed first because they're waiting.   12
3 Its quiet movement is a sign that it's operating very well.   12
4 Do you know who's riding in whose jeep for the noon parade?   12
  | 1 | 2 | 3 | 4 | 5 | 6 | 7 | 8 | 9 | 10 | 11 | 12
```

30-SECOND SPEED TIMINGS

Take two 30-second speed timings on lines 5 and 6. Then take two 30-second speed timings on lines 7 and 8. Or type each sentence twice.

```
5 When did she go to the city and pay them for the world maps   12
6 which I ordered several months ago but did not pick up yet?   24

7 If you're ready to go, I will get your friend, who's trying   12
8 to find out whose jacket was left in his auto last evening.   24
  | 1 | 2 | 3 | 4 | 5 | 6 | 7 | 8 | 9 | 10 | 11 | 12
```

FORMATTING BUDGET REPORTS

To format a budget report:

1. Use standard format for unbound reports.
2. Arrange financial data as a table within the body of the report.
3. Do not use a byline. Budget reports are submitted by the person who prepares them. Use a writer's identification as in minutes of a meeting.

FORMATTING REVIEW

Tables in Reports

1. Leave 3 blank lines above and below a table in a report.
2. Single-space the table.
3. Center the table horizontally.
4. Keep the table within the margins. Reduce space between columns if necessary.

BUSINESS AND OFFICE EDUCATION

Computer Instruction Program

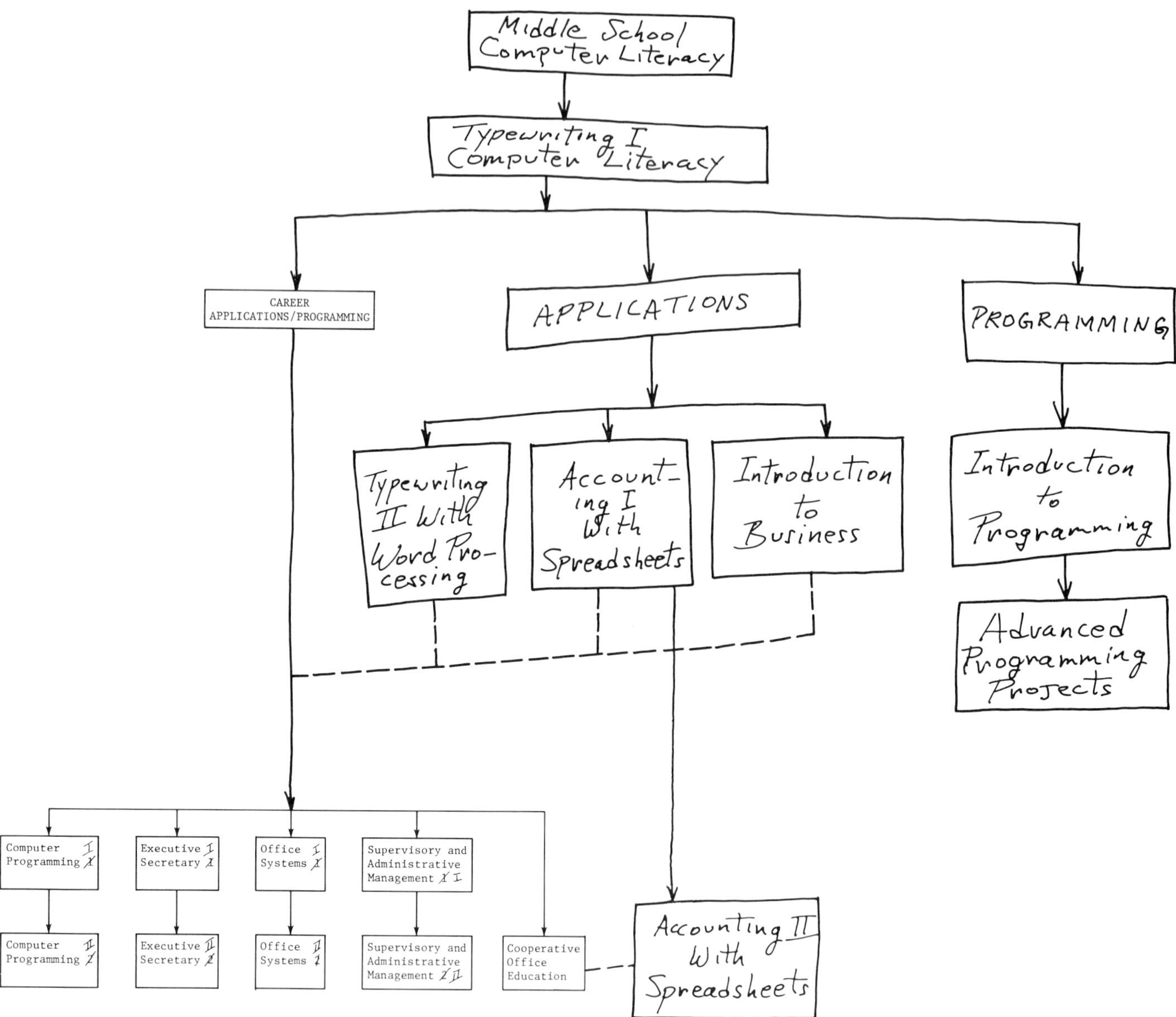

Note: Introduction to Business, Accounting, Career Computer Programming, and SAM do not require Typewriting I, but students will be more able to use the computer if they have taken it before enrolling in these courses.

——Strongly recommended
- - -Optional

JOB 204 A. BUDGET REPORT

Standard format.

BUDGET REPORT FOR THE YEAR 19— 19
UNITED WAY OF SENECA COUNTY 37

A $400,000 goal has been tentatively set by 49
United Way of Seneca County for this year's fall 59
campaign. It's the highest goal ever established 69
for the countrywide fund drive—about 8 percent 78
higher than last year's $371,655 goal. 86

The United Way Budget Committee, chaired by 96
Jo Ann Lance, spent more than two weeks re- 105
viewing agency requests before making final 113
recommendations to the Board. Here is the list 123
they drew up: 126

Association for the Blind—$22,524 138
Boy Scouts—$21,386 144
Community Ambulance Service—$15,960 153
Community Services of Seneca County— 161
$15,307 164
Decision House—$14,416 170
Family Service and Children's Aid Society— 180
$30,327 182
Freemont YMCA—$40,198 189
Freemont YWCA—$42,231 195
Girl Scouts—$22,371 201
Red Cross of Freemont—$35,008 209
Red Cross of Troy City—$37,530 217
Salvation Army of Seneca County—$43,527 227
United Services Organization—$4,019 236
United Way of Seneca County—$52,177 246
Youth Alternative, Inc.—$3,019 254

Ruby Montgomery, the chairperson of the 19— 267
campaign, said she feels the $400,000 goal is a 276
realistic one to achieve. Recruitment of cam- 285
paigners is on target, and the campaign cabinet 295
will meet for the first time at 8 p.m. on August 305
10 to review plans for the total operation. 314

Dan Vogelbacker, Secretary 326
Budget Committee 331

JOB 204 B. REPORT TO A COMMITTEE

Standard format.

REPORT TO BOROUGH PLANNING COMMISSION ON EXIT DE- 29
VELOPMENT ON INTERSTATE 80 45

By Paul S. Hardy, Planning Consultant 69

I have done a thorough study of the possibility for development of the 86
land near Exit 10 of I-80. In my opinion, such a project should be post- 101
poned. 102

The development of the land near Exit 10 requires the construction of 117
utilities, such as water, sewage, and power lines. Costs for these installa- 132
tions are high. Also, the development plans have to be approved by state 147
and federal authorities, possibly a lengthy process. 158

While the land near exits may develop overnight, other tracts may never 173
reach the level of growth that is hoped for by local governments, business- 188
people, and property owners. 194

FORMATTING ALTERNATE
If a chart will not fit on one page, use these variations:

1. Stack boxes vertically instead of horizontally.
2. Vary the size of some boxes. Use as few different sizes as possible. Use good judgment.

JOB 266 A. CHART

Standard format. Sideways on the page. Hold on to this job for use in Lesson 267.

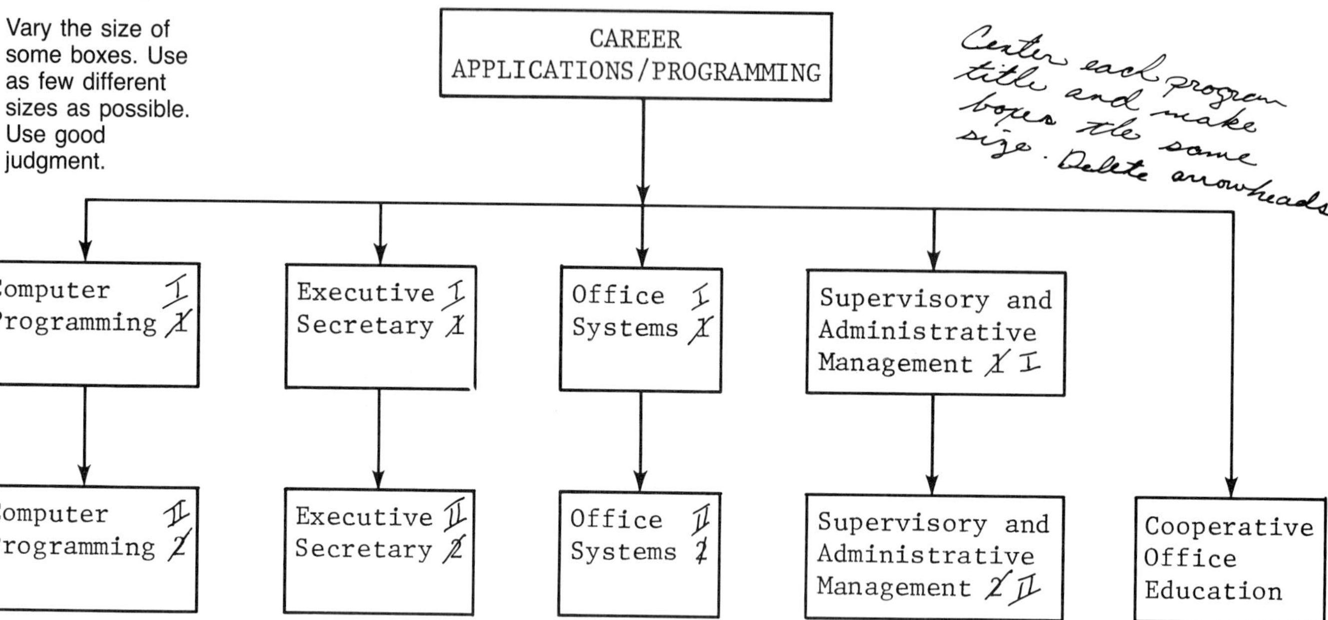

LESSON 267

■ GOALS
To use confusing words correctly while typing sentences.
To type a two-page chart.

■ FORMAT
Single spacing 60-space line

LAB 32
Confusing Words

Type lines 1–4 once, selecting the appropriate word from those enclosed in parentheses. Edit your copy as your teacher reads the answers. Then retype lines 1–4 from your edited copy.

1 I can (access, assess) our computer's ability to gain (access, assess) to data.
2 I hope that my speech has a positive (affect, effect) on our workers.
3 Our foreign (correspondence, correspondents) must submit daily sales reports.
4 Permission to (precede, proceed) must (precede, proceed) your departure for Utah.

JOB 267 A. TWO-PAGE CHART

Format the hierarchy chart on page 432 using two pages. Decide where you can break the chart for each page so that it can be easily taped together when you are finished. The chart you prepared in Job 266 A is the reduced section of the two-page form. Use the chart you prepared when typing that section; do not try to read the reduced copy.

■ GOALS
To use contractions and possessive pronouns correctly while typing sentences.
To type 44/5'/4e.
To format and type an annotated bibliography.

■ FORMAT
Drills: Single spacing 60-space line
5-Minute Timings: Double spacing 5-space tab

LAB 24

Contractions and Possessive Pronouns

Type lines 1–4 once, providing the appropriate answers. Edit your copy as your teacher reads the answers. Then retype lines 1–4 from your edited copy.

(Its/It's) an excellent choice because (its/it's) price has just fallen.
(Your/You're) responsible for handling (your/you're) dozen accounts, Myrna.
(Their/They're) quick decision surprised us, but (their/they're) right to go.
(Their/They're) agent, Jack Waverly, said that (their/they're) eager to sell.

PREVIEW PRACTICE

Type each line twice as a preview to the 5-minute timings below.

Accuracy: quaint prized unique example Damnoen boardwalk satisfactory
Speed: suspended tourist ability prices depend visit make with can

5-MINUTE TIMINGS

Take two 5-minute timings on lines 7–25.

When shopping, in this country we generally accept the price tag on merchandise as being the final price the store will consider. If we want the item, we pay the amount that is asked. In some countries, however, prices may fluctuate from moment to moment, depending on the purchaser's ability to bargain. Then it becomes a matter of both the buyer and the seller reaching a satisfactory price.

A simple example of this process awaits the tourist in Bangkok who visits the floating market at Damnoen Saduak, a charming place of quaint beauty. Located outside the city, this stilt village resembles a boardwalk-like structure, or suspended streets, or open-air shops built above the water.

Cruising to the center of the village, your canoe will make a stop where you can disembark and wander through many shops lining the boardwalk. There's a friendly atmosphere, with a tremendous selection of unique and prized handcrafts made in Thailand. Prices, of course, depend upon how adept you are at bargaining. Haggling is just a well-established way to conduct their everyday business.

SI 1.59

JOB 265 B. CHART

Standard format.

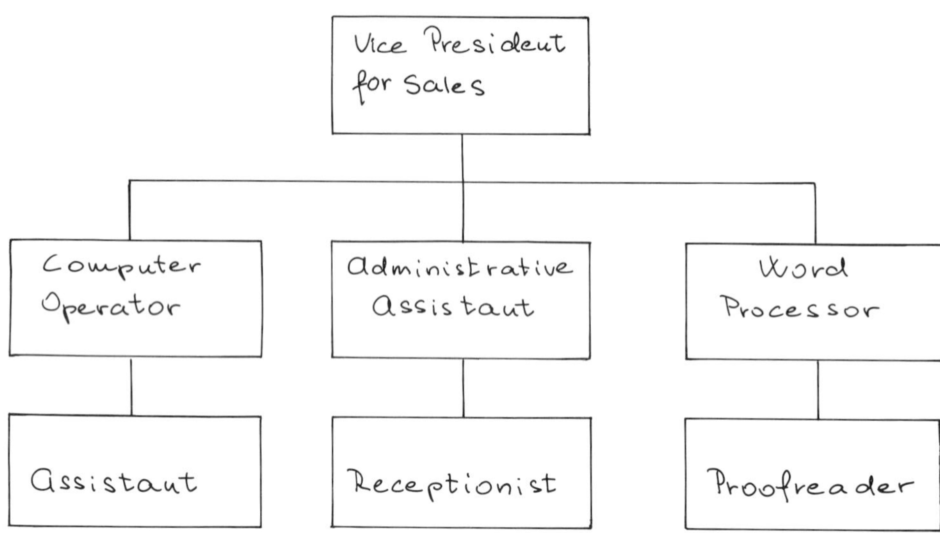

JOB 265 C. CHART

Design an organizational chart headed by Ann Williams, Regional Manager. Reporting to Ms. Williams are three district managers: Joan V. DiMarco, Edward J. Riley, and Jacob Hirschen. Each of them has, respectively, one field manager: Andrew Lin, Donna P. Merrill, and Owen C. Taylor. Standard format.

LESSON 266

■ **GOALS**
To identify the correct use of confusing words while typing sentences.
To type 49/5′/3e.
To type a hierarchy chart sideways.

■ **FORMAT**
Drills: Single spacing 60-space line
5-Minute Timings: Double spacing 5-space tab

LAB 32 Confusing Words

Type lines 1–4 once. Then repeat lines 1–4 or take a series of 1-minute timings.

```
1  The agenda shows that they will assess the access tomorrow.   12
2  Regardless of what is said, they cannot affect the outcome.   12
3  I expect my secretary to handle all routine correspondence.   12
4  He will precede us in the parade; it will proceed up Fifth.   12
   | 1 | 2 | 3 | 4 | 5 | 6 | 7 | 8 | 9 | 10 | 11 | 12
```

5-MINUTE TIMINGS

Take two 5-minute timings on lines 5–25 on page 433.

FORMATTING ANNOTATED BIBLIOGRAPHIES

An annotated bibliography lists not only some books on a certain subject but also a brief description of the contents of each book. To format an annotated bibliography, follow these instructions:

1. Use a full sheet of paper.
2. Margins: 5-inch line (or margins to match report).
3. On line 13, center the title
   ANNOTATED BIBLIOGRAPHY
   Triple-space after the heading.
4. Single-space each entry; double-space between entries.
5. Begin each entry at the left margin. Indent turnover lines 5 spaces.
6. Begin the description on a new line, a double space below the publication information. Indent all lines of the description 5 spaces.
7. List the entries alphabetically by author, last name first. Do not number the entries.

JOB 205 A. ANNOTATED BIBLIOGRAPHY

Standard format.

Arnold, David, Getting Started With the IBM PC and XT, Simon & Schuster, New York, 1984, 208 pages, softcover.

In his attempt to guide readers to a minimum proficiency in using the PC, Arnold has included the minimum information required. Two of the best sections are computer ergonomics and menu-driven software. There is a practical hard-disk introduction.

Goodman, Danny, Going Places With the New Apple IIc: All You'll Need to Know to Get There, Pocket Books, New York, 1984, 256 pages, softcover.

The first book on the new Apple IIc to hit the bookstores, this is a machine-specific computer selection guide rather than a guide to applications or operations. Goodman has provided an informative overview that potential buyers of the Apple IIc will find rewarding.

Heiney, Mildred A., Software Author's Guide, Datamost, Chatsworth, CA, 1983, 208 pages, softcover.

This guide provides prospective software authors with solid advice on packaging their code and a directory of software publishers looking for specific kinds of programs. Legal guidelines and some tips on self-marketing are among the articles that provide solid advice.

Phillips, Gary, IBM PC Public Domain Software, Vol. I, Ashton-Tate, Culver City, CA, 1983, 547 pages, softcover.

This book is easily the best critical guide to the vast library of free software. The author evaluates hundreds of these programs and tells you how to obtain them. Though expensive compared with other directories of this type, it is well worth the price. There's no listing of "user-supported" programs that readers like for their reference source.

LESSON 265

■ GOALS
To recognize the correct use of confusing words while typing sentences.
To format and type organizational charts.

■ FORMAT
Single spacing 60-space line

LAB 32
Confusing Words

Type lines 1–4 once. Then repeat lines 1–4 or take a series of 1-minute timings.

```
1 They will assess how much access employees should not have.  12
2 The correspondence was sent to our overseas correspondents.  12
3 The effects of the recent legislation will not affect them.  12
4 Research must precede our approval for the team to proceed.  12
  | 1 | 2 | 3 | 4 | 5 | 6 | 7 | 8 | 9 | 10 | 11 | 12
```

access: the right to enter, a means of approach
assess: to make a judgment, to determine

correspondence: letters
correspondents: those who write

affect: to bring about, to cause a change
effect: result, outcome, consequence

precede: to go before
proceed: to advance

30-SECOND "OK" TIMINGS

Type as many 30-second "OK" (errorless) timings as possible out of three attempts on lines 5–7.

```
5 Maizie quickly paid Joan for the five new taxis she bought.  12
6 Jack's man found exactly a quarter in the woven zipper bag.  24
7 Weekly magazines request help by and for junior executives.  36
  | 1 | 2 | 3 | 4 | 5 | 6 | 7 | 8 | 9 | 10 | 11 | 12
```

FORMATTING CHARTS

An organizational chart is a common form. To format:

1. All boxes should be the same size: For width, add 2 spaces to the longest line of type. For depth, add 2 blank lines to the copy that has the most lines of type. Thus the boxes in Job 265 A are 18 spaces wide (2 spaces wider than "Thomas A. Easton") and 4 lines deep (2 lines for typed copy and 2 lines for blanks).
2. For vertical placement, count lines as you would for ruled tables. In Job 265 A the page is turned lengthwise and the copy requires 12 lines. Thus 51 − 12 = 39, and 39 ÷ 2 = 19.5; begin on line 19.
3. For horizontal placement, decide how many boxes will be placed side by side, and multiply by the length of each box. In Job 265 A, 3 boxes × 18 spaces/box = 54 spaces, plus 6 spaces between boxes, gives a total of 66 spaces. Backspace 33 spaces (half of 66) from the center of the page.

Type underscores the correct width for the top and bottom of each box and for the horizontal connecting line. Type colons for, or pen in, the vertical lines.

JOB 265 A. CHART

Full page, sideways. Note the penned-in spacing directions as you format this organizational chart.

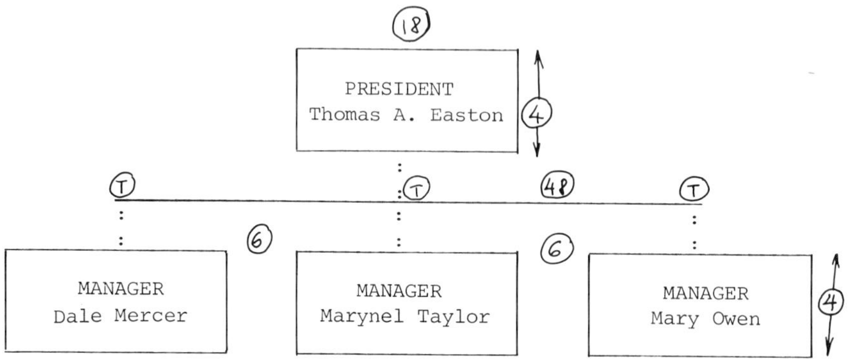

LESSON 206

CLINIC

GOAL
To build competency on selected keyboard reaches.

FORMAT
Single spacing   60-space line   5-space tab

KEYBOARDING SKILLS

Type lines 1–4 once. Then practice using your shift key by typing line 5 twice. Repeat lines 1–4, or take a series of 1-minute timings.

Speed 1 When did he go to the city and pay them for the world maps? 12
Accuracy 2 The wizard's dogs quickly jumped over one pyramid of boxes. 12
Numbers 3 I checked lockers 10, 29, 38, 47, and 56, but not 65 or 74. 12
Symbols 4 Wow! Whose painting is it? Who's the artist? It's great! 12
Technique 5 Ruth Mary Zora Paul Rick Kate Dora Jean M.D. B.C. N.Y. N.J.
| 1 | 2 | 3 | 4 | 5 | 6 | 7 | 8 | 9 | 10 | 11 | 12

PRETEST 1

Take two 2-minute timings on lines 6–9. Circle and count your errors on each.

6 I was confident that all packages were delivered with care. 12
7 Eleven local farmers departed during the first of the week. 24
8 The judge gave us the rules to use for the sporting events. 36
9 The guide lowered the ropes to those standing on the ledge. 48
| 1 | 2 | 3 | 4 | 5 | 6 | 7 | 8 | 9 | 10 | 11 | 12

PRACTICE 1

Type lines 10–15 five times.

10 who deck grade license handled packages confident president
11 how farm spray quarter secured surgical operators departure
12 typed seals moved parts fixed guide lower cloth farms early

13 sense rules plant ready means grass judge legal local extra
14 show past lost ours send sole does gets idea lift hose feed
15 bed eat get kit par tag use hot way fat lie red sea dry are

POSTTEST 1

Repeat Pretest 1 to see how much your skill has improved.

PRETEST 2

Take two 2-minute timings on lines 16–19. Circle and count your errors on each.

16 Did you ever think of the phenomenon that normally the 12
17 fish is a truly active animal? Some fish do the minimum of 24
18 swimming, but the group is small; the busy fish abides in a 36
19 bowl, and the hungry fish that slows down is soon devoured. 48
| 1 | 2 | 3 | 4 | 5 | 6 | 7 | 8 | 9 | 10 | 11 | 12

PRACTICE 2

Type lines 20–24 five times.

20 ion nation motion station portion rations position donation
21 oin points joints coining appoint joining pointing adjoined
22 min mining minute minting minimum mineral trimming minerals
23 imp import impose imposes imports impress imposing imported
24 ill chills drills fulfill willing billing goodwill waybills

POSTTEST 2

Repeat Pretest 2 to see how much your skill has improved.

FORMATTING QUESTIONNAIRES

Questionnaires may be formatted in several ways, depending upon the types of questions you have and how simple you want the form to appear. For example, you can use any of the following styles for displaying short responses:

Yes ____	A ruled line.	(X)	A circle.
[X]	A box.	(Yes) No	Ask the respondent to circle a word.

Use typed lines or open spaces for long responses.

JOB 264 A. QUESTIONNAIRE

Select the most appropriate style or styles, and format the questionnaire for Western Paradise Resort. Full sheet of paper. Allow space for comments or suggestions at the end of the questionnaire. Try not to crowd the questions.

DID YOU ENJOY YOUR STAY WITH US?

We hope that you enjoyed your visit with us and that you found our services and facilities to your liking. Before you leave, however, we would appreciate your giving us your opinion by completing this questionaire of the avarious aspects of our service. so that we can continue to offer our guests the best possible vacation pacage of it's kind in the country circle your answers:

1. What facilites did you use during you visit? Swimming pool Tennis courts Golf course Sauna Riding Bowling allys Paddle ball courts Health club

2. Whast organized sports did you particite in? Baseball Volleyball Tennis tourment Golf Tournment Maountain climbing

3. What organized social activities did you participate in? Sqare dancing Disco dancing contest Waltz contest Wine and cheese party Bengo Bridge Las Vagas night Indian artsfestival Rodeo

4. How would you rate our food? Excellent Good Poor

5. How would yourate our house keeping? Excellent Good Poor

6. How would you rate your sarvice? Excellent Good Poor

7. How would you ate your total experence? Excellent Good Poor

JOB 264 B. QUESTIONNAIRE FROM ROUGH-DRAFT COPY

Format Job 264 A on an 8 by 5 card. Use both sides.

LESSON 207

UNIT 34 Formatting Correspondence

UNIT GOAL 44/5'/4e

■ GOALS

To use contractions and possessive pronouns correctly while typing sentences.

To format and type letters with a company name in the closing.

■ FORMAT

Single spacing   60-space line

LAB 24

Contractions and Possessive Pronouns

Workbook 397–398.

Type lines 1–4 once, providing the appropriate answers. Edit your copy as your teacher reads the answers. Then retype lines 1–4 from your edited copy.

1 (Whose/Who's) fixtures are these, and (whose/who's) going to ship them all?
2 When (your/you're) ready, quickly send (your/you're) order to Rosa Jiminez.
3 (Their/They're) ready, but (their/they're) supervisor, John, is not here yet.
4 (Its/It's) exciting to have our firm enjoying (its/it's) best year ever.

12-SECOND TIMINGS

Type each line three times, or take three 12-second timings on each line. For each line, type with no more than 1 error.

```
5 We hired six women--you did say six, didn't you?--to check.
6 If the eight men do the work right, they may make a profit.
7 I like to watch her zip through the job with lots of speed.
```

FORMATTING COMPANY NAMES

A company name typed in the closing is used to emphasize that the letter is being written by a representative of the company, not by the writer as an individual. To format company names in the closing:

1. Type the company name in all-capital letters a double space below the complimentary closing.
2. Type the writer's name and title 4 lines below the company name.
3. Add 20 words to the body count to determine placement.

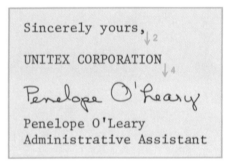

```
Sincerely yours, ↓2
UNITEX CORPORATION ↓4
Penelope O'Leary
Penelope O'Leary
Administrative Assistant
```

JOB 207 A. LETTER

Standard format. Workbook 399–400. Body 107 words.

Ms. Pamela Chew, Manager, Office Technology, 17
Hi-Com Corporation, 180 Wells Avenue, New- 24
ton, MA 02159-4680, Dear Ms. Chew: For over 35
40 years PRO has been in the business of design- 45
ing and making computers. Today we're proud 54
to introduce the PRO Personal Computer. 62
¶ What makes the PRO Personal Computer spe- 71
cial is its ability to run most current business 81
software. It operates as a standalone unit or as an 91
intelligent workstation in an integrated computer 101
network. Moreover, costly options on some 110
other PCs are standard features on the PRO Per- 119
sonal Computer—features such as color graph- 128
ics; clock/calendar display; monitor tilt; plus 138
multiple expansion slots to add extra printers, 147
memory, and other plug-in options. ¶ To get 157
more information, just call your local PRO sales 167
office at 555-5000. Sincerely, PRO CORPORA- 179
TION, Jerrald V. Zar, Sales Manager 192

Some word processing systems contain a function to replicate lines. This is a good application of that principle.

JOBS 263 A AND 263 B. FORMS

Prepare two forms from the copy shown. Use a half sheet of paper for each. Arrange the copy attractively on the page.

WEEKLY RUNNING LOG

	Date	Course	Distance	Time	Comments
M					
T					
W					
T					
F					
S					
S					

INDIVIDUAL PROGRESS CHART

Type of Membership_______ Name_________________________Phone__________

Is spouse a member?______ Address______________________________________

Date Enrolled____________ ____________________________________Age______

■ GOAL
To format and type a questionnaire in two formats.

■ FORMAT
Single spacing 60-space line

KEYBOARDING SKILLS

Type lines 1–4 once. Then use the shift lock for the last word as you type line 5. Repeat lines 1–4, or take a series of 1-minute timings.

Speed	1	She may make the girls do the theme for their eighth panel.	12
Accuracy	2	With all kinds of gripes, Buz rejected every required exam.	12
Numbers	3	Was the number 10, 29, 38, 47, or 56? Can you remember it?	12
Symbols	4	Max & Erma's has a new sign; it's brighter than Al & Joe's.	12
Technique	5	If you type Chicago with the shift lock down, it's CHICAGO.	

| 1 | 2 | 3 | 4 | 5 | 6 | 7 | 8 | 9 | 10 | 11 | 12

12-SECOND TIMINGS

Type each line three times, or take three 12-second timings on each line. For each timing, type without error.

6 He said that they will rule that page with four long lines.
7 They will note this thin line when they look over this job.
8 They must have good jobs with very good pay; they told her.

5 10 15 20 25 30 35 40 45 50 55 60

JOB 207 B. LETTER

Retype Job 207 A (page 342), adding the paragraph in the right column as the third paragraph of the letter. Address the letter to Mr. Jeremy Hawk, 196 Westlea Terrace, Brockton, MA 02401-0163. Block format. Workbook 401–402. Body 149 words.

For solutions to all your business problems, the new PRO software really applies itself, with a wide range of new applications. We've created a Business Management Series to perform a full range of management functions from financial analysis to sales agreement.

LESSON 208

■ **GOALS**
To type 44/3′/3e.
To type a memo.
To compose a memo.

■ **FORMAT**
Drills: Single spacing 60-space line
3-Minute Timings: Double spacing 5-space tab

KEYBOARDING SKILLS

Type lines 1–4 once. Then practice using your editing skills as you type line 5. Repeat lines 1–4, or take a series of 1-minute timings.

Speed	1	I am to go to work for the audit firm by the fourth of May.	12
Accuracy	2	Jacqueline was vexed by the folks who got the money prizes.	12
Numbers	3	She moved out of Rooms 10, 28, and 39 into Rooms 47 and 56.	12
Symbols	4	Be sure to write Janet before 7/25 or phone her before 8/8.	12
Technique	5	we asked bill to point out tim clark and hugh green for us.	

PRETEST

Take a 3-minute timing on lines 6–17. Circle and count your errors.

```
 6      It is not easy to list all that local governments have  12
 7 to do.  The departments of most local agencies include some  24
 8 of these:  police and fire, public safety, justice, sanita-  36
 9 tion, parks and recreation, and schools.                     44
10      Local governments today employ a large number of resi-  12
11 dents.  They also receive and expend major sums of money as  24
12 well as make decisions that affect the lives of all persons  36
13 who reside within that local zoned area.                     44
14      Therefore, it's important for each person to learn how  12
15 his or her local government functions and be aware of every  24
16 action that is being taken.  The quality of your local gov-  36
17 ernment is determined by alert citizens.                     44
                                                          SI 1.59
```

PRACTICE

Take a 1-minute timing on each paragraph of the Pretest.

POSTTEST

Take another 3-minute timing on lines 6–17 to see how much your skill has improved.

PRETEST

Take a 3-minute timing on lines 5–17. Circle and count your errors.

```
5       Businesses are finding that the management of the many   12
6  records they have to keep is sometimes best performed by an   24
7  automated data control center.  Data can be communicated by   36
8  a terminal from an individual's business to a center across   48
9  town or across the country.  It's amazing how efficiently a   60
10 data control center operates.                                  66
11      Both financial records and correspondence are recorded   78
12 for a firm to replay, edit, or merge.  A center offers many   90
13 ways to store and retrieve data with such exactness that it  102
14 justifies its existence for most big firms.  A company that  114
15 requires that data be compared and analyzed is impressed by  126
16 the amount of labor saved when many different kinds of data  138
17 are quickly merged, printed, and distributed.                 147
   | 1 | 2 | 3 | 4 | 5 | 6 | 7 | 8 | 9 | 10 | 11 | 12        SI 1.68
```

PRACTICE

In the chart below find the number of errors you made on the Pretest. Then type each of the designated drill lines four times.

Pretest errors	0–1	2	3+
Drill lines	20–23	19–22	18–21

Accuracy

```
18 justify recorded analyzed companies distributed efficiently
19 existence performed automated financial retrieval exactness
20 amazing management individual's communicated correspondence
```

Speed

```
21 center replay offers labor saved kinds firms such will when
22 that many they have keep best data from down both firm edit
23 large ways are the can how and for its of to is by an be or
```

POSTTEST

Take another 3-minute timing on lines 5–17 to see how much your skill has improved.

CREATING FORMS

Often a company needs a new form. It is typed, and then it is duplicated or sent to a printer.

To format a form:

1. Decide whether the form is to be filled out in handwriting or filled in on the typewriter.
2. Use at least double spacing if the form will be filled in on the typewriter.
3. Use at least one and a half spacing if the form will be filled out in handwriting.
4. Make sure ruled lines are long enough for the information that is to be filled in.
5. Center column headings over the columns, if used. Make sure the column is wide enough for the column heading.
6. Vertical rules may be typed or penned in. If penned in, be sure to use a ruler.

JOB 208 A. MEMO

Standard format. Workbook 403–404.

[*To:*] All Employees, [*From:*] Marlo Castellucci, [*Date:*] January 7, 19—, [*Subject:*] Computers and Your Health, Here are some guidelines for making your daily interactions with micros much easier and more comfortable. ¶ Your keyboard, your screen, and any papers you're working on should be about equal distances from your eyes. This also means that you may need to put a manual or some other documentation on the desktop—not your lap. ¶ Ideally, the screen should be about 20 degrees below your line of sight. Most of the time you want to be able to look directly ahead with your head fully upright, your eyes more or less level with the top of the display, or slightly above it. ¶ The keyboard, researchers say, should be about 26 inches from the floor, not 28 inches, which is common to most desktops. This is about the height of a typing table. You can tell if a keyboard is at the right height when your wrists and forearms are about parallel to the floor when you type. Lights in your office or workspace need to be placed in such a way as not to reflect on your screen or cause glare. The screen should be placed either at right angles to windows or facing away—and certainly far enough away so that there's no reflection. Also, clean your screen regularly because static electricity attracts dust. ¶ I hope these suggestions will help make your jobs easier.

JOB 208 B. COMPOSE A MEMO

Compose a short memo for Marlo Castellucci to Shelly DeHoven in response to the electronic message below. Thank Ms. DeHoven for bringing the chair problem to your attention. Indicate that adjustable chairs are needed but are not in this year's budget. Express concern, and promise to read the report issued by the government. Standard format. Workbook 405 top.

```
DATE:  JANUARY 15,19--
TO:    MARLO CASTELLUCCI
       VICE PRESIDENT
FROM:  SHELLY DEHOVEN
       MANAGER, TECHNOLOGY
SUBJ:  CHAIRS IN COMPUTER ROOM
THANK YOU FOR SHARING YOUR SUGGESTIONS
CONCERNING HEALTH AND COMPUTERS.  ALL
THOSE WHO WORK IN THE COMPUTER ROOM AP-
PRECIATE YOUR CONCERN FOR THEIR PHYSI-
CAL COMFORT.  BECAUSE OF YOUR INTEREST,
I WOULD LIKE TO CALL YOUR ATTENTION TO
THE FACT THAT THE CHAIRS IN THE COM-
PUTER ROOM POSE A HEALTH HAZARD BECAUSE
THEY ARE STATIONARY.  PLEASE READ THE
CHAPTER ON CORRECT SEATING IN THE RE-
PORT ISSUED BY THE GOVERNMENT, WHICH I
AM SENDING YOU.
```

LESSON 209

■ GOALS
To recognize the correct use of abbreviations while typing sentences.
To format and type cover letters.

■ FORMAT
Single spacing 60-space line

LAB 25

Abbreviations

Type lines 1–4 once. Then repeat lines 1–4 or take a series of 1-minute timings. As you type each line, note the abbreviations.

```
1 Mr. and Mrs. Davis just left for a cruise around the world.  12
2 Quintex Box Co. is hiring students who can type accurately.  12
3 Alvin Zembling, Jr., is studying economics and world trade.  12
4 Our plane left at 7:10 a.m. and landed in Peru at 6:15 p.m.  12
  | 1 | 2 | 3 | 4 | 5 | 6 | 7 | 8 | 9 | 10 | 11 | 12
```

(Continued on next page)

8 the jab rat you rot yes red ore vat her nor hat big lit aft
9 long hats pure jets gone navy club part bond jack flue puff
10 ghost earth ready virus think teach spunk vague yearn yacht

POSTTEST 1

Repeat Pretest 1 on page 424. Proofread and note your improvement.

PRETEST 2

Take two 2-minute timings on lines 11–14. Proofread both, and note the more accurate of the two scores.

11 The river runs in all seasons, but not once has ice formed. 12
12 The women were given a refund and made a fortune in prizes. 24
13 It is much too soon to detect minor defects in the new car. 36
14 Now is the moment to save and protect our younger citizens. 48
| 1 | 2 | 3 | 4 | 5 | 6 | 7 | 8 | 9 | 10 | 11 | 12

PRACTICE 2

Type lines 15–20 five times. Repeat individual lines for speed gain if you had two or fewer errors on Pretest 2; otherwise, repeat each block of lines for accuracy gain.

15 joining matched utmost saying zones place unit text act run
16 protect routine season invest women river pins mill inn nor
17 utilize younger paying refund serve thing army live won bid

18 fortune exposed making prompt using prize done none ton gun
19 correct defects gained detect minor night save much now son
20 appoint citizen finish import aimed catch once soon fun ice

POSTTEST 2

Repeat Pretest 2. Proofread and note your improvement.

LESSON 263

UNIT 43 Processing Forms

UNIT GOAL 49/5′/3e

- GOALS
  To use confusing words correctly while typing sentences.
  To type 49/3′/2e.
  To create forms.
- FORMAT
  Drills: Single spacing 60-space line
  3-Minute Timings: Double spacing 5-space tab

LAB 31

Confusing Words

Type lines 1–4 once, selecting the appropriate word from those enclosed in parentheses. Edit your copy as your teacher reads the answers. Then retype lines 1–4 from your edited copy.

1 I will not (accede, exceed) to his proposals; they (accede, exceed) our limits.
2 The ship's (complement, compliment) deserves a (complement, compliment) for its effort.
3 My school (principal, principle) expects us to maintain high (principals, principles).
4 The (stationary, stationery) cabinets contain my supplies and (stationary, stationery).

Abbreviations are very commonly used in technical writing for emphasis and quick comprehension: *g* for *gram* or *grams, in* for *inch* or *inches,* and so on. In nontechnical business writing, abbreviations are generally limited to the most commonly used abbreviations, some of which are never spelled out:

Mr. Mrs. Ms. Dr. Jr. Sr. a.m. p.m. Inc. Co. Ph.D.

Note the use of periods with the above abbreviations. Standard and metric abbreviations for measurements, such as *g, cm, km, in, qt,* and *ft,* however, need no periods.

30-SECOND "OK" TIMINGS

Type as many 30-second "OK" (errorless) timings as possible out of three attempts on lines 5–7.

```
5 Yes, my students must keyboard with expertise various kinds   12
6 of business forms so that they will be ready to zip through   24
7 these jobs:  memos, invoices, requisitions, and statements.   36
  | 1 | 2 | 3 | 4 | 5 | 6 | 7 | 8 | 9 | 10 | 11 | 12
```

FORMATTING COVER LETTERS

When a long document, report, or résumé has been prepared for submission to others, a cover letter is attached to explain the purpose of the document. Any letter style may be used.

JOB 209 A. COVER LETTER ON BARONIAL STATIONERY

Standard format. Workbook 405–406 bottom. Body 54 words.

Dr. B. John Haselen, Professor of 15
Personnel Management, San 20
Juan University, San Juan, 25
Puerto Rico 00910, Dear Dr. 31
Haselen: As you requested 38
during our discussion at 43
the convention of International 49
Safety and Health Directors 55
in Bonn, West Germany, I 60
have attached a copy of 65
the report issued by the 70
federal government concerning 76
computers and worker's health. 82
¶ I hope you can use this 88
information in your 92
research on ergonomics 96
as it relates to computers. 102
Sincerely, Shelly DeHoven, 108
Manager, Technology 117

JOB 209 B. COVER LETTER WITH SUBJECT LINE

Block format. Insert the years where instructed to do so. Workbook 407–408. Body 82 words.

The Honorable John Doyle Neuberg, Governor of Ohio, Columbus, OH 43215, Dear Governor Neuberg: Subject: Annual Report--State Human Services Council

As head of the State Human Services Council, I am happy to submit to you our annual report, as required by law under Section 2 of the Comprehensive Employment and Training Act. ¶ This report covers the period from July 1, (last year's date), to

(Continued on next page)

JOB 261 A. FORM LETTERS WITH INSERTS

Standard format. Allow room for the date, the inside address, the salutation, and inserts in the body. If you are using a typewriter, use Workbook 607–610. If you are using a computer or word processor, save on a disk.

GSD-1. Subject: Policy No. [*insert number*]

In approximately [*4 spaces*] days, a renewal bill will be mailed for this policy. This is the anniversary of your "Good Student Discount." For you to retain this discount, we will require a new "Good Student" certificate, Form GU-6866A, which must be received by [*14 spaces*]. ¶ If we have not received the certificate by that date, your premium will be billed without the "Good Student Discount," and you will not be eligible for the discount until the next renewal date. ¶ This is the only notification that you will receive regarding this discount. Sincerely,

LCC-2. Subject: Policy No. [*insert number*]

This letter is to advise you that we are canceling your limited collision coverage as of [*40 spaces*]. ¶ This notice is in line with the "Conditions" of the policy. Your policy now covers property damage liability, bodily injury liability, medical payments, and protection against uninsured motorists within the limits shown in your policy. ¶ Our action was influenced by information in a consumer report regarding the value of limited collision coverage on older cars. Very truly yours,

JOB 261 B. ADDRESSING FORM LETTERS WITH INSERTS

Use the information below and your client information to complete the two letters you typed in Job 261 A. If you are using a typewriter, fill in the form letters you prepared. If you are using a computer or word processor, use the merge function. Date: June 20, 19—. Signature: Terry Daniels, Client Representative.

GSD-1: Sarah J. Catalano, 40, July 20, 19—.
LCC-2: Aida Johnson, 12:01 a.m. EDT, September 1, 19—.

LESSON 262

CLINIC

- **GOAL**
  To build competency on selected keyboard motions and reaches.
- **FORMAT**
  Single spacing   60-space line

PRETEST 1

Take two 2-minute timings on lines 1–4. Proofread both, and note the more accurate of the two scores.

```
1 Mark ought to clear enough money from our pipes to go home.  12
2 Carl bought a sixty-pound crate of cotton from that farmer.  24
3 Leonard wrote to you last month about coming to our picnic.  36
4 I doubt Ruth won a hat as one of the prizes at the meeting.  48
  | 1 | 2 | 3 | 4 | 5 | 6 | 7 | 8 | 9 | 10 | 11 | 12
```

PRACTICE 1

Type lines 5–10 five times. Repeat individual lines for speed gain if you had two or fewer errors on Pretest 1; otherwise, repeat each block of lines for accuracy gain.

```
5 you won pin out add sad are fly one hat mar ate coy mat lye
6 toys adds tone clad spur flag come glad song size pure road
7 wrong adapt woman flags doubt touch roads ought prize spurs
```

(Continued on next page)

JOB 209 B (CONTINUED)

June 20, (this year's date). It contains a state wide review of the success of the HHS pro gram and an appendex which gives a summary of expendtures, training, as-signments, and enrollees characteristics for each ofthe 28 prime sponsors in the state. Sincerely, Shirley Rush

JOB 209 C. COVER LETTER WITH SUBJECT LINE

Standard format. Insert the year where instructed to do so. Workbook 409–410. Body 95 words.

The Honorable Thomas S. Farro, Governor of Michigan, Lansing, MI 48924, Dear Gov-ernor Farro Subject: Annual Report--Commission onthe States of Women

The Commission on the Status of Wommen is plaesed to sub mit its Annual report for the year (current year). The commission carried out it's charge to be be a strong vote for the rights of woman in the state" though the program designed to correct in equities and to provide women with information to assist them in attaining equal right and equal opportu-nity. We are proud ofthe work that has has been accomplish this year in the fields of credit education, employment, criminal justice, legislation. We look forward to further progress and accom-plishment inthe year a head. Sincerely yours, Alda S. Wexler, Executive Director

■ GOALS
To identify the correct use of abbreviations while typing sentences.
To format and type coupon letters.

■ FORMAT
Single spacing 60-space line

LAB 25

Abbreviations

Type lines 1–4 once. Then repeat lines 1–4 or take a series of 1-minute timings.

```
1 The order was sent to Frances Weiler-Zeeb, Ph.D., in April.   12
2 Please let me know if Beman Company, Inc., can do this job.   12
3 They met for dinner at 6:30 p.m. and got home about 10 p.m.   12
4 Mrs. Exeter will check the manuscript for Dr. Vera Nuquist.   12
  | 1 | 2 | 3 | 4 | 5 | 6 | 7 | 8 | 9 | 10 | 11 | 12
```

12-SECOND TIMINGS

Type each line three times, or take three 12-second timings on each line. For each timing, type with no more than 1 error.

```
5 Most of the good guys in the movie were wearing white hats.
6 Her jolly friends have been glad that she has done so well.
7 He has found that a bit of music is a help when he studies.
  5 10 15 20 25 30 35 40 45 50 55 60
```

■ **GOALS**
To use confusing words correctly while typing sentences.
To type 48/5′/3e.
To type and address form letters with inserts.

■ **FORMAT**
Drills: Single spacing 60-space line
5-Minute Timings: Double spacing 5-space tab

LAB 31

Confusing Words

Type lines 1–4 once, selecting the appropriate word from those enclosed in parentheses. Edit your copy as your teacher reads the answers. Then retype lines 1–4 from your edited copy.

1 To get the maximum votes, I must (accede, exceed) to the proposition.
2 I would like to (complement, compliment) you on a job that was well done.
3 The (principal, principle) reason she failed was her lack of (principals, principles).
4 Each one of the computers in the center must be (stationary, stationery).

PREVIEW PRACTICE

Type each line twice as a preview to the 5-minute timings below.

Accuracy
```
5 matrix expansions requirements sophisticated microcomputers
```
Speed
```
6 more that will gave from when have with this some made wide
```

5-MINUTE TIMINGS

Take two 5-minute timings on lines 7–23.

7 As microcomputers become more and more common in homes and of- 13
8 fices, the software that is being produced will offer more options to the 28
9 users. First editions of software gave users different word processing, 43
10 spreadsheet, and data base functions in separate packages. More recent 57
11 versions offer users combined packages in which all three operations 71
12 merge to allow single reports to be produced with text as well as tables 85
13 from a variety of different documents. 93
14 When more sophisticated software began to be developed for the mar- 107
15 ket, the new software required that the computer running the software have 122
16 additional memory. With this new requirement came a flood of new pe- 136
17 ripheral items that could be attached to existing computers. Some manu- 150
18 facturers made a variety of cards to be inserted into special slots on the 165
19 computer. Others offered expansions by adding more drives. Still others 180
20 concentrated on printer options that offer the users letter-quality and dot 195
21 matrix options, color options, and a wide choice of type styles and sizes. 210
22 Microcomputer users will see even more advances in the future as hard- 224
23 ware and software giants join ventures in the pursuit of greater technology. 240

| 1 | 2 | 3 | 4 | 5 | 6 | 7 | 8 | 9 | 10 | 11 | 12 | 13 | 14 | 15 | SI 1.70

NATIONAL ASSOCIATION OF MAYORS

P.O. Box 2173 Washington, D C 20013 (202) 555-4739

October 10, 19-- ↓5

No inside address; subject/salutation covers all addressees.

To All NAM Members
Who Plan to Attend the
Chicago Convention:

This letter is to remind you that only paid-up Association members will be admitted to the convention sessions we will hold in November at the Drake Hotel in Chicago. Membership dues can, of course, be paid at the registration desk upon arrival at the convention, but the charge there will be $25 more per individual than dues paid in advance. So we urge you to remit your dues in advance.

You may use the coupon below. Just fill it in, attach your check for $75, and mail them in the enclosed envelope to our offices in Washington. Your membership card will be sent immediately.

Informal complimentary closing.

See you at the convention!

Initials may be on same line as signer's identification to allow room for coupon.

ts
Enclosure

Beverly T. Prescott
Executive Director ↓1

Date ______________ ↓2

↓2

National Association of Mayors
P.O. Box 2173
Washington, DC 20013

Enclosed is my check for $75 in payment of my Association dues. ↓2

Name ______________ Mayor of ______________ ↓2

Address ______________ City ______ State ______ ZIP ______

12-SECOND TIMINGS

Type each line three times, or take three 12-second timings on each line. For each timing, type without error.

```
5  Jane will sell four lots when they find the cash they need.
6  They will sell him some more lots when they need more cash.
7  Jane will give them back the money they gave her last week.
```

5 10 15 20 25 30 35 40 45 50 55 60

FORMATTING LETTERS FROM BOILERPLATE FILES

A *boilerplate file* is a file of previously written standard paragraphs that can be stored and then combined in a variety of ways to produce individualized letters; for examples see the paragraphs below. Read each paragraph carefully for content. Note that the first ones (PC01–PC03) are *introductory* paragraphs, the next ones (PC11–PC14) are *middle* paragraphs, and the last ones (PC21–PC24) are *closing* paragraphs.

JOBS 260 A TO 260 D. LETTERS FROM BOILERPLATE FILES

Compose four letters using the paragraphs below and the potential-client information you prepared in Lesson 257. Date the letters June 20, 19—, and use the signature "Terry Daniels, Client Representative." Workbook 599–606. If you are using a microcomputer or a word processor, first store each paragraph as a separate document, naming each document using the codes.

A. Jennifer Shapiro (new college graduate)
B. Mr. and Mrs. Lippman (new baby girl)
C. John Allen (new resident)
D. Sherri Atworst (new resident) Do not make her letter exactly like the one to Mr. Allen. Each letter must sound as if it were written especially for each client.

PC01. Congratulations on the arrival of your new baby! We'd like you to accept our gift along with the others you have received for the new arrival.

PC02. Congratulations on your graduation from college! We know that you are anxious to begin your career, and we would like you to accept a gift from us along with the others you have received.

PC03. Welcome to Atlanta! We hope that you will learn to love the charm of the city as we do. Please accept our gift as a welcome to our city.

PC11. We offer this gift to acquaint you with the services that Americana has to offer. We offer insurance plans for life, health, home, and auto. Our company is a family company that has been in business for 40 years.

PC12. We offer you this gift to acquaint you with the special services that we have to offer new families in our community. Thousands of new parents are choosing our plan.

PC13. We offer you this gift to acquaint you with information about a plan that enables you to wrap up your family's insurance protection in one convenient, low-cost program.

PC14. We offer you this gift to acquaint you with the special services that we have to offer young adults in regard to health and life insurance coverage.

PC21. For information about our insurance coverage, just mail the postpaid card. No signature is required, and there is no obligation whatsoever.

PC22. In the next few days, I will call to arrange a brief appointment at your convenience. I know you will find the services we have to offer well worth the few minutes we will need to discuss them.

PC23. In the next few days, I will call to arrange a mutually convenient appointment. I know that you will find this service well worth the small amount of time it requires.

PC24. May I call on you within the next few days to explain to you our special coverage? I know that the few minutes needed will be well spent.

FORMATTING COUPON LETTERS

Sometimes business letters are formatted so that there is room at the bottom for a tear-off coupon for the convenience of the person receiving the letter to respond to some request. To format a coupon letter:

1. Use any letter style, but set margins for a long letter—6-inch line.
2. Separate the coupon from the letter with a line of spaced underscores or hyphens. Single-space before the line; double-space after it.
3. Reference initials and enclosure notations, if used, may be raised to align with the last line of the writer's identification.
4. Use double spacing between lines of underscores to allow room for the insertions.

Note: Coupon letters are form letters, so they often contain a "subject/salutation" instead of an inside address and salutation.

JOB 210 A. COUPON LETTER

Type the coupon letter on page 347. Standard format. Make one carbon copy. Workbook 411–412. Body 124 words.

JOB 210 B. COUPON LETTER

Block format. Personalize the letter by using an inside address and salutation. Workbook 413–414. Body 124 words.

Mr. C. W. Cyphert, 214 Seminole Street, Bradford, PA 16701

In answer to numerous requests, we can now supply a selection of PENN NEWS covers in a size and format suitable for framing. A set of four covers, all by famous artists, now is available. ¶ These are full-color prints, enlarged to 9″ by 12″ on heavy, coated paper, without the magazine logo or overprinting. The set includes the Philadelphia harbor from the April issue, Salmon Creek from the July issue, Gettysburg from the September issue, and Amish farms from the December issue. These prints are not available in stores. ¶ The price is $3 per set, delivered. Clip the coupon below, fill it in, and attach your check. Make your check or money order payable to the Pennsylvania State Commission. Order your set today. Sincerely yours, Harvey Laird, Jr., Executive Director

\- -

Date ____________

Pennsylvania State Commission
P.O. Box 1011
Harrisburg, PA 17108

Enclosed is a check for $_____ for _____ set(s) of the four covers of PENN NEWS.

Please send to ______________________
Name
____
Address
____
City State ZIP

■ GOALS
To use abbreviations correctly while typing sentences.
To type 44/5′/4e.
To type a memo and coupon letter.

FORMAT
■ Drills: Single spacing 60-space line
5-Minute Timings: Double spacing 5-space tab

LAB 25

Abbreviations

Type lines 1–4 once, providing standard abbreviations for the underscored words. Edit your copy as your teacher reads the answers. Then retype lines 1–4 from your edited copy.

1 <u>Doctor</u> Jennie Felix works at the new Mercy Hospital in Dayton.
2 I sent a memo to George Van Sickle, <u>Senior</u>, about the problem.
3 Isabel's class meets at 11:30 <u>ante meridiem</u> on Mondays and Tuesdays.
4 Zuppello Electronics, <u>Incorporated</u>, built a factory in New Zealand.

JOB 258/259 B (CONTINUED)

CSP-1

An investment in four years of college may cost anywhere from $10,000 to $30,000 or more. For most parents, even the lower figure is a problem.

Americana has some ideas that have provided solutions for a great number of parents. We would like to share these ideas with you.

At the same time we'd like to give you, with our compliments, a current copy of <u>College Costs</u>.

this booklet contains information about tuition, fees, and room and board for just about every college in the country.

One of our agents will call to arrange a brief talk with you. You'll find the few minutes well spent. Cordially yours,

JOB 258/259 C. ADDRESSING FORM LETTERS

If you are using a typewriter, use the client information you typed on index cards to fill in the date, name and address, and appropriate salutation. If you are using a word processor, use the client information list to prepare a document containing the date, name and address, and appropriate salutation. Then use the merge function to address the letters (Workbook 587–598).

Send the following letters to the people indicated. Date the letters June 18, 19—, and use the signature "Terry Daniels, Client Representative."

FPC-1: Chuck Dickerson (client)
FPC-2: Dr. and Mrs. Hatton (client)
FPC-3: Todd Ruppert (potential client)
CSP-1: Aida Johnson (client)
LIU-4: Elizabeth Townsend (client)
YAS-2: Sarah J. Catalano (client)

LESSON 260

GOALS
To identify the correct use of confusing words while typing sentences.
To format and type standard paragraphs.
To create form letters from boilerplate files.

FORMAT
Single spacing 60-space line

LAB 31

Confusing Words

Type lines 1–4 once. Then repeat lines 1–4 or take a series of 1-minute timings.

```
1  If you exceed the speed limit, your license may be revoked.  12
2  I am looking for a blouse that will complement my new suit.  12
3  Does the principal know what principle affected the choice?  12
4  He redesigned the letterhead for our new office stationery.  12
   | 1 | 2 | 3 | 4 | 5 | 6 | 7 | 8 | 9 | 10 | 11 | 12
```

PREVIEW PRACTICE

Type lines 5 and 6 on page 339 twice as a preview to the 5-minute timings on page 339.

5-MINUTE TIMINGS

Take two 5-minute timings on lines 7–25 on page 339.

JOB 211 A. MEMO

Standard format. Workbook 415–416.

[DATE:] Today's, [TO:] Jerrald Zar, Sales Man- 4
ager, [FROM:] Kazuhiko Toshiba, Vice Presi- 17
dent, [SUBJECT:] Vendor Demonstration 23
Last evening I had a call from one of my neigh- 34
bors, Dr. Sadaharu Arakawa, president of Dal- 43
ton Engineering. ¶ He received your sales letter 54
concerning the features of our new PRO Per- 62
sonal Computer and is very much interested in 71
our product. I suggested to him that you and 81
your staff do an in-house demonstration for him 90
and his managers. He liked the idea. ¶ Please 100
contact him regarding a vendor demonstration. 114

JOB 211 B. COUPON LETTER

Standard format. Workbook 417–418.

Dr. Sadaharu Arakawa, President, Dalton Engineering, P.O. Box 303, Dalton, MA 01226-0303, Dear Dr. Arakawa: Our vice president, Dr. Kazuhiko Toshiba, has told me about your interest in our PRO Personal Computer and requested that I arrange an in-house demonstration for you and your managers. I am delighted to do this. ¶ To schedule a demonstration at your site, please fill in the tear-off section at the bottom of this letter and return it to me in the enclosed envelope. I will call you to finalize the date and time. ¶ Thank you for your interest in the PRO Personal Computer. Sincerely, PRO CORPORATION, Jerrald V. Zar, Sales Manager

- -

Date ________________

Mr. Jerrald V. Zar, Sales Manager
PRO Corporation
35 Wheeler Street
Cambridge, MA 02138-6822

We would like a vendor demonstration of the PRO Personal Computer.

Company Name	Contact Person
Address	Telephone
City State ZIP	Preferred Dates (3)

LESSON 212

CLINIC

■ GOAL
To build competency on selected keyboard reaches.

■ FORMAT
Drills: Single spacing 60-space line Tabs every 13 spaces
2-Minute Timings: Double spacing

KEYBOARDING SKILLS

Type lines 1–4 once. Then practice using your tab key by typing line 5 twice. Repeat lines 1–4, or take a series of 1-minute timings.

Speed	1	The profit she got for the corn and hay may make them rich.	12
Accuracy	2	Jack quietly moved up front and seized the big ball of wax.	12
Numbers	3	By June 10 ship 29 seats, 38 stoves, 47 tents, and 56 cots.	12
Symbols	4	Visitors may park in locations #10, #29, #38, #47, and #56.	12
Technique	5	Abcde Fghij Klmno Pqrst Uvwxyz	

| 1 | 2 | 3 | 4 | 5 | 6 | 7 | 8 | 9 | 10 | 11 | 12

JOB 258/259 A (CONTINUED)

Futures Planning Service is a financial service. It can actually increase the value of your present life insurance without any further expense to you. By means of a simple analysis, your present financial situation and future financial needs and assets are clearly shown.

The service can give you a complete understanding of your social security benefits and how they relate to your life insurance program. You will know exactly where you stand in terms of family security and retirement income.

One of our agents will call within a few days to find the most convenient time to provide this service. Sincerely,

FPC-3. Subject: Futures Planning Conference

Futures Planning is a service that almost invariably increases the value of a person's present insurance. It starts with a conference based on two premises:

1. No effort will be made to sell anything during that conference.
2. You will not be contacted again unless you request it.

These two premises set the stage for a fair, relaxed discussion.

The service can give you a complete understanding of your social security and other benefits and how they relate to your life insurance program. You'll know exactly where you stand in terms of family security and retirement income.

One of our agents will call you within a few days to arrange an appointment. Cordially yours,

JOB 258/259 B. FORM LETTERS

Format the following form letters. Code them as you did the letters in Job 258/259 A. Use letterhead (Workbook 593–598) if using typewriters; save on a disk if using word processors.

LIU-4

Your birthday is an important insurance date. On that day, any additional life insurance you might need will cost more than it does today.

That fact alone is not a reason for you to buy new insurance, but it is a good reason to review your present insurance. Not only does your own life situation change from year to year, but life insurance plans and benefits change and improve from year to year too.

In the next few days, one of our agents will call to arrange a brief appointment. I know you will find it well worth the few minutes needed to review your program.

Cordially yours,

YAS-2

May we introduce you to a savings plan that thousands of other promising young adults have found attractive?

At your age the plan is available at a modest cost and can guarantee that you will be able to obtain life insurance later when your needs and ability to pay increase. It may also have tax and other advantages.

The idea can be explained in just 15 minutes. One of our agents will give you a call soon to arrange a convenient appointment. Cordially,

(Continued on next page)

PRETEST 1

Take two 2-minute timings on lines 6–9. Circle and count your errors on each.

```
6  Phyllis Hinkimin wore a kinky kimono of nylon on Mt. Looke.  12
7  A pupil in hilly Joplin sold Lou that oil monopoly in June.  24
8  A plump puppy limped in as Johnny looked at the oily pools.  36
9  My polo pony looked jolly as Phillip pulled him in my pool.  48
   | 1 | 2 | 3 | 4 | 5 | 6 | 7 | 8 | 9 | 10 | 11 | 12
```

PRACTICE 1

Type lines 10–15 four times.

```
10 hip ill joy kin lip mop nip oil pin you hop imp lop mum nun
11 kink lily milk nook only pill upon yolk honk join limp mill
12 imply lumpy onion hominy kimono limply pinion unhook minion

13 ohm ply hum ink mom non pop hun inn nil pun him pip pup Lon
14 noon oily pink hook kiln lion mink noun plum polk loop jump
15 nylon phony pupil phylon unholy linkup uphill poplin pippin
```

POSTTEST 1

Repeat Pretest 1 to see how much your skill has improved.

PRETEST 2

Take two 2-minute timings on lines 16–19. Circle and count your errors on each.

```
16 Adam Fallan, an Anzac man, can scan a ban as calmly as Sam.  12
17 Jack slams a handball hard, and Alan lacks a hard backhand.  24
18 Ben commonly banks a maximum sum of money in his zinc mine.  36
19 Zoe expects to watch a mammoth zebra at the zoo next month.  48
   | 1 | 2 | 3 | 4 | 5 | 6 | 7 | 8 | 9 | 10 | 11 | 12
```

PRACTICE 2

Type lines 20–24 four times.

```
20 next elms name exam ribs fear zeal acts vent zero been mine
21 index zebra exact dozen human, puzzle mummy, critic pom-pom
22 numb zinc buzz bomb back comb comma maxim venom annex axiom
23 black balsa blank balls class lacks small calls basal chalk
24 Ezra Saxon said the old lax law on pizzas was quite quaint.
```

POSTTEST 2

Repeat Pretest 2 to see how much your skill has improved.

LESSON 213

UNIT 35 Formatting Forms

UNIT GOAL 44/5'/4e

- **GOALS**
  To use abbreviations correctly while typing sentences.
  To format and type credit memorandums.
- **FORMAT**
  Single spacing   60-space line

LAB 25

Abbreviations

Type lines 1–4 once, providing standard abbreviations for the underscored words. Edit your copy as your teacher reads the answers. Then retype lines 1–4 from your edited copy.

1 The Zambro Company will need to check the work with Mister Zambro.
2 The board measures 6 feet long; however, they need 2 feet more.
3 He purchased 2 quarts of milk; she purchased 18 quarts of gasoline.
4 He drove the race car at 256 kilometers per hour and won the prize.

■ GOALS
To recognize the correct use of confusing words while typing sentences.
To type 48/5′/3e.
To format, type, and address form letters.

■ FORMAT
Drills: Single spacing 60-space line
5-Minute Timings: Double spacing 5-space tab

LAB 31

Confusing Words

Type lines 1–4 once. Then repeat lines 1–4 or take a series of 1-minute timings.

```
1  If we do not accede to the cuts, we will exceed the budget.   12
2  To say that I complement you is a very touching compliment.   12
3  The principle upon which this principal was hired is clear.   12
4  A stationary wall unit is used to store our new stationery.   12
   | 1 | 2 | 3 | 4 | 5 | 6 | 7 | 8 | 9 | 10 | 11 | 12
```

accede: to consent, agree
exceed: to surpass, go beyond

complement: (n.) officers and crew
(v.) to complete or bring to perfection
compliment: (n.) praise, a flattering statement
(v.) to praise

stationary: fixed, unmovable
stationery: writing materials, paper

principal: (adj.) chief, leading
(n.) a person in a leading position
principle: rule, code of conduct

PRETEST

Take a 5-minute timing on lines 7–26 on page 416. Circle and count your errors.

PRACTICE

Take a 1-minute timing on each paragraph of the Pretest on page 416.

POSTTEST

Take another 5-minute timing on lines 7–26 on page 416 to see how much your skill has improved.

FORMATTING FORM LETTERS

As a word processing secretary, you are to key form letters into a CPU (central processing unit). These letters will be recalled later. No dates, addresses, or salutations are keyed at this time; allow space for them.

JOB 258/259 A. FORM LETTERS

Some companies have several letters that are slightly different in their wording. Format the following form letters. Code the letters FPC-1, FPC-2, and FPC-3. If you are using a typewriter, code the letters in the lower left corner, about 3 lines from the bottom of the page; use letterhead (Workbook 587–592). If you are using a word processor, store each letter as a separate document, naming each document using the codes. Save the letters on a disk.

FPC-1. As an Americana Insurance Company policy owner, you are entitled to periodic review of your life and health insurance programs.

Such things as beneficiary designations, use of dividends, social security benefits, and other matters need periodic checking. You will find it worth your while to take a few minutes for this service.

One of our agents will give you a call in the near future to arrange an appointment at your convenience. Cordially yours,

FPC-2. As an Americana Insurance policy owner, you are eligible to receive, free and without obligation, the benefits of our Futures Planning Service.

(Continued on next page)

12-SECOND TIMINGS

Type each line three times, or take three 12-second timings on each line. For each timing, type with no more than 1 error.

```
5  Laura will go to the store in the a.m. to get a qt of milk.
6  They will move home from the city when they need more cash.
7  How soon can you help them get some cash to move back here?
```

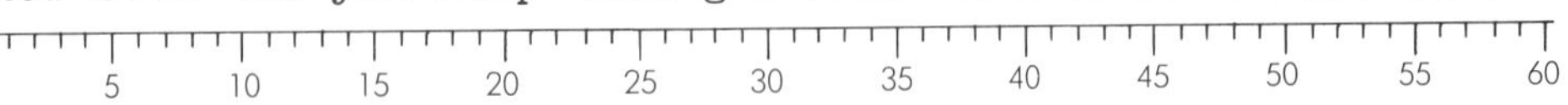

FORMATTING CREDIT MEMORANDUMS

A credit memorandum is a form used to let a customer know that a credit (deduction) has been made to his or her account.

To format a credit memorandum:

1. Use the standard format for business invoices.
2. Type the words *Total amount credited* (instead of *Total amount due*) aligned with the *D* in *Description.*
3. Format any adjustments as follows:

Amount credited	75.15
5% Sales tax refund	3.76
Transportation refund	3.45
Total amount credited	82.36

ELLIS INDUSTRIES 7812 Hillcrest Avenue Dallas, Texas 75225 — Credit Memorandum

TO: Williams and Finch, Inc.
181 Danvers Street
Normal, IL 61761

DATE: October 8, 19--

Your account has been credited as follows:

QUANTITY	DESCRIPTION	UNIT PRICE	AMOUNT
6	Regulation Type F Basketballs, damaged in transit	11.90	71.40
1	Basketball Inflation Pump and Needle, not ordered	3.75	3.75
	Amount credited		75.15
	5% Sales tax refund		3.76
	Transportation refund		3.45
	Total amount credited		82.36

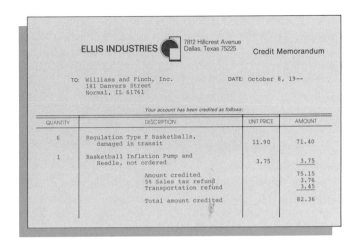

JOB 213 A. CREDIT MEMORANDUM

Workbook 419–420 top.

[*To:*] Alamosa Sports Equipment, 204 Main Street, Alamosa, CO 81101 [*Credits:*]

10 Racquetball rackets, Model 75H (handle wrapping defective) [*Unit price*] 19.50 [*Amount*] 195.00

5 Racquetball gloves, right hand (elastic torn) [*Unit price*] 4.75 [*Amount*] 23.75

Amount credited	218.75
Transportation refund	17.50
Total amount credited	236.25

JOB 213 B. CREDIT MEMORANDUM

Workbook 419–420 bottom.

[*To:*] C & R Sports Inc., 378 Delaware Avenue, NE, St. Petersburg, FL 33703 [*Credits:*]

3 Fastdart dart boards, 36″ (boards not ordered) [*Unit price*] 15.65 [*Amount*] 46.95

12 Bullseye darts, #4560 (dart tips damaged) [*Unit price*] 12.50 [*Amount*] 150.00

Amount credited	196.95
Transportation refund	8.76
Total amount credited	205.71

JOB 213 C. CREDIT MEMORANDUM

Calculate the amounts. Workbook 421–422 top.

[*To:*] Ms. Celeste Van Dis, Freedom High School, 1340 Freedom Way, Jacksonville, FL 32250 [*Credits:*]

12 Regulation Type XL basketballs (incorrect model) [*Unit price*] 18.89

2 Type K hoops (broken on arrival) [*Unit price*] 31.35

Transportation refund 24.78

JOB 213 D. CREDIT MEMORANDUM

Calculate the amounts. Workbook 421–422 bottom.

[*To:*] New Bedford Junior College, 9200 West Evans Avenue, Denver, CO 80227 [*Credits:*]

2 Regulation Type A footballs (deflated—will not hold air) [*Unit price*] 22.95

24 Helmets, assorted sizes (wrong color) [*Unit price*] 46.80

Transportation refund 42.50

FORMATTING CLIENT INFORMATION

Form letters are used in business when the same information needs to be transmitted to a number of people. Insurance companies make a great use of form letters. In order to rapidly process this routine correspondence, they must maintain client information in data banks. The information can be recalled by client name, policy number, type of policy, or even renewal date. In this lesson you will develop client records that will be used in the remaining lessons of this unit. If you are using a typewriter, keep these records on 5 by 3 index cards. If you are using a word processor or microcomputer, prepare the information as a list and save it on a disk.

```
Ortega:  Juan, Marie (Mr. and Mrs.)

   1863 Peachtree Road
   Atlanta, GA 30309

Automobile        Homeowners
728A392-80        928763H
September 30      September 30

Life              Life
L0738-6432        L0738-6433
September 30      September 30
Juan              Marie
12/03/55          06/15/58
```

JOB 257 A. PREPARING CLIENT INFORMATION

Use the format illustrated to prepare the following client information. If you are using cards, type one client per card (Workbook 583–584). If you are making a list, leave 3 blank lines between clients.

Dr. and Mrs. James (Phyllis) Hatton, Chatham Apartments, 669 Abercorn Street, Savannah, GA 31401, Homeowners 846032H November 1; Life (James, 02/11/40) L0723-4998, July 15; Life (Phyllis, 11/22/39) L0723-4999, July 15.

Mrs. Aida Johnson, 155 Forrest Lane, Albany, GA 31707, Life (05/31/57) L0736-1005, September 1; Automobile 724A436-80, September 1.

Ms. Elizabeth Townsend, Coronado Apartments, #317, 200 23d Avenue, Columbus, GA 31903, Life (09/04/60) L0739-6082, August 10.

Mr. Chuck Dickerson, 712 Forrest Lane, Albany, GA 31707, Automobile 822A491-78, August 1; Life (10/21/56) L0735-1148, January 2; Health GH3725M/H, September 15.

Miss Sarah J. Catalano, Armstrong College, 11845 Abercorn Street, Savannah, GA 31406, Automobile 715A098-84, July 30.

PREPARING POTENTIAL-CLIENT LISTS

Many companies, insurance companies in particular, often send routine letters to potential customers. They get the names of these people from real estate documents (new homeowners) and from newspaper articles about promotions, recent graduates, births in the city, and so on. Use the standard format for index cards. Type the purpose of the letter at the tab stop, a double space below the address.

JOB 257 B. PREPARING POTENTIAL-CLIENT LISTS

Use cards (Workbook 585–586) or a list as appropriate.

Mr. Todd Ruppert, Armstrong College, 11935 Abercorn Street, Savannah, GA 31406, new college graduate.

Ms. Jennifer Shapiro, 22 Peachtree Avenue, Atlanta, GA 30305, new college graduate.

Mr. and Mrs. Geoffrey Lippman, 38 Meadow Park Drive, Atlanta, GA 30315. They have a new baby girl.

John Allen, a business executive, recently moved to Atlanta, GA; 10 Parkview Circle, 30337.

Sherri J. Atworst, Apartment K, Willowwood Court, Atlanta, GA 30345, new to the community.

LESSON 214

■ **GOALS**
To type 45/3'/2e.
To format and type statements of account.

■ **FORMAT**
Drills: Single spacing 60-space line
3-Minute Timings: Double spacing 5-space tab

KEYBOARDING SKILLS

Type lines 1–4 once. Then practice using your editing skills in line 5 to capitalize wherever necessary. Repeat lines 1–4, or take a series of 1-minute timings.

Speed 1 We do not yet know all that we would like to know about it. 12

Accuracy 2 Jack was quite amazed to see the taxes paid by Mrs. Wagner. 12

Numbers 3 I watched for 10, 28, and 39. Jerry watched for 47 and 56. 12

Symbols 4 Hat sale: $29 hats for $10, $47 for $38, and $100 for $56. 12

Technique 5 judd and cox protested when lee and poe sued huff and park.

| 1 | 2 | 3 | 4 | 5 | 6 | 7 | 8 | 9 | 10 | 11 | 12

PRETEST

Take a 3-minute timing on lines 6–17. Circle and count your errors.

6 Resorts have been popular since Colonial times, but it 12

7 was not until the spread of the railroads that the business 24

8 really expanded. Then Americans began to travel to seaside 36

9 and mountain resorts, hot springs, and spas. 45

10 Traditionally, resorts were fancy hotels which offered 12

11 to their clients large rooms, good food, outdoor games, and 24

12 quaint places for sight-seeing and shopping. These resorts 36

13 were usually open just during the summertime. 45

14 The industry now includes year-round as well as summer 12

15 resorts. Some of the most popular are ski resorts, many of 24

16 which are open all year. Tropical resorts are very popular 36

17 for getting away from the long winter freeze. 45

| 1 | 2 | 3 | 4 | 5 | 6 | 7 | 8 | 9 | 10 | 11 | 12 SI 1.57

PRACTICE

Take a 1-minute timing on each paragraph of the Pretest.

POSTTEST

Take another 3-minute timing on lines 6–17 to see how much your skill has improved.

PRACTICE 1

Type lines 5–10 five times. Repeat individual lines for speed gain if you had two or fewer errors on Pretest 1; otherwise, repeat each block of lines for accuracy gain.

5 bay mad tax map tab mar van nab car ink can jam bat jab man
6 baby mast vary mall sack pack care jack bank hymn tack jobs
7 enemy vault blame clams mulch bands truck track bulbs nails

8 cab mob bag mix vat men bin lob act inn bar nob may bad vim
9 back maze bake navy calm mast many came zany cage bend mint
10 meant coach manly basic naval cable lemon canal money candy

POSTTEST 1

Repeat Pretest 1 on page 416. Proofread and note your improvement.

PRETEST 2

Take two 2-minute timings on lines 11–14. Proofread both, and note the more accurate of the two scores.

11 She informs me that the boy was running by the office door. 12
12 Just for the fun of it, I gave my aunts one cent for lunch. 24
13 We have to admit that the stones somehow broke the windows. 36
14 Tod doubts the main brakes have a chance of working anyhow. 48

| 1 | 2 | 3 | 4 | 5 | 6 | 7 | 8 | 9 | 10 | 11 | 12

PRACTICE 2

Type lines 15–20 five times. Repeat individual lines for speed gain if you had two or fewer errors on Pretest 2; otherwise, repeat each block of lines for accuracy gain.

15 windows somehow timely office print night tiny pain act nor
16 unknown tactful prompt stones round smoke skin main sun any
17 orchard shelves lesson motive hints exact room noon mob run

18 primary running expand having lunch knife inch aunt ice cry
19 leading mounted chance driven bench count gave from win beg
20 informs helping anyhow brakes doubt admit have cent fun one

POSTTEST 2

Repeat Pretest 2. Proofread and note your improvement.

LESSON 257

UNIT 42 Processing Correspondence

UNIT GOAL 48/5′/3e

■ GOALS
To use confusing words correctly while typing sentences.
To format and type client information for mailing lists.

■ FORMAT
Single spacing   60-space line

LAB 30

Confusing Words

Type lines 1–4 once, selecting the appropriate word from those enclosed in parentheses. Edit your copy as your teacher reads the answers. Then retype lines 1–4 from your edited copy.

1 I agree that no one (accept, except) Phillip should (accept, except) the award.
2 In (addition, edition) to my order, send a new (addition, edition) of the catalog.
3 Lee has been vacationing in Europe for the (passed, past) two months.
4 Only (to, too, two) people felt that there were (to, too, two) many things (to, too, two) do.

FORMATTING STATEMENTS OF ACCOUNT

A statement of account summarizes a customer's transactions during a specific period (usually a month). To format a statement of account:

1. Align fill-ins in the heading with guide words.
2. Begin typing the body a double space below the horizontal rule; single-space the body.
3. Visually center the date in the first column. Abbreviate long months. To align numbers on the right, space twice before typing one-digit numbers.
4. Begin items in the Reference column 2 spaces after the vertical rule.
5. Visually center amounts of money in the Charges, Credits, and Balance columns.

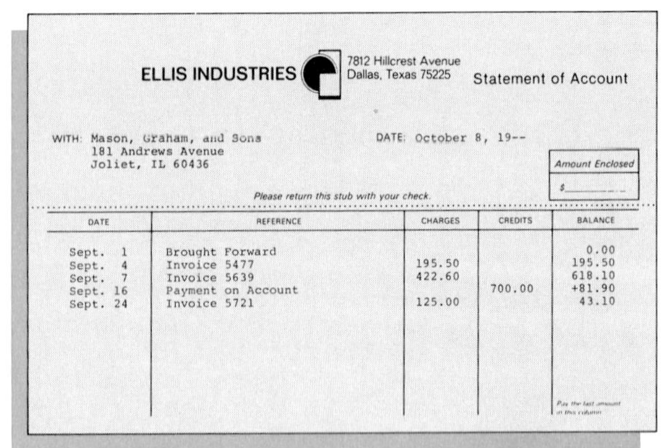

ELLIS INDUSTRIES 7812 Hillcrest Avenue Dallas, Texas 75225 Statement of Account

WITH: Mason, Graham, and Sons
181 Andrews Avenue
Joliet, IL 60436

DATE: October 8, 19--

Amount Enclosed $______

Please return this stub with your check.

DATE	REFERENCE	CHARGES	CREDITS	BALANCE
Sept. 1	Brought Forward			0.00
Sept. 4	Invoice 5477	195.50		195.50
Sept. 7	Invoice 5639	422.60		618.10
Sept. 16	Payment on Account		700.00	+81.90
Sept. 24	Invoice 5721	125.00		43.10

Pay the last amount in this column

Note: Invoices are *charges* to the account and are added to the balance. Payments are *credits* and are subtracted from the balance.

JOB 214 A. STATEMENT OF ACCOUNT

Standard format. Workbook 423–424 top.

[*Date*] May 1, 19—, [*With*] Professional Travel Service, 1600 Broad Street, Chicago, IL 60608

April 1 Brought Forward [*Balance*] 00.00
12 Invoice T-2939 [*Charges*] 16.75 [*Balance*] 16.75
14 Invoice T-3008 [*Charges*] 133.00 [*Balance*] 149.75
20 Payment on Account [*Credits*] 100.00 [*Balance*] 49.75
23 Invoice T-4071 [*Charges*] 10.75 [*Balance*] 60.50

JOB 214 B. STATEMENT OF ACCOUNT

Standard format. Save for use in Job 216 A. Workbook 423–424 bottom.

[*Date*] May 1, 19—, [*With*] Red's Sport Shop, Park Acres Shopping Center, Winnetka, IL 60093

April 1 Brought Forward [*Balance*] 72.00
10 Payment [*Credits*] 72.00 [*Balance*] 00.00
15 Invoice 3559 [*Charges*] 234.00 [*Balance*] 234.00
27 Credit Memo 496 [*Credits*] 35.10 [*Balance*] 198.90

JOB 214 C. STATEMENT OF ACCOUNT

Standard format. Compute the balances for the statement of account at the top of the next column. Save for use in Job 216 A. Workbook 425–426 top.

[*Date*] May 1, 19—, [*With*] Parkway Plaza, 3202 Parkway Drive, Peoria, IL 61611

April 1 Brought Forward [*Balance*] 120.00
3 Invoice T-1688 [*Charges*] 56.50
12 Payment [*Credits*] 75.00
22 Invoice T-4026 [*Charges*] 164.23

JOB 214 D. STATEMENT OF ACCOUNT

Standard format. Compute the balances. Save for use in Job 216 A. Workbook 425–426 bottom.

[Date] May 1 [With] Hampshire House
181 Andrews Boulevard, Joliet, IL 60436
4/1 Brought Forward [Balance] 00.00
4/4 Invoice T-1732 [Charges] 195.50
4/7 Invoice T-1846 [Charges] 422.60
4/24 Payment on Account [Credit] 500.00
4/30 Invoice T-4150 [Charges] 125.00

JOB 214 E. STATEMENT OF ACCOUNT

Standard format. Compute the balances. Save for use in Job 216 A. Workbook 427–428 top.

[Date] May 1 [With] The Carriage Inn
676 State Street, Chicago, IL 60605
4/1 Brought Forward 115.85
4/10 Payment 115.85
4/20 Invoice T-3998 176.50
4/24 Invoice T-4087 218.75
4/30 Payment 100.00

5-MINUTE TIMINGS

Take two 5-minute timings on lines 7–26.

7 Word processors are making many typewriting tasks much 12
8 easier to complete. Correcting a keyboarding error is very 24
9 simple. Just backspace and key correct characters over the 36
10 top of incorrect characters. The changes are done quickly. 48
11 Making major changes in business communications always 60
12 frustrates even the most proficient typist. Words or lines 72
13 left out mean retyping the complete document. Even a small 84
14 error that was not found before may mean retyping the page. 96
15 Major changes on the CRT screen are called editing. A 108
16 text may need different margins, different line spacing, or 120
17 different positioning of characters, lines, and paragraphs. 132
18 Word processors allow for quick movement within a document. 144
19 Combining data from two or more sources into one docu- 156
20 ment is called merging. Individual addresses can be easily 168
21 added to form letters. Form letters can be personalized by 180
22 merging key phrases into spaces in letters by using a code. 192
23 When documents will be used again—even with changes— 204
24 they can be stored on magnetic tape or diskettes. Rekeying 216
25 isn't necessary; documents can be reprinted as they are, or 228
26 they can be edited to incorporate whatever change you need. 240

| 1 | 2 | 3 | 4 | 5 | 6 | 7 | 8 | 9 | 10 | 11 | 12 | SI 1.70

JOB 255 A. MULTIPAGE BROCHURE

Finish the 16-page brochure you started in Lessons 252/253.

LESSON 256

CLINIC

GOAL
To use intensive drill to improve basic skills.

FORMAT
Single spacing 60-space line

PRETEST 1

Take two 2-minute timings on lines 1–4. Proofread both, and note the more accurate of the two scores.

1 Frank knows about the campus campaign to back a labor vote. 12
2 Carol gave six tubs of shrubs to enable the band to travel. 24
3 Scott and Elmer called the track coaches about those races. 36
4 Benjamin will carry about nine heavy loads to the big barn. 48

| 1 | 2 | 3 | 4 | 5 | 6 | 7 | 8 | 9 | 10 | 11 | 12 |

■ GOALS
To recognize all-capital abbreviations while typing sentences.
To type on ruled lines.
To format and type receipts and checks.

■ FORMAT
Single spacing 60-space line

All-Capital Abbreviations

Type lines 1–4 once. Then repeat lines 1–4 or take a series of 1-minute timings.

```
1  The FBI will investigate the journals for the UAW officers.  12
2  Those students will visit the U.S.A. in the next few years.  12
3  The text revolves around a happening in Iraq about 300 B.C.  12
4  Patricia Gazer earned her M.A. degree in English from Yale.  12
   | 1 | 2 | 3 | 4 | 5 | 6 | 7 | 8 | 9 | 10 | 11 | 12
```

Most all-capital abbreviations are typed without periods:

FBI CBS UN UNESCO UAW IBM RCA

Some all-capital abbreviations (geographic names, academic degrees, and a few miscellaneous abbreviations, such as *R.S.V.P., P.O., A.D.*) do use periods:

U.S. U.S.A. U.S.S.R. M.D. M.B.A. R.S.V.P. P.O.

30-SECOND SPEED TIMINGS

Take two 30-second speed timings on lines 5 and 6. Then take two 30-second speed timings on lines 7 and 8. Or type each sentence twice.

```
5  The juniors who excelled did not find the quiz very taxing,  12
6  but I found that I could not exceed their very fine record.  24

7  You may do your best work when you are happy with yourself;  12
8  so I try to like myself and like what I am doing each week.  24
   | 1 | 2 | 3 | 4 | 5 | 6 | 7 | 8 | 9 | 10 | 11 | 12
```

FORMATTING REVIEW

Typing on Ruled Lines

1. Preliminary step: On a blank sheet, type your name and underscore it. Note (*a*) exactly where the underscore touches or almost touches the aligning scale and (*b*) exactly how much room is between the letters and line.

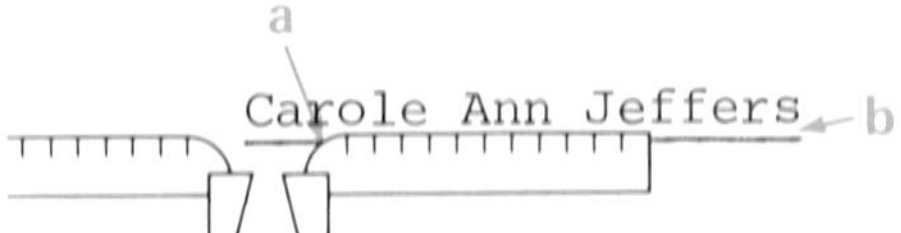

2. Then insert the paper with the ruled lines, and adjust it so that one of the ruled lines is in the position of an underscore. The ruled line should look like this:

3. Type what is to be on the line.

Practice: At various places and angles on a page, type underscore lines 30 spaces long. Remove the paper. Reinsert it. Type your name on each line.

Puerto Vallarta, Zihuatanejo, Acapulco, and Cabo San Lucas. Disembark in Los Angeles on Saturday, December 28. D $1942, E $1878, F $1815, G $1781, H $1680, I $1589

Page 1 (Cover). Cruises Internationale
July 1, 19—, to December 31, 19—
182 Broadway (Your City, State, ZIP)
1-800-555-4896

■ GOALS
To identify the correct use of confusing words while typing sentences.
To type pages of a multipage brochure.

■ FORMAT
Single spacing 60-space line

LAB 30
Confusing Words

Type lines 1–4 once. Then repeat lines 1–4 or take a series of 1-minute timings.

```
1 Our motto will be "We will accept nothing except the best."  12
2 The new edition of the textbook won't be out until January.  12
3 Marybeth has always enjoyed doing her homework in the past.  12
4 Which two people said that there were too many items to do?  12
  | 1 | 2 | 3 | 4 | 5 | 6 | 7 | 8 | 9 | 10 | 11 | 12
```

JOB 254 A. MULTIPAGE BROCHURE

Continue preparing the 16-page brochure you began in Lessons 252/253.

■ GOALS
To use confusing words correctly while typing sentences.
To type 48/5′/3e.
To type pages of a multipage brochure.

■ FORMAT
Drills: Single spacing 60-space line
5-Minute Timings: Double spacing 5-space tab

LAB 30
Confusing Words

Type lines 1–4 once, selecting the appropriate word from those enclosed in parentheses. Edit your copy as your teacher reads the answers. Then retype lines 1–4 from your edited copy.

1 Jean will (accept, except) all of the program (accept, except) the fifth entry.
2 My brother (passed, past) his political science course in the (passed, past).
3 Is the new staff (addition, edition) in our (addition, edition) of this directory?
4 In (to, too, two) months several of us will go (to, too, two) that university (to, too, two).

PREVIEW PRACTICE

Type each line twice as a preview to the 5-minute timings on page 416.

```
Accuracy  5 retyping characters keyboarding personalized communications
Speed     6 work just mean that from form code when used with they tape
```

FORMATTING RECEIPTS AND NEGOTIABLE INSTRUMENTS

To format receipts and negotiable instruments (such as checks and promissory notes):

1. The ruled line should be in the position of the underscore.
2. Backspace the month and day from the end of the ruled date line.
3. Begin all other lines as close to the start of the ruled line as possible.
4. After the name and the amount, fill in the rest of the line with hyphens. Do not space before or after the hyphens.
5. When spelling out amounts of money, capitalize the first word and express cents as a fraction.

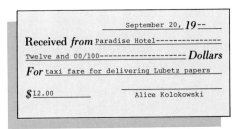

September 20, *19--*

Received *from* Paradise Hotel---------------

Twelve and 00/100------------------- *Dollars*

For taxi fare for delivering Lubetz papers

*$*12.00 Alice Kolokowski

WESTERN RANCH 23-157/1020

PAY TO THE ORDER OF Carmen Esposito---------------------------- $ 37.50

July 5, 19-- No. 340

Thirty-seven and 50/100----------------------------------- DOLLARS

Denver Trust
Plaza Branch

Memo

Willa Horne
AUTHORIZED SIGNATURE

⑈1020⑈0157⑆ ⑈108⑈5172321⑈

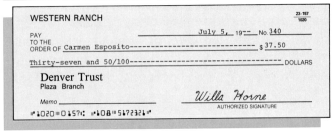

JOB 215 A. RECEIPTS

Standard format. Workbook 427–428 bottom.

You work for the Paradise Hotel. If suppliers are paid in cash rather than by check, they must sign receipts acknowledging receipt of the money. Prepare receipts for the two following cash transactions on July 2, 19—.

1. Prepare a receipt to be signed by Adam McKensie (from Specialty Desserts) in the amount of $135 for a double sheet cake for the Lee banquet.
2. Prepare a receipt to be signed by Janine LeQueux (LaFleur) in the amount of $58.75 for two floral pieces for the Lee banquet.

JOB 215 B. CHECKS

Checks are to be made out to students who were temporaries at Western Ranch; they were paid $4.75 an hour; yours is the authorized signature. Format four checks—no erasing on a check. Compute the amount due. Date all checks July 5, 19—. Workbook 429–430.

1. Terry O'Connors—7 hours.
2. Chris Rubinski—8½ hours.
3. Celeste Corey-Miller—11 hours.
4. Ernie L. Lum—18 hours.

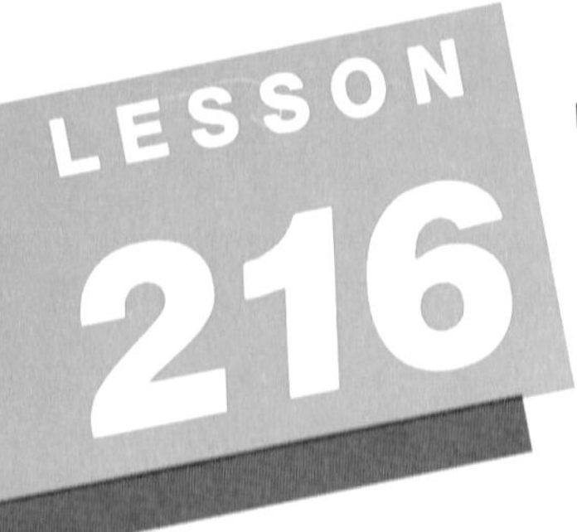

■ GOALS
To identify all-capital abbreviations while typing sentences.
To format and type voucher checks.
To format and type expense reports.

■ FORMAT
Single spacing 60-space line

LAB 26

All-Capital Abbreviations

Type lines 1–4 once. Then repeat lines 1–4 or take a series of 1-minute timings.

```
1 In the fall Ms. Polinski will visit the U.S.S.R. and Japan.  12
2 I wrote R.S.V.P. on the invitations to the wedding banquet.  12
3 My address is P.O. Box 165--not 156, as shown on this form.  12
4 Zoe has accepted a position with the CIA for work overseas.  12
  | 1 | 2 | 3 | 4 | 5 | 6 | 7 | 8 | 9 | 10 | 11 | 12
```

Page 4. Summer Alaska Aboard the Royale
Sail from San Francisco on Tuesday, July 16, for 10 days. Cruise to the ports of Vancouver, Juneau, Glacier Bay (cruising only), Sitka, and Victoria. Disembark in San Francisco on Friday, July 26.
D $2848, E $2560, F $2496, G $2416, H $1952

Page 5. Summer Hawaii Aboard The Aloha
Sail from Honolulu on Saturday, August 10, for 7 days. Cruise to the ports of Kahului, Hilo, Kona, and Nawiliwili. Disembark in Honolulu on Saturday, August 17. D $1555, E $1470, F $1385, G $1299

Page 6. Summer Caribbean Aboard The Sky Wind
Sail from Miami on Saturday, July 13, for 11 days. Cruise to the ports of Curaçao, Caracas, Grenada, Martinique, St. Thomas, St. John, and Nassau. Disembark in Miami on Wednesday, July 24. D $2029, E $1961, F $1897, G $1861, H $1813, I $1745

Page 7. Summer Mediterranean Aboard The Pacifica
Sail from Naples on Monday, August 12, for 12 days. Cruise to the ports of Messina, Heraklion (Crete), Alexandria, Haifa, Rhodes, Delos, and Mykonos. Disembark in Athens on Saturday, August 24. D $3377, E $3204, F $2724, G $2517

Page 8. Summer British Isles Aboard The Blue Viking
Sail from Tilbury (London) on Sunday, July 14, for 10 days. Cruise to the ports of Dublin (Ireland), Portree, Lerwick (Scotland), Bergen, Flaam, Gudbangen (Norway), and Leith (Scotland). Disembark in Tilbury on Wednesday, July 24. D $2790, E $2680, F $2560, G $2240, H $2180, I $1960

Page 9. Summer Danube River Cruise Aboard the Ulricha
Sail from Passau, Germany, on Saturday, July 6, for 7 days. Cruise to the ports of Durnstein, Budapest, Esztergom, Bratislava, Vienna, and Melk. Disembark in Passau on Saturday, July 13. D $1180, E $1095

Page 10. Summer Black Sea Cruise Aboard The Sea Knight
Depart the United States on Saturday, August 3. Stay overnight in London and sail from Piraeus on Monday, August 5, for 17 days. Cruise to the ports of Mount Athos Peninsula, Istanbul, Trabzon, Batumi, Sochi, Yalta, Constanta, Varna, Nessebur, Skiathos, and Skyros. Disembark in Piraeus on Thursday, August 22. D $3972, E $3203, F $3064, G $2965, H $2879

Page 11. Fall New England Aboard The Canadian Viking
Depart from New York on Saturday, September 21, for 14 days. Cruise to the ports of Bar Harbour, Halifax, Quebec, Montreal, Charlottestown, Sydney, Boston, and Newport. Disembark in New York on Saturday, October 5. D $4032, E $3864, F $3696, G $3052, H $2954, I $2660

Page 12. Fall Caribbean Aboard The Sky Wind
Sail from Miami on Saturday, November 16, for 11 days. Cruise to the ports of Cozumel, Grand Cayman, Panama Canal, San Blas Islands, Ocho Rios, and Nassau. Disembark in Miami on Wednesday, November 27. D $2023, E $1955, F $1891, G $1855, H $1823, I $1807

Page 13. Fall Hawaii Aboard The Aloha
Sail from Honolulu on Saturday, October 12, for 7 days. Cruise to the ports of Kahului, Hilo, Kona, and Nawiliwili. Disembark in Honolulu on Saturday, October 19. D $1555, E $1470, F $1385, G $1299

Page 14. Fall Mediterranean Aboard The Pacifica
Sail from Naples on Tuesday, September 17, for 12 days. Cruise to the ports of Dubrovnik, Venice, Corfu, Itea, Livorno, and Villefranche. Disembark in Naples on Sunday, September 29. D $3361, E $3188, F $2708

Page 15. Holiday Hawaiian Aboard The Aloha
Sail from Honolulu on Saturday, December 21, for 7 days. Cruise to the ports of Kahului, Hilo, Kona, and Nawiliwili. Disembark in Honolulu on Saturday, December 28. D $1725, E $1640, F $1555, G $1470

Page 16. Holiday Mexico Aboard The Seaway
Sail from Los Angeles on Wednesday, December 18, for 10 days. Cruise to the ports of Mazatlán,

(Continued on next page)

FORMATTING VOUCHER CHECKS

A voucher check is a check with a tear-off stub. The stub includes the payee's name and address and can therefore be inserted in a window envelope to save typing time. The stub also includes an explanation of the payment—very helpful to the payee.

To format a voucher check:

1. Check half: Standard format for checks (page 355).
2. Stub half:
   a. Type the reason for the check, aligned with the amount, 3 lines below the top of the stub.
   b. Type the name and address a double space below the top of the address box, 2 spaces in from the left edge of the box.

PROFESSIONAL TRAVEL SERVICE
1600 Broad Street, Chicago, Illinois 60606

2 - 523
710

May 10, 19-- No. 396

PAY TO THE ORDER OF T & G Printing-------------------------------- $60.50

Sixty and 50/100-- DOLLARS

Reliable Bank of Chicago
212 South State Street
Chicago, IL 60604

Memo

Sylvia Wong
AUTHORIZED SIGNATURE

⑆0710⑈0523⑆ ⑈324⑈9846307⑈

DETACH AND RETAIN THIS STATEMENT • The attached check is in payment of items described below. If not correct, notify us promptly.

In settlement of your statement of May 1, 19--.

T & G Printing
403 South Wacker Drive
Chicago, IL 60607

JOB 216 A. VOUCHER CHECKS

Prepare voucher checks in payment of the statements you typed in Jobs 214 B to 214 E, page 353. Date all checks May 10, 19—. Standard format. Workbook 431–434.

FORMATTING EXPENSE REPORTS

To be reimbursed for business expenses such as travel and entertainment expenses, workers must fill out detailed expense reports. For each expense, the report shows the date, the reason, and the actual cost. The report provides space for the payee's signature and an approval signature.

To format an expense report, follow standard format for business forms.

Note: If the Amount column contains a vertical rule separating dollars and cents, align the numbers 1 space from the rule.

Pay to Mary Beth Keith (Claimant to insert name) Date March 11, 19--

Address 219 Dellafield Avenue, Brockton, MA 02402 (Claimant to insert address)

MONTH	DAY	ITEMS OF EXPENDITURE	DOLLARS	CENTS
3	10	Transportation to Boston airport	17	50
		Plane fare to Washington--round trip	167	00
		Transportation to FBI Building	11	75
		Luncheon ticket	10	00
		Transportation to Washington airport	11	75
		Transportation from Boston airport	17	50
		Total	235	50

Signature of Claimant Mary Beth Keith

Approved: L. R. Denyski

JOB 216 B. EXPENSE REPORT FORMS

Standard format. Compute totals. Date each form the day after the last date of the trip. Save for use in Job 217 A. Workbook 435–438.

Robert Carberry, 3900 Fourth Avenue, Macon, GA 31201. March 2: Airfare to/from Charleston, SC, $87.21; Limousine from airport, $8.75; Convention registration fee, $15.00; Hotel Pecan, including porter's tip, $57.50; Meals, including banquet, $25.00. March 3: Transportation to Charleston airport, $8.75.

Y. K. Pao, 214 Sunset Lane, Atlanta, GA 30344. March 7: Luncheon at La Normande Restaurant for customers—Dr. Albert T. Karr (research specialist) and Dr. Greta Speer-Hagen (Dr. Karr's associate), both of I. T. Fragen, Inc., Federal Republic of Germany—and two staff members, $89.50.

Robert Carberry, 3900 Fourth Avenue, Macon, GA 31201. March 18: Bus to/from Atlanta for GCA meeting, $27.18; Registration fee (including lunch), $25.

(Continued on next page)

Speed
30 least fails skills often those paper alone tasks every some
31 must able task with also both very well work word this many
32 need team when will the has two you any and job for who are
33 each all can put via on at be to of is an in do no it an or

POSTTEST Take another 5-minute timing on lines 5–25 on page 412 to see how much your skill has improved.

JOB 252/253 A. MULTIPAGE BROCHURE

For the next several lessons you will be preparing a 16-page brochure that will be typed on both sides of the paper. First, prepare a dummy of the entire brochure.

1. Cut 2 sheets of paper in half (the 4 pages will measure 8½ by 5½ inches). Hold the pages together and fold them in half.
2. Number each page, front and back, 1 through 16. Mark what is to be placed on each page.
3. Follow the dummy when preparing the brochure. Type all four pages on each half sheet before going on to a new sheet.
4. After you have typed all 16 pages, gather the pages together in the correct sequence and staple them on the fold line.

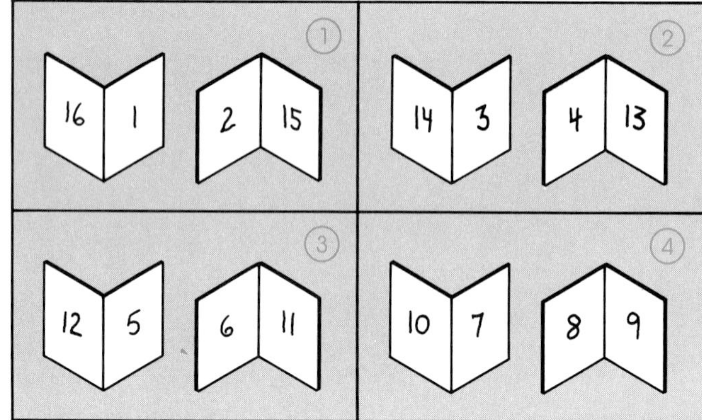

5. Copy the illustrations below for pages 2 and 3. Pages 4–16 will follow the same format as page 3. Arrange the cover material attractively on page 1.

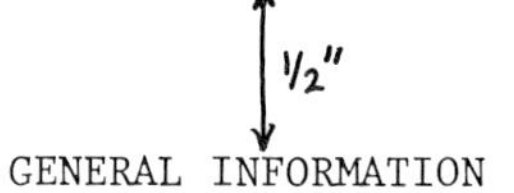

GENERAL INFORMATION

½" These special prices are available to all persons who enjoy fun and want to relax for a few days on a cruise ship. ½"

For reservations on any of the cruises listed in this brochure, call 1-800-555-4896. There will be a reservation clerk on duty 24 hours a day.

TYPES OF ACCOMMODATIONS

Category	Description
D	Outside stateroom, veranda
E	Outside stateroom, Deck 3
F	Outside stateroom, Deck 2
G	Outside stateroom, Deck 1
H	Inside stateroom, Deck 3
I	Inside stateroom, Deck 2

2

½"

SUMMER MEXICO

ABOARD THE SEAWAY

Sail from Los Angeles on Saturday, July 20, for 11 days.

Cruise to the ports of Guadalupe Island, Mazatlan, Acapulco, Zihuatanejo, Manzanillo, Puerto Vallarta, and Cabo San Lucas. Disembark in Los Angeles on Wednesday, July 31.

Category	Price
D	$1753
E	1693
F	1630
G	1596
H	1531
I	1438

3

JOB 216 B (CONTINUED)

Lucille Sanchez, 14 Washington Road, Atlanta, GA 30344. March 14: Limousine to airport, $6.50; Airfare to/from New York, $198.81; Transportation from airport to Rockefeller Center (taxi), $16.00; Dinner, Hotel Ingram, $13.75; Hotel Ingram, $98.35. March 15: Meals, $21.50; Transportation from Rockefeller Center (taxi), $16.00; Limousine from Atlanta airport, $6.50.

■ GOALS
To use all-capital abbreviations correctly while typing sentences.
To type 45/5′/4e.
To type voucher checks.

■ FORMAT
Drills: Single spacing 60-space line
5-Minute Timings: Double spacing 5-space tab

LAB 26
All-Capital Abbreviations

Type lines 1–4 once, providing the standard abbreviations for the underscored words. Edit your copy as your teacher reads the answers. Then retype lines 1–4 from your edited copy.

1 Texas National Airlines flies into John F. Kennedy Airport at 12:30 p.m. on Thursdays only.
2 After her visit to the Union of Soviet Socialist Republics, Jan will get to the United States of America.
3 Bredel sponsors a quiz program on the American Broadcasting Company network each day.
4 Zora will earn her Master of Arts degree in English this fall, right?

30-SECOND "OK" TIMINGS

Type as many 30-second "OK" (errorless) timings as possible out of three attempts on lines 5–7.

5 Some persons say they would like to jog, but they're afraid 12
6 of friends laughing at them. Once they experience the zest 24
7 and value that comes from jogging, they'll learn its worth. 36

| 1 | 2 | 3 | 4 | 5 | 6 | 7 | 8 | 9 | 10 | 11 | 12

PREVIEW PRACTICE

Type each line twice as a preview to the 5-minute timings on page 358.

Accuracy 8 zoos fixing prevent doctors required city-type veterinarian
Speed 9 Kentucky health giving their paid work with such may but do

5-MINUTE TIMINGS

Take two 5-minute timings on lines 5–24 on page 358.

JOB 217 A. VOUCHER CHECKS

Prepare voucher checks to reimburse employees for their business expenses reported on the expense report forms you prepared in Job 216 B, pages 356–357. Workbook 439–442.

accept: (v.) to take willingly
except: (prep.) other than

passed: (v.) moved ahead, proceeded, elapsed
past: (adj.) not current, gone, over

addition: something that is added
edition: one version of a publication

two: (n.) a number
too: (adv.) also, in addition to
to: (prep.) in the direction of, toward

PRETEST

Take a 5-minute timing on lines 5–25. Circle and count your errors.

```
     Succeeding on the job always has at least two aspects.    12
You must be able to perform any task required of you with a    24
degree of accuracy and speed.  You must be able to complete    36
a task pleasantly, cooperatively, and dependably also.  The    48
blending of both skills and attitudes on the job is often a    60
very challenging task for veterans as well as for those who    72
are beginners.                                                 75
     As surveys indicate, however, the human element in all    87
work situations is extremely important.  The growth of word    99
processing centers emphasizes this point.  No longer do all   111
office workers complete assignments alone.  Many tasks need   123
to be completed as team efforts, with every person within a   135
cluster responsible for a section of the completed job.  It   147
can be very frustrating when someone fails to cooperate.      158
     Many persons will be responsible for a completed docu-   170
ment in a large company.  An author dictates the message to   182
a central processing unit; a word processor transcribes the   194
message onto a screen and formats it attractively to be put   206
on printed paper or to be transmitted via satellite to some   218
business located halfway around the globe.  Each communica-   230
tion is quickly received and the response returned.           240
| 1 | 2 | 3 | 4 | 5 | 6 | 7 | 8 | 9 | 10 | 11 | 12           SI 1.66
```

PRACTICE

In the chart below find the number of errors you made on the Pretest. Then type each of the designated drill lines below and on page 413 four times.

Pretest errors	0–1	2–3	4+
Drill lines	28–33	27–32	26–31

Accuracy

```
screen veterans required attitudes processing cooperatively
degree received accuracy beginners emphasizes communication
quickly cooperate satellite extremely dependably succeeding
challenging assignments frustrating responsible transcribes
```

(Continued on next page)

UNIT 36 In-Baskets

UNIT GOAL 45/5′/4e

■ **GOALS**
To use all-capital abbreviations correctly while typing sentences.
To type 45/5′/4e.
To prioritize and format related office communications.

■ **FORMAT**
Drills: Single spacing 60-space line
5-Minute Timings: Double spacing 5-space tab

LAB 26

All-Capital Abbreviations

Workbook 443–444.

Type lines 1–4 once, providing the standard abbreviations for the underscored words. Edit your copy as your teacher reads the answers. Then retype lines 1–4 from your edited copy.

1 Alice went with our class to visit the <u>United Nations</u> in New York City.
2 We bought our typewriters from <u>International Business Machines</u>, which is a big company.
3 Our regular doctor earned her <u>Doctor of Medicine</u> degree in the Near East.
4 We hope they will visit the <u>United States</u> with the group from China.

PRETEST

Take a 5-minute timing on lines 5–24. Circle and count your errors.

```
 5      What do the Kentucky Derby, the circus, zoos, and many   12
 6  farms throughout this country all have in common?  They are   24
 7  all places where animals can be found.  And where there are   36
 8  animals, there is usually a veterinarian near.                45
 9      Veterinarians are doctors who are trained to treat and   12
10  prevent diseases in animals.  Although they go to different   24
11  medical schools than doctors trained to treat people, their   36
12  courses of study and training are much alike.                 45
13      Veterinarians are required to do all aspects of animal   12
14  health care, such as giving shots to prevent sickness, fix-   24
15  ing broken bones, helping owners plan a safe and sound type   36
16  of diet, and doing all kinds of major surgery.                45
17      Many veterinarians limit their practice to one kind of   12
18  animal, such as horses.  These doctors are highly paid, for   24
19  they may care for priceless racehorses.  A few doctors work   36
20  with or do special research on wild animals.                  45
21      Doctors of veterinary medicine may travel with a rodeo   12
22  or circus, live in the wilderness, or care for animals in a   24
23  zoo.  Many, however, help farmers with cattle, hogs, and so   36
24  on; but most others help with city-type pets.                 45
    | 1 | 2 | 3 | 4 | 5 | 6 | 7 | 8 | 9 | 10 | 11 | 12         SI 1.57
```

FORMATTING A FOUR-FOLD BROCHURE

When you prepare a four-fold brochure, which will have copy printed on all pages, you will need to prepare a "dummy" copy first. To prepare the dummy:

1. Fold a full sheet of paper into fourths. Each page measures 4¼ by 5¼ inches (42P/51E wide, 33 lines deep).
2. Keeping the folds at the top and the left, number each page, front and back, 1 through 4.
3. Unfold the dummy to see where the copy for each of the pages is to be typed.

To type the brochure:

1. Fold a clean sheet of paper into fourths. Unfold the paper, and type the copy for each page in the appropriate quarter page.

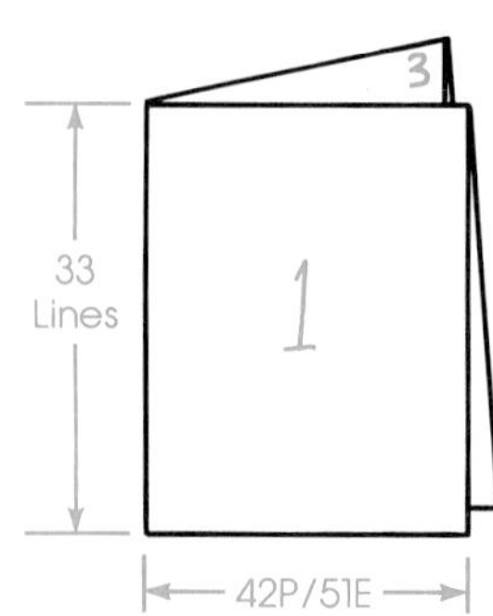

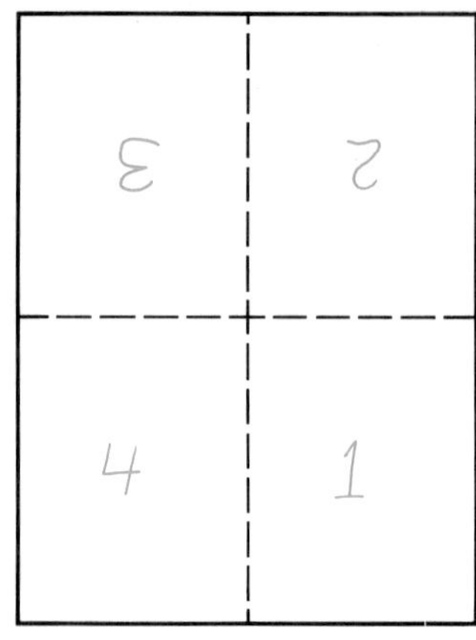

2. Arrange the copy attractively in each quarter. Center vertically; center horizontally or use a minimum of 1/2-inch side margins.

JOB 251 B. FOUR-FOLD BROCHURE

Use any display style.

[Page 1] The Sixth Annual Baxter High School Computer Conference, Saturday, April 12, 19—

[Page 2] 9 a.m.: Registration and Exhibits; 10 a.m.: Determining Your Needs; 11 a.m.: Selecting a Computer; 12 noon: Luncheon; 1:30 p.m.: Selecting Software; 2:30 p.m.: Using Your Modem; 4 p.m.: Exhibits close

[Page 3] Luncheon Menu: Fresh Fruit Cup; Fried Chicken, Ham, Turkey, Roast Beef; Potato Salad; Rolls and Butter; Soda, Milk; Ice Cream; $3.50

[Page 4] Visit the Exhibits
Computers: The Computer Shop, Computer World; Software: Video Shack, SoftWorld; Books: The Book Nook; Supplies: Masden's Computer Supplies; Demonstrations: Baxter High School's Computer Club

■ GOALS
To recognize the correct use of confusing words while typing sentences.
To type 48/5′/3e.
To format and type pages of a multipage brochure.

■ FORMAT
Drills: Single spacing 60-space line
5-Minute Timings: Double spacing 5-space tab

LAB 30

Confusing Words

Type lines 1–4 once. Then repeat lines 1–4 or take a series of 1-minute timings.

```
1  Why did she accept all of the program except the one entry?  12
2  The most recent edition of the math book stresses addition.  12
3  In the past few weeks the quarterback passed for 200 yards.  12
4  Two people said that there were too many changes to review.  12
   | 1 | 2 | 3 | 4 | 5 | 6 | 7 | 8 | 9 | 10 | 11 | 12
```

Homonyms are words that sound alike but are spelled differently. There are also a number of words that sound similar but are also spelled differently. These words and homonyms are grouped together as *confusing words.* Study their definitions.

(Continued on next page)

PRACTICE Take a 1-minute timing on each paragraph of the Pretest on page 358.

POSTTEST Take another 5-minute timing on lines 5–24 on page 358 to see how much your skill has improved.

IN-BASKET C:

Working for a Civic Association

You have volunteered to work in the offices of the Animal Rescue League, 6020 Hamilton Avenue, Chicago, IL 60607. Ms. Carolyn A. Heppenstahl is the executive director, and Dr. Henrietta Ludwig is the staff veterinarian. Today is August 10, 19—. Use letterheads and forms where appropriate. Workbook 445–466.

PRIORITY SHEET AND TIME LOG

Read through the entire in-basket, and then complete the priority sheet. Be sure to keep an accurate time log as you complete each job.

COUPON LETTER

Standard format with indented paragraphs. Prepare three carbon copies for use in addressing coupon letters and envelopes.

All Chicago area residents under the age of 18 years are invited to register their favorite dogs and cats now in the ARL Dog and Cat Show to be held Saturday, September 3, 19—, at 1 p.m. at the League's Rosedale Kennels, 600 Hoffman Lane, Hoffman Estates, IL 60195.

There is no entry fee for the show. Each exhibitor may show one dog or cat. All pets must be leashed and must have received a distemper vaccination within the past year.

You can use the coupon below to register. Please fill it out and return it to the League offices at 6020 Hamilton Avenue, Chicago, IL 60607, by August 30, 19—.

Prizes will be awarded in 11 classes, so indicate on the coupon the class in which you want your pet to compete.

Sincerely, Carolyn A. Heppenstahl, Executive Director

- -

ARL DOG AND CAT SHOW

Name____________________________________Age________

Address____

____

Pet's Name________________________ Dog Cat (Please circle one.)

Class in which you wish your pet to be entered (please circle one):

Shaggiest Dog	Best Groomed	Droopiest Ears (Dogs Only)
Furriest Cat	Smartest	Longest Whiskers (Cats Only)
Most Colorful	Prettiest Tail	Friendliest
Most Typical	Saddest Eyes	

ADDRESSING COUPON LETTERS AND ENVELOPES

Address the four coupon letters to the new members.

LESSON 251

UNIT 41 Formatting Brochures

UNIT GOAL 48/5'/3e

■ **GOAL**
To format and type brochures.

■ **FORMAT**
Single spacing 60-space line Tabs every 9 spaces

KEYBOARDING SKILLS

Type lines 1–4 once. Then use the tabulator as you type line 5. Repeat lines 1–4, or take a series of 1-minute timings.

```
Speed       1  Janet is busy with the key, so the man is to do the panels.   12
Accuracy    2  Roxie jumped off the van quickly when we saw the big plaza.   12
Numbers     3  They found Invoices 10, 29, 38, 47, and 56 in the corridor.   12
Symbols     4  "Here we are," he said.  "We have $30 (in change) to give."   12
Technique   5  Set      tabs     nine     spaces    apart;    then     type.
               | 1 | 2 | 3 | 4 | 5 | 6 | 7 | 8 | 9 | 10 | 11 | 12
```

FORMATTING BROCHURES

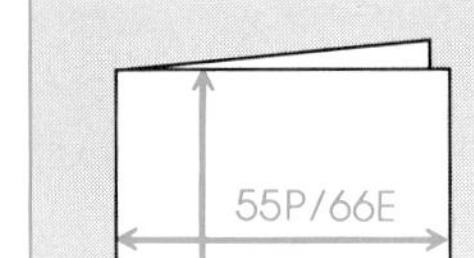

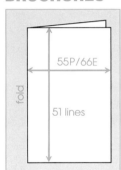

A brochure is a small pamphlet or booklet and is often used to display a program.

To format a single-fold, four-page brochure:

1. Fold a standard-sized sheet of paper in half from top to bottom.
2. Turn the paper so that the fold is at the left. The measurement of each "page" is 55P/66E wide and 51 lines deep.
3. Display the title in any display format on the front cover.
4. Divide the copy as evenly as possible, and display it on the two inside pages. (Leave the back cover blank unless the copy is too long to fit on the middle two pages.)

JOB 251 A. SINGLE-FOLD BROCHURE

Use any display style, such as spread centering, block centering, underscoring, all-capital letters, leaders.

PROGRAM
Thursday, March 9
Opening Session, 7 p.m., Grand Ballroom, Speaker: Dr. Barry Brechak, Topic: "World Marketing in the 1990s"
Friday, March 10
Session 1, 9:30 a.m., Suite A, Speaker: Joe LaVigne, Topic: "The Effects of Grain Embargoes on Domestic Pricing"
Session 2, 11 a.m., Suite C, Speaker: Phatama Shih, Topic: "The Growing Market of Software Products"
Luncheon, 12:30 p.m., Grand Ballroom, Speaker: Alison Aker, Station WTWC
Session 3, 2 p.m., Suite C, Speaker: Noriko Hagashima, Topic: "The World Car Concept in Transition"
Session 4, 3:30 p.m., Suite A, Speaker: Leah Chuang, Topic: "Trends in the Telecommunications and Computer World"
Dinner and Entertainment, 7 p.m., Grand Ballroom, Speaker: Jeffrey Meyer, Topic: "Trends in Language Requirements for Marketing Positions"

Use the copy below for the cover.

National Conference / World Marketing Trends / March 9–10 / Waldorf-Astoria Hotel / New York City

INDEX CARDS

Format 5 by 3 cards for the new members to the ARL so that their names and addresses can be added to your mailing list. All are Chicago, IL. Standard format.

Ms. Mattie Bradley, 1214 Manor Road, 60110
Mr. Nick Valenti, 215 Lenore Drive, 60002
Mrs. Wilma Volk 894 McCoy Road, 60208
Mr. and Mrs. Michael Sullivan, 3101 Grand Avenue, 60043

COMPOSE A LETTER

Compose a rough draft of a short letter that can be sent to the four new members. Thank them for contributing to the Animal Rescue League and for being concerned about the humane treatment of animals in the city of Chicago. Explain that their names have been placed on the ARL mailing list to receive the monthly League NEWSLETTER. Invite them to an open house at League Headquarters on Sunday, August 20, from 2 to 5 p.m. If they need further information, suggest that they call the League at 555-6452. The executive director of the League will sign the letter. Use plain paper.

FORM LETTER

Prepare the letter you composed for new members in block format. Use a subject salutation, such as *To All New Members of the Animal Rescue League.* Do not use an inside address. Prepare an original and three copies. Address a large envelope to each new member.

SPEECH

Standard format. Triple-space. Prepare for the League's veterinarian.

WHAT KIND OF DOG DO YOU WANT TO OWN?

If you are thinking of getting a dog, close one who's disposition, size, and appearance appeal to you. There are threegroups of dogs, according to their orginal uses: (1) sporting dogs, such as setters, spanells, and hounds, were bred as hunters; (2) working dogs, such as sheperds, collies, and sheep dogs, were used as herdders; (3) toy dogs and nonsporting dogs, such as Boston terriers and podles, were pets and companions. It helps to be able to recognize breed characteristics in order to predict adultsize and behavior.

families with pre school children ought to look for medium-size breeds that have good temperment and can endure ough play. If you live the city, you might have difficulty providing out door space for lage sporting dogs and hounds, which neeed plenty of runing room. The dachshund and cocker spaniel, for example, demand less out door exercise and adapt better to "city life."

Many dog owners prefer an animal that does not require frequent grooming. Most breeds shed there coats once a year; but with regular brushings excessive loss of fur shouldnot be a problem around

When you can only guess at the ancestry of a puppy,

Note: Dr. Ludwig will give this speech tonight at a PTA meeting.

LEVEL 11

GOALS

1. Demonstrate keyboarding speed and accuracy on straight copy with a goal of 49 words a minute for 5 minutes with 3 or fewer errors.
2. Correctly proofread copy for errors and edit copy for revision.
3. Apply advanced production skills in keyboarding and formatting copy for business documents from a variety of input modes.
4. Apply rules for correct use of homonyms and confusing words in written communications.
5. Prioritize and make appropriate formatting decisions while completing two in-baskets.

thehouse. Some dogs are light shedders--wire haired terriers and podles, for example. Heavy-sheding breeds include the dalmaian and german sheperd.

pupies offered for sale or adoption should always be atleast 6 weeks old. A healthy animal will have bright eyes, a glossy coat white teeth, and pink gums. Do not consider a puppy that shows any signs of illness--a runn nose, watery eyes, or fever--or exhibits temper problems, such as snappyness or extreme shyness.

Data for Table

1 = 15	11 = 60
2 = 24	12 = 64
3 = 28	13 = 68
4 = 32	14 = 72
5 = 36	15 = 76
6 = 40	16 = 80
7 = 44	17 = 84
8 = 48	18 = 88
9 = 52	19 = 92
10 = 56	20 = 96

TABLE

Standard format. Full sheet of paper. Title: HOW OLD IS YOUR DOG? Title of column 1: Age of Dog (Years). Title of column 2: Equivalent Age of Human (Years). A 1-year-old dog is equated with the human equivalent age of 15—shown in the data as 1 = 15. Use the data given in the margin on the left.

MEDICAL CERTIFICATES

Complete two certificates of vaccination for Dr. Ludwig, who has just examined the two dogs described below. Their owners are in the waiting room.

1. Owner: Jennie Pugh; dog, collie with black/white markings, male, four years old, weight 75 lb, named Max. Lives at 42 Glen Arden Drive, Chicago, IL 60610. Vaccination tag #5754. Owner's telephone: 555-8132. Vaccination for distemper and rabies.
2. Owner: Hilda Schiller; dog, German shepherd with brown and gray spots, female, six years old, weight 95 lb, named Minerva. Lives at 517 Amberson Place, Hoffman Estates, IL 60195. Vaccination tag #5755. Owner's telephone: 555-9101. Vaccination for rabies, distemper, and hepatitis.

Newsletter
goes to press
August 11

NEWSLETTER COLUMN

The column was written by Dr. Ludwig. Edit the copy as you type it. Standard format for enumerations. Full sheet of paper.

QUESTIONS AND ANSWERS

Q. What are the most prevelent allergy problems in cats?

A. cats do not have allergy conditions nearly as frequently as dogs; but when cats do have allergy conditions, they are usually sever. The causes of allergys in cats are not as well defined or understood as in dogs, but there is generally a good response to proper treetment.

Q. is flea allergy in cats as sereous as in dogs?

A. yes this can be a sever condition in cats.

Q. Can cats have allergic reactions to foods?

A. food allergys are very hard to identify; consult your veterinarian.

JOB 249/250 D. INCOME STATEMENT

Complete the figures on the income statement. Standard format.

IGLOO SPORTSWEAR
SUMMARY INCOME STATEMENT
FOR THE MONTH ENDED FEBRUARY 28, 19—

SALE OF GOODS		$21,570.00
COST OF GOODS SOLD		
GOODS IN SHOP FEB. 1, 19—	$ 9,231.18	
GOODS PURCHASED DURING MONTH	4,507.00	
TOTAL AVAILABLE GOODS FOR SALE	$13,738.18	
GOODS IN SHOP FEB. 28, 19—	9,418.30	
COST OF GOODS SOLD		4,319.88
GROSS PROFIT ON GOODS SOLD		
EXPENSES		
RENT OF SHOP	$ 400.00	
UTILITIES	180.00	
TOTAL EXPENSES		
NET INCOME FOR MONTH OF FEBRUARY		

JOB 249/250 E. JOB DESCRIPTION

Standard format.

Position Title: Supervisor
Department: Vocational Education
Reports to: Director of Vocational Education

Description of Position: Supervises the improvement of instruction and learning, and functions as a leader in his or her capacity in the instructional procedure. Contributes to the effective change and general improvement of the educational process.

Duties:

1. Directs the development of an evolving curriculum that is relevant to the world of work.
2. Fosters professional improvement of staff.
3. Supervises the development of both immediate and long-range goals.
4. Recommends to the director of vocational education selections for library and audio-visual aids and reference materials.
5. Works cooperatively with other personnel.
6. Supervises and encourages formal and informal research projects.
7. Promotes good public relations.
8. Assists in the orientation of new teachers and substitute teachers.

LESSONS 221–223

■ GOALS
To type 45/5′/4e.
To prioritize and format related office communications.

■ FORMAT
Drills: Single spacing 60-space line
5-Minute Timings: Double spacing 5-space tab

KEYBOARDING SKILLS

Type lines 1–4 once. Then practice using your backspace and underscore keys by typing line 5 twice. Repeat lines 1–4, or take a series of 1-minute timings.

Speed	1	Both the men may go to town if he pays them for their work.	12
Accuracy	2	Five wizards very quickly jumped into the box on the stage.	12
Numbers	3	By June 10 ship 29 seats, 38 stoves, 47 tents, and 56 cots.	12
Symbols	4	Quotation marks (") set off exact words: "Fire!" he cried.	12
Technique	5	The first week of <u>Time</u>, <u>Newsweek</u>, and <u>People</u> has been sent.	

| 1 | 2 | 3 | 4 | 5 | 6 | 7 | 8 | 9 | 10 | 11 | 12

PREVIEW PRACTICE

Type each line twice as a preview to the 5-minute timings below.

Accuracy	6	sizes equipment handlebar mechanized customized inexpensive
Speed	7	bicycle future blends riding shapes their autos city may of

5-MINUTE TIMINGS

Take two 5-minute timings on lines 8–27.

8 Motorcycles are the result of our mechanized age, even 12
9 though their basic model has been with us since the bicycle 24
10 was invented. Their design blends the simple basics of the 36
11 bicycle with the advanced technology that is used in autos. 48
12 The result is a lightweight vehicle, inexpensive to operate 60
13 and maintain and great fun to ride. 67
14 Like all good ideas, motorcycles do have some features 79
15 that are bad. They carry only two passengers, and most are 91
16 uncomfortable for long-distance riding. Hauling equipment, 103
17 luggage, or even a bag of groceries home from the store can 115
18 be an impossible task because motorcycles have no trunk. A 127
19 snowstorm or severe rainfall can be a major problem for the 139
20 motorcycle operator: skidding on wet roads. 148
21 Just like automobiles, motorcycles come in many shapes 160
22 and sizes. There are trail bikes for riding off the street 172
23 or for racing on lonely back roads, city bikes, and mopeds, 184
24 which are ideal for running errands. Some motorcycles have 196
25 been customized by their owners, using fancy handlebars and 208
26 painted gas tanks. In the future each of us may use a bike 220
27 to promote energy economy. 225

| 1 | 2 | 3 | 4 | 5 | 6 | 7 | 8 | 9 | 10 | 11 | 12 SI 1.58

JOB 249/250 A. LETTER WITH MULTIPLE ADDRESSEES

Standard format. Workbook 575–576.

Mr. Fred Kilburn Ms. Marla Wentz, 15
Campaign Headquarters 11134 Mill Road, 22
Cincinnati, OH 45506, Dear Mr. Kilburn 31
and Ms. Wentz: As regional campagn 39
chairperson for the midest, I have 46
been asked by Mr. Matthews to arrange 54
for his official candidacy announced 63
in your city. There are a numberof 70
strong supporters in Cincinnati and 77
we feel that any opening remakrs 84
would recieve strong support & good 92
media coverage. Would you please 99
check to see if the area around the 108
fountain during lunch time is avail- 111
able. A larger crowd might be drawn 122
to such a location during that time 129
of day. Please let me secretary know 136
as soon as possible. There will be 145
approximately forty people with the 158
campaign in Cincinnati. We shall 166
need about 34 rooms and a hospitality 173
suite to acommodate everyone. I as- 180
sume that the City Center Motel will 190
be the best location. Thank you for 199
your help in this important part of 212
the campaign. Sincerely, Tony A. 222
Makato, Regional CAmpaign Chairperson 231

JOB 249/250 B. LETTER WITH MULTIPLE SIGNATURES

Block format. Workbook 577–578.

Ms. Ginette Williams, 483 South Broad 15
Street, Chicago, IL 60608, Dear Ms. 23
Wiliams: We have rearanged our sched- 32
ules so that we can spend a half day 39
with you on Tuesday March 22. We will 47
be enroute to Detroit to meet with Al 55
DeMonaco and can stop long enough for 63
us to plan the campaign for Illinois. 71
We will arrive on american 574 at ap- 79
proximately 2:10 on Tuesday afternoon, 87
and have arranged to stay at the air 94
port Hotel so that we can leave imme- 101
diately on Wednesday morning for 108
Detroit. Please bring your list of 116
workers with you so that we can orga- 123
nize our efforts. We have special 131
brochures that should be of help to 139
you. One explains the telephone cam- 147
paing, and the other offers sugges- 153
tions for dinners and receiptions. 160
We look forward to working ith 168
you in march. Best wishes, Tony A. 179
Makato, Regional Campaign Chairperson, 186
Roy A. Grimes, National Chairperson 198

JOB 249/250 C. DICTATED LETTER

Send this letter to Mountain Construction Company, 45 West Broadway, Jackson, Wyoming 83001. It needs to be edited as it is typed. Workbook 579–580.

gentlemen and ladies this leter is to confirm the telephone conversation that we had earlier this weak i have decided that i do want to expand the display area of the shop the storage area also needs to be expanded by about ten feet as i look at the volume of business, it appears that some time during the month of may would be the best time to complete the project most of the skiers will be gone and the summer tourists will have started to come in enclosed is the bid request form which you sent to me it should help in figuring costs of remodelling please let me know if these requests can be completed by the end of may sincerely [*Sign your own name as owner or manager of the Igloo Sportswear Shop.*]

IN-BASKET D:

Working for a Small Shop

You are working in the office of The Cycle Shop, which is located at 4100 Graham Blvd., Houston, TX 77052. The shop buys and sells bicycles, mopeds, and motorcycles, as well as parts and accessories. The owners are Nancy and Harry DiSalenti. Today is April 2, 19—. Use letterheads and forms where appropriate. Workbook 467–482.

PRIORITY SHEET AND TIME LOG

Read through the entire in-basket, and then complete the priority sheet. Be sure to keep an accurate time log as you complete each job.

PURCHASE ORDERS

Prepare purchase orders for parts from the supplier's motorcycle parts list shown below. Standard format.

Sumoto Corporation, 7800 Grand Avenue, San Diego, CA 92101.
No. 1754. Order six each of items 13, 16, 17, and 18 listed below. Calculate the total. Rush order for good customer.

No. 1755. Order six each of items 7, 8, and 9 listed below. Calculate the total. Rush order for good customer.

SUMOTO MOTORCYCLE PARTS

Item	Number	Description	Unit Price
1	070037	Tank, Fuel	$42.50
2	071076	Cap, Fuel Tank	2.25
3	710032	Fitting, Tank	.79
4	070020	Hose, Rubber	1.52
5	070011	Screen	.40
6	071087	Fitting Assembly	2.38
7	710017	Filter, Fuel	1.86
8	071066	Hose, Insulating	1.15
9	071072	Line, Fuel	3.16
10	051147	Carburetor Assembly	18.51
11	710033	Fitting, "T"	1.15
12	021192	Cable, Throttle	5.25
13	091236	Wire Assembly, Choke	7.49
14	051151	Manifold, Air Intake Inner	4.89
15	720005	Screw, Allen	.45
16	720004	Retainer, Cable	6.65
17	720006	Nut, Self-Locking	.38
18	051156	Rod	.73

TEST

■ **GOALS**
To type 47/5'/3e.
To demonstrate competency in producing appropriately formatted communications from unarranged, handwritten, rough-draft, and unedited copy.

■ **FORMAT**
Double spacing 60-space line 5-space tab

PREVIEW PRACTICE

Type each line twice as a preview to the 5-minute timings below.

Accuracy 1 input firm's quarter analyze expenses expresses summarizing
Speed 2 future handle their names vital firm what with owns and its

5-MINUTE TIMINGS

Take two 5-minute timings on lines 3–22.

3 If a firm contracts with a data control center to pre- 12
4 pare its records, the center will handle at least four main 24
5 financial documents--balance sheets, income statements, and 36
6 schedules of accounts receivable and accounts payable. 47
7 The relationship between what a business owns and what 59
8 it owes is revealed on a balance sheet. It, too, is needed 71
9 each month, quarter, and year. The balance sheet expresses 83
10 how a company's assets and liabilities are distributed. 94
11 An income statement contains the income and expenses a 106
12 company has for a month, a quarter, or a year. Summarizing 118
13 these two categories in one report allows a firm to analyze 130
14 the vital relationship between its income and expenses. 141
15 Businesses must keep a close record of their customers 153
16 and their creditors. Customers are referred to as accounts 165
17 receivable, and creditors are called accounts payable. The 177
18 lists are prepared with names, amounts owed, and dates. 188
19 A data control center has the capability to input data 200
20 or readjust data, permitting numerous analyses and compari- 212
21 sons. The firm's future depends upon an ability to analyze 224
22 its statements and make careful long-range predictions. 235

| 1 | 2 | 3 | 4 | 5 | 6 | 7 | 8 | 9 | 10 | 11 | 12 | SI 1.72

RECEIPTS

Type receipts for the four customers who gave you cash for the tickets they ordered. They are waiting for the receipts. (The Cycle Shop does not charge for handling the ticket orders.) Standard format.

LETTER

Block format.

Sumoto Corporation, 7800 Grand Avenue, San Diego, CA 92101 Gentlemen and Ladies: Subject: Malfunctions in Model ST-520, During the past two or three months we have had many owner complaints about a breakdown of their Sumoto Super-Twin Motorcycles, Model ST-520. ¶As you know, the points and condenser on the left side of the engine attach around the end of the crankshaft. After 2000 miles of travel the oil seal breaks down, letting oil into the points and condenser. As a result, the engine loses ignition. ¶We feel that all your Model ST-520s need an improved seal, and we suggest a recall. Your authorized dealers need something to restore the public's confidence in Sumoto. Sincerely, Harry DiSalenti.

ORDER FORMS

Complete four fill-in order forms for tickets for customers who plan to attend the Super Motorcross in Dallas on April 30, 19—. Tickets are scarce, so there is a need to process the orders immediately.

Ticket Prices

Covered box seats: $20
Open box seats: $18
Bleachers: $15
Upper bleachers: $12
No reserved seats.

1. Louise Koegler, 1640 Jancey, Houston, TX 77051: 6 tickets @ $18.
2. Jerome Liskowitz, 117 Braddock Road, Houston, TX 77046: 2 tickets @ $20 and 3 @ $15.
3. Norman Stumpf, 104 Church Avenue, Houston, TX 77037: 7 tickets @ $20.
4. Nancy and Harry DiSalenti, The Cycle Shop, 8 tickets @ $18 and 8 @ $12.

MANUSCRIPT

Type on a 40-space line, single-spaced. The editor needs it by noon today.

EDITOR'S CORNER

You've finaly made it. You either have your first job or are look for one, or you may be sitting in a dormitory on a campus somewhere facing your first college exam. Its a new feeling one that is challenging and frustrating at the same time. DIMES 'N' DOLLARS is designed to give you suggestions along the way. The cover story focuses on the changing economic conditions and the effect on todays youth. You'll also read about the ups and down of 3 young office workers, some super exercises thatyou can do to keep in shape, and what you role can be as a new voter.

The special feature of this issue is about Ms. Alicia Fezer, who has been a personnel assistant for 2 years. There's a fun quiz to test your knowledge of current events too. We think that you will find DIMES 'N' DOLLARS interesting and useful reading and we welcome any comments or suggestions for future issues. Let us hear from you.

TABLE WITH LEADERS

Set this up as a table of employees and positions. We need it for our 10 a.m. staff meeting today.

Editor in Chief, Marion Weaver; Assistant Editor, James T. Riley; Art Director, Valerie Randolph; Senior Editors, Robin Byer, Joseph Madison, Lorraine Reade, Darryl Geller; Art Editors, Katharine Vito, Ruth Pavlov, Joan Greif; Research Editor, Bonnie Daignelt; Copy Editor, Susanne Manelli; Production Editor, Paul Covell; Promotion Director, Alta Warner; Business Manager, Paulette Zucker; Advertising Manager, Grigsby Jones; Publisher, Jeanne Ziegler

RULED TABLE

The advertising manager wants this information in table form immediately. The main heading is *Youth, Inc., 2112 Avenue of the Americas, New York, NY 10019-1095.* The column headings are *Size* and *Advertising Rates*. 1/8 page is $200, 1/4 page is $300, 1/2 page is $500, 1 full page is $800, the back cover is $1000, and 1 column inch is $75. Put a note at the bottom that it is $100 extra for two-color displays.

LETTER

The cover story for DIMES 'N' DOLLARS was submitted by Calvin Ellston, a professor of economics at Wellston University in Hanover, Indiana. He lives at 1156 College Avenue, Hanover, IN 47243. Please compose a letter to him thanking him for his manuscript. Give him the same information as Ms. Fetzer, but make the following changes: Tell him that his article was selected for the cover story since it best reflects the theme of the magazine. Add that he will receive a $200 check for the article.

DISPLAY NOTICE

Use an attractive format for the safety instructions below, which will be posted at The Cycle Shop for the information of customers who are thinking about buying new bicycles.

PROTECT YOUR bicycle

- Lock your bicycle every time you must laeve it un attended. Don't the mistake of leaving it unlocked and unattendedfor "just a minute
- when you are not riding your bicycle put it way in a locked room, garage, or basement. Don't leave your eycycle in a drive way or yard where it can be seen.
- always use a quality lock and case hardened chain or high-quality cable to lock your new bicycle. Avoid locks that can be easily broken and chains and cables that are light an readily cut with wire cutters.
- record the cereal number of your bicyclein a safe place and keep it with your permenent records. If possible registeryour bicycle with your local police department.
- If your family has a homeowners or apartment insurance check to see if the policycovers bicycels.
- When you lock your bicycle be sure to put the chin through both wheels, the frame, and the rack or other stationery object towhich you are on securing it.

INVOICES

The Cycle Shop marks up the prices in the Sumoto catalog 15 percent for selling to its customers. Prepare invoices for the customers shown below, using marked-up prices. Standard format.

G. T. Miller, 1643 Warren Avenue, Houston, TX 77049. Invoice 351. Purchased one each of items 10, 11, 13. Sales tax, 6%.

Cyrus von der Byl, 171 Canton Court, Houston, TX 77045. Invoice 352. Purchased one each of items 1, 2, 3, and 9. Sales tax, 6%.

COMPOSE A LETTER

Compose a letter to Dallas International Classics, P.O. Box 165, Dallas, TX 75221. Indicate that you want to stock some T-shirts for the Dallas Super Motorcross. Inquire as to the prices, sizes, colors, and shipping arrangements, since you would like the shirts at least one week before the event. You select the format.

ADDRESS CARDS

The following names need to be added to the computer list of subscribers. Make address cards for each, and then alphabetize them.

Mr. Jay Yeary, 84A Wildhurst Apartments, Paintsville, KY 41240
Ms. Deanna Zbacnik, 47 Tipperary Court, Nageezi, NM 87037
Mr. George L. Weitkamper, 422 Jahrom Lane, Modesto, CA 95355
Mr. Alvin MacGregor, 738 Hawthorne Circle, Skokie, IL 60076
Ms. Marilyn Pearson, 8830 Carberry Drive, Hiko, NV 89017
Ms. Marla Patrick, 975 Willow Street, Huntington, WV 25701
Mrs. Tamara Meulendyke, 4830 Decker Drive, Tivoli, TX 77990

REPLY CARDS

Two different reply cards are needed—one for CURRENT SPORTS and one for DIMES 'N' DOLLARS. Make the cards 4¼ by 6 inches. Arrange them attractively. They must be delivered to the printer by tomorrow afternoon.

The CURRENT SPORTS card should have this beginning paragraph:

Every month 250,000 people open their mail to CURRENT SPORTS. Each issue is packed with information, insights, and ideas. Start your subscription now with this card. You'll save over 50% off CURRENT SPORTS's newsstand price of $1.50. *Type three lines for name, address, and city/state/ ZIP. Below these double-spaced lines, type* Send me 25 ($18), 40 ($28), or 60 ($40) issues. *Put a small box beside each choice. Below that, also using boxes, type* Payment enclosed *and* Bill me later.

The DIMES 'N' DOLLARS card should have this beginning paragraph:

Save over 15% on a charter subscription to DIMES 'N' DOLLARS. *Below that, and with a box in front of it, type* Starting with the premier issue, please enter a one-year charter subscription to DIMES 'N' DOLLARS for me at the current low price of only $8 (regular rate: $10). *Below that, with another box preceding, type* I prefer two years at $15 for an additional saving. *Below that, with boxes in front, type* Payment enclosed *and* Bill me later. *At the bottom, double-spaced, type a line for name, a line for address, and a line for city/state/ZIP.*

TABLE

Type a geographic listing of the names of the new subscribers as well as an alphabetic listing. Add the following names:

Ms. Penny McNab, 68 Elton Street, Eagle, WI 53119; Mr. Sidney Meehan, 385 J-Mar Drive, Franklin, OH 45005; Mrs. Ellen Thompson, Centerburg High School, Brookville, IN 47012. [*Put an asterisk after her name, and make a note at the bottom of the page that it is for 20 copies at school rate.*]

DICTATED LETTER

Type the following letter to Alicia Fetzer, 1783 West Berwyn Avenue, Chicago, IL 60640. The letter is unedited—watch for spelling and punctuation!

thank you very much for submiting your artical on job interviews to our editor dimes n dollars is a new publication and will be circulating its first issue next month your artical is exactly what we were looking for to complete the section on employment since you have been working in personal for sometime i am sure that our subscribers are going to be interested in reading your excellant suggestions as soon as this issue is printed you will recieve advance copies and a check for 100 dollars thank you for your contribution to our new magazine sincerly james t. riley

TEST

■ **GOALS**
To type 45/5'/4e.
To demonstrate competency in formatting and producing a variety of correctly typed documents from numerous sources.

■ **FORMAT**
Double spacing 60-space line 5-space tab

PREVIEW PRACTICE

Type each line twice as a preview to the 5-minute timings below.

Accuracy: degree career readily cluster average elsewhere competently
Speed: work type paid make it's this with then but pay if do so or

5-MINUTE TIMINGS

Take two 5-minute timings on lines 3–21.

```
     The degree of ability needed by a word processing typ-     12
ist depends on whether you work in a standalone, a cluster,     24
or a center.  In all three types you are really expected to     36
complete numerous kinds of operations, but it is clear that     48
the standalone demands the broadest experience, the cluster     60
next, and the center least.  In other words, a beginner can     72
be employed readily in a center but possibly not elsewhere.     84
     Pay scales are not standardized, but you will probably     96
be paid according to the operations you can demonstrate.  A    108
standalone operator earns more, in most offices, because he    120
or she should be able to do more jobs that make the machine    132
prove it is cost-effective and as productive as advertised.    144
     If there's something to be acquired from these remarks   156
about word processing, it's probably this:  A little knowl-    168
edge and a little experience are not enough.  If you intend    180
to pursue a career using this new technology, learn to type    192
with above-average speed and accuracy.  Then master all the    204
operations that your word processing machine is designed to    216
do so that you are able to work competently.                   225
| 1 | 2 | 3 | 4 | 5 | 6 | 7 | 8 | 9 | 10 | 11 | 12          SI 1.59
```

JOB 224/225 A. CREDIT MEMO
Standard format. Calculate balances. Workbook 483–484.

[*To*] Clark's Sports Center, Washington Shopping Center, Villa Park, IL 60181

July 27 Letterhead order (Invoice 3575) was short 200 sheets. [*Amount*] $36.00
5.25% Sales tax refund

JOB 224/225 B. STATEMENT OF ACCOUNT
Standard format. Calculate balances. Workbook 483–484.

[*To*] Clark's Sports Center, Villa Park

July	1	Brought Forward	35.50
	15	Invoice 3575	189.45
	18	Payment	100.00
	27	Credit Memo 512	

IN-BASKET F: Publishing

You are a typist for a publisher of magazines. They have two magazines on the market and are preparing to begin publication of a third. It is your job to type the following communications. Workbook 563 bottom–574.

PRIORITY SHEET AND TIME LOG

Read through the entire in-basket and then complete the priority sheet. Be sure to keep an accurate time log as you complete each job.

FORM LETTER

Set up a copy of this form letter on plain paper. Remember to leave room for the date, inside address, and salutation.

Welcome to the world of DIMES 'N' DOLLARS. We are sure that you are going to be pleased with every issue of our young adult consumer magazine. Designed especially for persons who are beginning their first job or going on to college, DIMES 'N' DOLLARS is written by young adults between the ages of 18 and 25 who will assist you in finding an apartment, purchasing an automobile, and planning a budget. In addition, DIMES 'N' DOLLARS will inform you about the latest fashions for the working set and offer special seasonal pointers.

Your first issue of DIMES 'N' DOLLARS should arrive within the next two weeks. We know that you're going to enjoy all the advantages DIMES 'N' DOLLARS will bring you. Cordially, Paulette Zucker, Business Manager

FORM LETTER

Set up this letter on plain paper.

current sports is written for people who have a interest deep in the world--people like you that is why we're sending a free copy of this months issue. When you read and enjoy our clear concise article you will want to join the 250,000 other Readers who now enjoy CURRENT SPORTS every month. When decide you that you want CURRENT SPORTS--and you will--simle fill out the enclosed card and return it too us. We'll then send you CURRENT SOPORTS so that you can injoy the lively features on your favorite sprts personalites and sports teams. Cordially yours, paulette Zucker, Business Manager. PS. You are eligible for the multi year savings option shown on the enclosed card. Won't you put your card in the mail?

JOB 224/225 C. VOUCHER CHECKS

Standard format. Workbook 485–486.

1. Prepare a check in payment of the statement you prepared in Job 224/225 B, page 366.
2. Prepare a check to Ms. Michelle Bamonte, 401 Waterman Street, Providence, RI 02906, for a refund of a $200 deposit on a canceled trip.

JOB 224/225 D. LETTER WITH TABLE

Standard format. Date: August 15. Workbook 487–488. Body 167 words.

Ms. Debbie Schwazz, 1100 Oceana Drive, Aurora, OH 44202, Dear Schwartz: I am delighted that you thought of writing to to Worldwide Travel Agency for help with some of the travel questions you and your dlassmates are discuging in your course entitled world affairs. It is important for every one to know about the subject of travelexpenses and how to go about finding economical ways to bisit other countries. You particlarly asked me to identify high-cost forigen cities; that is the places in the world that are expensive to live in. Our latest source of information from the United States reports the following statistics.

High Cost-of-Living Cities

Country	City	Index *
Japan	Tokyo	199
Switzerland	Geneva	163
Belgium	Brussels	150
Denmark	Copenhagen	146
Netherlands	The Hague	143
France	Paris	136

Austria Vienna 138

* Based on a comparison with the costs of living in New York City, which is rated 100.

I hope that this information is complete and pertenent to your course work. Please do not hesitate to call Worldwide whenevee we can beof service to you. Sincerely, WORLDWIDE TRAVEL AGENCY, Holly Allen-Sloan, Manager

JOB 224/225 E. BOXED TABLE

Arrange the table in the letter to Ms. Schwartz on a full sheet of paper. Put the cities in the first column and the countries in the second column. Arrange the table body alphabetically by city. Standard format for a boxed table with 8 spaces between columns.

JOB 224/225 F. MEMO

Standard format. Workbook 489. Body 54 words.

[DATE:] Today's date, [TO:] All Client Representatives, [FROM:] Holly Allen-Sloan, [SUBJECT:] High Cost-of-Living Cities, Many of our business clients have indicated that they want an updated list of high cost-of-living cities throughout the world. ¶ Attached is a copy of the table containing the latest statistics that were released by the United Nations last Saturday. This information should be sent to your business clients who request it. HAS

JOB 224/225 G. ANNOTATED BIBLIOGRAPHY

Standard format.

Burrell, M. R., Are You an OK Boss? Fabin & Fabin, Inc., New York, 1979. Almost everyone is a boss at one time or another. In this practical text, the author takes a new look at "bossing," using sound techniques for good communication. You'll see how OK you are when it comes to directing others.

Everett, John C., Motivating People, Newman and Sons, Inc., Dallas, 1981. This book will introduce you to basic theories of communication and show you how to apply them in your place of business. Each of the 32 chapters includes case studies.

Scarlatti, Veronica, Everybody Wants to Win, Arris House, Sacramento, 1981. The author brings together comments of and programs for people throughout the country and explains how certain people have achieved good human relations by working with people in groups.

■ **GOALS**
To type 47/5′/3e.
To prioritize and format related office communications.

■ **FORMAT**
Drills: Single spacing 60-space line
5-Minute Timings: Double spacing 5-space tab

KEYBOARDING SKILLS

Type lines 1–4 once. In line 5, backspace and underscore the titles shown in italics. Repeat lines 1–4, or take a series of 1-minute timings.

Speed	1	It is the time for all of us to take the time to save more.	12
Accuracy	2	The Zanzibar Express was jolting us four but moved quickly.	12
Numbers	3	Would you like to see 10, 29, 38, 47, or 56 new characters?	12
Symbols	4	Adam (my colleague) paid $6.95 a ream for 20# tinted paper.	12
Technique	5	Please make plans to peruse *Future Shock* or *The Third Wave*.	

| 1 | 2 | 3 | 4 | 5 | 6 | 7 | 8 | 9 | 10 | 11 | 12

PREVIEW PRACTICE

Type each line twice as a preview to the 5-minute timings below.

Accuracy	6	quality requests explosion magazines existence experiencing
Speed	7	language glance formal cities shapes their goals signs work

5-MINUTE TIMINGS

Take two 5-minute timings on lines 8–27.

8 Walk into a bookstore and take a look at the magazines 12
9 on display. They are published in all sizes and shapes and 24
10 in just about any language. The topics range from a formal 36
11 literary work to the most trivial aspects of modern living. 48
12 Magazines are just one of the signs of the huge information 60
13 explosion we are experiencing as technology advances. 71
14 The real magazine explosion was seen over a century or 83
15 more ago. The spread of education became important, and an 95
16 even more important goal was the reduction of illiteracy in 107
17 the country. People began to gather in large cities, where 119
18 magazines could be sold more easily. Printing presses were 131
19 improved; they were faster and of better quality. 142
20 Throughout their existence, magazines have served as a 154
21 voice in the influencing of culture and the interpreting of 166
22 society. Early magazines printed special literary works of 178
23 their time, and eventually some women's journals and sports 190
24 magazines were added. Modern editors and publishers branch 202
25 out to reach as many new marketing areas as they can. They 214
26 flood potential customers with requests for the purchase of 226
27 magazines which are entertaining and informative. 235

| 1 | 2 | 3 | 4 | 5 | 6 | 7 | 8 | 9 | 10 | 11 | 12 SI 1.72

GOALS

1. Demonstrate keyboarding speed and accuracy on straight copy with a goal of 47 words a minute for 5 minutes with 3 or fewer errors.
2. Correctly proofread copy for errors and edit copy for revision.
3. Apply advanced production skills in keyboarding and formatting copy for business documents from a variety of input modes, including dictation.
4. Apply rules for correct use of prefixes, compound nouns, and compound adjectives in written communications.
5. Prioritize and make appropriate formatting decisions while completing two in-baskets.

STATEMENT OF OPERATIONS

Mail this with the report to stockholders.

PRECAST TECHNOLOGY, INC.
Consolidated Statement of Operations
For Quarter Ended March 31, 19--

Summary Items	This Year	Last Year
Net Profit After Taxes	$ 48,247	$ 123,642
Federal and State Income Tax	10,700	128,521
Sales	2,241,507	2,285,474
Resale Material Sales Cost	136,825	153,596
Delivery Sales Cost	137,314	89,542
Installation Sales Cost	392,910	395,923
Net Plant Sales	1,514,458	1,646,413
Orders	2,193,966	2,392,743
Backlog	932,605	1,042,329
Employees	70	67
Stockholders	127	128
Stock Investment	182,915	183,915
Shares	16,855	16,772
Book Value per Share	22.18	19.42
Net Earnings per Share	2.86	7.52

MEETING AGENDA

Change order of items so that they follow in more logical order.

Agenda
Annual Meeting of the Stockholders
Precast Technology, Inc.
3 p.m., April 28, 19—

1. Report by Charlene Grimes, V.P. in Charge of Operations, explaining new methods of erecting precast.
2. Presentation by James T. Hilgeman about plans for expansion of plant facilities.
3. Report by Richard Wilkins concerning new research in precast surfaces.
4. Report of financial status by Richard Wilkins.
5. Further discussion of plant expansion led by James T. Hilgeman.
6. Election of board of directors.
7. Dinner at the Inn to be served immediately following the meeting.

ACCIDENT REPORT

[*Client*] Juan Dimetro; [*Date reported*] 3/15/—; [*Address*] Apartment A, 54 Main Street, Springfield, OH 45502; [*Phone*] None; [*Explanation of accident*] Juan Dimetro works as an employee on the loading dock for Precast Technology, Inc. On the morning of March 15, 19—, Mr. Dimetro slipped on some ice on the dock and fell between the dock and the trailer, twisting his back as he fell. The client did require a doctor—Dr. Theodore Garland, 14 South Ludlow Street, Springfield, OH 45507 (Phone 555-5038). Mr. Dimetro was taken to Springfield City Hospital at 25 South Ludlow Street. The client is insured with National Cross, 237 Allendale Drive, Columbus, OH 43227. Witnesses to the accident were Richard Sizemore, Barry Coppock, and Michael Smith. Person in charge was Charlene Grimes.

UNIT 37 Processing Reports

UNIT GOAL 46/5′/3e

GOALS
To type 46/5′/3e.
To format and type a policy manual.

FORMAT
Drills: Single spacing 60-space line
5-Minute Timings: Double spacing 5-space tab

KEYBOARDING SKILLS

Type lines 1–4 once. Then use the shift lock for the words in all-capital letters as you type line 5. Repeat lines 1–4, or take a series of 1-minute timings.

Speed	1	Their firm is paid to paint half the signs for those towns.	12
Accuracy	2	Francis and Max proved quite lucky with the big jazz bands.	12
Numbers	3	The prefix 123 replaces 789, so my new listing is 123-0564.	12
Symbols	4	The Myer & Lippet Co. is selling "special" T-shirts for us.	12
Technique	5	Is ACME-APEX the brand of that company, or is it APEX-ACME?	

| 1 | 2 | 3 | 4 | 5 | 6 | 7 | 8 | 9 | 10 | 11 | 12

12-SECOND TIMINGS

Type each line three times, or take three 12-second timings on each line. For each timing, type without error.

6 When will she be able to amend the bill that she supported?
7 He sent a letter about an issue to two members of Congress.
8 When you take a tour, you may see the new Congress at work.

PRETEST

Take a 5-minute timing on lines 17–36 on page 370. Circle and count your errors. Use the chart below to find the number of errors you made on the Pretest. Then type each of the designated drill lines five times.

PRACTICE

Pretest errors	0–1	2–3	4+
Drill lines	11–16	10–15	9–14

9 1948 1952 after million greater watched Congress candidates
10 although meetings selection officials difference television
11 American citizens exposures delegates elections conventions
12 caucusing campaigning commercials nominations participation

13 media quite their worth every first these state while heavy
14 called their party first when than time find that cost paid
15 will lead both such days were this came made mass when into
16 they for was not the our out and led has one are who pay by

POSTTEST

Take another 5-minute timing on lines 17–36 on page 370 to see how much your skill has improved.

LETTER

Signature: Richard Wilkins, President. Send special delivery.

Mr. Gregg R. Snapp, General Contractor, Box 44, Bowling Green, KY 42101, Dear Mr. Snapp: Your precast has been successfully delivered and was installed without incident at the building site. Your construction chief complimented our erecting crew on the professional job they performed. There is only one problem. We have not received your check in the mail.

Please help us complete the paperwork on this job by mailing us your check as soon as possible. As we are a new business, we do not have an excess in operating capital. We need your prompt payment.

Sincerely,

DICTATED LETTER

Signature: James T. Hilgeman, Vice President for Sales.

mid-atlantic precast concrete company 9914 elizabeth road waynesboro va 22980 gentlemen thank you for offering to share your display area with us at the national precast convention in minneapolis next month since we are new in the busness we appreciate your thoughtfulness at this time we are manufacturing a limited number of options but by next year we hope to have some additional ones with this in mind i shall be displaying twelve 12″ × 12″ blocks of our product samples we have the display racks to set them upright if you think that you will have room for them i look forward to seeing you in minneapolis sincerly

JOB DESCRIPTION

Personnel needs this by Thursday in order to include it in the job postings for next week.

Position Title: Plant Manager; Department: Operations; Reports to: Charlene Grimes, V.P. in Charge of Operations; Description of Position: To manage work load in the plant, report time spent making each piece of precast, to maintain safe working conditions. Duties: 1. Assigns specific work to employees, 2. Costs each piece of work on official report, 3. Reports condition of safety equipment weekly, 4. Reports any accidents on official report, 5. Schedules shipping of precast to erection sites, 6. Inspects quality of each piece of precast before shipment.

MEMO TO EMPLOYEES

This should be distributed to all employees as soon as possible.

[*To*] All Plant Employees of Precast Technology, Inc.; [*From*] Charlene Grimes, Vice President in Charge of Operations; [*Subject*] Plant Safety Our plant was recently inspected by federal officials, who found violations of some safety codes. Three employees were not wearing hard hats while working in the loading area, and four employees were not wearing safety glasses while operating the high-speed router and sanding equipment. The safety equipment has been provided by the company for your protection. Please use glasses and hard hats while on the job for both your protection and ours. CG

Although heavy campaigning for a number of months will 12
lead up to a national convention for both parties, such was 24
not the way it was done in earlier days of elections in our 36
country. At first, candidates used to be picked by members 48
of their party in Congress. This way of picking candidates 60
is called the caucus method. Caucusing was stopped after a 72
while, and then nominations were made by state officials in 84
mass meetings. These meetings are the basis of our present 96
practice of conventions. 101

When the national conventions began, they brought more 113
national participation into the selection process, and when 125
the first television cameras came in 1948, the exposure was 137
much greater than before. It has been judged that 68 to 70 149
million people watched the 1952 conventions. Today, almost 161
every American citizen has watched at least one convention. 173

The expenses for a national convention are quite high. 185
Citizens who become delegates find that their participation 197
is worth whatever it will cost. The parties do not pay for 209
television time. Sponsors pay for the commercials, and the 221
difference is paid for by the media itself. 230

| 1 | 2 | 3 | 4 | 5 | 6 | 7 | 8 | 9 | 10 | 11 | 12 SI 1.57

FORMATTING POLICY MANUALS

To format the pages of a policy manual:

1. Type the name of the institution or organization in all-capital letters on line 7.
2. Set margins for a 6-inch line (60P/70E), bound.
3. Number sections and subsections consecutively. Numbers hang in the margin.
4. Type section titles in all-capital letters. Type subsection titles in initial caps, underscored. Run in copy after the subsection titles.
5. Single-space sections and subsections but double-space between them.
6. If more than one paragraph is included in a section or subsection, double-space between paragraphs but do not use a paragraph indention.

SIX-COUNTY CAREER CENTER ↓ 2

CHAPTER II--BOARD OF EDUCATION POLICY ↓ 3

210 IDENTIFICATION

211 Name. The Board of Education of this district shall be known as the Six-County Career Center Board of Education.

212 Boundaries. The Six-County Career Center is composed of the territories that lie within the school districts of Butler, Clinton, Greene, Montgomery, Preble, and Warren.

213 Location. The Six-County Career Center is located at the corner of State Routes 48 and 122.

220 AUTHORITY, POWERS, AND PURPOSE

221 Authority. The supervision of the public schools of this district shall be conducted by the Board of Education, also hereinafter referred to as the "Board," which is constituted and is governed by Code 33 Educational Libraries of the Revised Code of the State of Ohio.

222 Member Powers. Board members as individuals do not separately possess the powers that reside in the Board of Education. The duties and powers

PRACTICE

In the chart below find the number of errors you made on the Pretest. Then type each of the designated drill lines four times.

Pretest errors	0–1	2–3	4+
Drill lines	27–30	26–29	25–28

25 Taj East Mahal Middle Greece Gothic Modern Baroque American
26 basic ornate durability usefulness magnificent architecture
27 textures skillful reinforced available sun-dried structures
28 their color blend often basic goals every world first ideas
29 that have been each were made with them used came more then
30 are one its the and two new now for not era own of to as in

POSTTEST

Take another 5-minute timing on lines 5–24 on page 398 to see how much your skill has improved.

IN-BASKET E:
Architecture

You are employed as a full-time secretary for an architectural precast concrete firm. The firm has three principals who need paperwork to be completed by you—the Vice President for Sales, the Vice President in Charge of Operations, and the President. Today is Wednesday, April 10. Use letterheads and forms where appropriate. Workbook 555–563 top.

PRIORITY SHEET AND TIME LOG

Read through the entire in-basket and then complete the priority sheet. Be sure to keep an accurate time log as you complete each job.

REPORT TO STOCKHOLDERS

First Quarter Report: Precast Technology, Inc.

~~I~~ We have three pieces of information to share with you for this quarter. ¶ 1. It has been only an average year so far. Last quarter we told you that we were quite concerned about the business scene for the next two quarters. Our concern was well placed: We are caught in a squeeze between rising costs and firm resistance to rising costs. As the enclosed state^ment^ shows, the result~~s~~ of that squeeze has been a lower sales ~~c~~volum^e^, and, therefore, less profit and lower net earnings ^per^ share; however, we have turned the corner and expect the rest of the year to be normal, or even better than normal.

2. We are planning an expansion of our plant. Our sale^s^ staff has been working overtime to secure a wider market, and their work has paid off. New plant plans will be explained at the meeting.

3. New research in the area of precast concrete reveals promising possibilit~~y~~ies of ~~two~~ three new surfaces. M~~o~~lds are now being designed to allow us to produce these surfaces.

~~I~~ We hope that you will be able to attend the annual stockholders' meeting on April 28. ~~I look forward to seeing you there.~~

JOB 226/227 A. POLICY MANUAL

Standard format.

CARRER CENTER

Chapter II--BOARD OF EDUCIAION POLICY

210 IDENTIFICATION

211 Name. The Board of Education of this district shall be known as the Career Center Board of Education.

211 Boundaries. The Kareer Center is composed of the territories that lie within the school districts of

213 Location. The Career Center is located at the corner of Routes 48 and 122.

220 AUTHORITY, POWERS, AND PURPOSE

221 Authority. The supervision of the public schools of this disthrrict shall be conducted by the Board of Education, also hereinafter referred to as the "Board," which is constituted and is governed by Code 33 Educational Libraries of the Revised Code of the State of Ohio.

222 Member Powers. Board members as individuals do not separately possess the powers that reside in the Board of Education. The duties and powers that a member is given under the law can be exercised only when the Board is in session. Board members as individuals have no control ofer the schools. No Board Member shall be denied facts or materials required for the proper performance of his or her duties.

If, in the opinion of the superintendent of the treasurer, a board members request for information is administratively unreasonable or represents significant expense in time or material to the district, the request shall be referred to the Board for disposition.

223 Board Purpose. The Board is an administrative, legislative, and quasi-judicial agenr established by the Ohio General Assembly as a political subdivision of the state responsible to maintain, manage, and control the public school system of the district within the Board's jurisdiction. The Board plays a leadership role in educational affairs through it's superintendent and professional staff in the provision of free education for all eligable youth of the district.

224 Legislative. The Board shall exercise its rulemaking authority by adopting bylaws and policies for the organization and operation ofthe school district.

(Continued on next page)

LESSONS 243–245

UNIT 40 In-Baskets

UNIT GOAL 47/5'/3e

■ GOALS

To use compound adjectives correctly while typing sentences.
To type 47/5'/3e.
To prioritize and format related office communications.

■ FORMAT

Drills: Single spacing 60-space line
5-Minute Timings: Double spacing 5-space tab

LAB 29

Compound Adjectives

Workbook 553–554.

Type lines 1–4 once, providing the missing hyphens. Edit your copy as your teacher reads the answers. Then retype lines 1–4 from your edited copy.

1 She wore an old fashioned dress to the late night jamboree.
2 We enjoy cross country skiing and some big league baseball.
3 Discuss tax free imports as well as up to date zoning laws.
4 It's a well known fact that Val quit working a 12 hour day.

PRETEST

Take a 5-minute timing on lines 5–24. Circle and count your errors. Use the chart on page 399 to determine which lines to type for practice.

The history of a people is often traced via the structures they have made. Architectural history shows just how humans built structures in each period of time blending the usefulness, durability, and beauty of each style. Although several differences appear for each period of architecture, each one displays a distinctive blend of these goals.

Every area of the world offers different materials and designs. In the Middle East, structures were first created of rushes and sun-dried bricks. Two walls were constructed with an arch between them. Eastern architecture used giant carvings and created such magnificent structures as the Taj Mahal. With classical architecture came the famous columns of Greece and those huge arches and vaults of Rome. Design became more ornate with Gothic and Baroque styles; American architecture blended the best to create new ideas.

Modern architecture now uses reinforced concrete for a durable structure and precast concrete for special textures or colors not otherwise available. Each new era brings new excitement as architects realize the wealth of choices they made possible through skillful research and design.

SI 1.68

Those by laws and policies that are not directed by the statues or policies and regulations of the State Board of Education or ordered by the superintendent of of Public Instruction or a court of competent authority may be adopted, amended, and repealed by a majority vote of the full Board, pursuant to section ~~000~~ 293.

The adoption, modification, repeal, or suspension of a Board bylaw or policy shall be recorded in the minutes of the Board. All bylaws and policies shall be printed in the Board Policy Manual.

232 ~~225~~ Executive. The Board shall exercise its executive authority by the appointment of a superintendent of schools who shall enforce the statutes of Ohio, rules of the State Board of Education, and the policies of the Board of Education.

233 ~~226~~ Judicial. The Board of Education may assume jurisdiction over any dispute or controversy arising within this school district and concerning any matter in which authority has been vested in the Board by statute, rule, contract, or policy of ~~the~~ this Board.

240 MEMBERSHIP

242 ~~241~~ Compensation. Board members shall be compensated for each meeting attended and for the number of meetings attended each year in an amount equal to the maximum allowable ~~by~~ under law.

~~242~~ 241 Number. The Board ~~will~~ shall consist of 7 members.

243 Qualifications. Each member of the Board of Education shall be a duly appointed member of one of the 6 participating school districts. Each participating district will appoint a member to the board, with the 7th member coming from one of the participating districts on an alphabetical basis rotation beginning with Butler.

Insert (A) from next page

244 Term of office. Board members are to be appointed by their respective Boards of Education. Effective the next calendar year, the terms shall be for 2 years. The term of office of each member shall begin on the 1st Monday in January.

245 Oath of Office. Each member of the Board shall, before

(Continued on next page)

30-SECOND SPEED TIMINGS

Take two 30-second speed timings on lines 5 and 6. Then take two 30-second speed timings on lines 7 and 8. Or type each sentence twice.

5 Recently, those who sell clothing came up with a crazy 12
6 idea. They put the labels of the designers on the outside. 24

7 Well, the idea was a real winner and greatly increased 12
8 sales. Labels on the outside have now become very stylish. 24

| 1 | 2 | 3 | 4 | 5 | 6 | 7 | 8 | 9 | 10 | 11 | 12

JOB 242 A. TWO-PAGE COMPARATIVE INCOME STATEMENT

Standard format.

Martin and Bellingham, Inc.

COMPARATIVE INCOME STATEMENT ~~SUMMARY~~

For the Months Ended April 30, May 31, June 30, and July 31, 19--

	April 30		May 31	
SALES		$48,431		$59,651
COST OF GOODS SOLD				
Beginning Merchandise Inventory, ~~April 1~~	$16,401		$16,512	
Merchandise Purchases	35,208		33,147	
Total Available for Sale	$51,609		$49,659	
Ending Merchandise Inventory, ~~April 30~~	16,512		14,185	
Cost of Merchandise Sold		35,097		35,474
GROSS PROFIT ON SALES		$13,334		$24,177
EXPENSES				
Depreciation of Equipment	$ 400		$ 400	
Utilities Expense	361		450	
Rent Expense	2,500		2,500	
Sales Expense	4,341		4,518	
Total Expenses		7,602		7,868
NET INCOME BEFORE TAXES		$ 5,732		$16,309

June 30		July 31	
	$63,074		$62,749
$14,185		$12,011	
20,000		47,000	
$34,185		$59,011	
12,011		15,832	
	22,174		43,179
	$40,900		$19,570
$ 400		$ 400	
425		465	
2,500		2,500	
4,210		4,160	
	7,535		7,525
	$33,365		$12,045

assuming the duties of the office, take an oath to support the constitution of the United States and the Constitution of the State of Ohio and to perform faithfully the duties of the office. Such oath may be administered by the treasurer or any other member of the Board.

246 Orientation. The Board shall encourage each new member to understand the function of the board, to acquire knowledge of matters related to the operation of the district, and to learn Board procedures.

247 Vacancies. A vacancy on the Board for any reason shall be filled by action of the participating district represented by the vacancy. A vacancy may be caused by death, nonresidence, resignation, removal from office, failure to qualify, or absence from Board meetings for a period of (90) days for reasons declared to be insufficient by two-thirds vote of the remaining members.

Insert (A)

¶ A member may not have, directly or indirectly, any pecuniary interest in any contract of the Board or be employed for compensation by the Board except as treasurer.

250 ORGANIZATION

251 Organization Meeting Date. The Board shall hold its annual organization meeting on or before the 15th of January of each year. The time and date are to be determined at the regular meeting in December or as provided by statute. The organization meeting will be called to order by the immediate past president or, in his or her absence, the immediate past vice president, who will act as presiding officer pro tempore.

252 Election of Officers. The Board shall elect a president and vice president by a majority of the full Board who shall serve for one year and until their respective successors are elected. In the event that the office of president becomes vacant, the vice president shall fill the office for the remainder of the term.

In the event that the office of the vice president becomes vacant, the Board shall fill the vacancy for the unexpired term in the same manner as the election conducted at the organization meeting.

253 Appointment of Treasurer. At the organization meeting, the Board shall appoint a treasurer to serve on a full-time basis. The treasurer shall initially serve a two-year probationary term and thereafter, if reappointed, shall serve for a four-year term. Removal of the treasurer shall be pursuant to the provisions of the Ohio Revised Code.

254 Treasurer's Compensation. The Board shall fix the compensation of the treasurer at the organization meeting yearly.

255 Treasurer's Bond. Before taking office, the treasurer shall execute a bond to an amount and with surety as approved by the Board payable to the State with a certified copy filed with the county auditor. The Board shall pay the premium on the Treasurer's bond.

256 Committees. The Board may provide for standing or special committees of Board members

(Continued on next page)

JOB 241 A. BALANCE SHEET

Standard format. Compute totals.

Central City Cleaners
Balance Sheet
December 31, 19--

Assets		
Cash	$14,000.00	
Accounts Receivable	400.00	
Equipment	12,100.00	
Machinery	65,000.00	
Supplies	100.00	
Total Assets		$
Liabilities		
Loans Payable	$ 5,000.00	
Income Taxes Payable	3,230.00	
Total Liabilities		$
Partners' Equity		
J. Barnheiser, Capital	$41,685.00	
W. Barnheiser, Capital	41,685.00	
Total Partners' Equity		
Total Liabilities and Partners' Equity		$

LESSON 242

- GOALS
  To use compound adjectives correctly while typing sentences.
  To type a two-page comparative income statement from rough-draft copy.
- FORMAT
  Single spacing 60-space line 5-space tab

LAB 29

Compound Adjectives

Type lines 1–4 once, providing the missing hyphens. Edit your copy as your teacher reads the answers. Then retype lines 1–4 from your edited copy.

1 Buy these water repellent jackets in finest quality fabric.
2 He likes a wide collar shirt made of high priced materials.
3 Now government owned land may be leased at an amazing cost.
4 Her up to date accounts are excellent low risk investments.

appointed by the president to conduct studies and make recommendations, acting only in an advisory capacity. Special committees may be created by the president or by Board action, and the Board may function as a committee of the whole. Special committees shall be appointed for specific purposes and shall be discontinued when their work is completed. A committee created by the president shall choose one of its own members to serve as chairperson. When the Board functions as a committee of the whole, the president shall serve as chairperson.

260 MEETINGS

261 Parliamentary Authority. Parliamentary authority governing the Board shall be Robert's Rules of Order in all cases in which it is not inconsistent with statute administrative code or these bylaws.

262 Presiding Officer. The president shall preside at all meetings and be responsible for the dispatch of business, start all meetings promptly at the appointed hour, and state the type of meeting and its purpose. In the absence of the president, the vice president shall assume the duties of the president. If neither person is available, any member shall be designated to preside by a plurality of those present. The act of any person so designated shall be legal and binding.

263 Regular Meetings. Regular meetings shall be public and held in accordance with the schedule adopted at the organization meeting unless changed by a majority vote of the Board. Agendas shall be made available to the public at the time of Board meetings. It shall be the responsibility of the superintendent and/or the treasurer to prepare an agenda of items of business to come before the Board and to deliver the agenda to each Board member at least two days prior to the meeting date. Board members or others who want to include special items on the agenda should place requests with the superintendent or treasurer at least five days prior to the meeting date.

264 Special Meetings. Special meetings of the Board shall be public. They may be called by the president or the treasurer or by any two members of the Board by serving a written notice of the time, place, and purpose of such meetings upon each Board member at least two days in advance of the meeting.

News media that have requested notification shall receive notice of any special meeting at least 24 hours prior to such meeting except in cases of emergency where the immediate notification of such media is sufficient.

265 Emergency Meeting. An emergency meeting follows the same procedure as outlined for special meetings and is a special meeting except that the 24-hour media notification and the two-day member notice are waived.

266 Recess of a Meeting. The Board may at any time recess or adjourn a meeting to a special time, date, and place. The adjourned or recessed meeting shall take up its business at the point on the agenda where the motion to recess was acted upon. Procedures for recessing or adjourning meetings shall be consistent with Robert's Rules of Order.

267 Executive Session. The Board reserves the right to meet privately in executive session only at a regular or special meeting as provided in the Ohio Revised Code. No official action may be taken at an executive session. The minutes shall record those present in the executive session.

After the regular or special meeting is convened, a Board member may make a motion for an executive session stating therewith the purpose of the session.

Discussion in executive sessions is permitted only for special purposes: personnel matters, to

(Continued on next page)

■ GOALS
To identify compound adjectives while typing sentences.
To type 47/5'/3e.
To type a balance sheet.

■ FORMAT
Drills: Single spacing 60-space line
5-Minute Timings: Double spacing 5-space tab

LAB 29

Compound Adjectives

Type lines 1–4 once. Then repeat lines 1–4 or take a series of 1-minute timings.

1 Joan Mendez signed a two-year contract with Vickers Metals. 12
2 Al's municipal-bond investments give him a tax-free income. 12
3 Doctors use X-ray treatment to cure some kinds of sickness. 12
4 Fourth-quarter sales for many high-priced items have risen. 12

| 1 | 2 | 3 | 4 | 5 | 6 | 7 | 8 | 9 | 10 | 11 | 12

PREVIEW PRACTICE

Type each line twice as a preview to the 5-minute timings below.

Accuracy 5 variety equipment apparatus exercises whirlpool manipulated
Speed 6 bicycle provide also when with body spa own and sit the may

5-MINUTE TIMINGS

Take two 5-minute timings on lines 7–26.

7 The management of a health spa means handling quite an 12
8 array of equipment. Every spa boasts about its own special 24
9 apparatus. Some equipment forces your body in a variety of 36
10 directions, while other pieces of equipment must be manipu- 48
11 lated by different parts of your body. 56
12 Almost every spa has numerous bicycles that assist you 68
13 in warmups and toning exercises which precede more rigorous 80
14 exercises. Some spas provide belts and rollers to warm up, 92
15 tone up, and generally get started. Extra areas might also 104
16 be provided for just stretching your muscles without having 116
17 equipment to help you, and spas may provide exercise music. 128
18 Additional equipment is available to give variety when 140
19 warmups are finished. A twister reduces a bulky waist, but 152
20 fat legs require pushing weights overhead with your legs as 164
21 you lie on your back or sit. Pulleys and presses have some 176
22 possibilities for development and reduction. An individual 188
23 program can be built especially for anyone. Of course, the 200
24 sauna, whirlpool, steam room, and swimming pool attract the 212
25 tired body at the conclusion of rigorous exercise and add a 224
26 zip to a routine, which gives you a worthwhile feeling. 235

| 1 | 2 | 3 | 4 | 5 | 6 | 7 | 8 | 9 | 10 | 11 | 12 SI 1.67

consider the sale or purchase of property, conferences with an attorney concerning disputes involving possible court action, reviewing negotiations or bargaining sessions with public employees, matters required to be kept confidential by federal law rules or state statutes, and specialized details of security arrangements where disclosure of matters might reveal information that could be used for the purpose of committing or avoiding prosecuting for a violation of the law.

268 Board Committee Sessions. The Board may meet in public as a committee of the whole to discuss issues and formulate motions to be acted upon at a subsequent regular or special meeting except that no official action may be taken.

A Board committee of the whole session may be called at any time by the president. The president shall call such a committee session when requested by two members of the Board. The treasurer shall provide notice of a Board committee session in accordance with section 263 of these bylaws.

269 Voting. All motions shall require for adoption a majority vote of those present and voting, except as provided by statute, these bylaws, or parliamentary authority upon the demand of any member of the Board.

LESSON 228

■ GOALS
To recognize when to hyphenate prefixes while typing sentences.
To continue typing a policy manual.

■ FORMAT
Single spacing   60-space line   5-space tab

LAB 27

Prefixes

Type lines 1–4 once. Then repeat lines 1–4 or take a series of 1-minute timings.

```
1  My mother took a trip to Florida to see her great-grandson.    12
2  That new self-service gasoline station is always very busy.    12
3  We can't afford new furniture, so we will re-cover the old.    12
4  There must be an antidote for anti-American demonstrations.    12
   | 1 | 2 | 3 | 4 | 5 | 6 | 7 | 8 | 9 | 10 | 11 | 12
```

Prefixes usually are not separated from the root word by a hyphen. However, if a word may be mistaken for another, use a hyphen after the prefix.

re-cover (to cover again)	recover (regain)
re-lease (to rent again)	release (to let go)
co-op (cooperative)	coop (a pen or cage for birds)

Use a hyphen after the prefixes *self, great,* and *quasi.*

self-esteem	self-satisfied	self-contained
great-grandfather	quasi-judicial	

Use a hyphen after a prefix when the root word begins with a capital letter.

un-American	post-Civil War	mid-July

JOB 240 A

Schroeder and Van Tine

COMPARATIVE INCOME STATEMENT

For the Months Ended April 30, 19--, and May 31, 19--

	April		May	
SALES		$29,453.28		$26,943.35
COST OF MERCHANDISE				
Beginning Inventory, ~~April 1~~ ?	$15,267.00		$12,613.50	
Inventory Purchases	8,476.50		18,732.90	
Total Available	$23,743.50		$	
Ending Inventory, ~~April 30~~ ?	12,613.50		19,290.60	
Cost of Merchandise Sold		11,130.00		
GROSS PROFIT ON SALES		$18,323.28		$
EXPENSES				
Depreciation of Equipment	$ 1,000.00		$1,000.00	
Utilities Expense	520.43		481.30	
Rent Expense	2,500.00		2,500.00	
Sales Expense	5,436.84		5,109.20	
Total Expenses		9,457.27		
NET INCOME BEFORE TAXES		$ 8,866.01		$

JOB 240 B

Data for This Year
Inpatient:
$83,586,000
Outpatient:
$9,128,000
Other:
$4,611,000
Deductions:
$4,610,000
Salaries:
$48,988,000
Supplies:
$19,319,000
Utilities:
$10,157,000
Depreciation:
$4,642,000
Interest:
$4,949,000

Note: You will have to calculate the missing figures from the data given you.

City Medical Center

STATEMENT OF OPERATIONS

December 31, 19--

REVENUE		
Inpatient	$ 96,385,000	
Outpatient	11,763,000	
Other	5,112,000	
	$113,260,000	
Deductions	8,124,000	
Total Revenue		$105,136,000
EXPENSES		
Salaries and Benefits	$ 55,854,000	
Supplies and Expenses	21,836,000	
Purchased Services and Utilities	12,236,000	
Depreciation and Amortization	4,669,000	
Interest and Insurance	5,144,000	
Total Expenses		99,739,000
NET GAIN		$ 5,397,000

JOB 228 A. POLICY MANUAL

Standard format.

Continue with the policy manual you started in Job 226/227 A on pages 371–375.

■ GOALS
To identify when to hyphenate prefixes while typing sentences.
To format and type job descriptions.

■ FORMAT
Single spacing   60-space line   5-space tab

LAB 27
Prefixes

Type lines 1–4 once. Then repeat lines 1–4 or take a series of 1-minute timings.

```
1 We will be taking a trans-Canadian flight in mid-September.  12
2 Gina and Bob just bought a stove with a self-cleaning oven.  12
3 A cooperative apartment is commonly referred to as a co-op.  12
4 Last week I went to visit my great-grandmother in Honolulu.  12
  | 1 | 2 | 3 | 4 | 5 | 6 | 7 | 8 | 9 | 10 | 11 | 12
```

30-SECOND SPEED TIMINGS

Take two 30-second speed timings on lines 5 and 6. Then take two 30-second speed timings on lines 7 and 8. Or type each sentence twice.

```
5      You can be a part of the work of our nation in so many  12
6 ways.  It is very easy to do your part for good government.  24
7      When you write a letter to a senator, vote on election  12
8 day, or just keep up on the news, you are a part of it all.  24
  | 1 | 2 | 3 | 4 | 5 | 6 | 7 | 8 | 9 | 10 | 11 | 12
```

FORMATTING JOB DESCRIPTIONS

Job descriptions are used in evaluating salary levels of various jobs and in filling vacancies. The job description identifies the tasks that are performed on a specific job. It helps define the skills and qualifications that an applicant must possess. To format a job description:

1. Set margins for a 6-inch line (60P/70E).
2. Type the title on line 13 in all-capital letters.
3. Align words in the heading 2 spaces after the colon following the longest guide word. Double-space between items in the heading.
4. Single-space the position description; double-space before and after it.
5. Use hanging-indented format for the enumeration of the duties.

JOB DESCRIPTION

Position Title: Word Processing Specialist

Department: Administrative Support, Word Processing Services

Reports to: Office Personnel Director

Description of Position: To offer word processing services to ten legislative principals of the federal government in a shared communications atmosphere.

Duties:

1. Receives, codes, sorts, and routes incoming documents.
2. Keyboards all communications into terminals and stores them in the CPU.
3. Proofreads and edits all copy for typographical, formatting, spelling, grammatical, and content errors.
4. Prints out final draft of documents and routes them to supervisor.

GOALS
To recognize compound adjectives while typing sentences.
To format and type comparative income statements.

FORMAT
Single spacing   60-space line   Tabs as needed

LAB 29

Compound Adjectives

Type lines 1–4 once. Then repeat lines 1–4 or take a series of 1-minute timings.

```
1 Henry just sent various duty-free imports by quick express.  12
2 The board of directors held a high-level conference Friday.  12
3 Please prepare an up-to-date report for the talk in Zurich.  12
4 The owner said that she wants to erect a 50-story building.  12
  | 1 | 2 | 3 | 4 | 5 | 6 | 7 | 8 | 9 | 10 | 11 | 12
```

A compound adjective—two or more words joined to modify a noun—is usually hyphenated when it goes before a noun but not hyphenated when it follows a noun: a *well-known* actor (**but:** an actor who is *well known*), an *up-to-date* study (**but:** a study that is *up to date*). Exceptions are proper adjectives (a *New York* firm, the *United States* position) and very commonly used compounds (a *high school* teacher).

30-SECOND "OK" TIMINGS

Type as many 30-second "OK" (errorless) timings as possible out of three attempts on lines 5–7.

```
5      Exercise gives your body the zip it needs to adjust to  12
6 a pace required to live in this modern society.  Walking is  24
7 just one way that you are likely to add years to your life.  36
  | 1 | 2 | 3 | 4 | 5 | 6 | 7 | 8 | 9 | 10 | 11 | 12
```

FORMATTING COMPARATIVE INCOME STATEMENTS

A comparative income statement allows a company to "compare" the income summary of one quarter with another, one month with another, and so on. To format a comparative income statement:

1. Use standard format for financial statements (page 389).
2. Center a braced heading over the appropriate columns.
3. Type an underscore below the braced heading the full width of the columns being braced.

JOB 240 A. COMPARATIVE INCOME STATEMENT

Prepare the material at the top of page 394 as a comparative income statement. Standard format. Turn the paper lengthwise.

JOB 240 B. COMPARATIVE INCOME STATEMENT

Prepare the material at the bottom of page 394 as a comparative income statement. Add the figures for this year, indicated in the column on the left, and make the appropriate changes in the headings. Standard format. Turn the paper lengthwise.

JOB 229 A. JOB DESCRIPTION

Standard format. Make a copy for use in Lesson 230.

JOB Description 9

Position Title: WP Specialist 20

Department: WP Center 29

Reports to: WP Supervisor 39

Description of Position: Must possess 48

excellent keyboarding, formatting, edit- 56

ing, and transcription skills and be able to 65

work in a team situation with 8 other 73

specialists. 76

Duties: 79

1. Keyboards all communications on 87

terminal and stores them in CPU. 95

2. Performs editing functions for all documents called up from cpu for 102 109

revision. 113

3. Proofreads and edits all copy for 120

typographical, spelling, grammatical, 131

formatting, and content errors. 136

4. Prints out final draft of docu- 143

ments and routes them to supervisor. 152

5. Keeps daily log of number of lines 160

keyed on terminal. 165

6. Works with other specialists to 172

complete production deadlines. 179

7. Reports all required maintenance of 187

terminal to supervisor. 193

8. Participates in weekly in-service 201

program. 204

9. Performs other duties as designated 212

by supervisor. 216

JOB 229 B. JOB DESCRIPTION

Standard format. Make a copy for use in Lesson 230.

Job Description 9

Position Title: Word Processing 18

Supervisor 20

Department: Word Processing Center 29

Reports to: Office Personnel 37

Director 38

Description of Position: Must 46

be able to work well with 51

people in a time-pressured 56

situation. Must be able to 62

direct regular in-service 67

programs for subordinates. Must 74

possess excellent knowledge 79

of English and formatting skills. 86

Duties: 89

1. Receives, codes, sorts, and 96

routes incoming documents. 103

2. Keeps weekly log of center 109

production. 113

3. Keeps up-to-date coding 118

file for all documents pro- 125

duced in the center. 130

4. Routes all completed documents 137

to authors. 141

5. Communicates with authors 147

concerning efficiency of 153

operation of the center. 159

6. Conducts daily "spot checks" of 166

documents being produced in 173

the center. 176

7. Conducts weekly in-service 182

programs for specialists and 189

authors. 192

8. Authorizes maintenance of 198

equipment in center. 204

9. Performs other duties as 209

designated by office per- 215

sonnel director. 219

JOB 239 A. BALANCE SHEET

Standard format. Fill in missing figures.

In very detailed balance sheets, major entries are spread centered. (Backspace once for every 2 letters and spaces. Leave 3 spaces between words.)

You will know that your figures are correct if your Total Assets line is the same as your Total Liabilities and Partners' Equity line. The same totals show that the balance sheet "balances."

Schroeder and Van Tine

BALANCE SHEET

December 31, 19--

A S S E T S

Current Assets		
Cash	$ 7,000.00	
Petty Cash	15.00	
Exchange Fund	25.00	
Notes Receivable	4,000.00	
Interest Receivable	160.00	
Accounts Receivable (Less Allowance for Bad Debts)	5,489.00	
Merchandise Inventory	34,000.00	
Prepaid Insurance	800.00	
Total Current Assets		$
Fixed Assets		
Land	$ 6,000.00	
Building (Less Accumulated Depreciation)	14,600.00	
Delivery Equipment (Less Accumulated Depreciation)	3,690.00	
Office Equipment (Less Accumulated Depreciation)	4,749.00	
Total Fixed Assets		
Total Assets		$

L I A B I L I T I E S

Current Liabilities		
Notes Payable	$ 2,600.00	
Interest Payable	150.00	
Accounts Payable	7,000.00	
Salaries Payable	290.00	
Employees' Withholding Taxes Payable	300.00	
FICA Taxes Payable	200.00	
Sales Taxes Payable	400.00	
Total Current Liabilities		$
Long-Term Liabilities		
Mortgage Payable		12,000.00
Total Liabilities		$

P A R T N E R S ' E Q U I T Y

George S. Schroeder, Capital	$28,794.00	
James Van Tine, Capital	28,794.00	
Total Partners' Equity		
Total Liabilities and Partners' Equity		$

■ GOALS
To hyphenate prefixes correctly while typing sentences.
To type 46/5′/3e.
To revise and type job descriptions.

■ FORMAT
Drills: Single spacing 60-space line
5-Minute Timings: Double spacing 5-space tab

LAB 27

Prefixes

Type lines 1–4 once, providing hyphens where appropriate. Edit your copy as your teacher reads the answers. Then retype lines 1–4 from your edited copy.

1 Your paintings are excellent recreations of the originals.
2 Aunt Adrienne, my greataunt, invited me to visit her home.
3 Selfdiscipline is the basis of most college honor systems.
4 They will be studying for midsemester exams in midOctober.

PREVIEW PRACTICE

Type each line twice as a preview to the 5-minute timings on page 382.

Accuracy 5 exact receive request legislator President's scrutinization
Speed 6 through signed while means than also both some have may the

5-MINUTE TIMINGS

Take two 5-minute timings on lines 6–25 on page 382.

JOB 230 A. JOB DESCRIPTION

Retype Job 229 A on page 377 making the changes given below. Mark the changes on the copy you prepared. Standard format.

Position Title: Data Entry Specialist
Department: Data Processing Center
Reports to: Data Processing Supervisor
Description of Position: Must possess excellent keyboarding, records management, computer operating system, and file handling skills and be able to work in a team situation with other specialists.
2. Load and unload input and output devices and monitor processing.
3. Download programs from CPU and make changes in data as designated.

JOB 230 B. JOB DESCRIPTION

Retype Job 229 B on page 377 making the changes given below. Mark the changes on the copy you prepared. Standard format.

Position Title: Data Processing Supervisor
Department: Data Processing Center
Description of Position: *Delete the last sentence and add* Must possess excellent knowledge of computer operating system and general knowledge of BASIC and COBOL.
Change the word "authors" *to* "principals" *wherever it occurs in the list of duties.*

LESSON 239

■ **GOALS**
To type 47/5′/3e.
To type a balance sheet.

■ **FORMAT**
Drills: Single spacing 60-space line
5-Minute Timings: Double spacing 5-space tab

KEYBOARDING SKILLS

Type lines 1–4 once. Then practice using the apostrophe in line 5. Repeat lines 1–4, or take a series of 1-minute timings.

Speed	1	They may end the big fight by the lake by the usual signal.	12
Accuracy	2	Igor amazed Pat by how quickly he waxed a single jumbo van.	12
Numbers	3	The dates to remember are 1910, 1928, 1939, 1947, and 1956.	12
Symbols	4	Two hyphens typed without spaces--like this--make the dash.	12
Punctuation	5	it's they're weren't you'll Mary's Joneses' writers' lion's	

| 1 | 2 | 3 | 4 | 5 | 6 | 7 | 8 | 9 | 10 | 11 | 12

PRETEST

Take a 5-minute timing on lines 6–25. Circle and count your errors.

```
6       Managing a clothing shop in a tourist area requires an    12
7  amazingly high degree of proficiency in business skills.  A    24
8  venture into the business means you'll be a salesperson, an    36
9  accountant, and a secretary--and you must try to excel.        47
10      As a salesperson, you will design exciting displays of    12
11 your merchandise.  Assisting customers in purchasing unique    24
12 items as gifts or selecting garments for themselves will be    36
13 your major task.  Making decisions will take much time.        47
14      When you are the accountant, you'll find yourself busy    12
15 with purchasing, pricing, and inventorying.  Closing state-    24
16 ments must be prepared monthly; growth requires a staff and    36
17 payroll records; tax reports will be a great challenge.        47
18      As secretary, you will prepare all the communications,    12
19 and you will have to type them too.  Prioritizing the tasks    24
20 will not be easy; you will have to meet each of the demands    36
21 of the manager, salesperson, accountant, and secretary.        47
22      Although your life may seem hectic, the opportunity of    12
23 owning your own business makes it worthwhile.  Perhaps that    24
24 explains why some businesses survive in spite of high risk.    36
25 Being your own manager and decision maker is exciting.         47
```

| 1 | 2 | 3 | 4 | 5 | 6 | 7 | 8 | 9 | 10 | 11 | 12 SI 1.64

PRACTICE

Take a 1-minute timing on each paragraph of the Pretest.

POSTTEST

Take another 5-minute timing on lines 6–25 to see how much your skill has improved.

LESSON 231

CLINIC

GOAL
To build competency on selected keyboard reaches.

FORMAT
Single spacing   60-space line

PRETEST 1

Take a 30-second timing on each line. Circle and count your errors.

```
1  I may not buy any more amber boxes before Craig moves home.  12
2  It may be my turn to direct more waltz music on prom night.  12
3  May played on cymbals for the evening musical in September.  12
4  The crane moved very near the north corner of the building.  12
   | 1 | 2 | 3 | 4 | 5 | 6 | 7 | 8 | 9 | 10 | 11 | 12
```

PRACTICE 1

Type lines 5–10 four times. If you averaged two or fewer errors in Pretest 1, repeat individual lines for speed; otherwise, repeat each block of lines for accuracy.

```
5  not may very more night amber played before evening cymbals
6  any bet near turn crane boxes bright corner directs musical
7  nor tax raze prom lines moves umpire climbs nearing waltzes

8  now vat vine numb venom broom mostly zenith victims minutes
9  bow con mice cede mixes money notion crafty credits invites
10 cry mit note oxen crumb exert blazes victor innings mixture
```

POSTTEST 1

Repeat Pretest 1 to see how much your skill has improved.

PRETEST 2

Take a 30-second timing on each line. Circle and count your errors.

```
11 Someone must review the mistake to perfect the main device.  12
12 It was wrong to think that the closing balances were fixed.  12
13 Why not join the best debate teams and have fun as you win?  12
14 Our members were trying their best, but they could not win.  12
   | 1 | 2 | 3 | 4 | 5 | 6 | 7 | 8 | 9 | 10 | 11 | 12
```

PRACTICE 2

Type lines 15–20 four times. If you averaged two or fewer errors in Pretest 2, repeat individual lines for speed; otherwise, repeat each block of lines for accuracy.

```
15 ton mix text from movie kinds member extent furnace extreme
16 gun bed over main river pound reveal paints someone perfect
17 act pin acre very wrong think verify trying mistake reviews

18 not won best join fixed doubt levels ignore drawing created
19 any ice have much above copes device atomic closing balance
20 fun son save twin brown among coding debate animals country
```

POSTTEST 2

Repeat Pretest 2 to see how much your skill has improved.

JOB 238 A. FINANCIAL STATEMENTS: THE BALANCE SHEET

Standard format. 65-space line.

The Foundation Club

BALANCE SHEET

June 30, 19-- ↓3

Major entry—all caps.

Subentry—initial caps; indent 5 spaces.

Total line—initial caps; indent 10 spaces.

Grand total—indent 15 spaces.

ASSETS		
Supplies on Hand	$231.60	
Cash in Bank	478.59	
Accounts Receivable	166.42	
Total Assets		$876.61 ↓2
LIABILITIES		
Accounts Payable	$265.98	
Refunds on Memberships	75.00	
Total Liabilities		$340.98 ↓2
EQUITY		
Capital	$415.75	
Profit from Club Activities	119.88	
Total Equity		535.63
Total Liabilities and Equity		$876.61

JOB 238 B. FINANCIAL STATEMENTS: THE INCOME STATEMENT

Standard format. 60-space line.

Baker and Brown Inc. ↓2

SUMMARY INCOME STATEMENT ↓2

For the Month Ended June 30, 19-- ↓3

SALES		$38,564.39 ↓2
COST OF GOODS SOLD		
Beginning Inventory	$26,378.00	
Inventory Purchases	9,587.60	
Total Available	$35,965.60	
Ending Inventory	23,724.60	
Cost of Goods Sold		12,241.00 ↓2
GROSS PROFIT ON SALES		$26,323.39 ↓2
EXPENSES		
Selling Expense	$ 6,536.96	
Rent Expense	3,699.50	
Heat and Light	731.54	
Depreciation of Equipment	2,250.50	
Total Expenses		13,218.50 ↓2
NET INCOME BEFORE TAXES		$13,104.89

LESSON 232

UNIT 38 Processing Correspondence

UNIT GOAL 46/5'/3e

■ GOALS
To hyphenate prefixes correctly while typing sentences.
To format reports in memo form.
To review formatting distribution lists.
To type two reports in memo form.

■ FORMAT
Single spacing 60-space line

LAB 27

Prefixes

Workbook 517–518.

Type lines 1–4 once, providing hyphens where appropriate. Edit your copy as your teacher reads the answers. Then retype lines 1–4 from your edited copy.

```
1 Are you going to take that selfdefense course with Robert?
2 I will use my mobile transceiver on my transAmerican trip.
3 Were her greatgrandparents born here or did they emigrate?
4 After the 2-day sale, we had to remark all the price tags.
```

12-SECOND TIMINGS

Type each line three times, or take three 12-second timings on each line. For each timing, type without error.

```
5 She counted one, two, three, four, five, six, seven, eight.
6 Her speech was very good; she will do well in the election.
7 I read all of the issues when I voted; some were very long.
```

5 10 15 20 25 30 35 40 45 50 55 60

FORMATTING REPORTS IN MEMO FORM

A report that has been prepared for another person or group of people is often formatted as a memo. This format saves the time of typing the report and a covering memo. To format a report in memo format:

1. Follow memo format.
2. Type the title as the subject.
3. Do not type the writer's initials at the end of the report.

FORMATTING REVIEW

Distribution lists:
If a memo is addressed to a number of people and their names will not fit after the guide word *To:*, use a distribution list.

1. After *To:*, type *See distribution below.*
2. Type *Distribution* (initial caps, underscored) a triple space below the last notation, at the left margin.
3. Type each name on a separate line at the left margin under the word *Distribution:*.

JOB 232 A. REPORT IN MEMO FORM WITH DISTRIBUTION LIST

Standard format. Workbook 519–520.

This memo should be sent to the following committee members: Mr. Larry Schenck, Ms. Robert Uhl, Dr. John Smith, Mr. Gordon Perkins, and Miss Rosa Pieratt. This memo is from the committee chairperson, Mr. Oliver Dunkin. The subject is Energy Alternatives.

A review of energy options has not produced any politically acceptable alternatives for cutting the uses of energy. This means that we must continue to seek new ways to replace the oil imports. Although Congress does not favor the import fee, it may be the only alternative left once other avenues have been explored.

Several alternatives have been expressed by other members of Congress. The first of these is to remove the price controls from gasoline and allow the oil companies to operate under a situation of decontrol for a while. A second alternative, which has been discussed before, is that we give serious con-

(Continued on next page)

LESSON 238

UNIT 39 Processing Tables

UNIT GOAL 47/5'/3e

■ GOALS
To use compound nouns correctly while typing sentences.
To format and type financial statements.

■ FORMAT
Single spacing   60-space line

LAB 28 Compound Nouns

Type lines 1–4 once, providing the missing hyphens where necessary. Edit your copy as your teacher reads the answers. Then retype lines 1–4 from your edited copy.

1 Let's have one more run through before the final rehearsal.

2 Can they have a get together next week and discuss the job?

3 Ken's supper dance next evening may be quite an eye opener.

4 Jan Zorn, a senior vice president, gave a press conference.

12-SECOND TIMINGS

Type each line three times, or take three 12-second timings on each line. For each timing, type without error.

5 His disks are stored so that the hot sun cannot touch them.
6 She will copy this data from one disk to another with ease.
7 It is a good practice to make a backup copy of vital files.

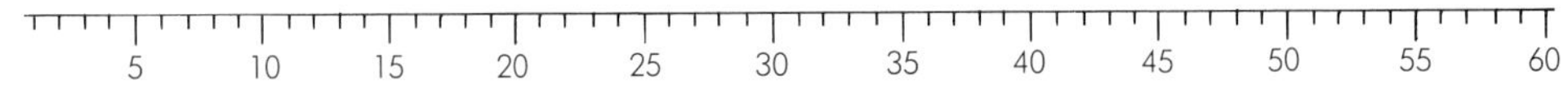

FORMATTING FINANCIAL STATEMENTS

Workbook 551.

Periodic financial statements help businesses to analyze cash flow, profit and loss, and other important financial information. Among the monthly, quarterly, or yearly statements that are commonly used in business are the balance sheet and the income statement.

Because it is important to compare current financial statements with past statements, they should be formatted consistently.

To format financial statements:

1. Vertically center the statement. Use single spacing.
2. Set margins to an assigned line length (usually 60, 65, or 70 spaces).
3. Position money columns only 2 spaces apart (not 6) for easiest reading. Set tabs for the money columns by backspacing from the desired line-ending point.
4. Type major entries in all-capital letters. Double-space before major entries.
5. Capitalize the first letter of each major word in subentries.
6. Use leaders to carry the eye from the first column to the second column.
7. Indent subentries 5 spaces from the left margin.
8. Indent *Total* lines 5 spaces from the beginning of the line above.
9. Type a single rule to separate groups of numbers that must be added or subtracted.
10. Type a double rule to indicate totals. Use the platen release lever as you turn up the paper for the second line. (The platen release lever allows you to temporarily change the line of writing.)

JOB 232 A (CONTINUED)

sideration to reducing the import of foreign oil. We are continuing to reduce our consumption each year. This reduction may allow us to eliminate the need for any import of oil in the future.

It has been noted with some optimism that new sources of energy are now being discovered in other parts of the country. Additional funds to encourage more exploration at this level will need to be given important time in the next session of Congress. One or two large finds along the coast would certainly relieve the pressure on the domestic scene. With the growing pressures on the American economy, it is indeed a risky move to consider adding to the burden of the consumers.

JOB 232 B. REPORT IN MEMO FORM WITH DISTRIBUTION LIST

Standard format. Workbook 521–522.

This memo should be sent to the following committee members: Dr. Alberta Zelwig, Miss Martina Lopez, Mr. James Edwards, Dr. Woodrow Lorenz-Meyer. The memo is from the committee chairperson, Dr. June Albritten. The subject is Results of Recent Survey on Energy Attitudes.

The results of the recent survey conducted concerning the attitudes of Americans regarding the use of energy sources have been tabulated. Three major groups were surveyed, and the results follow.

Although the topic of an energy crisis has been before the public for a number of years, the American people still do not want to accept the fact that there is a crisis. Different reasons for not wanting to take on the responsibility for dealing with a crisis are given by different segments of the population.

The oil producers, of course, always favor full decontrol so that there will be no limit to what the domestic businesses and OPEC can demand for oil. They would like to have full rein to determine what costs are necessary to operate at an acceptable margin of profit.

The automobile industry wants more and more time to make the changes in technology and marketing necessary to allow them to keep a profitable business going.

The public does not want to give up any of its conveniences either. Doing so would mean performing a few more tasks manually. In our society, which has witnessed many technological advances, manual operation of anything is considered unreasonable. It would mean putting "we" ahead of "me" in order to make progress.

LESSON 233

■ GOALS
To type 46/5'/3e.
To format and type letters with multiple addressees.

■ Format
Drills: Single spacing 60-space line
5-Minute Timings: Double spacing 5-space tab

KEYBOARDING SKILLS

Type lines 1–4 once. Then spell out the numbers in line 5 as you type it. Repeat lines 1–4, or take a series of 1-minute timings.

Speed	1	I am to go to work for the audit firm by the eighth of May.	12
Accuracy	2	Seizing the wax buffers, Jensen quickly removed a big spot.	12
Numbers	3	They had rooms 10 and 28. We had rooms 39, 47, and 56 too.	12
Symbols	4	The room went from 10° to 28° to 39° to 47° to 56° Celsius.	12
Number Usage	5	Please send us 6 clerks, 4 typists, and 1 secretary.	

| 1 | 2 | 3 | 4 | 5 | 6 | 7 | 8 | 9 | 10 | 11 | 12 |

LESSON

237

CLINIC

■ GOAL
To build competency on selected keyboard reaches.

■ FORMAT
Single spacing 60-space line

PRETEST 1

Take a 30-second timing on each line. Circle and count your errors.

1 Now is the moment to save and protect our younger citizens. 12
2 The river runs in all seasons, and not once has ice formed. 12
3 The women were given a refund and made a fortune in prizes. 12
4 It is much too soon to detect minor defects in the new car. 12
| 1 | 2 | 3 | 4 | 5 | 6 | 7 | 8 | 9 | 10 | 11 | 12

PRACTICE 1

Type lines 5–10 four times. If you averaged two or fewer errors in Pretest 1, repeat individual lines for speed; otherwise, repeat each block of lines for accuracy.

5 won bid live army thing serve refund paying utilize routine
6 nor inn mill pins river women invest season protect younger
7 act run text unit place zones saying utmost joining matched

8 ice fun soon once catch aimed import gained correct defects
9 gun now much save night minor detect gained appoint exposed
10 won ton none done prize using prompt making fortune citizen

POSTTEST 1

Repeat Pretest 1 to see how much your skill has improved.

PRETEST 2

Take a 30-second timing on each line. Circle and count your errors.

11 We have to admit that the stones somehow broke the windows. 12
12 Tod doubts the main brakes have a chance of working anyhow. 12
13 She informs me that the mob was running to the office room. 12
14 Just for the fun of it, I gave my uncle one cent for lunch. 12
| 1 | 2 | 3 | 4 | 5 | 6 | 7 | 8 | 9 | 10 | 11 | 12

PRACTICE 2

Type lines 15–20 four times. If you averaged two or fewer errors in Pretest 2, repeat individual lines for speed; otherwise, repeat each block of lines for accuracy.

15 nor act tiny pain print might timely office windows somehow
16 sun any skin main round smoke prompt stones unknown tactful
17 mob run room noon hints exact lesson motive orchard shelves

18 ice cry line inch lunch knife expand having primary running
19 win beg from gave bench count chance driven leading mounted
20 fun one have cent doubt admit brakes anyhow informs helping

POSTTEST 2

Repeat Pretest 2 to see how much your skill has improved.

PRETEST Take a 5-minute timing on lines 6–25. Circle and count your errors.

Have you ever wondered [1] just how someone is able [2] to get 12
an idea proposed [3] in Congress? Only someone [4] who is a member 24
of the [5] legislature can propose [6] a bill. Bills can originate [7] 36
anywhere, but a representative [8] must sponsor them. [9] 46

Once it is introduced [10] by a legislator, a [11] bill receives 12
a number. [12] The bill is routed to a committee. [13] While in the [14] 24
committee, the bill can be [15] killed, amended, or rewritten [16] in 36
a special way. [17] Legislators may request hearings. [18] 46

If a bill [19] survives the committee, [20] it will be routed to 12
the Rules [21] Committee before its [22] scrutinization on the floor. [23] 24
Some bills are approved [24] by the House faster than [25] others. A 36
bill may also [26] be amended or returned [27] to committee. 46

After [28] a bill survives the House, [29] it is referred to the [30] 12
Senate in a similar manner. [31] Both houses of the legislature [32] 24
must finally approve [33] exact versions of a [34] bill. Approval of 36
a bill [35] allows its assignment to [36] a different level. 46

[37] Presidential consideration [38] of a bill means it has been [39] 12
through both houses [40] and can be signed by the President. [41] It 24
may become [42] law even without the President's [43] signature after [44] 36
a certain number of days pass [45] without a decision. [46] 46

| 1 | 2 | 3 | 4 | 5 | 6 | 7 | 8 | 9 | 10 | 11 | 12 | SI 1.58

PRACTICE Take a 1-minute timing on each paragraph of the Pretest.

POSTTEST Take another 5-minute timing on lines 6–25 to see how much your skill has improved.

JOB 233 A. LETTER

Standard format. Workbook 523–524.

Miss Marie Gabbard, 98 Nutmeg Place, 15
Urbana, OH 43078. Dear Marie: 22
Subject: Air Force Academy 29
Appointment I shall be very 35
happy to recommend you for 41
an appointment to the Air Force 47
Academy for next fall. Your fine 54
academic standing and the numerous 61
recommendations from your high school 68
teachers and principal make you 75
an excellent candidate. 80
Your participation in debate at the 88
national level and your extensive 95
leadership skills demonstrated in your 103
community place you among the best 110
qualified for the work required at the 117
academy. 119
I shall contact you by phone as 127
soon as the official announcements 134
have been made. Sincerely, Sarah 147
Jacot, Representative, third District 157

PREVIEW PRACTICE

Type each line twice as a preview to the 3-minute timings below.

```
Accuracy  5  taxes citizen lawmakers inquiries Washington representative
Speed     6  with what whom want most mail make many they that some send
```

3-MINUTE TIMINGS

Take two 3-minute timings on lines 7–18.

```
 7       Businesses and individuals can write letters to people    12
 8   in Washington.  There are several persons to whom you might   24
 9   send a letter.  You could write to the President, to a sen-   36
10   ator, or to a representative.  Each person who's elected to   48
11   go to Washington takes a staff along who can answer most of   60
12   the mail citizens send.  Using the mail is one way that the   72
13   legislators continually keep in touch with what is going on   84
14   in their individual congressional districts.                  93
15       People send inquiries on many subjects.  They may want   105
16   to express a positive feeling, or they may want to complain  117
17   about taxes, pollution, or foreign policy.  Some letters do  129
18   influence how lawmakers make their decisions.                138
     | 1 | 2 | 3 | 4 | 5 | 6 | 7 | 8 | 9 | 10 | 11 | 12          SI 1.63
```

JOB 236 A. LETTER

Standard format. Workbook 543–544 top.

I need to send four letters to members of the staff. I'll give you the main parts of the message, but please word each letter just a little differently. I would not want the staff to compare letters and find the same message in all four letters.

The first letter goes to David L. Martin. He lives here in Indianapolis at 593 North Street, 46227. Please make one carbon of the letter, and address envelopes for all the letters.

Dear Mr. Martin: Congratulations on your recent appointment as chairperson of the Indianapolis campaign. It must be a great satisfaction to you to know that other members of your group respect you so much. I am sure that the campaign will be very successful under your leadership. I should like to invite you and your wife to an informal social gathering at my home at seven o'clock on April 4. I hope that you will be able to join us. Very cordially yours, Tony A. Makato [*Title*]

JOBS 236 B TO 236 D. LETTERS TO BE COMPLETED

Standard format. Workbook 543–547.

There are three other members of the staff who must receive letters. Ms. Molly Alsop lives at 56 Ninth Street, 46204. She will be the assistant to the chairperson for this campaign. She has served on campaign committees for several years and is always responsible for seeing that large numbers of volunteers help with last-minute tasks for the campaign.

Mrs. Andrea Kilran will be the treasurer for the campaign. Her address is 67 Valleyview Drive, 46227. She was very efficient in her work as treasurer for the past two campaigns.

Mr. Richard Callahan, 462 Northern Avenue, 46208, is the new secretary and has worked on just one campaign before. He has been active in supporting local candidates and has become interested in being part of this national campaign. Invite his wife also.

Please sign these letters for me, and get them in today's mail. I want them to have plenty of notice about this social gathering. Thanks.

FORMATTING MULTIPLE ADDRESSEES IN LETTERS

When a letter is addressed to two or more people at the same address, format as follows:

1. Type the name of each addressee on a separate line.
2. Do not use business titles or department names unless they are common to all the addressees.
3. Use the names in the salutation or use a group salutation, such as *Dear Authors:, Ladies:*.

JOB 233 B. LETTER

Standard format. Workbook 525–526.

Mrs. Beverly Chung, Mr. Saul Greenblat, 16
OEA Advisers, Jane Addams 21
High School, 45 Meadowgrove, 26
Delaware, OH 43015 30
Dear Mrs. Chung and Mr. Greenblat: 38
It is with a great deal of 44
pleasure that I congratulate you 51
on the fine contribution that 57
you and your chapter of OEA 63
students have made to the 68
Special Olympics this year. 74
Because yours is one of twelve 81
chapters in the country that 87
contributed over $3000 toward 93
the program this year, we are 99
honoring you with a special 104
plaque, which should arrive 110
within the next two weeks. We 116
hope that your chapter will 122
display it proudly. Best 129
wishes, Sarah Gacot, Represen- 139
tative, Third District 146

JOB 233 C. LETTER

Standard format. Workbook 527–528.

Mr. Stan Babno, Mr. Jerry Lopez, 14
Washington Memorial High School, 1411 22
Arlington Avenue, Dayton, OH 45402 28
Gentlemen: 32
Congratulations to you and your team 40
on a fine season. Your contribution 48
to the growth of soccer in our state 55
is most appreciated. 59
I am looking forward to meeting 67
you and your team at your annual 73
honors assembly in May. A plaque 80
will be given to your school in 87
your honor. Cordially, Sarah Gacot, 100
Representative, Third District 107
Copy to Dan Davidson, Superintendent 116

LESSON 234

GOALS
To recognize compound nouns while typing sentences.
To type letters from dictated copy.
To format and type letters with multiple signatures.

FORMAT
Single spacing   60-space line

LAB 28

Compound Nouns

Type lines 1–4 once. Then repeat lines 1–4 or take a series of 1-minute timings.

```
1  I hope to work as a clerk-typist for Joe Zwick next summer.   12
2  I will mail the invitations for our October 6 get-together.   12
3  The salesclerk said good-bye to the company vice president.   12
4  We do our banking at a drive-in quite close to Xenia, Ohio.   12
   | 1 | 2 | 3 | 4 | 5 | 6 | 7 | 8 | 9 | 10 | 11 | 12
```

(Continued on next page)

JOB 235 A (CONTINUED)

of a once beautiful countryside and see only ash-covered ground and miles of devastated land which once held dense forests of trees one of the photographers in the area describes the event as the transformation of an area from a postcard-symmetrical cone 9677 feet high to an ugly flattop 1300 feet lower geologists say the blast had 500 times the punch of the bomb which hit hiroshima some actual statistics which ive been able to secure note that the eruption blew down 150 square miles of timber worth about 200 million dollars; caused an estimated 222 million dollars in damage to wheat, alfalfa, and other crops; and created a 20-mile-long logjam along the snow mountain river, which blocked shipping in both washington and oregon a number of residents and visitors who were in the area when the eruption occurred are still being interviewed by the media and by my staff as the threat of more eruptions hangs over the area, it is very difficult for residents to calm down and regain composure the official reports from the geologists and photographers are still being compiled as more and more evidence is gathered, i shall keep you apprised of the situation

JOB 235 B. DICTATED REPORT IN MEMO FORM

Workbook 541–542.

to the president of the united states from representative john glengale concerning the aftermath of the zenith tornado ive just returned from a trip to the southern part of my state and want to report to you some of the sites which i witnessed while their the once-populated city is now completely flattened except for a few concrete structures which amazingly withstood the high winds more than a thousand people have lost their homes and almost every business there has been destroyed both the red cross and the numerous insurance companies have moved in to try to bring comfort to the residents but its very difficult to do so at present the governor had visited the sight the day before i arrived and there is no doubt in either of our minds that federal funds must be used to help restore this community to some kind of normalcy as quickly as possible im sure that a visit from you at this time would be greatly appreciated arrangements will be coordinated with your office to make the visit as worthwhile as possible your immediate attention to this disaster site will be very much appreciated

■ GOALS
To use compound nouns correctly while typing sentences.
To type 46/3′/2e.
To create final drafts of letters that are unarranged and incomplete in their present form.

■ FORMAT
Drills: Single spacing 60-space line
3-Minute Timings: Double spacing 5-space tab

LAB 28

Compound Nouns

Type lines 1–4 once, providing the missing hyphens where necessary. Edit your copy as your teacher reads the answers. Then retype lines 1–4 from your edited copy.

```
1 This year our dinner dance will be at the big Jonquil Club.
2 The homeowners want the work done as a time saver for them.
3 We cannot expect the vice president to solve these puzzles.
4 Everything was at a standstill when the night light failed.
```

Nouns such as *vice president, father-in-law,* and *paycheck* are compound nouns—two or more words joined into one noun. When the compound noun shows that one person or thing has two functions, as in *clerk-typist* and *dinner-dance,* the noun is hyphenated.

For all other compound nouns, check your dictionary to see whether the noun is spelled as two words (*double entry*), is hyphenated (*get-together*), or is spelled as one word (*checkbook*).

TRANSCRIBING FROM DICTATED COPY

Much of the material in this program might normally be transcribed from shorthand notes or a machine transcriber, but it will be presented here in typed unarranged copy and will be labeled "Dictated Letter," "Dictated Report," and so on. You will have to supply capitalization, punctuation, and paragraphing. You will also have to check spelling; many words sound alike but are spelled differently.

JOB 234 A. DICTATED LETTER

Standard format. Workbook 529–530.

ms nadine bergman 757 newscastle drive akron ohio 44313 dear nadine thank you for designing the letterhead for our regional campaign both the artwork and the slogan are most appropriate for our candidate i am mailing you under seperate cover our ideas for the billboards please feel free to modify them in any way that you wish if you can possible do it we would like to have the artwork to give to the printer by next month please let me know whether you can met that deadline cordially tony a makato regional campaign chairperson

JOB 234 B. DICTATED LETTER

Standard format. Workbook 531–532.

mr duke bellas 1044 state street marysville ohio 43040 dear duke thank you for agreeing to prepare the copy for the special brochure highlighting the political history of our candidate my secretary will send you a number of photographs which you may want to include in the brochure our budget will allow us to have too 8½ by 11 pages printed on both sides thus making for pages in all the printer has set a deadline of the first of the month for all copy would you please let my secretary know this week whether you will be able to meet such a deadline thanks again for volunteering your time toward the campaign sincerely tony a makato [*title*]

JOB 234 C. DICTATED LETTER

Standard format. Workbook 533–534.

doctor aileen madison 5649 centennial drive reynoldsburg ohio 43068 dear aileen i recieved your script for the three-minute television spots we have planned for next month they are extremely creative and do an excellant job of highlighting the good points about our candidate the film is being shot this week and should be ready for editing by next monday would you please check your schedule to see if you could come to indianapolis on monday to assist us with this operation the photographer has agreed to take a number of poses for each portion of the script to allow us a number of alternatives when we edit and combine the too please call my secretary and let her know if you will be able to help with the editing best wishes tony a makato [*title*]

FORMATTING MULTIPLE SIGNATURES IN LETTERS

Letters are sometimes signed by two people jointly. When this occurs, signature blocks must be provided for each of the signers. To format multiple signatures:

1. Type the salutation as usual.
2. Space down 4 lines and type the first signature line.
3. Space down another 4 lines and type the second signature line.
4. If the letter is running long, reduce the space for the signature to 2 blank lines (space down 3 lines).

JOB 234 D. DICTATED LETTER MULTIPLE SIGNATURES

Standard format. Workbook 535–537.

mr alfred demonaco 44 circle avenue lansing michigan 48901 dear mr demonaco we have rearranged our schedules so that we can arrive in detroit and buffalo next week we are sending you our flight numbers so that you can meet us in detroit and continue with us to buffalo we will arrive in detroit at 9:45 wednesday morning on united 847 and stay at the motel with you on wednesday and thursday evenings we will leave detroit on united 582 at 10:15 on friday morning and arrive in buffalo an hour later we will plan to stay with you threw the weekend returning to indianapolis on monday evening please let us know weather this schedule will coincide with your schedule and whether you will be able to make reservations on the same flight to buffalo cordially tony a makato regional campaign chairperson roy a grimes national chairperson

■ GOALS
To identify compound nouns while typing sentences.
To type reports in memo form from dictated copy.

■ FORMAT
Single spacing   60-space line   5-space tab

LAB 28
Compound Nouns

Type lines 1–4 once. Then repeat lines 1–4 or take a series of 1-minute timings.

```
1 The secretary-treasurer has the know-how to help us manage.  12
2 Their trade-in is of little value to the company right now.  12
3 We need to employ a clerk-typist to help us type the bills.  12
4 Jacqueline organized an exciting get-together for our club.  12
  | 1 | 2 | 3 | 4 | 5 | 6 | 7 | 8 | 9 | 10 | 11 | 12
```

30-SECOND "OK" TIMINGS

Type as many 30-second "OK" (errorless) timings as possible out of three attempts on lines 5–7.

```
5      Please send seven boxes of election fliers to my south  12
6 precinct as quickly as you can.  We just realized that they  24
7 were going to run out.  Thank you for helping me with this.  36
  | 1 | 2 | 3 | 4 | 5 | 6 | 7 | 8 | 9 | 10 | 11 | 12
```

JOB 235 A. DICTATED REPORT IN MEMO FORM

Workbook 539–540.

to the secretary of the interior from senator marilyn heuser about my trip to see the results of the snow mountain volcanic explosion

the cloud of ash cleared for a few hours during the days when i visited the area where snow mountain exploded its very humbling to gaze at the sight

(Continued on next page)